Population, Evolution, and Birth Control

SECOND EDITION

Population
Evolution
and
Birth Control

A COLLAGE OF CONTROVERSIAL IDEAS

Assembled by

Garrett Hardin
UNIVERSITY OF CALIFORNIA, SANTA BARBARA

W. H. Freeman and Company
San Francisco

Grateful acknowledgment is made to the authors and publishers of the selections listed below and identified by number:
17. Reprinted with the permission of Charles Scribner's Sons and Russell & Volkening, Inc., from *The Prevalence of People*, pp. 150–152, by Marston Bates. Copyright © 1955 Marston Bates. **22.** From *Deserts on the March* by Paul B. Sears. University of Oklahoma Press. Copyright © 1935. **23.** From a chapter by Lee Merriman Talbot in *Wildlands in our Civilization*, David Brower, editor, Sierra Club. Copyright © 1964. **24.** Reprinted with permission of The Macmillan Company from *The Last Horizon* by Raymond F. Dasmann. Copyright © by Raymond F. Dasmann 1963. **26.** From *The Challenge of Man's Future* by Harrison Brown. Copyright © 1954 by Harrison Brown. Reprinted by permission of The Viking Press, Inc., and McIntosh and Otis. **30.** From *The Politics of Population* by William Petersen. Copyright © 1964 by William Petersen. Reprinted by permission of Doubleday & Company, Inc., and Victor Gollancz Ltd. **31.** From *Freedom and Control in Modern Society*, M. Berger, T. Abel, and C. H. Page, editors. D. Van Nostrand Co., Inc. Copyright © 1954. **32.** From *The Ethical Basis of Medical Practice* by Willard L. Sperry. Harper & Row, Publishers, Inc. Copyright © 1950. **36.** From *China: The Land and the People* by Gerald F. Winfield. Copyright © 1948 by Gerald F. Winfield by permission of William Morrow and Company, Inc. **37.** From *The Image* by Kenneth E. Boulding. University of Michigan Press. Copyright © 1956. **39.** From *Hungry Nations* by William and Paul Paddock, by permission of Little, Brown and Co. Copyright © 1964, by William and Paul Paddock. **42.** From *Where Winter Never Comes* by Marston Bates. Charles Scribner's Sons. Copyright © 1952. **43.** From *Eden Was No Garden* by Nigel Calder. Copyright © 1967 by Nigel Calder. Reprinted by permission of Holt, Rinehart and Winston, Inc., and Martin Secker & Warburg Limited. **44.** From remarks by Raymond B. Cowles in *The Meaning of Wilderness to Science*, David Brower, editor, Sierra Club. Copyright © 1960. **45.** From *Ulendo* by Archie Carr. Alfred A. Knopf, Inc. Copyright © 1964. **47.** From "Population Density and Social Pathology" by John B. Calhoun. Copyright © 1962 by Scientific American, Inc. All rights reserved. **53.** From an article by Kenneth E. Boulding in *Environmental Quality in a Growing Economy*, Henry Jarrett, editor. The Johns Hopkins Press. Resources for the Future, Inc. Copyright © 1966. **55.** From *The Human Use of Human Beings* by Norbert Wiener. Houghton Mifflin Company. Copyright © 1950. **56.** From *Famine—1975!* by William and Paul Paddock, by permission of Little, Brown and Co. and Weidenfeld & Nicolson. Copyright © 1967, by William and Paul Paddock. **79.** From *Nature and Man's Fate* by Garrett Hardin. Copyright © 1959 by Garrett Hardin. Reprinted by permission of Holt, Rinehart and Winston, Inc. **82.** From *Essays in the History of Ideas* by Arthur O. Lovejoy. The Johns Hopkins Press. Copyright © 1948. **88.** From *The First Five Lives of Annie Besant* by Arthur H. Nethercot. The University of Chicago Press. Copyright © 1960. **89.** From *The Birth Controllers* by Peter Fryer. Martin Secker & Warburg Limited. Copyright © 1965. **90.** Quoted, by permission, from *An Autobiography*, by Margaret Sanger. Copyright © 1938 by Margaret Sanger. All rights reserved. **93.** From *Birth Control and Catholic Doctrine* by Alvah W. Sulloway. Beacon Press. Copyright © 1959. **96.** From "Birth Control: Catholic Opinion Varies Widely on Rock's New Book" by Daniel S. Greenberg. *Science*, 140:791–792. 17 May 1963. Copyright © 1963 by the American Association for the Advancement of Science. **103.** From *The Right to Life* by Norman St. John-Stevas. Copyright © 1963, 1964 by Norman St. John-Stevas. Reprinted by permission of Hodder and Stoughton Limited and Holt, Rinehart and Winston, Inc. **108.** From *Studies in Population* edited by G. F. Mair. Princeton University Press. Copyright © 1949. **109.** From *Life, Death and the Law* by Norman St. John-Stevas. Indiana University Press and Eyre & Spottiswoode (Publishers) Ltd. Copyright © 1961. **116.** From *Modern Science and the Human Fertility Problem* by Richard L. Meier. John Wiley & Sons, Inc. Copyright © 1959. **117.** From *Complete Poems of Robert Frost*. Copyright © 1916 by Holt, Rinehart and Winston, Inc. Copyright © 1944 by Robert Frost. Reprinted by permission of Holt, Rinehart and Winston, Inc., and Laurence Pollinger Limited. **118.** From "Raising Per Capita Income Through Fewer Births" by Stephen Enke. General Electric—TEMPO. Publication 68 TMP-9. March 1968. **119.** From remarks by Raymond B. Cowles in *The Meaning of Wilderness to Science*, David Brower, editor, Sierra Club. Copyright © 1960. **120.** From pp. 135–6 *The Meaning of the 20th Century* by Kenneth E. Boulding. (Harper & Row, 1964). **121.** "Population Policy: Will Current Programs Succeed?" by Kingsley Davis. *Science*, 158:730–739. 10 November 1967. Copyright © 1967 by the American Association for the Advancement of Science. **122.** From *The Population Bomb* by Dr. Paul R. Ehrlich, published by Ballantine Books, Inc. Copyright © 1968 by Paul R. Ehrlich. **123.** "The Tragedy of the Commons" by Garrett Hardin. *Science*, 162:1243–1248. 13 December 1968. Copyright © 1968 by the American Association for the Advancement of Science.

Grateful acknowledgment is made to the living authors of the selections listed below for their permission to reprint. The editors of the following journals gave their permission to reprint several selections, which are indicated by number:
ASA Newsletter, 101; *The Catholic Messenger*, 97; *The Catholic World*, 104; *Journal of Heredity*, 52; *Journal of Marriage and the Family*, 105; *Nature*, 35, 50, 70; *National Catholic Reporter*, 99; *New Scientist*, 27, 57; *Perspectives in Biology and Medicine*, 40, 98; *Population Bulletin*, 19, 20, 100; *Population Review*, 48, 54; *Population Studies*, 91; *Science*, 41, 94, 96, 121, 123; *Scientific American*, 47; *Thought*, 38.

to Jane

Introduction

The emerging history of population is a story of disaster and denial—disaster foreseen, but disaster psychologically denied in our innermost being. Our reaction to the signals assaulting us is perfectly understandable: they foretell an event that has never happened before. How can one believe in something—particularly an unpleasant something—that has **never** happened before? This necessity must have been a terrible problem for Noah. Unfortunately the Bible is silent about Noah's psychological experience, surely the most significant aspect of his ordeal. If it was wisdom that enabled Noah to believe in the never-yet-happened we could use some of that wisdom now.

Kenneth Galbraith has remarked that "Nothing in our economic policy is so ingrained, and so little reckoned with by economists, as our tendency to wait and see if things do not improve by themselves." This tendency is not limited to economic affairs. At the outset of the Second World War, as Roberta Wohlstetter has shown in her **Pearl Harbor: Warning and Decision,** American authorities received repeated warning over a period of many months of the coming attack on Hawaii. They did nothing. A small coterie of "Monday-morning quarterbacks" later decided that treason in high places was the cause of the lack of preparation at Pearl Harbor. I don't think this hypothesis is supported by the evidence. A simpler and more plausible explanation is this: none of the men in power were Noahs. They could not believe in their bones (where the action must begin) that what had never happened before would happen now.

In similar circumstances, would **we** behave any better? I think we have our chance now, in respect to population problems. Many thoughtful population experts are forecasting an imminent population catastrophe of unprecedented dimensions. The signals (from nature in this case) are ambiguous (just as the pre-Pearl Harbor signals were). But if we correct for our natural anti-Noah bias, the meaning of the signals is, I think, undeniable. If this be true, what shall we do? What can we do, usefully?

To a society that is faced with an unavoidable catastrophe we can offer two good reasons for "thinking about the unthinkable" ahead of time. The more obvious one is that by advance preparation we may be able to ameliorate the agony somewhat; ninety per cent of a catastrophe is better than the whole lump. More importantly, if the disaster impending is one of a conceivable series, then, as Kenneth Boulding has put the matter:

> the critical question . . . is whether disaster can be a learning process, a kind of shock treatment, as it were, for a society which can increase its self-awareness and hence can create an image of a social process which leads to the avoidance of disasters in the future. Disastrous floods often lead to flood control measures. The Irish famine of 1846 created a sharp learning process in the Irish by which they learned to restrict their population growth. It may be, therefore, that the best way to learn from disasters is to prepare people for them, for there are also many occasions in human history in which people have not learned anything from disasters at all.

The required increase in self-awareness can, and should, begin now. To further this is the purpose of this book. Significant sections of historical classics are presented because I agree with John Maynard Keynes that **a study of the history of opinion is a necessary preliminary to the emancipation of the mind.** The progress of opinion is never straightforward. There is never one question, but many; with imperfectly seen, and constantly changing, regions of contact. Intellectual progress in things that really matter is never neat, never linear. The picture (if honestly presented) is a sort of patchwork; hence my choice of the word **collage** for this collection. Not everything that is truly relevant is obviously so at first glance—but determining the relevance is half the excitement! At least I have found it so in putting together this collage; I hope the reader does, too.

Hereafter, comments by the editor and essays by the editor that are original to this volume—i.e., not reprinted from other publications—are printed in sans serif type like this, without explicit attribution.

Contents

II. Evolution

III. Birth Control

Population, Evolution, and Birth Control

I

Population

1
Malthus Starts
the Argument

Every year Malthus is proven wrong and is buried—only to spring to life again before the year is out. If he is so wrong, why can't we forget him? If he is right, how does he happen to be so fertile a subject for criticism?

The career of Thomas Robert Malthus was begun by a controversy—a personal controversy with his father, who was an admirer of the Frenchman Condorcet and the Englishman Godwin. These great optimists, just after the French Revolution, foresaw increasing and unlimited progress for man as he threw off the shackles of reactionary human institutions. Not so, said young Malthus, who reasoned that great natural principles limited man's progress. So persuasively did he argue that his father urged him to state his views in print. The resultant **Essay** attracted immediate notice and determined the career of its author, who devoted a major share of his life thereafter to revising and defending his book. The first edition genuinely deserved to be called an essay, for it was written easily—"off the top of his head," as we would say now. Subsequent editions, documented to twice the size of the first, really deserve to be called treatises on population. It is from the first edition that I have drawn the extracts presented here.

Malthus said many things, not all of which are true; and implied many more. **What did Malthus say?** This is the first question we must tackle. **Was he the first to say it?** This is our second question. And finally: **What have we learned since Malthus' time?**

3

2

An Essay on
the Principle of Population

Thomas Robert Malthus
1766–1834

1798

Chapter I

The great and unlooked for discoveries that have taken place of late years in natural philosophy, the increasing diffusion of general knowledge from the extension of the art of printing, the ardent and unshackled spirit of inquiry that prevails throughout the lettered and even unlettered world, the new and extraordinary lights that have been thrown on political subjects which dazzle and astonish the understanding, and particularly that tremendous phenomenon in the political horizon, the French revolution, which, like a blazing comet, seems destined either to inspire with fresh life and vigour, or to scorch up and destroy the shrinking habitants of the earth, have all concurred to lead many able men into the opinion that we were touching on a period big with the most important changes, changes that would in some measure be decisive of the future fate of mankind.

It has been said that the great question is now at issue, whether man shall henceforth start forwards with accelerated velocity towards illimitable, and hitherto unconceived improvement, or be condemned to a perpetual oscillation between happiness and misery, and after every effort remain still at an immeasurable distance from the wished-for goal.

Yet, anxiously as every friend of mankind must look forwards to the termination of this painful suspense, and eagerly as the inquiring mind would hail every ray of light that might assist its view into futurity, it is much to be lamented that the writers on each side of this momentous question still keep far aloof from each other. Their mutual arguments do not meet with a candid examination. The question is not brought to rest on fewer points, and even in theory scarcely seems to be approaching to a decision.

The advocate for the present order of things is apt to treat the sect of speculative philosophers either as a set of artful and designing knaves who preach up ardent benevolence and draw captivating pictures of a happier state of society only the better to enable them to destroy the present establishments and to forward their own deep-laid schemes of ambition, or as wild and mad-headed enthusiasts whose silly speculations and absurd paradoxes are not worthy the attention of any reasonable man.

The advocate for the perfectibility of man, and of society, retorts on the defender of establishments a more than equal contempt. He brands him as the slave of the most miserable and narrow prejudices; or, as the defender of the abuses of civil society, only because he profits by them. He paints him either as a character who prostitutes his understanding to his interest, or as one whose powers of mind are not of a size to grasp any thing great and noble, who cannot see above five yards before him, and who must therefore be utterly unable to take in the views of the enlightened benefactor of mankind.

In this unamicable contest the cause of truth cannot but suffer. The really good arguments on each side of the question are not allowed to have their proper weight. Each pursues his own theory, little solicitous to correct or improve it by an attention to what is advanced by his opponents.

The friend of the present order of things condemns all political speculations in the gross. He will not even condescend to examine the grounds from which the perfectibility of society is inferred. Much less will he give himself the trouble in a fair and candid manner to attempt an exposition of their fallacy.

The speculative philosopher equally offends against the cause of truth. With eyes fixed on a happier state of society, the blessings of which he paints in the most captivating colours, he allows himself to indulge in the most bitter invectives against every present establishment, without applying his talents to consider the best and safest means of removing abuses and without seeming to be aware of the tremendous obstacles that threaten, even in theory, to oppose the progress of man towards perfection.

It is an acknowledged truth in philosophy that a just theory will always be confirmed by experiment. Yet so much friction, and so many minute circumstances occur in practice, which it is next to impossible for the most enlarged and penetrating mind to foresee, that on few subjects can any theory be pronounced just, that has not stood the test of experience. But an untried theory cannot fairly be advanced as probable, much less as just, till all the arguments against it have been maturely weighted and clearly and consistently refuted.

I have read some of the speculations on the perfectibility of man and of society with great pleasure. I have been warmed and delighted with the enchanting picture which they hold forth. I ardently wish for such happy improvements. But I see great, and, to my understanding, unconquerable difficulties in the way to them. These difficulties it is my present

5

purpose to state, declaring, at the same time, that so far from exulting in them, as a cause of triumph over the friends of innovation, nothing would give me greater pleasure than to see them completely removed.

The most important argument that I shall adduce is certainly not new. The principles on which it depends have been explained in part by Hume, and more at large by Dr. Adam Smith. It has been advanced and applied to the present subject, though not with its proper weight, or in the most forcible point of view, by Mr. Wallace, and it may probably have been stated by many writers that I have never met with. I should certainly therefore not think of advancing it again, though I mean to place it in a point of view in some degree different from any that I have hitherto seen, if it had ever been fairly and satisfactorily answered.

The cause of this neglect on the part of the advocates for the perfectibility of mankind is not easily accounted for. I cannot doubt the talents of such men as Godwin and Condorcet. I am unwilling to doubt their candour. To my understanding, and probably to that of most others, the difficulty appears insurmountable. Yet these men of acknowledged ability and penetration, scarcely deign to notice it, and hold on their course in such speculations, with unabated ardour and undiminished confidence. I have certainly no right to say that they purposely shut their eyes to such arguments. I ought rather to doubt the validity of them, when neglected by such men, however forcibly their truth may strike my own mind. Yet in this respect it must be acknowledged that we are all of us too prone to err. If I saw a glass of wine repeatedly presented to a man, and he took no notice of it, I should be apt to think that he was blind or uncivil. A juster philosophy might teach me rather to think that my eyes deceived me and that the offer was not really what I conceived it to be.

In entering upon the argument I must premise that I put out of the question, at present, all mere conjectures, that is, all suppositions, the probable realization of which cannot be inferred upon any just philosophical grounds. A writer may tell me that he thinks man will ultimately become an ostrich. I cannot properly contradict him. But before he can expect to bring any reasonable person over to his opinion, he ought to shew, that the necks of mankind have been gradually elongating, that the lips have grown harder and more prominent, that the legs and feet are daily altering their shape, and that the hair is beginning to change into stubs of feathers. And till the probability of so wonderful a conversion can be shewn, it is surely lost time and lost eloquence to expatiate on the happiness of man in such a state; to describe his powers, both of running and flying, to paint him in a condition where all narrow luxuries would be contemned, where he would be employed only in collecting the necessaries of life, and where, consequently, each man's share of labour would be light, and his portion of leisure ample.

I think I may fairly make two postulata.

First, That food is necessary to the existence of man.

Secondly, That the passion between the sexes is necessary and will remain nearly in its present state.

These two laws, ever since we have had any knowledge of mankind, appear to have been fixed laws of our nature, and, as we have not hitherto seen any alteration in them, we have no right to conclude that they will ever cease to be what they now are, without an immediate act of power in that Being who first arranged the system of the universe, and for the advantage of his creatures, still executes, according to fixed laws, all its various operations.

I do not know that any writer has supposed that on this earth man will ultimately be able to live without food. But Mr. Godwin has conjectured that the passion between the sexes may in time be extinguished. As, however, he calls this part of his work a deviation into the land of conjecture, I will not dwell longer upon it at present than to say that the best arguments for the perfectibility of man are drawn from a contemplation of the great progress that he has already made from the savage state and the difficulty of saying where he is to stop. But towards the extinction of the passion between sexes, no progress whatever has hitherto been made. It appears to exist in as much force at present as it did two thousand or four thousand years ago. There are individual exceptions now as there always have been. But, as these exceptions do not appear to increase in number, it would surely be a very unphilosophical mode of arguing, to infer merely from the existence of an exception, that the exception would, in time, become the rule, and the rule the exception.

Assuming then, my postulata as granted, I say, that the power of population is indefinitely greater than the power in the earth to produce subsistence for man.

Population, when unchecked, increases in a geometrical ratio. Subsistence increases only in an arithmetical ratio. A slight acquaintance with numbers will shew the immensity of the first power in comparison of the second.

By that law of our nature which makes food necessary to the life of man, the effects of these two unequal powers must be kept equal.

This implies a strong and constantly operating check on population from the difficulty of subsistence. This difficulty must fall some where and must necessarily be severely felt by a large portion of mankind.

Through the animal and vegetable kingdoms, nature has scattered the seeds of life abroad with the most profuse and liberal hand. She has been comparatively sparing in the room and the nourishment necessary to rear them. The germs of existence contained in this spot of earth, with ample food, and ample room to expand in, would fill millions of worlds in

7

the course of a few thousand years. Necessity, that imperious all pervading law of nature, restrains them within the prescribed bounds. The race of plants, and the race of animals shrink under this great restrictive law. And the race of man cannot, by any efforts of reason, escape from it. Among plants and animals its effects are waste of seed, sickness, and premature death. Among mankind, misery and vice. The former, misery, is an absolutely necessary consequence of it. Vice is a highly probable consequence, and we therefore see it abundantly prevail, but it ought not, perhaps, to be called an absolutely necessary consequence. The ordeal of virtue is to resist all temptation to evil.

This natural inequality of the two powers of population and of production in the earth and that great law of our nature which must constantly keep their effects equal form the great difficulty that to me appears insurmountable in the way to the perfectibility of society. All other arguments are of slight and subordinate consideration in comparison of this. I see no way by which man can escape from the weight of this law which pervades all animated nature. No fancied equality, no agrarian regulations in their utmost extent, could remove the pressure of it even for a single century. And it appears, therefore, to be decisive against the possible existence of a society, all the members of which should live in ease, happiness, and comparative leisure; and feel no anxiety about providing the means of subsistence for themselves and families.

Consequently, if the premises are just, the argument is conclusive against the perfectibility of the mass of mankind.

I have thus sketched the general outline of the argument, but I will examine it more particularly, and I think it will be found that experience, the true source and foundation of all knowledge, invariably confirms its truth.

Chapter II

I said that population, when unchecked, increased in a geometrical ratio, and subsistence for man in an arithmetical ratio.

Let us examine whether this position be just.

I think it will be allowed, that no state has hitherto existed (at least that we have any account of) where the manners were so pure and simple, and the means of subsistence so abundant, that no check whatever has existed to early marriages, among the lower classes, from a fear of not providing well for their families, or among the higher classes, from a fear of lowering their condition in life. Consequently in no state that we have yet known has the power of population been left to exert itself with perfect freedom.

Whether the law of marriage be instituted or not, the dictate of nature and virtue seems to be an early attachment to one woman. Supposing a liberty of changing in the case of an unfortunate choice, this liberty would not affect population till it arose to a height greatly vicious; and we are now supposing the existence of a society where vice is scarcely known.

In a state therefore of great equality and virtue, where pure and simple manners prevailed, and where the means of subsistence were so abundant that no part of the society could have any fears about providing amply for a family, the power of population being left to exert itself unchecked, the increase of the human species would evidently be much greater than any increase that has been hitherto known.

In the United States of America, where the means of subsistence have been more ample, the manners of the people more pure, and consequently the checks to early marriages fewer than in any of the modern states of Europe, the population has been found to double itself in twenty-five years.

This ratio of increase, though short of the utmost power of population, yet as the result of actual experience, we will take as our rule, and say, that population, when unchecked, goes on doubling itself every twenty-five years or increases in a geometrical ratio.

Let us now take any spot of earth, this Island for instance, and see in what ratio the subsistence it affords can be supposed to increase. We will begin with it under its present state of cultivation.

If I allow that by the best possible policy, by breaking up more land and by great encouragements to agriculture, the produce of this Island may be doubled in the first twenty-five years, I think it will be allowing as much as any person can well demand.

In the next twenty-five years, it is impossible to suppose that the produce could be quadrupled. It would be contrary to all our knowledge of the qualities of land. The very utmost that we can conceive, is, that the increase in the second twenty-five years might equal the present produce. Let us then take this for our rule, though certainly far beyond the truth, and allow that by great exertion, the whole produce of the Island might be increased every twenty-five years, by a quantity of subsistence equal to what it at present produces. The most enthusiastic speculator cannot suppose a greater increase than this. In a few centuries it would make every acre of land in the Island like a garden.

Yet this ratio of increase is evidently arithmetical.

It may be fairly said, therefore, that the means of subsistence increase in an arithmetical ratio. Let us now bring the effects of these two ratios together.

The population of the Island is computed to be about seven millions, and we will suppose the present produce equal to the support of such a number. In the first twenty-five years the population would be fourteen millions, and the food being also doubled, the means of subsistence would be equal to this increase. In the next twenty-five years the population would be twenty-eight millions, and the means of subsistence only equal to the support of twenty-one millions. In the next period, the population would be fifty-six millions, and the means of subsistence just sufficient for half that number. And at the conclusion of the first century the population would be one hundred and twelve millions and the means of subsistence only equal to the support of thirty-five millions, which would leave a population of seventy-seven millions totally unprovided for.

A great emigration necessarily implies unhappiness of some kind or other in the country that is deserted. For few persons will leave their families, connections, friends, and native land, to seek a settlement in untried foreign climes, without some strong subsisting causes of uneasiness where they are, or the hope of some great advantages in the place to which they are going.

But to make the argument more general and less interrupted by the partial views of emigration, let us take the whole earth, instead of one spot, and suppose that the restraints to population were universally removed. If the subsistence for man that the earth affords was to be increased every twenty-five years by a quantity equal to what the whole world at present produces, this would allow the power of production in the earth to be absolutely unlimited, and its ratio of increase much greater than we can conceive that any possible exertions of mankind could make it.

Taking the population of the world at any number, a thousand millions, for instance, the human species would increase in the ratio of—1, 2, 4, 8, 16, 32, 64, 128, 256, 512, &c. and subsistence as—1, 2, 3, 4, 5, 6, 7, 8, 9, 10, &c. In two centuries and a quarter, the population would be to the means of subsistence as 512 to 10: in three centuries as 4096 to 13, and in two thousand years the difference would be almost incalculable, though the produce in that time would have increased to an immense extent.

No limits whatever are placed to the productions of the earth; they may increase for ever and be greater than any assignable quantity; yet still the power of population being a power of a superior order, the increase of the human species can only be kept commensurate to the increase of the means of subsistence, by the constant operation of the strong law of necessity acting as a check upon the greater power.

The effects of this check remain now to be considered.

Among plants and animals the view of the subject is simple. They are all impelled by a powerful instinct to the increase of their species, and this instinct is interrupted by no reasoning or doubts about providing for their offspring. Wherever therefore there is liberty, the power of increase is exerted, and the super-abundant effects are repressed afterwards by want of room and nourishment, which is common to animals and plants, and among animals, by becoming the prey of others.

The effects of this check on man are more complicated. Impelled to the increase of his species by an equally powerful instinct, reason interrupts his career and asks him whether he may not bring beings into the world, for whom he cannot provide the means of subsistence. In a state of equality, this would be the simple question. In the present state of society, other considerations occur. Will he not lower his rank in life? Will he not subject himself to greater difficulties than he at present feels? Will he not be obliged to labour harder? and if he has a large family, will his utmost exertions enable him to support them? May he not see his off spring in rags and misery, and clamouring for bread that he cannot give them? And may he not be reduced to the grating necessity of forfeiting his independence, and of being obliged to the sparing hand of charity for support?

These considerations are calculated to prevent, and certainly do prevent, a very great number in all civilized nations from pursuing the dictate of nature in an early attachment to one woman. And this restraint almost necessarily, though not absolutely so, produces vice. Yet in all societies, even those that are most vicious, the tendency to a virtuous attachment is so strong that there is a constant effort towards an increase of population. This constant effort as constantly tends to subject the lower classes of the society of distress and to prevent any great permanent amelioration of their condition.

The way in which these effects are produced seems to be this.

We will suppose the means of subsistence in any country just equal to the easy support of its inhabitants. The constant effort towards population, which is found to act even in the most vicious societies, increases the number of people before the means of subsistence are increased. The food therefore which before supported seven millions must now be divided among seven millions and a half or eight millions. The poor consequently must live much worse, and many of them be reduced to severe distress. The number of labourers also being above the proportion of the work in the market, the price of labour must tend toward a decrease, while the price of provisions would at the same time tend to rise. The labourer therefore must work harder to earn the same as he did before. During this season of distress, the discouragements to marriage, and the difficulty of rearing a family are so great that population is at a stand. In the meantime the cheapness of labour, the plenty of labourers, and the necessity of an increased industry amongst them, encourage cultivators to employ more labour upon their land, to turn up fresh soil, and to manure and improve more completely what is already in tillage, till ultimately the means of subsistence become in the same proportion to the population as at the period from which we set out.

The situation of the labourer being then again tolerably comfortable, the restraints to population are in some degree loosened, and the same retrograde and progressive movements with respect to happiness are repeated.

This sort of oscillation will not be remarked by superficial observers, and it may be difficult even for the most penetrating mind to calculate its periods. Yet that in all old states some such vibration does exist, though from various transverse causes, in a much less marked, and in a much more irregular manner than I have described it, no reflecting man who considers the subject deeply can well doubt.

Many reasons occur why this oscillation has been less obvious, and less decidedly confirmed by experience, than might naturally be expected.

One principal reason is that the histories of mankind that we possess are histories only of the higher classes. We have but few accounts that can be depended upon of the manners and customs of that part of mankind, where these retrograde and progressive movements chiefly take place. A satisfactory history of this kind, of one people, and of one period, would require the constant and minute attention of an observing mind during a long life. Some of the objects of enquiry would be, in what proportion to the number of adults was the number of marriages, to what extent vicious customs prevailed in consequence of the restraints upon matrimony, what was the comparative mortality among the children of the most distressed part of the community and those who lived rather more at their ease, what were the variations in the real price of labour, and what were the observable differences in the state of the lower classes of society with respect to ease and happiness, at different times during a certain period.

Such a history would tend greatly to elucidate the manner in which the constant check upon population acts and would probably prove the existence of the retrograde and progressive movements that have been mentioned, though the times of their vibration must necessarily be rendered irregular, from the operation of many interrupting causes, such as the introduction or failure of certain manufactures, a greater or less prevalent spirit of agricultural enterprize, years of plenty, or years of scarcity, wars and pestilence, poor laws, the invention of processes for shortening labour without the proportional extension of the market for the commodity, and, particularly, the difference between the nominal and real price of labour, a circumstance which has perhaps more than any other contributed to conceal this oscillation from common view.

It very rarely happens that the nominal price of labour universally falls, but we well know that it frequently remains the same, while the nominal price of provisions has been gradually increasing. This is, in effect, a real fall in the price of labour, and during this period the condition of the lower orders of the community must gradually grow worse and worse. But the farmers and capitalists are growing rich from the real cheapness of labour. Their increased capitals enable them to employ a greater number of men. Work therefore may be plentiful, and the price of labour would consequently rise. But the want of freedom in the market of labour, which occurs more or less in all communities, either from parish laws, or the more general cause of the facility of combination among the rich, and its difficulty among the poor, operates to prevent the price of labour from rising at the natural period, and keeps it down some time longer; perhaps, till a year of scarcity, when the clamour is too loud, and the necessity too apparent to be resisted.

The true cause of the advance in the price of labour is thus concealed, and the rich affect to grant it as an act of compassion and favour to the poor, in consideration of a year of scarcity, and, when plenty returns, indulge themselves in the most unreasonable of all complaints, that the price does not again fall, when a little reflection would shew them that it must have risen long before but from an unjust conspiracy of their own.

But though the rich by unfair combinations contribute frequently to prolong a season of distress among the poor, yet no possible form of society could prevent the almost constant action of misery upon a great part of mankind, if in a state of inequality, and upon all, if all were equal.

The theory on which the truth of this position depends appears to me so extremely clear that I feel at a loss to conjecture what part of it can be denied.

That population cannot increase without the means of subsistence is a proposition so evident that it needs no illustration.

That population does invariably increase where there are the means of subsistence, the history of every people that have ever existed will abundantly prove.

And that the superior power of population cannot be checked without producing misery or vice, the ample portion of these too bitter ingredients in the cup of human life and the continuance of the physical causes that seem to have produced them bear too convincing a testimony.

Chapter III

It is well known that a country in pasture cannot support so many inhabitants as a country in tillage, but what renders nations of shepherds so formidable is the power which they possess of moving all together and the necessity they frequently feel of exerting this power in search of fresh pasture for their herds. A tribe that was rich in cattle had an immediate plenty of food. Even the parent stock might be devoured in a case of absolute necessity. The women lived in greater case than among nations of hunters. The men bold in their united strength and confiding in their power of procuring pasture for their cattle by change of place, felt, probably, but few fears

13

about providing for a family. These combined causes soon produced their natural and invariable effect on extended population. A more frequent and rapid change of place became then necessary. A wider and more extensive territory was successively occupied. A broader desolation extended all around them. Want pinched the less fortunate members of the society, and, at length, the impossibility of supporting such a number together became too evident to be resisted. Young scions were then pushed out from the parent-stock and instructed to explore fresh regions and to gain happier seats for themselves by their swords. "The world was all before them where to chuse." Restless from present distress, flushed with the hope of fairer prospects, and animated with the spirit of hardy enterprize, these daring adventurers were likely to become formidable adversaries to all who opposed them. The peaceful inhabitants of the countries on which they rushed could not long withstand the energy of men acting under such powerful motives of exertion. And when they fell in with any tribes like their own, the contest was a struggle for existence, and they fought with a desperate courage, inspired by the reflection that death was the punishment of defeat and life the prize of victory. . . .

Where there is any inequality of conditions, and among nations of shepherds this soon takes place, the distress arising from a scarcity of provisions, must fall hardest upon the least fortunate members of the society. This distress also must frequently have been felt by the women, exposed to casual plunder in the absence of their husbands, and subject to continual disappointments in their expected return.

But without knowing enough of the minute and intimate history of these people, to point out precisely on what part the distress for want of food chiefly fell, and to what extent it was generally felt, I think we may fairly say, from all the accounts that we have of nations of shepherds, that population invariably increased among them whenever, by emigration or any other cause, the means of subsistence were increased, and that a further population was checked, and the actual population kept equal to the means of subsistence by misery and vice.

For, independently of any vicious customs that might have prevailed amongst them with regard to women, which always operate as checks to population, it must be acknowledged I think, that the commission of war is vice, and the effect of it misery, and none can doubt the misery of want of food.

Chapter VI

The unwholesomeness of towns, to which some persons are necessarily driven from the nature of their trades, must be considered as a species of misery, and even the slightest check to marriage, from a prospect of the difficulty of maintaining a family, may be fairly classed under the same head. In short it is difficult to conceive any check to population which does not come under the description of some species of misery or vice.

Chapter VII

If there are no very great variations at particular periods in the proportions, it would appear, that the population of France and England has accommodated itself very nearly to the average produce of each country. The discouragements to marriage, the consequent vicious habits, war, luxury, the silent though certain depopulation of large towns, and the close habitations, and insufficient food of many of the poor, prevent population from increasing beyond the means of subsistence; and, if I may use an expression which certainly at first appears strange, supersede the necessity of great and ravaging epidemics to repress what is redundant. Were a wasting plague to sweep off two millions in England, and six millions in France, there can be no doubt whatever, that after the inhabitants had recovered from the dreadful shock, the proportion of births to burials would be much above what it is in either country at present. . . .

The only true criterion of a real and permanent increase in the population of any country is the increase of the means of subsistence. . . . .

The happiness of a country does not depend, absolutely, upon its poverty or its riches, upon its youth or its age, upon its being thinly or fully inhabited, but upon the rapidity with which it is increasing, upon the degree in which the yearly increase of food approaches to the yearly increase of an unrestricted population. This approximation is always the nearest in new colonies, where the knowledge and industry of an old State, operate on the fertile unappropriated land of a new one. In other cases, the youth or the age of a State is not in this respect of very great importance. It is probable, that the food of Great Britain is divided in as great plenty to the inhabitants, at the present period, as it was two thousand, three thousand, or four thousand years ago. And there is reason to believe that the poor and thinly inhabited tracts of the Scotch Highlands, are as much distressed by an overcharged population, as the rich and populous province of Flanders. . . . .

Famine seems to be the last, the most dreadful resource of nature. The power of population is so superior to the power in the earth to produce subsistence for man, that premature death must in some shape or other visit the human race. The vices of mankind are active and able ministers of depopulation. They are the precursors in the great army of destruction; and often finish the dreadful work themselves. But should they fail in this war of extermination, sickly seasons, epidemics, pestilence, and plague, advance

15

in terrific array, and sweep off their thousands and ten thousands. Should success be still incomplete, gigantic inevitable famine stalks in the rear, and with one mighty blow, levels the population with the food of the world.

Chapter X

Mr. Godwin considers marriage as a fraud and a monopoly. Let us suppose the commerce of the sexes established upon principles of the most perfect freedom. Mr. Godwin does not think himself that this freedom would lead to a promiscuous intercourse, and in this I perfectly agree with him. The love of variety is a vicious, corrupt, and unnatural taste and could not prevail in any great degree in a simple and virtuous state of society. Each man would probably select himself a partner, to whom he would adhere as long as that adherence continued to be the choice of both parties. It would be of little consequence, according to Mr. Godwin, how many children a woman had or to whom they belonged. Provisions and assistance would spontaneously flow from the quarter in which they abounded, to the quarter that was deficient. And every man would be ready to furnish instruction to the rising generation according to his capacity.

I cannot conceive a form of society so favourable upon the whole to population. The irremediableness of marriage, as it is at present constituted, undoubtedly deters many from entering into that state. An unshackled intercourse on the contrary would be a most powerful incitement to early attachments, and as we are supposing no anxiety about the future support of children to exist, I do not conceive that there would be one woman in a hundred, of twenty-three, without a family.

With these extraordinary encouragements to population, and every cause of depopulation, as we have supposed, removed, the numbers would necessarily increase faster than in any society that has ever yet been known. I have mentioned, on the authority of a pamphlet published by a Dr. Styles and referred to by Dr. Price, that the inhabitants of the back settlements of America doubled their numbers in fifteen years. England is certainly a more healthy country than the back settlements of America, and as we have supposed every house in the island to be airy and wholesome, and the encouragements to have a family greater even than with the back settlers, no probable reason can be assigned why the population should not double itself in less, if possible, than fifteen years. But to be quite sure that we do not go beyond the truth, we will only suppose the period of doubling to be twenty-five years, a ratio of increase, which is well known to have taken place throughout all the Northern States of America.

3
Doubling Times and Population Growth

He who has not played with compound interest calculations is generally surprised at how rapidly a sum of money (or a population) increases at even the most modest rate of interest. The following table will help in appreciating the implications of different rates of population growth among the various peoples of the world.

Rate of Population Increase (Percent per Year)	Time Taken to Double Population (Number of Years)
0.01	6,930
0.1	693
0.5	139
1.0	70
1.5	47
2.0	35
2.5	28
2.8	25
3.0	23
3.5	20
4.0	18

4
Fecundity and Prosperity

Han Fei-Tzu
Chou Dynasty (ca. 500 B.C.)

In ancient times, people were few but wealthy and without strife. People at present think that five sons are not too many, and each son has five sons also and before the death of the grandfather there are already 25 descendants. Therefore people are more and wealth is less; they work hard and receive little. The life of a nation depends upon having enough food, not upon the number of people.

5
The Blessings of Catastrophes

Tertullian
ca. 160–ca. 230

From *De Anima*

The strongest witness is the vast population of the earth to which we are a burden and she scarcely can provide for our needs; as our demands grow greater, our complaints against nature's inadequacy are heard by all. The scourges of pestilence, famine, wars, and earthquakes have come to be regarded as a blessing to overcrowded nations, since they serve to prune away the luxuriant growth of the human race.

6
Utopia

Thomas More
1478–1535

1516

That the city neither be depopulated nor grow beyond measure, provision is made that no household shall have fewer than ten or more than sixteen adults; there are six thousand such households in each city, apart from its surrounding territory. Of children under age, of course, no number can be fixed. This limit is easily observed by transferring those who exceed the number in larger families into those that are under the prescribed number. Whenever all the families of a city reach their full quota, the adults in excess of that number help to make up the deficient population of other cities.

7
Trust in God

Martin Luther
1483–1546

Gott macht Kinder, der wird sie auch ernähren.

8

Observations Concerning the Increase of Mankind

Benjamin Franklin
1706–1790

1755

There is, in short, no bound to the prolific nature of plants or animals, but what is made by their crowding and interfering with each other's means of subsistence. Was the face of the earth vacant of other plants, it might be gradually sowed and overspread with one kind only, as, for instance, with fennel: and were it empty of other inhabitants, it might, in a few ages, be replenished from one nation only, as, for instance, with Englishmen. Thus there are supposed to be now upwards of one million of English souls in North America (though it is thought scarce 80,000 have been brought over sea), and yet perhaps there is not one fewer in Britain, but rather many more, on account of the employment the colonies afford to manufacturers at home. This million doubling, suppose but once in twenty-five years, will, in another century, be more than the people of England, and the greatest number of Englishmen will be on this side of the water. . . . In fine, a nation well regulated is like a polypus: take away a limb, its place is soon supplied: cut it in two, and each deficient part shall speedily grow out of the part remaining. Thus, if you have room and subsistence enough, as you may, by dividing ten polypuses out of one, you may, of one, make ten nations, equally populous and powerful; or, rather, increase the nation tenfold in numbers and strength.

9

Various Prospects of Mankind, Nature, and Providence

Robert Wallace
1697–1771

London: A. Millar

1761

Under a perfect government, the inconveniencies of having a family would be so intirely removed, children would be so well taken care of, and every thing become so favourable to populousness, that though some sickly seasons or dreadful plagues in particular climates might cut off multitudes, yet in general, mankind would encrease so prodigiously, that the earth would at last be overstocked, and become unable to support its numerous inhabitants.

How long the earth, with the best culture of which it is capable for human genius and industry, might be able to nourish its perpetually increasing inhabitants, is as impossible as it is unnecessary to be determined. It is not probable that it could have supported them during so long a period as since the creation of Adam. But whatever may be supposed of the length of this period, of necessity it must be granted, that the earth could not nourish them for ever, unless either its fertility could be continually augmented, or by some secret in nature, like what certain enthusiasts have expected from the philosophers stone, some wise adept in the occult sciences, should invent a method of supporting mankind quite different from any thing known at present. Nay, though some extraordinary method of supporting them might possibly be found out, yet if there was no bound to the increase of mankind, which would be the case under a perfect government, there would not even be sufficient room for containing their bodies upon the surface of the earth, or upon any limited surface whatsoever. It would be necessary, therefore, in order to find room for such multitudes of men, that the earth should be continually enlarging in bulk, as an animal or vegetable body.

Now since philosophers may as soon attempt to make mankind immortal, as to support the animal frame without food; it is equally certain,

21

that limits are set to the fertility of the earth, and that its bulk, so far as is hitherto known, hath continued always the same, and probably could not be much altered without making considerable changes in the solar system. It would be impossible, therefore, to support the great numbers of men who would be raised up under a perfect government; the earth would be over-stocked at last, and the greatest admirers of such fanciful schemes must foresee the fatal period when they would come to an end, as they are alto-gether inconsistent with the limits of that earth in which they must exist.

What a miserable catastrophe of the most generous of all human systems of government! How dreadfully would the magistrates of such commonwealths find themselves disconcerted at that fatal period, when there was no longer any room for new colonies, and when the earth could produce no further supplies! During all the preceding ages, while there was room for increase, mankind must have been happy; the earth must have been a paradise in the literal sense, as the greatest part of it must have been turned into delightful and fruitful gardens. But when the dread-ful time should at last come, when our globe, by the most diligent culture, could not produce what was sufficient to nourish its numerous inhabitants, what happy expedient could then be found out to remedy so great an evil?

In such a cruel necessity, must there be a law to restrain marriage? Must multitudes of women, be shut up in cloisters like the ancient vestals or modern nuns? To keep a ballance between the two sexes, must a pro-portionable number of men be debarred from marriage? Shall the Uto-pians, following the wicked policy of superstition, forbid their priests to marry; or shall they rather sacrifice men of some other profession for the good of the state? Or, shall they appoint the sons of certain families to be maimed at their birth, and give a sanction to the unnatural institution of eunuchs? If none of these expedients can be thought proper, shall they appoint a certain number of infants to be exposed to death as soon as they are born, determining the proportion according to the exigencies of the state; and pointing out the particular victims by lot, or according to some established rule? Or, must they shorten the period of human life by a law, and condemn all to die after they had compleated a certain age, which might be shorter or longer, as provisions were either more scanty or plentiful? Or what other method should they devise (for an expedient would be absolutely necessary) to restrain the number of citizens within reasonable bounds?

Alas! how unnatural and inhuman must every such expedient be accounted! The natural passions and appetites of mankind are planted in our frame, to answer the best ends for the happiness both of the individuals and of the species. Shall we be obliged to contradict such a wise order?

Shall we be laid under the necessity of acting barbarously and inhumanly? Sad and fatal necessity! And which, after all, could never answer the end, but would give rise to violence and war. For mankind would never agree about such regulations. Force, and arms, must at last decide their quarrels, and the deaths of such as fall in battle, leave sufficient provisions for the survivors, and make room for others to be born.

Thus the tranquility and numerous blessings of the Utopian governments would come to an end; war, or cruel and unnatural customs, be introduced, and a stop put to the increase of mankind, to the advancement of knowledge, and to the culture of the earth, in spite of the most excellent laws and wisest precautions. The more excellent the laws had been, and the more strictly they had been observed, mankind must have sooner become miserable. The remembrance of former times, the greatness of their wisdom and virtue, would conspire to heighten their distress; and the world, instead of remaining the mansion of wisdom and happiness, become the scene of vice and confusion. Force and fraud must prevail, and mankind be reduced to the same calamitous condition as at present.

10

Is Charity Compatible with Stability?

As we have seen, some writers before the latter half of the eighteenth century did have a few things to say about population; but what they said was said only in passing, without explicitly developing the consequence. Systematic, carefully reasoned discussions came only toward the end of the eighteenth century as observant men increasingly realized that something was wrong with the "poor laws"—various laws established for the relief of poverty by state-organized work schemes or state-supported charity. But, ever since their appearance in the sixteenth century, poor laws had been under fire as **poor** laws; there was more than a little suspicion that they actually increased the poverty they were supposed to ameliorate. Economists were developing the first vague ideas of systems and equilibria, and critics of the poor laws began to ask whether the poor laws tended to produce equilibria, and if so, where were the points of stability? These questions were not asked very clearly, or in these terms, but such questions are implicit in the best of the early discussions.

Among the most important of the premalthusian writers was Joseph Townsend, a selection from whose **Dissertation** follows. The title page of this work identifies the author only as a "Well-Wisher of Mankind." It was not fear or cowardice that caused Townsend to remain anonymous; he merely followed the custom of most well-born English gentlemen of the eighteenth and early nineteenth centuries. We find the same semblance of modesty in the scientific papers of today, in which "I observed" is avoided in favor of "it was found"; and the sometimes ambiguous phrase "the author" stands for a brief and clear "I."

11

A Dissertation on the Poor Laws
BY A WELL-WISHER TO MANKIND

Joseph Townsend
1739–1816

1786

To a man of common sensibility nothing can be more distressing, than to hear the complaints of wretchedness, which he hath no power to redress, and to be daily conversant with misery, which he can neither fly from, nor relieve. This at present is the situation of the clergy, who, in virtue of their office, are obliged to visit the habitations of the poor. . . .

These [poor] laws, so beautiful in theory, promote the evils they mean to remedy, and aggravate the distress they were intended to relieve. . . .

Hope and fear are the springs of industry. It is the part of a good politician to strengthen these: but our laws weaken the one and destroy the other. For what encouragement have the poor to be industrious and frugal, when they know for certain, that should they increase their store it will be devoured by the drones? or what cause have they to fear, when they are assured, that if by their indolence and extravagance, by their drunkenness and vices, they should be reduced to want, they shall be abundantly supplied, not only with food and raiment, but with their accustomed luxuries, at the expense of others. The poor know little of the motives which stimulate the higher ranks to action—pride, honour, and ambition. In general it is only hunger which can spur and goad them on to labour; yet our laws have said, they shall never hunger. The laws, it must be confessed, have likewise said that they shall be compelled to work. But then legal constraint is attended with too much trouble, violence, and noise; creates ill will, and never can be productive of good and acceptable service: whereas hunger is not only a peaceable, silent, unremitting pressure, but, as the most natural motive to industry and labour, it calls forth the most powerful exertions; and, when satisfied by the free bounty of another, lays a lasting and sure foundation for good will and gratitude. . . .

He, who statedly employs the poor in useful labour, is their only friend; he, who only feeds them, is their greatest enemy. Their hopes and fears should centre in themselves. . . .

Now a fixed, a certain, and a constant provision for the poor weakens this spring; it increases their improvidence, but does not promote their chearful compliance with those demands, which the community is obliged to make on the most indigent of its members; it tends to destroy the harmony and beauty, the symmetry and order of that system, which God and nature have established in the world. . . .

In the South Seas there is an island, which from the first discoverer is called Juan Fernandes. In this sequestered spot, John Fernando placed a colony of goats, consisting of one male, attended by his female. This happy couple finding pasture in abundance, could readily obey the first commandment, to increase and multiply, till in process of time they had replenished their little island. . . .

In advancing to this period they were strangers to misery and want, and seemed to glory in their numbers: but from this unhappy moment they began to suffer hunger; yet continuing for a time to increase their numbers, had they been endued with reason, they must have apprehended the extremity of famine. In this situation the weakest first gave way, and plenty was again restored. Thus they fluctuated between happiness and misery, and either suffered want or rejoiced in abundance, according as their numbers were diminished or increased; never at a stay, yet nearly balancing at all times their quantity of food. This degree of equipoise was from time to time destroyed, either by epidemical diseases or by the arrival of some vessel in distress. On such occasions their numbers were considerably reduced; but to compensate for this alarm, and to comfort them for the loss of their companions, the survivors never failed immediately to meet returning plenty. They were no longer in fear of famine: they ceased to regard each other with an evil eye; all had abundance, all were contented, all were happy. Thus, what might have been considered as misfortunes, proved a source of comfort; and, to them at least, partial evil was universal good. . . .

When the Spaniards found that the English privateers resorted to this island for provisions, they resolved on the total extirpation of the goats, and for this purpose they put on shore a greyhound dog and bitch. These in their turn increased and multiplied, in proportion to the quantity of food they met with; but in consequence, as the Spaniards had foreseen, the breed of goats diminished. Had they been totally destroyed, the dogs likewise must have perished. But as many of the goats retired to the craggy rocks, where the dogs could never follow them, descending only for short intervals to feed with fear and circumspection in the valleys, few of these, besides the careless and the rash, became a prey; and none but the most watchful, strong, and active of the dogs could get a sufficiency of food. Thus a new kind of balance was established. The weakest of both species were among the first to pay the debt of nature; the most active and vigorous preserved their lives. It is the quantity of food which regulates the numbers of the human species. In the woods, and in the *savage state,* there can be few inhabitants; but of these there will be only a proportionable few to suffer want. As long as food is plenty they will continue to increase and multiply; and every man will have ability to support his family, or to relieve his friends, in proportion to his activity and strength. The weak must depend upon the precarious bounty of the strong; and, sooner or later, the lazy will be left to suffer the natural consequence of their indolence. Should they introduce a community of goods, and at the same time leave every man at liberty to marry, they would at first increase their numbers, but not the sum total of their happiness, till by degrees, all being equally reduced to want and misery, the weakly would be the first to perish. . . .

With regard to celibacy, we may observe, that where things are left to a course of nature, one passion regulates another, and the stronger appetite restrains the weaker. There is an appetite, which is and should be urgent, but which, if left to operate without restraint, would multiply the human species before provision could be made for their support. Some check, some balance is therefore absolutely needful, and hunger is the proper balance; hunger, not as directly felt or feared by the individual for himself, but as foreseen and feared for his immediate offspring. Were it not for this the equilibrium would not be preserved so near as it is at present in the world, between the numbers of people and the quantity of food. Various are the circumstances to be observed in different nations, which tend to blunt the shafts of Cupid, or at least to quench the torch of Hymen. . . .

By establishing a community of goods, or rather by giving to the idle and to the vicious the *first* claim upon the produce of the earth, many of the more prudent, careful, and industrious citizens are straitened in their circumstances, and restrained from marriage. The farmer breeds only from the best of all his cattle; but our laws choose rather to preserve the worst, and seems to be anxious lest the breed should fail. The cry is Population, population! population at all events! But is there any reasonable fear of depopulation? . . .

It is true, by a statute made in the thirty-first year of Queen Elizabeth, there is a penalty on every person who shall build a cottage without assigning four acres of land to be held for ever with it: but this statute, with which her famous poor law is in perfect harmony, and which, if observed, would have prevented the greatest evils felt and to be feared from that neglected provision for the poor, has been long neglected, or perhaps was never regarded. The penalty is ten pounds for the first erection of the cottage, and forty shillings per month as long as it shall be occupied. Had this law remained in force, or had it been constantly observed, the poor would not have multiplied; but then the manufactures would not have flourished in the kingdom as they do at present.

12
What if the World Be an Island and We Have No Dogs?

Townsend also wrote **A Journey Through Spain in the Years 1786 and 1787,** which was published in 1791. Scattered about in this work are various remarks on population, of which the following is worth recording here:

Increase the quantity of food, or where that is limited, prescribe bounds to population. In a fully peopled country, to say, that no one shall suffer want is absurd. Could you supply their wants, you would soon double their numbers, and advance your population **ad infinitum,** which is contrary to the supposition. It is indeed possible to banish hunger, and to supply that want at the expence of another; but then you must determine the proportion that shall marry, because you will have no other way to limit the number of your people. No human efforts will get rid of this dilemma; nor will men ever find a method, either more natural, or better in any respect, than to leave one appetite to regulate another.

Townsend did not directly affect the history of thought nearly as much as Malthus. Nevertheless, his story, possibly apocryphal, of the goats on Juan Fernandes Island still haunts the minds of men. If all this great earth be no more than the Island of Juan Fernandes, and if we are the goats, how can we live "the good life" without a functional equivalent of the dogs? Must we create and sustain our own dogs? Can we do so, consciously? And if we can, what manner of beast will they be?

13

The Checks to Population

William Forster Lloyd
1794–1852

From Two Lectures on the Checks to Population,
delivered before the University of Oxford
in Michaelmas Term, 1832

1833

From what has been said, I draw one general inference, viz. that the simple fact of a country being over populous, by which I mean its population pressing too closely against the means of subsistence, is not, of itself, sufficient evidence that the fault lies in the people themselves, or a proof of the absence of a prudential disposition. The fault may rest, not with them as individuals, but with the constitution of the society, of which they form part. . . .

I do not profess to be here considering generally the merits of systems of equality, and, therefore, I shall not stop to inquire, whether any, and what substitute, for the motive of private interest, can be suggested, to stimulate exertion, to prevent waste, and to check the undue increase of population. My object, in now referring to them, has merely been to illustrate the principle of objection to them, derived from the theory of population—a principle, which to some may perhaps appear so plain and self-evident, as not to have required the notice I have bestowed on it, but which, while it exists in a considerable degree of force in the present condition of the labouring classes in this country, seems nevertheless, as to its bearing on those classes, in a great measure to have ecaped observation. . . .

It will serve to illustrate the subject, if we compare the relation subsisting between the cases of two countries, in one of which the constitution of society is such as to throw the burden of a family entirely on the parents, and in the other such that the children maintain themselves at a very early age, with that subsisting between the parallel cases of inclosed grounds and commons; the parallel consisting in what regards the degree of density, in which the countries are peopled, and the commons are stocked, respectively. Why are the cattle on a common so puny and stunted? Why is the common itself so bare-worn, and cropped so differently from the adjoining enclosures? No inequality, in respect of natural or acquired fertility, will account for the phenomenon. The difference depends on the difference of the way in which an increase of stock in the two cases affects the circumstances of the author of the increase. If a person puts more cattle into his own field, the amount of the subsistence which they consume is all deducted from that which was at the command, of his original stock; and if, before, there was no more than a sufficiency of pasture, he reaps no benefit from the additional cattle, what is gained in one way being lost in another. But if he puts more cattle on a common, the food which they consume forms a deduction which is shared between all the cattle, as well that of others as his own, in proportion to their number, and only a small part of it is taken from his own cattle. In an enclosed pasture, there is a point of saturation, if I may so call it (by which, I mean a barrier depending on consideration of interest) beyond which no prudent man will add to his stock. In a common, also, there is in like manner a point of saturation. But the position of the point in the two cases is obviously different. Were a number of adjoining pastures, already fully stocked, to be at once thrown open, and converted into one vast common, the position of the point of saturation would immediately be changed. The stock would be increased, and would be made to press much more forcibly against the means of subsistence. . . .

Now, the field for the employment of labour is in fact a common, the pasture of which is free to all, to the born and to the unborn, to the present tenants of the earth, and to all who are waiting for admission. In the common for cattle, the young animal begins an independent participa-

29

tion in the produce, by the possession of a set of teeth and the ability to graze. In the common for man, the child begins a similar participation, by the possession of a pair of hands competent to labour. The tickets for admission being so readily procurable, it cannot happen otherwise, than that the commons, in both cases, must be constantly stocked to the extreme point of saturation. . . .

Mr. Malthus, in treating of the effects which would result to society from the prevalence of moral restraint, infers, that 'if it were generally adopted, by lowering the supply of labour in the market, it would, in the natural course of things, soon raise its price.' And we may readily allow, that, abstinence from marriage, if generally and almost universally prevalent, would have this effect. But, if the principles laid down in the last Lecture be correct, it is idle to imagine, that, among labourers who have only the sale of their labour on which to depend for their maintenance, such abstinence can ever generally prevail; and this for the simple reason, that, against it, there are the natural passions which prompt to marriage, and the substantial benefits derivable from marriage; while, in favour of it, to oppose these, there is no adequate individual benefit to be derived from abstinence. . . .

For, for the sake of argument, suppose it to prevail, and, by consequence, that the money wages of labour will command a considerable quantity of food. All labourers, therefore, without distinction, have apparently a greater power of maintaining with decency a large family. If all continue to abstain, they will retain this power. But here I ask, what is there to hinder individuals, who do not enter into the common feeling, from taking advantage of the general forbearance? What rule of prudence would they violate by doing so? Would they lower their rank in life? Would they be unable to transmit to their children the same advantages which they had themselves possessed? They might indeed have for a few years to deny themselves a few luxuries of dress or furniture, or otherwise, possibly, to submit to harder work and harder fare in order to retain them. . . .

Dr. Chalmers follows in the track of Mr. Malthus, and assumes, that by the operation of the moral preventive check, we may hope to see wages kept permanently high. And this effect he proposes to produce, through the means 'both of common and Christian education.' It is also to be the immediate fruit, 'not of any external or authoritative compulsion, but of the spontaneous and collective will of the working classes of society.' . . .

Let us examine this question by reference to a case, which, though not exactly similar, is yet sufficiently so for the present purpose. Were unanimity essential to the enactment of every law, and, not only to its enactment, but also to its continuance, there would evidently be great difficulties in the way of government. Could we entertain the hope of removing these difficulties by means of education? And in like manner I would ask, will education produce unanimity among the working classes of society? And, if it will not, how can effect be given to their collective will, without authoritative compulsion to coerce a dissentient minority? How can we expect that some will abstain from marriage, when others may step in to take advantage of their abstinence? . . .

The fact is, that the wages of the lowest description of labour, in every old country where competition has been tolerably free, have always bordered on the minimum necessary for maintenance. It was an observation of Swift, a hundred years ago, that there were few countries in which one third of the people were not extremely stinted even in the necessaries of life; and, were the point doubtful, similar remarks, applicable to almost every period of history, might be gleaned from other writers. We may expect them to remain at least in the structure of society, which shall furnish hopes of an advancement in station, leaving less to chance, and, at the same time, producing a degree of isolation, by which the consequences, whether good or evil, flowing from the actions of individuals, may be more fully appropriated to the authors of them. . . .

The common reasons for the establishment of private property in land are deduced from the necessity, of offering to individuals sufficient motives for cultivating the ground, and of preventing the wasteful destruction of the immature products of the earth. But to these there is another added, by the theory of population, from which we infer, that, since the earth can never maintain all who can offer themselves for maintenance, it is better that its produce should be divided into shares of a definite magnitude, sufficient each for the comfortable maintenance of a family, whence the number of families to be maintained would be determined from the number of such shares, than that all, who can possibly enter, should be first admitted, and then the magnitude of each share be determined from the number of admissions. . . .

Men are attracted upwards by the example of others who are richer than themselves. At the top of the scale this attraction is wanting. At that point, therefore, it is necessary that there should be a title to wealth without the labour of producing it. A state of perfect equality, by its effect in lowering the standard of desire, and almost reducing it to the satisfaction of the natural necessities, would bring back society to ignorance and barbarism. Still, the same principle of population, which furnishes a reason for the institution of property, prescribes a limit to its concentration. To a plank in the sea, which cannot support all, all have not an equal right; the lucky individuals, who can first obtain possession, being justified in appropriating it to themselves, to the exclusion of the remainder. Where property is much concentrated, and where, by consequence, the class of mere labourers is great, the principle of population would warrant the application of the same argument, to justify the appropriation of the field of employment, and a monopoly of labour. But, since such a monopoly is not easily maintainable, we are led to look for an equivalent in the diffusion of a sufficient degree of property throughout the whole fabric of society.

14
Malthus Under Attack

In the realm of theory the most important thing Malthus contributed to population doctrine was the cybernetic view of a balanced population in a static environment.[1] The view was only implicit in Malthus' writings, however; another century and a half was to pass before the ideas of cybernetics were to be made fully explicit by Norbert Wiener.

In a static environment the size of a population is controlled much as the temperature of a room is controlled by a thermostat. Fluctuations upward are damped by density-dependent mortality; fluctuations downward are erased by natural exponential growth. Metaphorically, one can say that the population is controlled by a **demostat.** The "carrying capacity" of the environment determines the **set point** of the demostat.

Unfortunately for his reputation, Malthus was living in a time when the set point was drifting upward, **but he didn't know it.** Edward Deevey, in his essay **The Human Population,**[2] identifies three great secular shifts in the set point of the human demostat, caused (in chronological order) by the toolmaking revolution, the agricultural revolution, and the scientific-industrial revolution (which is still continuing). The demostatic analysis of Malthus' writings implicitly refers to "normal," nonrevolutionary times. Had he written his **Essay** in the year 1000 probably no one would have contradicted him. He probably wouldn't have been noticed, either.

Unaware of the revolution he was living in, Malthus implied that any increase in the population of his own country in his own time would result in an increase in "misery and vice." History mocked him. In the fifth edition of his **Essay,** published in 1817, Malthus admits:

> The returns of the Population Act in 1811 undoubtedly presented extraordinary results. They showed a greatly accelerated rate of prog-

ress, and a greatly improved healthiness of the people, notwithstanding the increase of the towns and the increased proportion of the population engaged in manufacturing employment.

Not only in the towns, but throughout the nation, population and prosperity increased more or less hand-in-hand for all the years of Malthus' life, which continued until thirty-six years after the publication of the first edition of the **Essay.** The parallelism was not perfect, and there were fluctuations, but the contradiction of his prediction was still striking enough to furnish his critics with damaging ammunition.

Malthusian theory was vulnerable also in its conception of mechanism. A child of the eighteenth century, Malthus quite naturally developed his theory on the assumption that Man was wholly rational (though short-sighted). In prosperous times, rational men would marry and beget children, thus bringing about a diminution in the average prosperity. In hard times, men would rationally refrain from marriage and reproduction. But men are not wholly rational, at least not in this simple sense. On 26 October 1789 (when Malthus was only three years old) James Boswell recorded that his idol Samuel Johnson had remarked: "It is not from reason and prudence that men marry, but from inclination. A man is poor; he thinks, 'I cannot be worse, and so I'll e'en taken Peggy.' "

Cybernetically, this remark contains the germ of a theory that can quite properly be called anti-malthusian. If poverty causes people to breed more, and prosperity causes them to breed less, the result will be runaway feedback at both extremes of population density (with, presumably, a singularly unstable point of equilibrium between). The full implications of this remarkable theory have never been explicitly worked out, but in cryptic form it crops up every generation. Most recently, it was the thesis of Josué de Castro's **Geography of Hunger** (Boston: Little, Brown, 1952). The first expression of it, so far as I have been able to discover, was in an essay by T. R. Edmonds, published two years before Malthus' death; though Thomas Doubleday is usually given the credit, on the basis of a magazine article published in 1837 and expanded five years later into a book, **The True Law of Population shewn to be connected with the Food of the People.**

Although the anti-malthusian theory enjoys a perennial popularity with incurable optimists of a certain stripe, it has never been taken seriously by professional demographers. It hardly seems adequate for a broad, general theory of population dynamics. Nevertheless, there is a psychological truth at the base of this heterodox theory that must not be neglected in any attempt to control population growth.

---

[1] See Garrett Hardin, *Biology: Its Principles and Implications* (2nd ed.), San Francisco: W. H. Freeman and Company, 1966 (Chapter 9, "Population Dynamics").

[2] *Scientific American,* **203** (September 1960): 194–203. Reprinted in *39 Steps to Biology,* Garrett Hardin (ed.), San Francisco: W. H. Freeman and Company, 1968.

15

An Enquiry into the Principles of Population

exhibiting a System of Regulations for the Poor;
designed immediately to lessen, and finally to remove,
the evils which have hitherto pressed upon the
Labouring Classes of Society

Thomas Rowe Edmonds
1803–1889

Published anonymously

1832

Population does not actually increase in strict conformity with the received opinions upon that subject. It is quite possible for the ratio of increase to be small in countries possessing a lavish abundance of food. The labouring population may be in an elevated position, so that strong feelings of self-respect may be established which assimilate them in their habits to the better classes of society, and which render the operation of prudential restraint eminently efficacious. There has certainly been a deterioration in the condition of the English labourers; there is a great existing distress; and yet according to every authentic information the rate of increase is greater now than formerly, so complete has been the destruction of the feeling of self-respect. Amongst the great body of the people at the present moment, sexual intercourse is the only gratification; and thus, by a most unfortunate concurrence of adverse circumstances, population goes on augmenting at a period when it ought to be restrained. To better the condition of the labouring classes, that is, to place more food and comforts before them, however paradoxical it may appear, is the wisest mode to check redundancy. On this principle many singular anomalies in Ireland can be explained. The increase of poverty in that country, which has certainly taken place within the last generation, has increased the number of births, and probably also the adult population. Were that country to emerge from her present condition, and were the object to restrain a further supply of labourers, the wisest course would be to give the people a greater command over the necessaries of life. When they are better fed they will have other enjoyments at command than sexual intercourse, and their numbers, therefore, will not increase in the same proportion as at present.

16

The True Law of Population

Thomas Doubleday
1790–1870

London: Simpkin, Marshall & Co.

1842

In order to come in the clearest and fairest manner to the subject of this essay, the author deems the following to be the most advisable course. To state, first, in the tersest and at the same time, most lucid manner he can, the law by which he supposes population to be governed and regulated; next, to prove the existence and operation of this law from such facts as he has collected, which in his opinion tend to demonstrate either or both of these points. The GREAT GENERAL LAW then, which, as it seems, really regulates the increase or decrease both of vegetable and of animal life, is this, that whenever a *species* or *genus* is *endangered,* a corresponding effort is invariably made by nature for its preservation and continuance, by an increase of fecundity or fertility; and that this especially takes place whenever such danger arises from a diminution of proper nourishment or food, so that consequently the state of depletion, or the deplethoric state, is favourable to fertility, and that on the other hand, the plethoric state, or state of repletion, is unfavorable to fertility, in the ratio of the intensity of each state, and this probably throughout nature universally, in the vegetable as well as the animal world; further, that as applied to mankind this law produces the following consequences, and acts thus:—

There is in all societies a constant increase going on amongst that portion of it which is the worst supplied with food; in short, amongst the poorest.

Amongst those in the state of affluence, and well supplied with food and luxuries, a constant decrease goes on. Amongst those who form the mean or medium between these two opposite states, that is to say, amongst those who are tolerably well supplied with good food, and not overworked, nor yet idle, population is stationary. Hence it follows that it is upon the *numerical proportion* which these three states bear to each other in any society that increase or decrease upon the whole depends.

In a nation where the affluence is sufficient to balance, by the decrease which it causes amongst the rich, the increase arising from the poor, population will be stationary. In a nation highly and generally affluent and luxurious, population will decrease and decay. In poor and ill-fed communities, population will increase in the ratio of the poverty, and the consequent deterioration and diminution of the food of a large portion of the members of such communities. This is the real and great law of human population. . . .

Turning now to the vegetable kingdom, the author would point to the acknowledged existence of this principle in the theory and practice of all Horticulturists, Gardeners, and others engaged in the raising of trees, shrubs, flowers, and vegetables. It is a fact, admitted by all gardeners as well as botanists, that if a tree, plant, or flower, be placed in mould, either naturally or artificially made too rich for it, a plethoric state is produced, and fruitfulness ceases. In trees, the effect of strong manures and over-rich soils is that they run to superfluous wood, blossom irregularly, and chiefly at the extremities of the outer branches, and almost or entirely cease to bear fruit.

In order to remedy this state when accidentally produced, Gardeners and Florists are accustomed, by various devices, to produce the opposite or deplethoric state; this they familiarly denominate "giving a check." In other words, they put the species in danger in order to produce a correspondingly determined effort of nature to ensure its perpetuation, and the end is invariable attained. . . .

When a gardener wishes to save seed from a gourd or cucumber, he does not give the plant an *extra* quantity of manure or warmth. He does just the contrary: he subjects it to some *hardship* and takes the fruit that is *least* fine looking, foreknowing that it will be filled with seed, whilst the finest fruit are nearly destitute. . . .

There cannot be a doubt that, with the animal creation—including in that term birds and quadrupeds (of the habits of fish we know little or nothing)—fecundity is totally checked by the plethoric state, when induced, and increased, and rendered doubly certain, by the existence of the deplethoric or lean state; whilst a moderated prolificness is the effect of the state between the two. This is more or less the case even with the most prolific animals. The rabbit and the swine are extraordinary in this respect; yet every schoolboy knows that the doe, or female rabbit, and every farmer and breeder knows that the sow will *not* conceive if fed to a certain height of fatness; and that the number of the progeny is generally in the *ratio* of the *leanness* of the animal. All cattle breeders know the same law to be especially true in the cases of the mare, the cow, and the ewe, with which leanness is indispensable to conception; and upon their knowledge of this truth they invariably act. . . .

17

The Prevalence of People

Marston Bates
1906–

New York: Charles Scribner's Sons

1955

One of the most interesting theories has been developed by Josué de Castro in a book called *The Geography of Hunger*. The thesis of this book, if I may greatly oversimplify, is that overpopulation is caused by malnutrition. This, at least, is a refreshing reversal of the usual theory, that malnutrition is a result of overpopulation, though I am not persuaded by the logic of de Castro's book.

De Castro deals with the relationship between nutrition and reproduction at what might be called a physiological level; whereas I think that in man the cultural factors overwhelm any likely physiological effects. One may be able to show a relation between diet and litter size in rats, and there may well be a direct relation between the kind of food eaten and fertility in man. But when one examines actual situations, like Ireland, the explanation of changed fertility in man always seems to lie in things like marriage rates, birth control practices, infanticide, or such-like social factors, rather than in relative or absolute amounts of protein or vitamins or other things in the diet.

As far as I can see, most of the evidence from physiological studies indicates that malnutrition and famine tend to reduce fertility in man, so that the high reproductive rates in the Orient persist in spite of malnutrition rather than because of it.

One of the most interesting, and certainly the most thorough, of studies of the effects of starvation on man was carried out by Ancel Keys and a group of collaborators at the University of Minnesota, during World War II, using a group of volunteers from among "conscientious objectors." Their studies were written up and published in two huge volumes, which contain not only the results of their own observations, but also the results of combing through a vast literature.

One of the first effects of starvation on the men in the Minnesota group was a loss of all interest in sex. Their thoughts and dreams turned on food, not women; and their normal pattern of sexual activity, whether of coitus or masturbation, was broken.

> The diminution of the strength of the sex drive was so dramatic that the subjects were struck by the change and used colorful language to describe it. As one of them put it, "I have no more sexual feeling than a sick oyster. . . ." In the rehabilitation period, sexual impulses, needs and interests were very slow in regaining their pre-experimental intensity; they were still low at the end of the 12th week of rehabilitation.

Keys made all sorts of physiological measurements on his starvation subjects, including measurements of semen volume and sperm count. From these it appears that the men would probably have been sterile even if they had had the drive and opportunity for sex. Recovery was slow and the semen did not become normal until more than 20 weeks after rehabilitation had started.

The female reproductive system is surely also affected by starvation. The most direct evidence is the frequency of amenorrhea, or interruption of regular menstruation, under internment camp conditions. Keys quotes one observation, however, of a physician who noted that menstruation continued to be regular among emaciated Chinese women, suggesting an "adaptation to chronic starvation."

Direct evidence on fertility under actual famine conditions is hard to come by, because the conditions that lead to famine are not conducive to orderly statistical studies. Such evidence as there is, however, all tends to indicate greatly lowered fertility. For instance, during the severe famine in Madras in 1877, there were only 39 births in the relief camps, although more than 100,000 people were being cared for over a period of some months. The birth rate dropped early in the famine, probably as a consequence of the preceding near-famine conditions, and continued low for a considerable time. Nine months after the worst food shortage the birth rate was four to five per 1,000, as compared to a usual rate of 29 per 1,000 in the same districts.

Statistical services were maintained in the Netherlands all through World War II, and the record of births there is consequently one of the few available for famine conditions. In Rotterdam, for instance, there was no significant change in the birth rate from 1939 through 1944. Food was moderately restricted from the middle of 1940; but serious failure of food supply did not occur until September, 1944, with a low point in availability of food from January to April, 1945. The birth rate started to fall in July, 1945, ten months after the failure of food the previous September. By

October, 1945, births were less than half of normal (averaging 84 per week as compared with 210 to 245 per week in 1944). The birth rate in Rotterdam all through this period thus reflected neatly the food conditions prevailing nine or ten months previously.

18

1960: Cassandra Gets a Hearing

The Greeks had a keen ear for frustration. As a consequence of being kissed by a sacred snake Cassandra could correctly foretell the future—but no one would believe her. Biologists who lived through the first half of the twentieth century feel they understand what must have been her feelings of frustration. Like Cassandra prophesying the tragedy of the Trojan wars, biologists of the '30's and '40's insisted that the time of overpopulation was at hand—but the world did not believe them.

The inattention and scorn heaped on the biological Cassandras is understandable. Belief in the inevitability and rightness of perpetual expansion and growth required an ignoring of the finiteness of the world and a denial of the possibility of overpopulation. Those who asserted that there **was** a population problem implicitly attacked the religion of Progress, the only really universal religion of the time. They were regarded as pessimists, that is to say, apostates. Society does not hand out medals for killing Santa Claus.

The facts of historical development in the century after Malthus belied his gloomy predictions—at a superficial level. Not only did population grow faster than ever before, but per capita income grew even faster. Most un-malthusian! At least this is what happened in the "Western world," or "the Great Society"—roughly the literate world. What was happening in the illiterate world was quite another thing—but who knew about that? The religion of Progress was a religion of those who were rich enough to spare time for reading and writing about Progress and population; those who had to spend all their time grubbing out a living had no time to produce such a literature. Bias is more effective than censorship in producing conformity of thought.

Between 1924 and 1932 an English publisher put out a series of little books under the general title **Today and Tomorrow.** Nearly one hundred British intellectuals described their visions of the future. Not one of them mentioned the possibility of overpopulation, though J. B. S. Haldane, one of the brightest of the biologists, devoted some space to a discussion of the dangers of underpopulation.

For twenty years, beginning in 1934, the British historian A. J. Toynbee put out volume after volume of his monumental **Study of History.** When it was completed, the novelist Aldous Huxley thought he would use the index to see what the great historian had to say about population and related matters. This is what he found:

> In the index at the end of the sixth volume of Dr. Toynbee's **A Study of History,** Popilius Laenas gets five mentions and Porphyry of Batamaca, two; but the word you would expect to find between these names, Population, is conspicuous by its absence. . . . (One would like to know something about the Famines of earlier ages, but the nearest one gets to them in Mr. Toynbee's index is a blank space between Muhammad Falak-al-Din and Gaius Fannius.) . . . Agriculture (not referred to in Mr. Toynbee's index, though Agrigentum gets two mentions and Agis IV, King of Sparta, no less than forty-seven). . . . (One looks up Erosion in Mr. Toynbee's index but finds only Esarkaddon, Esotericism and Esperanto; one hunts for Forests, but has to be content, alas, with Formosus of Porto.)[1]

Even as Toynbee began the publication of his history several biologists were beginning to sound the alarm about population and the related topics of pollution, deforestation, soil erosion and famines. From 1930 to 1960 a number of excellent discussions were contributed by Karl Sax, Julian Huxley, William Vogt, Raymond Cowles and Robert C. Cook, to mention only a few. Biologists were impressed by this literature, but nonbiologists tended, on the whole, to ignore it, as one would ignore a rude noise in a polite gathering. Then, some time during the '50's, the tide began to change. The reasons for this change were no doubt complex; they have not been adequately studied from a historical point of view. A statistical indication of this change comes from the files of the Population Reference Bureau of Washington, D. C. This organization, largely the creation of Robert C. Cook, prepares objective, factual background studies of the population aspects of current political hot spots and distributes them as news releases to the press. The increase in the number of newspapers that use these releases and send courtesy copies back to the PRB—which not all of them do—gives a measure of public interest in population problems:

Year	Known Number of Press Clippings
1952	231
1960	1,216
1961	3,334
1962	5,725
1963	6,414

The biological Cassandras were finally heard. In the '60's, Toynbee himself wrote frequently and well about the importance of population in shaping the future history of the world, and lesser men followed in his wake. It is difficult now to imagine a time in the future when a new study of history might be written in which population would not be a major topic.

---

[1] Aldous Huxley, *Collected Essays,* New York: Bantam Books, 1960, p. 241.

19

One Man's Family

Glenn D. Everett
1921–

Population Bulletin, **17,** No. 8

1961

Recently, on the eve of his 95th birthday, John Eli Miller died in a rambling farmhouse near Middlefield, Ohio, 40 miles southeast of Cleveland, leaving to mourn his passing perhaps the largest number of living descendants any American has ever had.

He was survived by five of his seven children, 61 grandchildren, 338 great-grandchildren and six great-great-grandchildren, a grand total of 410 descendants.

Shortly before his death, which came unexpectedly from a stroke, I had the privilege of two long visits with John E. Miller, during which I learned the feeling of one man who had personally watched the population explosion of the 20th century. A national magazine had determined that the venerable Ohio farmer was head of what almost certainly was the largest family in the United States.

A Swedish newspaper in 1958 ran a competition for the largest family in that country and when a family named Hellander turned up with 265 members, headed by a 92-year-old great-grandmother, it asserted a claim to the Swedish and to the world championship.

Soon reports of even larger families were streaming in to editors, with an elderly Mormon couple in Utah claiming 334 living descendants taking the lead. However, I was certain that among the Old Order Amish

41

Mennonites, a sect in which families of more than 100 are commonplace, a family larger than this could be found. Through the medium of the Sugarcreek, Ohio, *Budget,* a unique weekly newspaper that is read by the Old Order Amish in all their communities throughout the Nation, it was soon ascertained that John Eli Miller, with his clan of more than 400, had the largest family among them. So far as could be learned, this family was the largest in America and probably the world's largest among monogamous peoples.

When John Miller and his family refused to pose for photographs because of their religious opposition to "graven images," the magazine gave up the idea of a story about this "largest family" but the interviews disclosed a number of facts about the impact of extremely rapid population growth on this family and the cultural group of which it is a part. These facts merit the serious attention of all students of population problems.

John Miller actually had seen with his own eyes a population explosion in his own lifetime. His data were not statistics on a graph or chart, but the scores of children at every family gathering who ran up to kiss Grandpa, so many that it confused a poor old man. His confusion can be forgiven for there were among them no less than 15 John Millers, all named in his honor. And what young man, much less an old one, could remember the names of 61 grandchildren and 338 great-grandchildren and keep straight just who their parents were?

The remarkable thing about this great clan of his was that it started with a family of just seven children. This was actually a little smaller than the typical family among the Amish, who have been found by one researcher to average 8.4 children per completed family. Two of his children died in early life: Samuel Miller, who left six children when he died at 40, and Lizzie (Mrs. Jacob Farnwald), who left four when she died at 28.

During most of his long life, therefore, John Miller's family was not unusually large. It is just that he lived long enough to find out what simple multiplication can do.

One of his daughters, Mary (Mrs. Jacob Mast), had only five children. But all four of his sons had quite large families. His son, John, Jr., with whom he lived at the family homestead, had six children by his first wife, who died in an accident, and nine more by his present wife, a total of 15. Andrew Miller had 12, Eli Miller, 11, of whom ten are living, and Joseph Miller, ten, of whom nine are living.

Of the 63 grandchildren born to John Miller's family, 61 lived to survive him, all but six now grown and married. And of 341 great-grandchildren born to the families of his 55 married grandchildren, only three had died, two in infancy, and one in an accident. All six of his great-great-grandchildren were born during the last year of his life and were healthy infants.

Thus, a major factor in the world-wide population crisis was vividly evident in John Miller's family: the fact that nearly all children born in the 20th century, who enjoy the benefits of modern medicine, are growing up to become adults and to have families of their own. A century ago, the ravages of smallpox, typhoid fever, tuberculosis, diphtheria and the many fatalities that occurred at childbirth would have left a far different picture in a large rural family. Even though the Amish live in rural areas, they avail themselves of the benefits of medical care. Now most Amish children are born in hospital delivery rooms.

While the sharp reduction in infant mortality and childhood disease is a happy development of science, it inevitably means that population grows with extraordinary rapidity. The Miller family offers a cogent example. John Miller had seven children; his children averaged nine offspring; and his married grandchildren had averaged six each when he passed away. Six married great-grandchildren had one apiece. These were not unusually large families among the Amish nor among the rural families of other Americans in the past century. Yet this clan numbered 410 when John Miller died.

Moreover, at the end of his life, the postman was bringing John Miller word of the birth of a new descendant on the average of once every ten days. This rate, we calculated, would have accelerated to one every other day as his more than 300 great-grandchildren reached marriageable age. Only eight were married when he died and six had had children by their first wedding anniversaries.

So great is the rate of progression of population growth that had John Miller lived one more decade he would have seen more descendants born to him than in all his 95 years of life and would in ten more years have counted at least 1,000 living descendants!

The rate at which population increases is almost unbelievable— even when a man is watching it happen within his own family. John Miller found it difficult to comprehend what was happening. When I told him that all available evidence indicated that he had the largest family in the United States, the kindly old man passed a gnarled hand before his failing eyes and shook his head in amazement. . . .

What did John Miller think about his family? Did it worry him to see it growing so large? Indeed it did. Significantly, his concerns were the very ones that the demographers, the economists, the sociologists, and other serious students of world population problems have been voicing. He was not an educated man, for the Amish still believe eight grades of education in a one-room country school is sufficient, but John Miller sum-marized it in one simple question he constantly repeated, "Where will they all find good farms?" . . .

Some day, at some point, John Miller's plaintive question, "Where will they all find farms?" will have to be answered in the bleak negative. They can continue now only by buying farms others will sell them. Some day no more farms anywhere will be for sale. A finite world is of limited size. So, ultimately, at some point, is the population it can hold.

20

How Many People Have Ever Lived on Earth?

Annabelle Desmond
1905–

Population Bulletin, **18**, No. 1

1962

How many people have ever been born since the beginning of the human race?

What percentage does the present world population of three billion represent of the total number of people who have ever lived?

These questions are frequently asked the Population Reference Bureau's Information Service. Because of the perennial interest and be-cause of the credence sometimes given to what would seem to be unrealistic appraisals, this issue presents an estimate prepared by Fletcher Welle-meyer, Manpower, Education and Personnel Consultant, Washington, D. C., with Frank Lorimer of American University, Washington, D. C., acting as advisor. This estimate, based on certain statistical, historic and demo-graphic assumptions set forth in an appendix, should be regarded as no more than a reasonable guess. It assumes that man first appeared about 600,000 years ago, a date which has been proposed for the dawn of the prehistoric era. However, this date obviously is a compromise, anthropologically speaking, between varying extremes.

Since then, it is estimated that about 77 billion babies have been born. Thus, today's population of approximately three billion is about 4.0 percent of that number. . . .

The estimate was made on the basis of three time periods:

	Period	Number of years in period	Number of births per year at beginning of period	Number of births per year at end of period	Number of births in period
I.	600,000– 6000 B.C.	594,000	"1"	250,000	12 billion
II.	6000 B.C.– 1650 A.D.	7,650	250,000	25,000,000	42 billion
III.	1650–1962 A.D.	312	25,000,000	110,000,000	23 billion
				Total	77 billion

To obtain the number of births at the beginning and end of these periods, certain assumptions were made regarding birth rates and the size of populations. It was assumed that at the beginning of the Neolithic era the population was five million and that the annual birth rate was 50 per thousand. The procedure assumes a smooth increase. The growth was undoubtedly irregular, but the estimates may fairly represent the net effect of the ups and downs.

By 1650, the annual number of births was estimated at 25 million, corresponding to a population of about 500 million. The 1962 world population of 3.05 billion, the number of births and birth rate of 36 per thousand are based on United Nations estimates.

The 600,000 years' duration of the Paleolithic era is based on the assumption that man-like types were then in existence but in very small numbers. Earlier dates have been given a few species by certain authorities, but some of these dates are questionable, and the earlier species may have been considerably less than man-like. The 600,000-year period seems a reasonable compromise between extreme possibilities.

Once the number of births at the dates indicated was determined, the total number of births for each period was calculated at a constant rate of increase for the period.

The estimated rates of increase differ sharply. For the long Paleo-lithic period, the average annual rate of increase was only 0.02 per thousand; during 6000 B.C. to 1650 A.D., it rose to 0.6; and during 1650–1962, it reached 4.35.

21
Denial and the Gift of History

"None believes in his own death," said Sigmund Freud. "In the unconscious everyone is convinced of his own immortality." He was not the first to say this. The poet Edward Young, more than two centuries earlier, wrote: "All men think all men mortal but themselves." Very likely others, even before Young, recognized this power of denial in man's life.

The operation of denial is evident in all literature, particularly heroic literature, which is the visible monument of this psychological process. "A thousand shall fall at thy right hand, ten thousand at thy left, but it [i.e., death] shall not come nigh thee," said the Psalmist. How our breast swells with confidence at these words! Religion must surely be good if it can instill in man this most useful confidence in his powers! So says the apologist for religion, after giving up the defense of its verity. It is a powerful apology. It is no doubt the cornerstone of the philosophy of life of both geniuses and habitual criminals. Arthur Koestler has reminded us that during the days when pickpockets were executed in England, the day of a hanging was a day of great profit for other pickpockets who circulated through the tense and orgasmic crowd. Statistics gathered from the early nineteenth century showed that out of 250 men hanged, 170 had, themselves, witnessed an execution. Denial plays havoc with the deterrence theory of punishment.

"Nothing can happen to me," said Freud's poor Hans, the road mender. Great kings are no wiser. When Croesus contemplated waging war against the Persians he consulted the oracle at Delphi, who replied, with her characteristic ambiguity: "If Croesus should send an army against the Persians he would destroy a great empire." Delighted with the reply, Croesus attacked, and the prophecy was fulfilled: a great empire was indeed destroyed —**his.**

Are we less the victims of denial now, two and a half millennia later? Consider an article published in the **Wall Street Journal** discussing the dangers of thermonuclear war. More than four columns were devoted to a glowing

46

description of how our stockpiles made us capable of destroying the Soviet Union "in several ways and several times over." But, as Jerome Frank has pointed out, the article included just two slight references to what the USSR could do to us. The oracle of Wall Street has spoken: "If we wage thermonuclear war, a great nation will be destroyed." Nothing could be clearer.

But perhaps it is only men of great affairs, practical men, who are the victims of the impulse of denial? Hardly; the biographies of scientists and scholars are replete with accounts of behavior that denies the implications of knowledge. Herbert Conn, a pioneer in the public hygiene movement, did not hesitate to use the public drinking cup **himself;** and though he warned that the housefly was a carrier of typhoid he did not bother to close his own screen doors. And Freud, who declared that children should receive sex instruction from their parents, left his own children to learn the facts of life "from the gutter," like everyone else.

How are we to explain the persistence and ubiquity of denial? As biologists we adhere to the working hypothesis that every trait has both genetic and environmental components. As evolutionists we ask, what is the selective advantage of the trait that the hereditary component should so persist through centuries and millennia? Does nonrealistic thinking have a survival value? Is denial superior to truth? These are unpleasant surmises. The problem is a difficult one, and it cannot be said that any man has the answer. But biologists know of a suggestive model—the sickle-cell trait. It is caused by genes.

In malarious regions of Africa the human population is genetically diverse with respect to this trait, and the diversity is stable (so long as we don't drain the swamps to kill mosquitoes or introduce atabrine to destroy the malarial parasites). The sickle-cell gene causes the red blood cells of the body, normally disc shaped, to become sickle shaped. Only the disc-shaped cells support the life of the parasite. But sickle cells are bad for the human; if a person has only sickle genes, he suffers from anemia, and usually dies young. In a malarious environment it is best to be a hybrid; such individuals are resistant to malaria, but do not suffer from anemia. Individuals having completely normal cells are not anemic, but suffer from malaria. To be hybrid is (individually) best, but a hybrid population is not stable; it constantly throws off some offspring having only genes for normal cells (these are eliminated by malaria) and some having only sickle-shaped cells (who are eliminated by anemia). Only some (50 percent) of the offspring are hybrid.

Is this perhaps the analogical model we need to explain the persistence of denial among humans? The purest deniers live in a world of magic; its lack of congruence with the real world causes the statistical early death of this group. Among these magicians we must number early aeronauts, men who go over Niagara Falls in a barrel, gold prospectors, and indeed all compulsive gamblers. At the other extreme are men of so realistic and cautious a disposition that they are left behind so long as there remains a frontier where rewards are great. A world made up only of such men of pure sensibleness would never invent the submarine or the airplane, never discover the New World. Denial, dangerous though it is, does have some survival value.

The power of denial, valuable though it may be to the individual competitive man of action, is a grave danger to society as a whole. The time scale of historical change, extending as it does over many human generations, makes denial easy and plausible. We tend to assume that as things are now, they have always been, and there's nothing to worry about in the future. The tourist of the Mediterranean lands naturally assumes that the picturesque and poverty striken countrysides of Spain, Italy, Greece, and Lebanon looked always thus, not realizing that these deserts and near deserts are the work of unconscious man. Plato, in his **Critias,** says:

> There are mountains in Attica which can now keep nothing but bees, but which were clothed, not so very long ago, with fine trees producing timber suitable for roofing the largest buildings, and roofs hewn from this timber are still in existence. There were also many lofty cultivated trees.
>
> The annual supply of rainfall was not lost, as it is at present, through being allowed to flow over a denuded surface to the sea, but was received by the country, in all its abundance—stored in impervious potter's earth—and so was able to discharge the drainage of the heights into the hollows in the form of springs and rivers with an abundant volume and wide territorial distribution. The shrines that survive to the present day on the sites of extinct water supplies are evidence for the correctness of my present hypothesis.

Every move today to preserve the beauty of the forests, the purity of the air, the limpidity of the streams, and the wildness of the seashore is opposed by practical and powerful men. The reasons they give are various, and are (of course) couched in the noblest terms. Freely translated, the voice of the practical man is that of Hans the Road Mender: **It can't happen to me.** Other Edens have become deserts, other empires have fallen, other peoples have perished—but not us. We deny the evidence of logic and our senses. As La Fontaine said, "We believe no evil till the evil's done."

The gift that history has to give us is freedom from denial. Historical decay takes longer than the efflorescence and decay of a single life, and so it is not easily perceived as a real process and a real danger. But the study of history, if it is to have any real worth, must convince us of the reality of processes that extend over more than a single life span. To achieve this goal we must explicitly state the therapeutic function of history, which is this: to reveal and neutralize the process of denial in the individual. If we fail in this our fate will be that which Santayana described: "Those who cannot learn from the past are doomed to repeat it."

22
Deserts on the March

Paul B. Sears
1891–

Norman: University of Oklahoma Press

1935

By the time of Charlemagne, who was an enlightened ruler, the onslaught against the forests of western Europe was under way, to continue through the thirteenth century. By the end of the Middle Ages the land was largely divested of its trees, as the Mediterranean region had been before the Christian era, and stringent laws against cutting came into being. Whatever advanced ideas had been inherited from Rome were soon lost to sight. Fields were used, then abandoned. Feudal lords shifted their headquarters from one castle to another, to get away, it has been said, from the accumulated filth. But the coefficient of toleration of filth was so high in those days that the moving was more likely to have been for the purpose of tapping new sources of food as the old sections of the fief played out. Eventually, after a period of rest, the abandoned fields had to be used again. Such a system is unsound. Recuperation takes too long, and too much of the land at a time remains idle. Paintings and sculptured figures of the period portray human beings who are wan and rickety, and since these portrayals were commonest in sacred art, most of us still have the feeling that anaemia and sainthood are inseparable. Actually the trouble was due to inadequate diet and malnutrition on a huge scale, such as we find in backward rural communities.

23

The Wail of Kashmir

Lee Merriman Talbot
1930–

From *Wildlands in Our Civilization,* David Brower, ed.
San Francisco: Sierra Club

1964

A striking example of man's growing impact on the land is the Great Thar Desert in western India. At the time of Christ, Indian rhinoceros roamed in grass jungles in the middle of what is now desert. And for the past 80 years the desert has been advancing into the rest of India at the rate of one-half mile a year along its whole long perimeter. That means that in 80 years, an estimated 56,000 square miles, or an area equal to that of Wisconsin, has been turned into shifting sand.

The mechanics of this land degradation seem clear. The starting point is the mature forest with its wildlife, fertile soil, and abundant water. The lumber is cut, often clear-cut with young growth destroyed. The land is then cultivated for a time, then grazed and overgrazed. There can be no replacement of trees or grass, for everything green is eaten by ravenous livestock. When there is nothing left for cattle, goats take over, and when the goats have left, nothing remains but sand or blowing dust. This story holds true, with the same plot and characters, but with different stage scenery and costumes, throughout much of the world.

To illustrate the effect of this land-use pattern on wilderness, let us consider Kashmir, the ancient Moguls' "paradise on earth." This is a lovely mountain land in northernmost India, lying at about the same latitude as San Francisco, and bordered by Tibet, China, and Pakistan. The British with the local maharajah set aside magnificent wild areas here. But when independence came, here as in most former colonies, the tendency during the first burst of nationalism was to reject all that smacked of the previous "imperialism" or "colonialism." Parks and wilderness areas were thought of as something kept away from the people by the former rulers rather than as a resource maintained for them, so the first reaction was to destroy them, to take "what was rightfully ours." On top of this came political and military unrest with a side effect of a large population suddenly armed but with little discipline. Among the results have been large-scale poaching leading to the virtual extermination of the Kashmir stag, heavy forest cutting, and overgrazing.

Through much of Kashmir up to and above timberline one runs into herders and livestock. In less than ten years much of this land changed from dense conifer forest or park lands like the best of our Sierra or Rockies, to what are approaching high-altitude deserts, with the vegetation pulled apart, cut, overgrazed, and burned out—and the soil too.

Economic need, destructive land use, and destructive nationalism from a constantly recurring pattern deadly to wilderness. Until all three of these factors are somewhat ameliorated it is hard to be optimistic about the future of wilderness lands throughout the world.

As my last example I would like to mention an area not usually thought of as living wilderness—the Middle East. Much of it is arid desert, but when Moses led the children of Israel through the Sinai wilderness, it was a live wilderness with wildlife and trees. Today one can go for days through that country and never see a living thing. The mountains above the Promised Land were cloaked with dense forest, with pine, oak, and cedar; and in the more open areas, Asiatic lions stalked abundant wildlife. Today these mountains are largely dead stone skeletons, and the last small remnant of the Asiatic lions is to be found 3,000 miles to the east. There are still two more or less living wilderness areas left—in northern Lebanon and western Syria. Until recently, protected by inaccessibility and unsettled conditions, the forest here remained intact; but within the last few years, lumbering and cultivation have begun to move into these last forests. When the land's fertility has been cropped out and the trees have been cut off, the crops will give way to grazing. Once overgrazing has gone far enough, the starving animals preventing grass, brush, and tree reproduction, the area will assume the desert aspect of most of the Middle East.

This remnant biblical wilderness illustrates one of the very real economic values of wilderness that, perhaps, is not often thought of in our country. It would be easy to say, looking at most of the desert Middle Eastern lands, that this area never did support much life, or that the old records of forests and crops are wrong, or that if there were trees here once there has since been a climatic change. But in these remaining wild forest areas we have the living proof that this was not the case. North Lebanon and western Syria provide a point of reference by which one may judge the condition of the land as it was, see what man has done to the rest of the land, and therefore see what can be done with what land is left.

24
Can Egypt Survive Progress?

Raymond F. Dasmann
1919–

From *The Last Horizon*
New York: Macmillan

1963

In Egypt the Nile forms flood plains and a delta. Over the millennia rich alluvial land has been built by the steady accretion of sediments garnered by the runoff from the far-off lands. Into this flood plain, Neolithic man, armed with some primitive ideas of farming techniques, moved and began to sow seeds. Finding the yield good, he remained and built in time a civilization.

For six thousand years or more, the Nile Valley has supported farming populations: supported them by soils that could not be depleted because they were added to each year when the Nile overflowed and left its fine layer of silt and organic materials behind. Pharaohs have come and gone, dynasties have risen and fallen, invasions have swept Egypt from the east, the south, and the north; but unlike the other civilizations of the Near East, Egypt has not collapsed. It survived Alexander, and Caesar, Mohammed, and the Crusade, the disruptions that followed on the Mongol invasions, and the spread of European dominion over Africa. Unlike its sister civilization in Mesopotamia, it remains populous and relatively wealthy today, because its soils have remained productive. But today, Egypt is encountering changes that can forever modify it. It is staking its existence on a big gamble with water and soil.

The beginnings of irrigation in Egypt were probably simple. Originally the Nile in flood covered the entire flood plain, and man's use was restricted in flood time to the area above the high-water mark. From here as the water retreated in the autumn months, he could sow seeds in the exposed mud, and harvest his grain before the flood rose again in the following summer. At some time, however, he began to build levees to keep the waters away from some of the higher lands. From this the next step was to enclose a basin of farming land with dikes, allowing water to flood in through openings parallel to the river, and then draining off the excess through a lower level opening. Thus there was built up, along that side of the river with the most flat land, a system of irrigation basins. The river was kept from washing over them by the levees built along its banks, irrigation water was led into them by openings along the banks that could be closed once enough water had covered the land. The other side of the river was kept for a while untouched, to accommodate excess flood waters and keep the river from jumping the banks into the fields. Eventually, as the demand for more land grew, basins were diked on either side of the river. The river then flowed through a restricted channel in flood time, elevated above the surrounding fields by its normal tendency to build up its own bed through deposition of excess silt. To take care of excess flood water, overflow basins were built, such as Lake Moeris near Fayum. In years of high floods, the excess water was drained into this lake where it could be held. When waters were low the lake could be drained back into the river, for further irrigation downstream.

This system of irrigation worked admirably over the long centuries. There were some troubles with unusually high floods, and years of famine when the floods failed, but in general the Nile took care of the farmers in its basin. Under this old system, however, the agriculture was seasonal and restricted to those crops which could be sown in winter and harvested in late spring. During the season of low water it was not possible to bring water up into the basins. Only the land near the levees could be irrigated, by hauling water up from the river by one device or another. Where this could be done, year-long cultivation could be carried out, and yields from the lands doubled.

The desire for higher crop production, particularly for those crops that had value for export such as sugar and rice, led to an increasing effort to bring more land under perennial irrigation instead of the seasonal basin irrigation. This led during the nineteenth century to the construction of barrages, which held water at a higher level during the dry season and permitted it to be led through irrigation canals onto the lands. Finally, in 1902, the first Aswan Dam was built to hold the Nile flood partly in check, and permit the stored water to be utilized through the year. Along with the dam additional barrages were built downstream and an elaborate canal network to bring the water to the lands.

In the nineteenth and early twentieth centuries, therefore, Egypt began to abandon the old basin irrigation scheme that had served it for five thousand years. In its place the dam-canal method was introduced. The immediate benefits were obvious. With perennial irrigation not only were more crops produced per acre of land, but acreage not readily flooded by the basin system could be brought into use. Agricultural yields were boosted, higher value crops were grown, and to those who owned or controlled the land came wealth. The damage from high floods and low water was mitigated, and the danger of crop failure reduced. But with these benefits came losses. The silt that had enriched the soil for centuries was held behind the dams and barrages to be scoured away to the sea during flood peaks. It no longer reached the croplands. The easy drainage of the old basins that had carried off excess salts was no longer possible. The drying and cracking of the land that had taken place after the crops were harvested and before the new floods arrived also ceased. This had served to aerate and warm the soil, to destroy weeds, and kill off harmful organisms, including mosquito larvae and fresh-water snails, before the land was again flooded.

The effects of these changes were soon felt. Although the canal-born water contained no more silt, it contained dissolved salts. When it moved up through the soil and evaporated from the land, the salts were left behind. Soon increasing salinization of the soil began to impair crop yields in some areas, and to force the abandonment of some kinds of crops. Without the fertilization by silt and without the aeration and insolation of the soil that had come with the seasonal drying, the soil fertility began to be exhausted. Soils that had grown crops from the beginnings of agriculture without chemical fertilizers had to be supplied with increasing amounts of imported chemicals to hold up crop yields. To fight salinization it was necessary to install elaborate drainage canals, and to use an excess of water to flush away the salts that had accumulated. In places, sufficient water was not available.

The change from basin to perennial irrigation had also other indirect but equally undesirable effects. It increased the incidence of certain diseases that have been crippling to the people of Egypt. Malaria has been known in Egypt since the days of the Pharaohs. But, with the change to perennial irrigation, standing water was left on the land through much of the year and provided a breeding ground for mosquitoes. The incidence of malaria in the population increased sharply. The water also provided a home for the snails that harbor the parasite causing bilharziasis, another major debilitating disease. In some areas the incidence of this disease increased more than tenfold following the shift to perennial irrigation. Other parasites, such as guinea worm, and various bacterial infections were also favored by the shift in irrigation methods. While most of these can be brought under control, the job of doing so is not easy. A high percentage of the population of Africa is still infected with malaria and with bilharziasis. In some places the incidence of these diseases has already forced the abandonment of irrigation projects. The maintenance of an effective, efficient irrigation system requires the presence of hard-working, healthy farmers. Diseases that lower the health and efficiency of the people cause neglect of necessary work on the irrigated lands. This in turn favors an increased incidence of the disease.

Today Egypt has problems not known in older times. The principal answer to these has been the plan for the High Aswan Dam to replace the old dam. This, when completed, will hold the entire Nile flood, in place of just part of it. It will mean the end of the Nile River in Egypt and of the remaining areas of basin agriculture. What was once the Nile will become a long irrigation canal carrying a regulated flow of water from the dam to the subsidiary canals. The entire silt load will be deposited behind the dam, instead of in the delta region. But there will be plenty of water for irrigation on all the old lands, and enough to bring two million new acres of land into year-round agricultural production. With the hydroelectric power generated from the dam it will be possible to produce nitrate fertilizer at home to take the place of expensive imports, and to replace in part the benefits of the old Nile flood. The excess water available should make it possible to flush and drain excess salts from the lands that have been made unusable through salinization. All this has seemed so important to the present Egyptian government that it was willing to defy the entire Western world, during the Suez crisis, in order to accomplish the objective of building the high dam. Through Soviet assistance it is now doing so.

A disturbing feature of the change in Egypt and the Nile is the wholesale abandonment of a tried-and-tested method of irrigation that has worked since the beginning of civilization, for a dam-and-canal system that has no long record of success anywhere, but many instances of complete or partial failure. The backing up of the entire silt load of the Nile behind a high dam is going to create a difficult problem of silt disposal. If this cannot be solved the life span of the dam will be reduced just as many of our major reservoirs in America are losing their storage capacity. Some in this country have already been abandoned after having been completely filled in by silt. Creation of a major reservoir in a desert region also creates a problem of water loss from evaporation. The magnitude of this is sufficient to cause some American water experts to recommend the abandonment of reservoir systems in any hot, dry area. Although this water loss can be cut down on smaller reservoirs by the spreading of a thin layer of certain alcohols, the effectiveness of this method breaks down on larger reservoirs where wind and wave action disrupt the surface film. Obviously the immediate benefits from the new dam in Egypt have been sufficiently attractive to override the consideration of possible long-term losses. Nevertheless, one wonders at the confidence of a nation in a modern technology of irrigation and soils that has only a few decades of practical experience behind it. Perhaps this faith in the sanity of mankind and the effectiveness of western technology will prove justified. If not, we in America who have set the example will have to share in the blame.

When the high dam is built and the new lands are brought into production, will the average Egyptian be better off than he is today? Here, indeed, is the rub. For the answer appears to be almost certainly, No. Along with the expansion of agriculture that started in the nineteenth century has come an expansion in Egypt's population. Where thirteen million people lived in 1920 there are over twenty-six million now. With a growth rate of 2.5 per cent per year, the gains in agricultural acreage and food production will be wiped out by the gain in population. A full-scale effort to slow down the population growth rate could change this picture, but no such effort appears likely to occur within the near future.

25

Nothing to Worry About

Sir John Boyd Orr
1880–

Proceedings of the International Congress on Population and World Resources in Relation to the Family
(Cheltenham, England, August 1948)

1948

When Darwin came forward with his theory of the survival of the fittest, that seemed to prove that the best thing to do was to let these people die out. That argument has been used to me—'Why reduce mortality? You only further overcrowd an already overcrowded planet.' I think you can take it, however, that if modern science is applied and Governments are willing to do it, we can feed and clothe and house as large a population as is likely to come in the next fifty or hundred years, and that is as far as we can see.

26

The Challenge of Man's Future

Harrison Brown
1917–

New York: Viking Press

1954

One ton of average granite contains about 4 parts per million (0.0004 percent) uranium and 12 parts per million (0.0012 percent) thorium. These are admittedly tiny amounts, but the energy content is impressive. If all the uranium and thorium could be extracted from 1 ton of rock and "burned" in a nuclear reactor, the energy release would be equal to that obtained from burning about 50 tons of coal. Thus, from the point of view of releasable energy, 1 ton of ordinary rock is equivalent to about 50 tons of coal.

It would be extremely difficult to extract economically all the uranium and thorium that is present in ordinary granite, but it should be possible to extract about 15 percent without undue difficulty. If a yield of approximately 15 percent should prove to be attainable, then 1 ton of rock would be equivalent in energy content to about 7½ tons of coal. This figure must be decreased still further, because energy is required to quarry the rock, transport it to the mill, and carry out the physical and chemical operations necessary for the extraction of the uranium and thorium. It seems likely that these operations could be carried out with an energy expenditure no greater than half a ton of coal for each ton of rock. Thus, without stretching our imaginations unduly, we can visualize a "net profit" of energy from 1 ton of rock equivalent to that produced by about 7 tons of coal. Thus, in principle, from the point of view of obtaining usable energy, all of the granites of the earth's crust are at our disposal.

Under our present economy it might cost 10 dollars to process 1 ton of rock for the purpose of extracting uranium and thorium. If a yield of 15 percent were obtained, about 200 tons of rock would have to be processed at a cost of 2000 dollars in order to obtain 1 pound of these elements. Although this might seem, at first glance, to be prohibitively expensive, particularly when compared with the existing uranium price of about 10 dollars per pound, the actual cost per unit of releasable energy would be quite modest. Since 1 pound of uranium and thorium is equivalent in energy content to about 1500 tons of coal, we see that, viewed solely from the point of view of energy content, uranium at existing price levels could compete successfully with coal costing less than 1 cent per ton, and, even at the high price of 2000 dollars per pound, uranium could compete with coal costing $1.50 per ton, if other factors were equal. In 1946, electric utilities in the United States paid about 5 dollars per ton for their coal.

It is clear that, per unit of releasable energy, the cost of nuclear fuel is already much less than the cost of coal, and that even when we are forced to process ordinary granite the cost per unit of releasable energy will be less than the cost of that obtained from coal today. . . .

In spite of the many difficulties, atomic energy now appears on the horizon as a major energy source of the future. If what now seems probable becomes actual, the operations involved will indeed be enormous. Let us imagine a world populated by perhaps 7 billion persons, who consume energy at a per capita rate equivalent to that derived from burning 10 tons of coal per person per year. Under such circumstances, uranium and thorium would be consumed at the rate of 23,000 tons per year, and yield losses might increase the consumption to 50,000 tons per year. The capital investment of uranium and thorium in the reactors would amount to over 10 million tons. Rock would be processed at a rate of nearly 20 billion tons per year, but an initial quantity amounting to perhaps 10 trillion tons of rock would have to be processed to provide the uranium and thorium "capital" required for the reactors. This capital investment would be equivalent to approximately 1000 cubic miles of rock.

Perhaps the main obstacle to world-wide utilization of atomic energy would be the enormous amounts of radioactivity that would be produced. The disposal problem would be tremendous. In a world powered largely by atomic energy, radioactivity will be without question a continuous major problem.

It should be stressed that supplies of uranium and thorium are finite; they should be looked upon, like coal and petroleum, as fossil fuels. If the world should come to rely largely upon these substances for its energy, the time would eventually arrive when the fuel would be exhausted. But at the rates of energy consumption foreseeable during the next century, the reserves in ordinary rocks should certainly last for tens of thousands of years, and more probably for millions of years.

In a way, since we know that our coal and petroleum will vanish in the near future, the prospect for atomic energy appears encouraging in spite of the purely technological difficulties. . . . If we were willing to be crowded together closely enough, to eat foods which would bear little resemblance to the foods we eat today, and to be deprived of simple but satisfying luxuries such as fireplaces, gardens and lawns, a world population of 50 billion persons would not be out of the question. And if we really put our minds to the problem we could construct floating islands where people might live and where algae farms could function, and perhaps 100 billion persons could be provided for. If we set strict limits to physical activities so that caloric requirements could be kept at very low levels, perhaps we could provide for 200 billion persons.

At this point the reader is probably saying to himself that he would have little desire to live in such a world, and he can rest assured that the author is thinking exactly the same thing. But a substantial fraction of humanity today is behaving as if it would like to create such a world. It is behaving as if it were engaged in a contest to test nature's willingness to support humanity and, if it had its way, it would not rest content until the earth is covered completely and to a considerable depth with a writhing mass of human beings, much as a dead cow is covered with a pulsating mass of maggots.

27
How Many People Can the World Support?

J. H. Fremlin
1913–

New Scientist, No. 415, 285–287

1964

The world population is now about 3,000 million and is increasing at a rate corresponding to a doubling in 37 years. In view of the increasing importance attached to the immediate effects of the rapid growth in human numbers, it is of interest to examine ultimate technical limits to this growth. Traditionally, these limits have usually been regarded as fixed by possible food supplies although, in practice, at least in historical times, the actual limiting factor has more often been disease.

Diseases are now nearly, and will soon be entirely, eliminated as effective controllers of population growth but it is not at all clear that difficulties in food production will take their place. It is true that there is a limit to the improvement of agricultural output by application of existing scientific knowledge, but by the time this limit is reached other methods of food-production will have been devised. In this article I shall explore the possibility that the real limits are physical rather than biological.

I shall assume throughout an effective degree of world cooperation in the application of food technology, etc. This is quite evidently essential if the maximum world population is to be reached. There are of course many ways of *not* reaching the maximum, but none of these will be discussed here.

In order to give a time scale, it is supposed that the rate of increase of population remains constant at the present value—that is to say, doubling every 37 years. In fact the rate is itself accelerating, so that, in the absence of limitations, this time scale will be too long.

Stage 1: up to 400,000 million in 260 years' time

Using existing crop plants and methods it may not be practicable to produce adequate food for more than four doublings of the world population, though the complete elimination of all land wild-life, the agricultural use of roofs over cities and roads, the elimination of meat-eating and the efficient harvesting of sea food might allow two or three further doublings —say seven in all. That would give us, with the present doubling time of 37 years, 260 years to develop less conventional methods, and would allow the population of the world to increase to about 130 times its present size, or about 400,000 million.

Stage 2: up to 3 million million in 370 years' time

The area of ice-free sea is some three times that of land. Photosynthesis by single-celled marine organisms may be more efficient than that of the best land plants. If organisms could be found capable of the theoretical maximum efficiency (8 percent of total solar radiation, according to A. A. Niciporovic) we should gain a factor of three in yield. We could then double our numbers a further three more times if all the wild-life in the sea, too, was removed and replaced by the most useful organisms growing under controlled conditions, with the optimum concentration of carbonates, nitrates and minerals. (Of course a reserve of specimens of potentially useful species could be preserved, perhaps in a dormant state.) Again, for maximum efficiency we must harvest and consume directly the primary photosynthesising organisms, rather than allow the loss of efficiency involved in the food-chains leading to such secondary organisms as zooplankton or fish.

By this stage, we should have had ten doublings, which at the present rate would take some 370 years, with a final world population of 3 million million. Since the world's surface (land and sea) is 500 million million square metres, each person would have a little over 160 square metres for his maintenance—about a thirtieth of an acre—which does not seem unreasonable by more than a factor of two, so long as no important human activity other than food production takes place on the surface.

No serious shortages of important elements need be envisaged so far, though extensive mining operations for phosphates might be needed, and we have not yet approached any real limit.

Stage 3: up to 15 million million in 450 years' time

At first sight, it seems that a very big leap forward could be taken if we use sources of power other than sunlight for photosynthesis. The solar power received at the earth's surface is only about 1 killowatt per square metre at the equator at midday, and the average value over the day and night sides of the globe is a quarter of this. Over half of it is in the regions of the spectrum of no use for photosynthesis.

About one kilowatt-year per square metre could be produced by the complete fission of the uranium and thorium in about 3 cm depth of the Earth's crust or by fusion of the deuterium in about 3 mm depth of seawater, so that adequate power should be available for some time. It is, however, difficult to see how the overall thermal efficiency from fuel to the light actually used for photosynthesis could be even as good as the ratio of useful to non-useful solar radiation (about 40 percent).

It would, therefore, be better to use large satellite reflectors in orbit to give extra sunlight to the poles and to the night side of the Earth. A large number of mirrors could be maintained in quasi-stable orbits about 1½ million kilometres outside the Earth's orbit, any deviations being controlled by movable "sails" using the pressure of sunlight. To double our total radiation income would require a total area of about 100 million square kilometres of mirror which, in aluminium a tenth of a micron thick, would weigh about 30 million tons. With plenty of people to design and make the equipment it should not be difficult by the time it would be required, and it would bring the whole Earth to equatorial conditions, melting the polar ice and allowing one further doubling of population.

A second doubling of radiation income would give the whole Earth midday equatorial conditions round the clock, which would be exceedingly difficult to cope with without serious overheating. The overall efficiency of local power sources for photosynthesis is likely to be less than that of sunlight, so that no real gain in ultimate population size can be expected from their use, without an even more serious overheating of the entire globe.

If, however, the mirrors outside the Earth's orbit were made of selectively reflecting material, reflecting only the most useful part of the spectrum, and if a further satellite filter were used, inside the Earth's orbit, to deflect the useless 60 percent of direct solar radiation, a further gain of a factor of 2½ should easily be possible without creating thermally impossible conditions, at the cost only of perhaps a 10–100 times increase of weight of mirror plus filter—not difficult for the larger population with an extra 50 years of technical development. We should then have attained a world population of 15 million million about 450 years from now.

Stage 4: up to 1,000 million million in 680 years' time

A considerably larger gain is in principle obtainable if the essential bulk foods: fats, carbohydrates, amino acids and so on, could be directly synthesised. Biological methods might still be permitted for a few special trace compounds. The direct rate of energy production resulting from the conversion of our food into our waste products is only about 100 watts per person and, if high-temperature energy from nuclear fuel (or sunlight) could be efficiently used, waste products could in principle be changed back into food compounds with the absorption of little more energy. Cadavers could be homogenised and would not, at least for physical reasons, need to be chemically treated at all. The fresh mineral material which would have to be processed to allow for population growth would be much less than 1 percent of the turnover, and its energy requirements can be neglected.

If we suppose that the overall efficiency could not be increased beyond 50 percent, a further 100 watts per person would be dissipated as heat in the process of feeding him. We have some hundreds of years to work up the efficiency to this value, so at least this ought to be possible. Some further power would be needed for light, operation of circulation machinery, communications etc., but 50 watts per person should suffice.

As we have seen, the long-term average heat income of the Earth's surface is at present about 250 watts per square metre, and this could be doubled without raising the temperature above the normal equatorial value. (The initial rate of rise would be low till the polar ice had gone, which might take 100 years.) We thus have 500 watts per head, could support 1,000 million million people altogether. The population density would be two per square metre, averaged over the entire land and sea surface of the Earth.

Stage 4a: up to 12,000 million million
in 800 years' time.   Dead end

Above two people per square metre, severe refrigeration problems occur. If the oceans were used as a heat sink, their mean temperature would have to rise about 1°C per year to absorb 500 watts per square metre. This would be all right for the doubling time of 37 years, at the end of which we should have four people per square metre. Half another doubling time could be gained if efficient heat pumps (which, for reasons of thermal efficiency, would require primary energy sources of very high temperature) could be used to bring the ocean to the boil.

Two more doublings would be permitted if the oceans were converted into steam, though that would create an atmospheric pressure comparable with the mean ocean bottom pressure at present. Since the resulting steam blanket would also be effectively opaque to all radiation, no further heat sink could be organised and this procedure would therefore seem to lead to a dead end.

Stage 5: up to 60,000 million million in 890 years' time

A preferable scheme would be the opposite one of roofing in the ocean to stop evaporation (this would, in any case, probably have been done long before, for housing) and hermetically sealing the outer surface of the planet. All of the atmosphere not required for ventilation of the living spaces could then be pumped into compression tanks, for which no great strength would be needed if they were located on ocean bottoms. Heat pumps could then be used to transfer heat to the solid outer skin, from which, in the absence of air, it would be radiated directly into space. The energy radiated from a black body goes up as T^4, where T is the absolute temperature (°K), but for a *fixed rate* of heat extraction from the living space, at a fixed temperature (say, 30°C or 303°K), the heat-power *radiated* must for thermodynamic reasons be proportional to T even if the refrigeration equipment is perfectly efficient (see any good textbook on the principles of refrigeration). Hence the rate of heat extraction will go up no faster than T^3 where T is the outer surface temperature.

All the same, this gives more promising results than would the use of the ocean as a temporary heat sink. An outer skin temperature of 300°C would give a heat extraction of 3 kW per square metre and 1,000°C would give an extraction ten times greater. If heat removal were the sole limitation, then we could manage about 120 persons per square metre for an outer skin temperature of 1,000°C—which represents nearly six further doublings of population after the end of Stage 4, with a world population of 60,000 million million in 890 years' time. 1,000°C may be a rather modest figure for the technology of A.D. 2854 and the population could, as far as heat is concerned, be able to double again for each rise of absolute skin temperature of $\sqrt[3]{2}$ or 26 percent. The difficulties in raising it much further while keeping all thermodynamic efficiencies high would, however, seem to be formidable. A rise to 2,000°C would give us less than three further doublings.

We seem, therefore, to have found one possible absolute limit to human population, due to the heat problem, which at the present rate would be reached 800–1,000 years from now, with a world population of 10^{16}–10^{18}.

I have not considered emigration to other planets because it seems to me unlikely that our technical capacity to do so will catch up with the population expansion. To keep world-population level we would have to be sending out 60 million people per annum *now*. It is so much cheaper to feed them here that this will not be done.

If, however, it were possible to export population on the scale required it would not make a great difference. Venus is much the same size as the Earth, so (assuming that it has all the raw materials needed) an extra 37 years would bring it to the same population density as the Earth. Mercury, Mars and the Moon together give half the same area, so that Venus and the Earth together would take them up to the same population density in a further 10 years. The moons of Jupiter and Saturn could give us another 2 years or so. It is not clear that normal human beings could live on Jupiter and Saturn themselves and impound their extensive atmospheres, and the outer planets would take a long time to reach; if all these extraordinary problems could be solved, nearly 200 years might be gained.

Other possible limitations than heat will doubtless have occurred to readers, but these do not seem to be absolute. The most obvious is perhaps the housing problem for 120 persons per square metre. We can safely assume, however, that in 900 years' time the construction of continuous 2000-storey buildings over land and sea alike should be quite easy. That would give 7½ square metres of floor space for each person in 1,000 storeys (though wiring, piping, ducting and lifts would take up to half of that) and leave the other 1,000 storeys for the food-producing and refrigerating machinery. It is clear that, even at much lower population densities, very little horizontal circulation of persons, heat or supplies could be tolerated and each area of a few kilometres square, with a population about equal to the present world population, would have to be nearly self-sufficient. Food would all be piped in liquid form and, of course, clothes would be unnecessary.

Raw materials should not be a problem. The whole of the oceans and at least the top 10 kilometres of the Earth's crust would be available, giving a wide choice of building, plumbing and machine-building materials. Even with 8 tons of people per square metre (reckoning 15 people to the ton) all the necessary elements of life could be obtained; some from air and sea (C, H, O, N, Na, Cl, Ca, K and some trace elements) and some from the top 100 metres of solid crust (Fe, S, P, I and remaining trace elements). Only after a further hundredfold increase in population would it be needful to go below the top 10 km of crust for some elements (N, S, P, I). Such an increase would need an outer skin temperature of 5,000°C (comparable with the surface of the Sun) to radiate away the body heat, which would seem to be well beyond the possible limits.

A question of obvious importance which is not easy to answer is whether people could in fact live the nearly sessile lives, with food and air piped in and wastes piped out, which would be essential. Occasional vertical and random horizontal low speed vehicular or moving-belt travel over a few hundred metres would be permissible, however, so that each individual could choose his friends out of some ten million people, giving adequate social variety, and of course communication by video-phone would be possible with anyone on the planet. One could expect some ten million Shakespeares and rather more Beatles to be alive at any one time, so that a good range of television entertainment should be available. Little heat-producing exercise could be tolerated. The extrapolation from the present life of a car-owning, flat-dwelling office-worker to such an existence might well be less than from that of the neolithic hunter to that of the aforesaid office-worker. Much more should be known about social conditioning in a few hundred years' time and, though it is difficult to be quite certain, one could expect most people to be able to live and reproduce in the conditions considered.

Many readers will doubtless feel that something unconsidered must turn up to prevent us from reaching the limiting conditions I have supposed. One point of this study is however to suggest that, apart from the ultimate problem of heat, we are now, or soon will be, able to cope with *anything* that might turn up. Anything which limits population growth in the future will, therefore, be something that we can avoid if we wish. It would be perfectly possible to choose not to eliminate some major killing disease or to neglect the world food problem and let famine do its work, but this would have to be a positive decision; it can no longer happen by mistake.

Consequently all methods of limitation of population growth will, from now on, be artificial in the sense that they are consciously planned for, whether or not the plan is carried out by individuals for themselves. We are, collectively, free to choose at what population density we want to call a halt, somewhere between the 0.000 006 per square metre of the present and the 120 per square metre of the heat limit; if we do not choose, eventually we shall reach that limit.

28

The Value of Life—
An Additive Function?

Some Noble Lords

News report of a debate in
the House of Lords, 6 June 1962
Eugenics Review, **54**:114

1962

Lord Walston wanted more food in the world: he also wanted a demographic institute. He thought that "it surely must be a confession of complete failure on the part of our civilization and the Western way of life if in fact we admit that we want fewer people in this world." With him the Earl of Longford—he to whom Lord Brabazon in the earlier debate had referred as "my Lord Cardinal Longford"—agreed "above all" in his "insistence that human life is good, that a large population is better than a small one."

29

What Is the Optimum Population?

P. K. Whelpton
1893–

*Proceedings of the International Congress
on Population and World Resources
in Relation to the Family*
(Cheltenham, England, August 1948)

1948

It seems to me that even in countries like the U.S.A., the population is above the economic optimum; that is, we have more people even there than is most desirable from the standpoint of the natural resources which we possess. That does not mean that a rapid decrease in population would be desirable, but I think it does mean that if we could choose between a stationary population of say, 100,000,000 and 150,000,000 or 200,000,-000 we should without question be better off with the former.

30

Marx versus Malthus

William Petersen
1912–

*From The Politics of Population
Garden City, N.Y.: Doubleday*

1964

The Speenhamland system, which assured a minimum family income to the poor irrespective of their earnings, had eventually obliterated the distinction between worker and pauper, and the ostensible protection of labor had become synonymous with its utter subordination. Malthus argued

67

for the Poor Law of 1834, which by a surgical operation on sentimentality transferred to each worker the responsibility for his own welfare. It would be difficult to overstate the importance, whether actual or theoretical, of this shift. Family allowances like those paid under the Speenhamland system are not only a social-welfare measure but very often a good index of what Karl Mannheim has termed the "basic intention" of the state. There is hardly a better bolster to conservatism than to strengthen the family, for so long as the older generation is able to set the thought and behavior patterns of the younger generation, social change is likely to be slow. Socialist parties have usually opposed family subsidies or, at most, half-heartedly supported them; for such a policy, while it does distribute aid to the poor and is therefore good, also contradicts the fundamental trade-union tenet of equal pay for equal work. Socialists have seldom noted, however, that the political effect of revoking the Speenhamland system was similarly ambiguous. The workers, told to depend on themselves, suffered for it; but this shift to a free labor market was a prerequisite to the later development of a self-conscious working class and the trade-union movement. Only when the traditionalist paternalism had been ended by emphasizing the self-dependence of the common people could they indeed become self-reliant.

Another important indication of Malthus' reactionary tendencies, according to Marx, was the fact that he was a curate of the Church of England, "Parson Malthus." [1] The point would be relevant if Marx had attempted to show that Malthus' ecclesiastical background introduced a consistent bias into his nontheological writings. Actually, as we noted earlier, many clergymen found his interpretation of Providence not to their liking. When Marx wrote that "an abstract law of population exists for plants and animals only," [2] he unwittingly set the minimum level at which a Malthusian approach must be taken as valid. If much of Malthus is an unacceptable as the work of any pioneer, he remains worth studying just because of his emphasis on the fact that man *is* an animal, living in a finite world. According to Engels, offering his final tribute to his lifelong collaborator at the latter's graveside, Marx's prime virtue, similarly, had been that he stressed man's biological necessities as basic: "As Darwin discovered the law of evolution in organic nature, so Marx discovered the law of evolution in human history: the simple fact, previously hidden under ideological growths, that human beings must first of all eat, drink, shelter and clothe themselves before they can turn their attention to politics, science, art and religion." [3]

If Malthus' social philosophy does not make him a reactionary, neither do his more specific policy recommendations. He is notorious for having opposed a poor law that had reduced free workers to pauperdom; but he is less well know for his support of the liberal measures listed in a previous chapter. Malthus' main reaction to the French Revolution and especially to some of its perfectibilist ideologues was negative; and such a political sentiment, personified best in England by Burke, has ordinarily been used to define modern conservatism. On the other hand, in several respects Malthus was markedly unconservative. The answer to this contradiction, perhaps, is that for figures as complex as Malthus or Marx the usual one-dimensional continuum from Left to Right is not a useful analytical model. This point can be illustrated by making use of one of the richest and most stimulating efforts to define one end-point of this continuum, namely, Mannheim's essay on conservative thought in the early nineteenth century.[4] One important difference between progressives and conservatives, Mannheim writes, is the way they experience time: "the progressive experiences the present as the beginning of the future, while the conservative regards it simply as the latest point reached by the past." But the whole thrust of Malthus' arithmetical and geometrical progressions was to the future; and Marx, though he hypothesized the extrapolation of present trends to a future utopia, concentrated in his writing on connecting the capitalist system with its historical past. Or: "The conservatives replaced Reason with concepts such as History, Life, the Nation." Malthus, on the contrary, extended the legitimate use of reason to the family, that sanctum of traditionalist norms, while for Marx reason was indeed subsumed in an irrepressible History. Or: The conservative "starts from a concept of a whole which is not the mere sum of its parts. . . . The conservative thinks in terms of 'We' when the liberal thinks in terms of 'I.' " Marxist analysis is wholly in terms of social classes, wholes greater than the sum of the individuals that make them up; and Malthus, like all who participated in developing the theory of market relations, began his analysis with the individual consumer or individual parent.

These paradoxes could be continued, but the point has been made: political reality ordinarily has more than one dimension. This is true of the differences between Marx and Malthus and, a fortiori, of those between Marxists and Malthusians. In the radical-liberal heyday, "Left" meant toward increased personal freedom; and then it acquired an additional meaning—toward increased state control over the economy. It is now apparent, however, that these two goals do not always lie in the same direction. With respect to population control, on the contrary, the right of individual parents to decide on the size of their family, established during one of the momentous struggles of the liberal era, is now often challenged because of the state's obsessive desire for more manpower.

In spite of these parallels between the two men, Marx rejected Malthus and his works, and did so in language strong even by his standards —"the contemptible Malthus," a "plagiarist," "a shameless sycophant of the ruling classes" who perpetrated a "sin against science," "this libel on the human race." The constant hyperbole suggests a polemical weakness: vituperation is no more a sign of strength with Marx than with any other social analyst. In order to preserve his faith in the inevitability of the socialist society, Marx found it necessary to discard Malthus' principle of population, for it undermined his entire system.

> If Malthus' theory of population is correct, then I can *not* abolish this [iron law of wages] even if I abolish wage-labor a hundred times, because this law is not only paramount over the system of wage-labor but also over *every* social system. Stepping straight from this, the economists proved fifty years ago or more that Socialism cannot abolish poverty, which is based on nature, but only *communalize* it, distribute it equally over the whole surface of society! [5]

---

[1] Indeed, according to Marx "most of the population-theory teachers are Protestant parsons . . . —Parson Wallace, Parson Townsend, Parson Malthus and his pupil, the arch-Parson Thomas Chalmers, to say nothing of the lesser reverend scribblers in this line." However, in contrast to other Protestant clergymen, who "generally contribute to the increase of population to a really unbecoming extent," Malthus "had taken the monastic vow of celibacy" (*Capital,* Chicago: Kerr, 1906, Vol. 1, pp. 675–676). That Marx did not know Malthus was a married man and the father of three children indicates that he knew rather little about the man whose character and motives he impugned.

[2] *Ibid.,* Vol. 1, p. 693.

[3] Franz Mehring, *Karl Marx: The Story of His Life,* New York: Covici-Friede, 1935, p. 555.

[4] Karl Mannheim, "Conservative Thought," *Essays on Sociology and Social Psychology,* New York: Oxford University Press, 1953, pp. 74–164.

[5] Marx, *Critique of the Gotha Program,* New York: International Publishers, 1933, p. 40.

31

The Demographic Foundations of National Power

Kingsley Davis
1908–

From *Freedom and Control in Modern Society,*
M. Berger, T. Abel, and C. H. Page, editors
New York: Van Nostrand

1954

From the standpoint of national power, an additional aspect of the problem needs emphasizing. Not only does national income cease at some theoretical point to grow in proportion to the rise in population, but the ways in which the income is produced and distributed are altered—and they are altered in such a way as to weaken the nation. That a population must have subsistence is axiomatic. The arts of war, propaganda, and diplomatic negotiation, however, require something beyond subsistence. Insofar as a national economic system, because of the density and rapid increase of numbers, must devote most of its economic effort to gaining mere subsistence for its people, it is in no condition to enjoy a high degree of industrial production for purposes of foreign trade, military might, and assistance to allies. It has the manpower but cannot put it to effective use. As war has grown more dependent upon intricate weapons produced by advanced industry, the capitalization of each soldier has increased tremendously. A country bogged down by excessive manpower in relation to both its natural resources and its existing technology cannot secure the necessary capitalization. Nor can it afford the nonmilitary avenues to foreign influence; propaganda by short-wave radio in foreign languages is expensive, as is the dissemination of literature overseas or the maintenance of economic and military missions on foreign soil. A country with a huge population, or even a large national income, may therefore be forced by its overpopulation into a defensive position in international affairs. It may tend to become the object of propaganda rather than the disseminator of it; it may focus its military force on defense rather than offense; it may receive rather than give aid. It may thus be forced into a secondary role which, with a more appropriate population, it could eschew.

An excessive population in relation to productive factors has other disadvantages. One is that an equitable distribution of the national product, if it should occur, would mean virtually no opportunity for capital development. Funds would be invested in immediate necessities rather than productive enterprise. By a sort of functional adaptation, therefore, most of the societies with excess numbers have evolved a rigid social stratification whereby a small but wealthy elite runs the government and the economy, the bulk of the population being in great poverty. The elite has surplus funds to invest; it does the investing and the managing, the rest of the population doing the hard physical work. While such an arrangement worked well enough in the antique world, it has a hard time surviving now. The state is today faced with the necessity of instituting basic reforms (thereby offending the rich and the powerful) or of doing nothing (thereby risking the pent-up and explosive resentment of the gradually awakening masses). Few states in heavily overpopulated agrarian countries have shown themselves capable of steering smoothly and firmly past the two horns of this dilemma. The usual history has been one of vacillation in the face of mounting domestic problems, which has of course weakened the nation in international affairs.

There are other disadvantages accruing from a redundant population, but these can be dealt with later in connection with birth and death rates. The main point to be stressed for the moment is that a country with a large population in relation to its resources is worse off, from an international point of view, than one with the same resources but with fewer people. It does not follow, then, that the bigger the population, the more powerful the nation. Whether or not a nation has too many people is independent of the absolute size of its total population, but depends rather on the relationship of population to resources and existing economic efficiency. Some small countries are overpopulated, some big ones are not. Our view is that India would have a much better chance to be one of the great powers if it had 100 million fewer citizens than it has. Egypt, Japan, Italy, China, Pakistan, Mexico, Haiti, Ceylon, and Israel would also be more powerful with fewer people. . . .

The disadvantages of high birth rates are not generally admitted for two reasons. First, quite independently of the facts, there is an ideological prejudice against admitting that a high birth rate can in any way be harmful, and so an anti-natalist policy does not generally appeal to politicians. Second, there is a widespread belief that an ever greater pool of manpower is a military and economic asset to a nation. It therefore comes as a shock to many people to hear it maintained that one of the demographic factors weakening a nation's power is a high birth rate. No one can maintain that a pre-industrial birth rate is always and in every way disadvantageous. In certain instances it may be an asset. But an analysis of the effect of birth rates on a nation's efficiency will show that in most cases today the advantage lies with a low rather than a high rate. . . .

If mortality has declined rapidly, the effect of a high birth rate in giving a country a heavy child burden is most marked, because the greatest lowering of the death rate occurs at ages zero to five. Also, a heavy emigration has the same tendency. Both of these conditions have prevailed in Puerto Rico and help account for its extraordinarily high proportion of children. Since there is probably an underenumeration of children in the Puerto Rican census, the percentage cited above may be lower than it should be.

One hears the argument that such an abundance of children is in the long run a good thing, since they will eventually be adults and can then contribute economically. But as long as the birth rate continues to be high, the age structure will continue to be weighted heavily in favor of children. The next generation, greatly expanded, will have a correspondingly expanded mass of children to support.

Not only does a country with a plethora of births have a child dependency burden, but it also tends to have a lesser proportion of its *adults* in the industrial labor force. The constant bearing and rearing of children take up the time of most women. In industrial countries women with young children are represented less in the labor force than women without any children or with only older children. In the United States in 1940, for instance, among women aged 18–64 who were married and living with their husband, 21.6 percent of those with *no* children under ten years of age were in the labor force whereas only 6.5 percent of those with two or more such children were in the labor force.[1] This fact explains why Hitler's early pro-natalist policy ran into difficulties. Originally he intended both to increase the birth rate and ease the unemployment problem in Germany by removing women from jobs and keeping them in the home. As the tempo of rearmament and army recruitment was intensified under the Third Reich, however, women were urgently needed in industry. The policy of keeping them at home was dropped in favor of other methods of stimulating the birth rate. . . .[2]

Children are of no value to a nation unless they are assimilated to the national culture, properly trained, and placed advantageously in the occupational structure. However, a huge increment of children every year in ratio to the total population interferes seriously with this process of "socializing" the young. Adequate educational facilities essential to the task are almost impossible to provide. Formal training is denied to many and is substandard in quality for those who receive it. . . .

In sum, a birth rate of 30 or more per 1000 inhabitants is a drag on any nation. It is certainly a drag from a short-run military point of view, because it loads the age structure with children who increase non-military costs; it withdraws women from the industrial labor force; it increases ill-health and mortality; and it places a great burden on educational and other facilities which must be either expanded or allowed to deteriorate. Accordingly, both Hitler and Mussolini were mistaken in their policy of trying to increase the birth rate. Both of them knew that they would shortly be at war. They should have known that the main task of a nation at war is to win the war. Had their population policies succeeded as they hoped, the flood of births would have made their chances of winning even less than they were. As it turned out, Mussolini did not succeed in raising the birth rate at all in Italy, and Hitler succeeded only in getting a normal post-depression rise earlier than usual. Eventually other countries, which had no pro-natalist policy at all, such as the United States, had a greater rise in the birth rate than did the Third Reich. As it turned out, therefore, the pro-natalist policies of the Fascist nations did not interfere with their war effort because they did not succeed.

[1] John D. Durand, *The Labor Force in the United States, 1890–1960,* New York: Social Science Research Council, 1948, p. 77. The percentages quoted are based on the groups when standardized for age.

[2] D. V. Glass, *Population Policies and Movements in Europe,* Oxford: Clarendon Press, 1940, pp. 289–290; Clifford Kirkpatrick, *Nazi Germany: Its Women and Family Life,* New York: The Bobbs-Merrill Company, 1938.

32

A Prerequisite to Sensitivity

Willard L. Sperry
1882–1954

From *The Ethical Basis
of Medical Practice*
New York: Paul B. Hoeber

1950

The climbers on Everest were occasionally asked what the landscape looked like as seen from the upper slopes of the mountain. They uniformly replied that they had no margins of attention to spare for sight-seeing. At an altitude where three breaths were required for every step upward they had to devote their minds to the single all-absorbing problem where next to put a foot. The aviator who finally flew over the summit of Everest was able from the cockpit of his plane to photograph the top of the mountain below him and the outspread panorama round about him.

33

Inescapable Materialism

The Panchatantra
(Fourth century A.D.)

Until a mortal's belly-pot
Is full, he does not care a jot
For love or music, wit or shame,
For body's care or scholar's name,

For virtue or for social charm,
For lightness or release from harm,
For godlike wisdom, youthful beauty,
For purity or anxious duty.[1]

---

[1] To which J. J. Spengler has added another line:

Nor yet for blessed Liberty.

34

The Necessity of Choice

The Bible

II Samuel 24:1–4 & 10–16
(King James version)

And again the anger of the Lord was kindled against Israel and he moved David against them to say, Go, number Israel and Judah.

For the king said to Joab the captain of the host, which was with him, Go now through all the tribes of Israel from Dan even to Beersheba, and number ye the people, that I may know the number of people.

And Joab said unto the king, Now the Lord thy God add unto the people, how many soever they be, an hundredfold, and that the eyes of my lord the king may see it: but why doth my lord the king delight in this thing?

Notwithstanding the king's word prevailed against Joab, and against the captains of the host. And Joab and the captains of the host went out from the presence of the king, to number the people of Israel. . . .

And David's heart smote him after he had numbered the people. And David said unto the Lord, I have sinned greatly in that I have done: and now, I beseech thee, O Lord, take away the iniquity of thy servant; for I have done very foolishly.

For when David was up in the morning, the word of the Lord came unto the prophet Gad, David's seer, saying,

Go and say unto David, Thus saith the Lord, I offer thee three things; choose thee one of them, that I may do it unto thee.

So Gad came to David, and told him, and said unto him, Shall seven years of famine come unto thee in thy land? or wilt thou flee three months before thine enemies, while they pursue thee? or that there be three days' pestilence in thy land? now advise, and see what answer I shall return to him that sent me.

And David said unto Gad, I am in a great strait; let us fall now into the hand of the Lord; for his mercies are great: and let me not fall into the hand of man.

So the Lord sent a pestilence upon Israel from the morning even to the time appointed: and there died of the people from Dan even to Beersheba seventy thousand men.

And when the angel stretched out his hand upon Jerusalem to destroy it, the Lord repented him of the evil, and said to the angel that destroyed the people, It is enough: stay now thy hand.

35

The Ethical Dilemma of Science

A. V. Hill
1886–

Nature, **170**:388–393

1952

The dilemma is this. All the impulses of decent humanity, all the dictates of religion and all the traditions of medicine insist that suffering should be relieved, curable diseases cured, preventable disease prevented. The obligation is regarded as unconditional: it is not permitted to argue that the suffering is due to folly, that the children are not wanted, that the patient's family would be happier if he died. All that may be so; but to accept it as a guide to action would lead to a degradation of standards of humanity by which civilization would be permanently and indefinitely poorer. . . .

Some might [take] the purely biological view that if men will breed like rabbits they must be allowed to die like rabbits. . . . Most people would still say no. But suppose it were certain now that the pressure of increasing population, uncontrolled by disease, would lead not only to widespread exhaustion of the soil and of other capital resources but also to continuing and increasing international tension and disorder, making it hard for civilization itself to survive: Would the majority of humane and reasonable people then change their minds? If ethical principles deny our right to do evil in order that good may come, are we justified in doing good when the foreseeable consequence is evil?

36

Response to Misery

Gerald F. Winfield
1908–

From *China: The Land and the People*
New York: William Sloane Associates

Gerald Winfield spent many years in China as a medical missionary. His observations may or may not be relevant to today's China—about which we in the West know little—but his conclusions must apply, with minor alterations, to at least a billion other people, if not to the Chinese. The ethical necessity of choice persists.

1948

I

There are times when I awake and hear again the cry of the dying beggar who wakened me one night in Chungking. I had seen him many times, a long, misshapen bag of discolored skin stretched over knotty, out-sized bones, lying beside the stone-paved trail that led up from the ferry landing to the house where I lived.

The first time I saw him he was already too weak to stand. He lay by the trail, well down the mountain near the upper edge of the village, begging between fits of coughing. The passersby were none too generous, but there were always a few dirty bills in the old cap that lay beside him. With them he bought a little food from passing vendors. Gradually, as the days went by, he began to work his way up the hill, a few feet at a time.

After he was dead, I heard his story. The only son of a family with a little property, he had, years before while still a young man, contracted tuberculosis. His family, after spending most of its resources on the ineffective treatments of old herb doctors, finally took him to a modern hospital where better care slowed the progress of the disease, although he was already too far gone for a cure to be effected. When his parents died he used up the rest of the family property to pay for his care. The hospital continued to treat and house him for many months after there was no money left to pay his ever-mounting costs. Finally, burdened by patients for whom there was some hope of cure, the needs of civilian and military war wounded, limited income, and rising expenses, the hospital authorities were forced to tell the old man that they could no longer keep him. An appeal was sent to the city welfare department and an official reply, belated as is the way with official replies anywhere, stated regretfully that there were no further funds available. The pain-wracked derelict left the hospital to beg in the streets.

As the weather turned colder, he eased his way up the hill toward my lodging. Several times I gave him money, yet I was ashamed to do so— ashamed because I knew that I was powerless to give enough to do anything more than prolong the slow pain of his dying—yet ashamed not to make some gesture of sympathy. Each time I saw him I was forced again to face the fact that there were thousands of shrunken creatures dying slowly beside the roads and trails of China, dying uncared for because millions were barely able to survive in a society that did not produce enough to support all its people and that was forced to burn huge quantities of what wealth it had to fight for its freedom.

At last he made his way to the shallow shelter of an old broken-down archway, a few tens of feet from the back wall of our compound. Then, in the small hours of the night when a light wind was blowing and a slow, cold rain was falling, I was wakened by the hoarse, pleading cry of the tubercular beggar. He was calling again and again the name of the woman in whose home I lived, begging for help.

The rest of the night I lay there sleepless, trapped between the quavering human cry in the night and the cold fact that forced me to know I could not save him or the thousands of others whose cries I could not hear. The next morning they came and told us that the beggar was dead.

His cry will haunt me the rest of my days, stinging me just as the cries of others like him will haunt those who come after me—driving all of us who hear to think and work and build, until at last the time can come when no one in China, or in any other land, need die of disease and starvation, uncared for in the shallow shelter of a broken-down archway.

II

Ultimately, however, the only means of enhancing the economic security of the family and the individual is the drastic raising of standards of living. So again one returns to the point where the vicious circle must be broken. The standard of living can be raised only as production is expanded and as population growth is checked to permit production to catch up. The limitation of the family becomes one of the most important factors in providing security for the family; and here is the most acute dilemma of all, in terms of both practical policy and moral values: existing checks on population growth must not be removed until the controls exerted by direct family limitation and industrialization are well established, perhaps for a period as long as thirty years. The death rate, therefore, must not be reduced too quickly. Medical-health policies must be shaped with great care with better health stemming from more knowledge and co-operation on the part of the people themselves and not from the super-imposition of preventive measures. It is obvious that the first objective of the medical-health program must *not* be the simple, natural one of saving lives: instead, it must be the development of means whereby the Chinese people will reduce their birth rate as rapidly as modern science can reduce the death rate.

The proposition is made with an acute awareness of its radical nature. For one trained in public health it will seem rank heresy to propose that during the next twenty to thirty years not even severe epidemics in China should be attacked with every means available to modern medicine. I suggest that public health measures which can save millions of lives should not be practiced in China on a nation-wide scale until the stage is set for a concurrent reduction of the birth rate. Existing misery and poverty can be permanently eliminated only when there are fewer, healthier people, with longer life expectancy and greater economic security. The future welfare of the Chinese people is more dependent on the prevention of births than on the prevention of deaths.

37

The Utterly Dismal Theorem

Kenneth E. Boulding
1910–

From *The Image*
Ann Arbor: University of Michigan Press

1956

A good example of these quasilatent models is the Malthusian theory. This is the famous dismal theorem of economics that if the only check on the growth of population is starvation and misery, then no matter how favorable the environment or how advanced the technology the population will grow until it is miserable and starves. The theorem, indeed, has a worse corollary which has been described as the utterly dismal theorem. This is the proposition that if the only check on the growth of population is starvation and misery, then any technological improvement will have the ultimate effect of increasing the sum of human misery, as it permits a larger population to live in precisely the same state of misery and starvation as before the change. . . .

The experience of Ireland is an extremely interesting case in point. In the late seventeenth century, the population of Ireland was about two million people living in misery. Then came the seventeenth-century equivalent of Point Four, the introduction of the potato, a technological revolution of first importance enabling the Irish to raise much more food per acre than they had ever done before. The result of this benevolent technological improvement was an increase in population from two million to eight million by 1845. The result of the technological improvement, therefore, was to quadruple the amount of human misery on the unfortunate island. The failure of the potato crop in 1845 led to disastrous consequences. Two million Irish died of starvation; another two million emigrated; and the remaining four million learned a sharp lesson which has still not been forgotten. The population of Ireland has been roughly stationary since that date, in spite of the fact that Ireland is a predominantly Roman Catholic country. The stability has been achieved by an extraordinary increase in the age at marriage.

38

To Feed the Hungry

Charles G. Wilber
1916–

Thought (Fordham University Quarterly), **38**:487–498

1963

In order to clarify the point of view which I, as a biological scientist, am taking in this discussion of goals for the next decade or two I should like the reader to share with me these fundamental ideas:

> Man was created to praise, reverence, and serve God our Lord, and by this means to save his soul; and the other things on the face of the earth were created for man's sake, and in order to aid him in the prosecution of the end for which he was created. Whence it follows, that man must make use of them in so far as they help him to attain his end, and in the same way he ought to withdraw himself from them in so far as they hinder him from it.—*The Spiritual Exercises of St. Ignatius Loyola.*

With this as my launching pad I wish to take off on an exploration of a few goals which I feel are essential to keep in view if humankind all over our planet is to be blessed with the right to "life, liberty, and the pursuit of happiness." . . .

The world food situation is unbalanced and dangerous. Miserably hungry people in South America, Asia, and parts of Africa gaze upon obese Americans and Europeans whose major food problem is overeating. We have a responsible agency of the United Nations publishing the conclusion that wheat is now and will continue to be a significant surplus on the world market, at a time when pitiful stories come from various corners of the world telling of death by starvation for throngs of children and adults.

It is my contention that human science and technology have, for the first time in the history of man, made hunger obsolete. But the fruits of science and technology have been badly and dangerously distributed. Only part of mankind has benefited whereas all have a right.

The question often arises, "Why feed the hordes of hungry people in the world? Let them die and relieve the population pressure." This question is usually followed by another, "How can we feed the mounting mobs of men even if we want to—there are too many mouths to feed?"

Both these questions derive from a pernicious attitude which I propose to call pagan pessimism. Mankind now and in the foreseeable future can be fed and must be fed. All men have a fundamental right to the good things of earth and they can have them. The problem is partly scientific but principally social and political. . . .

Such considerations give us pause. Do I have a moral right to three meals a day when my biological brother in South America is not sure of one? Is it ethical for my children to have two suits of clothing when their fellows in Asia have but rags? How do I justify my home with its various rooms and privacies when the father of a family in Africa must house his loved ones in a one-room hovel?

Of all these considerations the specter of hunger is most moving. We must feed our brothers throughout the world. We must reduce ourselves to subsistence level if that be necessary to bring all men to at least that level. This conclusion is to me a moral imperative. I do not like what I have concluded—but I cannot escape it and remain faithful to my commitment as a scientist. . . .

To the objection: "Such efforts will cost astronomical sums of money—we can't afford it," I answer that the cost will indeed be great—but morally we cannot afford not to do it. When I hear fellow scientists and our political leaders attempting to justify the great cost of flights to the moon and the planets, I am led to ask: "Is it not infinitely more important to satisfy the hunger of mankind than to photograph the other side of the moon?"

In conclusion, then, I should like to repeat the goals which I envision for the next two decades. They are simple: to feed the hungry, to clothe the naked, to give the cup of cold water in His Name; to be peacemakers. It will not be easy; the way is obscure; the cost will be painful. Pagan pessimism may discourage us. But I urge a Christian optimism based upon the truth that "With God all things are possible."

39
Hungry Nations

William and Paul Paddock
1921–
and 1907–

Boston: Little, Brown and Co.

William Paddock is a plant pathologist and agronomist with many years of experience in Central America. Paul Paddock is a retired Foreign Service Officer of the State Department. In their collaborative writing they feel that "we" and its derivatives are stilted, hence they use the first person singular, regardless of whether the observations are attributable to one or the other, or both.

1964

I

For four years my wife worked in a group of eight women who acted as agents of CARE in the distribution of food to two hundred fifty persons in a small, desolate village in Central America.

My experience with CARE has convinced me it is a well-administered organization and is efficient at verifying that its food is distributed to needy people. Its accounting system to keep track of this food is detailed, honest—and onerous.

Not generally known is that the food is distributed by volunteer workers. In these backward countries the volunteers usually are the type of civic-minded, conscientious women who in the United States are active in various social welfare organizations. Generally, in the remote areas this type of satisfying public service is not easily accessible to the local women. Hence they welcome the opportunity to act for CARE.

On TV in the United States recently my wife saw that the ten-millionth package that CARE had shipped abroad was being sent to Colombia. "Look!" she said. "Packages! Real packages! If we could only have seen one such package!"

The food received by her group for distribution arrived in large boxes or sacks or five-pound cans. It was hard physical work to open these and measure out the exact amounts per portion. The women claimed the cans were made out of cast iron and could be opened only by a blowtorch. Yet the cans had to be opened and the cheese sliced, the powdered milk measured out, and the beans and the rice. Have you ever measured out powdered milk for two hundred fifty people? Every Thursday? For four years?

Have you ever stood in a line of two hundred fifty persons waiting for a food ration? At each distribution without exception there would be fights. Children would fight. Women would fight. Big children would push aside little children. A woman would suddenly erupt in a fight over gossip about whose man was sleeping with whom. There would be arguments over the size of the piece of cheese received. If a woman did not get the amount of powdered milk to which she thought she was entitled, it would not be unusual for her to throw it on the ground or even, once, at one of the women distributing it.

Never, but never, was this a scene of joyous thanksgiving. The women distributing the food were often irritated because of the hard physical work and the lack of thanks they received. Only their sense of duty kept them there. Often they were accused of profiteering. Every three or four months a letter would be printed in the newspaper in the capital city of the country—which one of the persons receiving the food had presumably written—accusing this group of women of maltreatment and of stealing the food given to the village.

The people who received the food came to look upon it as their birthright. They never understood from where the food came and did not care anyway. They usually assumed it came from the president of the country as a personal, political gift, although in fairness to him he had never in any way tried to give such an impression, as I am told has occurred with executives in some countries in regard to American free food.

After four years the spirit of compassion toward the needy was exhausted and the eight women resigned. There was no one else in the community to whom CARE could turn over the job of distribution and so the service in this village ceased.

In reviewing their work the group decided that yes, it was likely some persons had been kept alive in this hungry village who otherwise probably would have weakened and died. Yet they agreed they had never improved the *health* of any person, nor had the village as a community been helped. This distribution of CARE food for four years had not, in their opinion, engendered any good will on the part of anyone among the villagers and definitely not the slightest iota of good will towards the United States.

During these years the group of women repeatedly had held meetings to determine how they might distribute the food so that good will, or rather a sympathetic understanding might be developed toward themselves, toward the CARE organization, or toward the American people who support CARE. No way was found. . . .

II

In 1954 Congress enacted Public Law 480 (reentitled by "public image" staffers as "Food for Peace"). Basically, this law enabled the shipment of American "surplus" foodstuffs abroad for free distribution to the needy or for sale to local governments for soft currencies which had to be left in the recipient countries. It has been a popular law. The do-gooders like it, the officials propagandizing foreign peoples like it, the politicians like it because it postpones their taking action on America's unbalanced modern agriculture, and the farmers like it because the politicians can postpone taking action on America's unbalanced agriculture.

Since enactment of the law, $12,000,000,000 worth of corn, sorghum, butter, cheese, wheat, rice and other basic foods have been shipped abroad under the program. In my opinion, only a naïve person blinded with rose-colored glasses would claim that the United States has received anything of value in return, either economic or political. . . .

The agricultural wealth of the United States is not inexhaustible, as proven in many a worn-out, thoroughly exhausted region. This can happen also in the Middle West, although research is keeping ahead, for the time being, of the steady draining away of the heritage of soil nutrients and of the virgin topsoil.

The agricultural value of Iowa farmland, it is estimated, is deteriorating at the rate of 1 per cent a year in relation to its inherent productivity of soil. Conservationists often claim the American standard of living has been bought by a permanent destruction of one-third of our topsoil.

The soils and nutrients in the soils of the Middle West are not inexhaustible. Remember how often writers used to say the forests of the United States were inexhaustible, the iron ore of Minnesota, the water supply for the cities, the buffalo, the passenger pigeons. Today one reads that the fish of the sea are inexhaustible food for the world's exploding population—when actually the expert knows how limited and capricious the fishing banks are.

I respectfully point out that the only genuine inexhaustibility in this world of ours is the use of the word.

If this "surplus" food being sent abroad [under P.L. 480] produced

86

tangible results either for American international policies in the Cold War or for financial returns to the national economy, there would be little cause for protest. But is it producing such benefits? If so, where? Egypt? Brazil? Pakistan? Indonesia? Mexico?

40

In Memory
of Malthus' Tragic Feast

Garrett Hardin
1915–

Perspectives in Biology and Medicine, **9:**225

1966

FROM MALTHUS

(*Out of the Second Edition of the Essay on Population*)

A man who is born into a world already possessed, if he cannot get subsistence from his parents on whom he has a just demand, and if the society do not want his labour, has no claim of right to the smallest portion of food, and, in fact, has no business to be where he is. At nature's mighty feast there is no vacant cover for him. She tells him to be gone, and will quickly execute her own orders, if he does not work upon the compassion of some of her guests. If these guests get up and make room for him, other intruders immediately appear demanding the same favour. The report of a provision for all that come, fills the hall with numerous claimants. The order and harmony of the feast is disturbed, the plenty that before reigned is changed into scarcity; and the happiness of the guests is destroyed by the spectacle of misery and dependence in every part of the hall, and by the clamorous importunity of those, who are justly enraged at not finding the provision which they had been taught to expect. The guests learn too late their error, in counter-acting those strict orders to all intruders, issued by the great mistress of the feast, who, wishing that all guests should have plenty, and knowing she could not provide for unlimited numbers, humanely refused to admit fresh comers when her table was already full.

TO MALTHUS

(Out of Wordsworth, Ill-Remembered, in Ill Times)

Malthus! Thou shouldst be living in this hour:
The world hath need of thee: getting and begetting,
We soil fair Nature's bounty. Sweating
With 'dozer, spray and plough we dissipate our dower
In smart and thoughtless optimism, blocking the power
Of reason to lay out a saner setting
For reason's growth to change, adapt and flower,
In reason's way, to weave that long sought bower
Of sweet consistency.—Great Soul! I'd rather be
Like you, logic-driven to deny the feast
To those who would, if saved, see misery increased
Throughout this tender, trembling world.
Confound ye those who set unfurled
Soft flags of good intentions, deaf to obdurate honesty!

41

A Medical Aspect of
the Population Problem

Alan Gregg
1890–1957

Science, **121**:681–682

1955

The medical aspects of what is called the population problem defy condensation into a brief paper. Even the relatively few factors we know something about are too numerous and too intricately involved with one another and with external circumstances to lend themselves to summary exposition. For this reason I propose to offer only one idea regarding the population problem. It hardly deserves to be called a medical aspect: it is rather the view of one who has had a medical training—a single idea around which subordinate reflections of a rather general sort present themselves.

In exposing this one idea I recall the Spartan custom of exposing infants to the rigors of the weather, in the conviction that such a practice weeds out the weaklings. To expose an infant idea to the rigors of a scientific atmosphere before providing the poor little thing with the support of experimental evidence or with the power of demonstrated predictive value may seem like Spartan treatment. But if the idea dies of exposure, its exit will be at least more dignified and permanent under AAAS auspices than under any other I could invite or invent. I should therefore witness its death with a very fair semblance of Spartan parental fortitude.

The way in which physicians estimate, by a sampling procedure, the number of white blood cells in the blood of a patient is generally known. In essence, it involves diluting a carefully measured amount of blood in a carefully measured amount of water, counting the number of cells found in a defined cubic volume of the blood thus diluted, and then computing the number of cells per cubic millimeter of blood. A similar method is applied to counting the red cells of the blood. Although such cell counts vary somewhat among individuals and in any one individual under varying conditions of activity, any variation of the order of 400 percent or more would usually justify the suspicion of being pathological. If, for example, a patient's white-cell count moved up within a month from 5000 to 23,000, a physician would think of the possibility that he was witnessing an early stage of leukemia—an uncontrolled growth in the numbers of white blood cells.

Now new growths of any kind (popularly called cancer) involve an increase in the number of some one kind of cell and, hence, a corresponding increase in the size of the organ or tissue involved. However, not all increases in the size of organs are the result of new growths: the heart hypertrophies—that is, grows larger—to make up for leaky valves and its lost efficiency as a pump; the uterus grows in volume remarkably during pregnancy; the organs and tissues of the growing child also present obvious increases in cellular numbers. But in these increases there appears to be a limit at which further cell reduplication stops or is in some way inhibited. Indeed, one has the mystified impression that there is a process involved that in its effect resembles self-restraint or self-limitation. One cannot, of course, attribute a sense of decorum to cells, even though we can give no better answer than ignorance to the question of why organs show a relative uniformity of size and shape in the normal state. But the fact remains that, in all but one instance, organs and tissues in their growth seem to "know" when to stop.

The exception, of course, is the whole category of new growths, or neoplasms (popularly called cancer), of which there are two main sorts— the benign and the malignant. Fibroids of the uterus furnish a good example of benign tumors; cancer of the stomach, of the malignant. I shall return to some of the more important characteristics of new growths, but now I would like, at this point, to introduce another set of considerations more apparently related to the population problem.

If we regard the different forms of plant and animal life in the world as being so closely related to and dependent on one another that they resemble different types of cells in a total organism, then we may, for the sake of a hypothesis, consider the living world as an organism. I would not merely admit that this is a hypothesis—I would insist that it is only a hypothesis. Perhaps more cautiously one would say that such a hypothesis is no more than a scaffolding. For a scaffolding may serve, but does not enter into, the final structure of established fact.

Let us look, then, at the different forms of life on this planet as a physician regards the federation or community of interdependent organs and tissues that go to make up his patient. What would we think if it became evident that within a very brief period in the history of the world some one type of its forms of life had increased greatly in number and obviously at the expense of other kinds of life? In short, I suggest, as a way of looking at the population problem, that there are some interesting analogies between the growth of the human population of the world and the increase of cells observable in neoplasms. To say that the world has cancer, and that the cancer cell is man, has neither experimental proof nor the validation of predictive accuracy; but I see no reason that instantly forbids such a speculation. If such a concept has any value at the outset, we should quite naturally incline to go further by comparing the other characteristics of new growths with the observable phenomena related to the extraordinary increase now noted in the world's population. An estimated 500 million in A.D. 1500 has grown, in 450 years, to an estimated population of 2 billion today. And the end is not in sight—especially in the Western Hemisphere.

What are some of the characteristics of new growths? One of the simplest is that they commonly exert pressure on adjacent structures and, hence, displace them. New growths within closed cavities, like the skull, exert pressures that kill, because any considerable displacement is impossible. Pressure develops, usually destroying first the function and later the substance of the normal cells thus pressed upon. For a comparison with a closed cavity, think of an island sheltering a unique form of animal life that is hunted to extinction by man. The limited space of the island resembles the cranial cavity whose normal contents cannot escape the murderous invader. Border warfare, mass migrations, and those wars that are described as being the result of population pressures resemble the pressures exerted by new growths. We actually borrow not only the word *pressure* but also the word *invasion* to describe the way in which new growths by direct extension preempt the space occupied by other cells or types of life. The destruction of forests, the annihilation or near extinction of various animals, and the soil erosion consequent to overgrazing illustrate the cancerlike effect that man—in mounting numbers and heedless arrogance—has had on other forms of life on what we call "our" planet.

Metastasis is the word used to describe another phenomenon of malignant growth in which detached neoplastic cells carried by the lymphatics or the blood vessels lodge at a distance from the primary focus or point of origin and proceed to multiply without direct contact with the tissue or organ from which they came. It is actually difficult to avoid using the word *colony* in describing this thing physicians call metastasis. Conversely, to what degree can colonization of the Western Hemisphere be thought of as metastasis of the white race?

Cancerous growths demand food; but, so far as I know, they have never been cured by getting it. Furthermore, although their blood supply is commonly so disordered that persistent bleeding from any body orifice suggests that a new growth is its cause, the organism as a whole often experiences a loss of weight and strength and suggests either poisoning or the existence of an inordinate nutritional demand by neoplastic cells—perhaps both. The analogies can be found in "our plundered planet"—in man's effect on other forms of life. These hardly need elaboration—certainly the ecologists would be prepared to supply examples in plenty of man's inroads upon other forms of life. Our rivers run silt—although we could better think of them as running the telltale blood of cancer.

At the center of a new growth, and apparently partly as a result of its inadequate circulation, necrosis often sets in—the death and liquidation of the cells that have, as it were, dispensed with order and self-control in their passion to reproduce out of all proportion to their usual number in the organism. How nearly the slums of our great cities resemble the necrosis of tumors raises the whimsical query: Which is the more offensive to decency and beauty, slums or the fetid detritus of a growing tumor?

One further analogy deserves attention. The individual cells of new growth often show marked variations of size, shape, and chemical behavior. This may be compared with the marked inequalities of health, wealth, and function so conspicuous among the human beings in over-populated countries. Possibly man's invention of caste and social stratification may be viewed in part as a device to rationalize and control these same distressing discrepancies of health, wealth, and status that increase as the population increases.

By now the main posts and planks of my scaffolding must be obvious. In the history of science there have been hypotheses that, although not true, have led to truth. I could hope that this somewhat bizarre comment on the population problem may point to a new concept of human self-restraint. Besides ennobling human life, it would, I think, be applauded by most other forms of life—if they had hands to clap with. Or are we deaf to such applause?

And finally, I submit that if some of the more thoughtful cells in, say, a rapidly growing cancer of the stomach could converse with one another, they might, quite possibly, reserve some afternoon to hold what they would call "a discussion of the population problem."

If Copernicus helped astronomy by challenging the geocentric interpretation of the universe, might it not help biology to challenge the anthropocentric interpretation of nature?

42

The First Fatal Steps
Toward Civilization

Marston Bates
1906–

From *Where Winter Never Comes*
New York: Charles Scribner's Sons

1952

How and why these first steps toward agriculture were taken we shall never know—which leaves a splendid field for speculation. The process was certainly slow and irregular. It seems likely that our savage ancestors were far from regarding agriculture as an unmixed blessing, since it soon involved such unpleasant features as regular habits and hard work. Agriculture is an insidious business, though. Once developed or adopted, it enables many more people to live on a given area of land, and human breeding habits being what they are, this population increase soon appears. The tribe is then saddled with agriculture for all eternity, since the old way cannot yield enough food for the numbers. . . .

A few food-gathering peoples resort to agriculture in emergencies when driven to such drastic action by prolonged scarcity of game. This shows that such people could be agricultural if they wanted to—but they avoid the necessity by desisting from agriculture as soon as game conditions return to normal and before their own population has made any untoward gain. Some of the Plains Indians of North America were enabled, by a lucky fluke, to escape the agricultural treadmill; they took to the horse when this appeared as a result of the Spanish intrusion, and when they discovered that their population could be maintained by this more efficient method of hunting, agriculture was abandoned forthwith. . . .

A few peoples apparently have never taken up with any of these insidious methods of food-producing: we find them living today in a food-gathering culture that seems not unlike the culture that probably characterized all of mankind fifteen or twenty thousand years ago. We call such people 'backward'—but maybe they are the cleverest of all in having managed to avoid, through all of these millennia, those first fatal steps toward the primrose-lined, ambition-greased, chute of civilization.

43

Eden Was No Garden

Nigel Calder
1931–

New York: Holt, Rinehart and Winston

1967

If men were intended to work the soil they would have longer arms. In truth, we evolved as hunters and we remain the most efficient predatory animals of all, shrewd of brain, infinitely adaptable of body, and with hands to make and wield weapons. Yet since the invention of agriculture some 10,000 years ago, most men have been obliged to bend their straight backs to cultivate the land. We have grown mightily in numbers, and have constructed remarkable civilizations on the basis of agriculture. But we have made it a distinctly boring world for most people; only in sport and in war can we recapture something of the excitement of the chase, which was the everyday occupation of the first of our species. . . .

If we pause to salute the hunter, before the Neolithic farmer, with his very different skills and systems, appears on the scene, our purpose is not to suggest an innocent nobility in the hunter, in any Rousseau-like sense. He was a rough, ignorant fellow. Yet when we read the evidence of Palaeolithic archaeology, or accounts of those disappearing remnants of essentially Palaeolithic tribes (the Eskimo, the Australian aborigine, the Bushman of the Kalahari) we find much that is admirable and ingenious.

How do you deal with an angry bull elephant, when all you have is a sharpened stone? You nip aside, slip in behind, and cut the tendons of his heel. What can you do to lure a giraffe, the most timid of large animals? You play on its curiosity for bright objects by flashing a polished stone in its direction. The Bushmen, according to Laurens Van der Post, would use lions as hunting "dogs," letting them kill game and eat a little, before driving them off with fire. Franz Boas tells how Eskimo approached deer, two men together, one stooping behind like the back end of a pantomime horse, the other carrying his bow on his shoulders to resemble antlers and grunting like a deer. The despised Australian aborigine can "travel light" with only a few wooden and stone implements and, by his knowledge of nature, survive indefinitely in the Great Sandy Desert. If we once let these echoes of our prehistory penetrate our sophisticated heads, they strike in us chords of excitement, if not of envy. . . .

It has taken many millennia of philosophy and revolution to dismantle the outrageous institutions of the kings and priests, created in the immediate wake of agriculture; and if the end is now possibly in sight it is because of the creation of affluence by technologies other than agriculture. Indeed, the ideals if not the practices of welfare capitalism, democratic socialism, and communism can be seen as various attempts to recreate, in the infinitely more complex world of today, something corresponding to the good-natured companionship of the hunting tribe. . . .

Yet, although it may seem that organized warfare is a consequence of civilization, rather than of the invention of agriculture, there are good reasons for attaching special significance to the latter. Why are soldiers glamorized? Why are war-narratives and war-movies so gripping? Why do small boys stalk one another with wooden rifles? Surely because the soldier to this day represents that missing hunter in each of us. When the fun (which I take to mean doing what comes naturally) went out of the daily occupations of most men, war provided a direct or vicarious relief of boredom. I do not believe that we shall ever eradicate war, even with the fear of nuclear annihilation, until we have properly diagnosed and treated this ultimate source of war's fascination. Any dreams of world order which seek to bottle up the aggressive urge in man, rather than to canalize it, are likely to fail. . . .

Consider other effects of agriculture on the mentality of mankind. Besides the notion of "harvest" it introduced two very important, closely related concepts into human affairs: "work" and "worth"—concepts that nowadays dominate all our lives.

Every clerk up from the suburbs to spend his day entering figures in a ledger, every fitter, shop assistant, or draughtsman working his stint, is living in the shadow of those Neolithic pioneers who found that if they did not tend their fields regularly the weeds would choke the crop. We need not doubt that their huntsman predecessor had chores to do, and invented routines for passing the day. But how could he have distinguished between "work," which was like our leisure, and "leisure" that was like our work? The idea of repetitive application of most of the daylight hours to a schedule determined by human policies, whose neglect would be disastrous—this surely arose from agriculture.

44

Wilderness and the Camel's Nose

Raymond B. Cowles
1896–

From *The Meaning of Wilderness to Science*
David Brower, editor
San Francisco: Sierra Club

1960

The demand for invasion of wilderness-sanctuary areas for water storage and power dams, oil rights, iron ore, irrigation, forests, farm lands, and so on is now but a gentle movement in comparison to what it will be with our predicted population of even forty years hence (which presumably will be two times our present one, or 340 million, to be fed with these resources that we have). I suspect that nothing having potentiality for satisfying the necessities, in the broad sense, can even briefly survive this kind of developing hunger.

It is not difficult to multiply examples: you have the pressures for lake fronts, stream sides, beach frontage, mountain property, anywhere there is beauty. These resources are as ample as they ever were, but not in terms of our present population size. You see, underlying everything is our population size, again and again. *This is the basic factor.* It isn't that we have used up or consumed some of these things, but that we have simply outgrown them in terms of numbers relative to available areas.

With continually mounting populations, by their sheer numbers, the pressure for property and the prices for natural scenic property anywhere can be expected to parallel the developments in waterfront property. As I see it, the stages that accompany population-density growth will take approximately the following insidious steps: First, we see the need for wilderness areas; for their beauty, their peace, their scientific value. We restrict the wilderness areas to foot travel or to horse travelers, but their numbers will increase along the trails until one is never out of sight or sound of others. Then there will be more trails added in order to dilute the density of the hikers on the trails; and we will probably have pack burros and horses increasingly to get to more remote areas and allow people to escape to the very thing for which wildlife and wilderness areas were established —solitude. So we will crowd, then develop more trails in more and more remote areas. Following this, there will be pressure for access roads—for fire protection, chiefly, or for those that don't have the hardihood to do it on their own feet or on horseback to traverse and merely see unspoiled nature. Then there will be requests for fixed campsites to localize the damage from an excess of people in the area. Then there will be demands for other campsites within the area so that more people can linger and enjoy the wilderness. A store, then stores, to supply food for more campers. I think most of you follow me; this is supposed to be a prediction, but I've seen it happening already. These stores will spread through the area to supply more food for more campers. Then we will see demands rising for the establishment of inns, as they will be called, but they will be hotels, and then more of these inns or hotels, in order to supply comfort for the people who are not rugged enough to take the wilderness by themselves. Then there will be demand for amusements associated with these inns and resting places to beguile the people who are bored during the hours of evening and night when they can't see anything. This will be repeated and there will be an insidious multiplication of these types of accommodations to take care of ever more people. And there will be more roads to give more fire protection, more accommodations, and to dilute the harmful effects of local pressures we will have a spreading web of roads, until there is no genuine wilderness left. Then there will be frank conversion of these accommodations to resort use. Ultimately—because we no longer have a wilderness—subdivision could logically follow. Who cares beyond that?

45

Has Hunting a Future?

Archie Carr
1909–

From *Ulendo*
New York: Knopf

1964

I heard of a woman once who said to Theodore Roosevelt, "Tell me, Mr. President, when will you ever get over your childish inclination to kill things?" Those were not the exact words, but the question was about like that, and in a way it was a good question. We are all going to have to get over killing things pretty soon, for one reason or another. But the problem is not as simple as the question makes it sound. Behind that well-fed woman there were too many millennia with less-well-fed women putting the question another way—saying, "Look, Gug, when are you going out and kill something?" Killing things is in one way childish. In another way though, it has till lately been not childish at all, but the most mature and necessary craft and craving a man could have, next to that for procreation. And when all the need to kill for survival was gone, the old bloodstirring urges stayed with us, as intact as our useless wisdom teeth. Like wisdom teeth they have been far slower to yield to changing times than the need to use them was. For a while men put the old juices to work for the fun of the chase, as a manly recreation. As long as men were fewer than ducks and deer, things went along all right that way.

But now I think fathers are creating misery for their sons when they build in them the false hope that there can be hunting in the man-ridden world to come. The cult of the pioneer is done. The axe and the gun are dead symbols, like the crossbow and the anvil. We are Cro-Magnon no longer; we are no longer Minute Men or Forty-niners. Whatever needs, joys, and rights our grandchildren may have, these will not include felling trees or felling bodies.

I saw a boy not long ago who seemed to embody the dilemma of the hunter in these times. I was waiting for my lunch in the dining room of an East African hotel. A party in the last stages of preparation for a safari came in, and the boy was one of the group. There were two big men in khakis, with shortsleeved tunics over shortsleeved shirts and bullet loops around the tunics. The boy was about thirteen, well grown and very like the men. Two women, clearly the wives of the men, walked in front of the hunters to the table the headwaiter showed them.

The men and the boy all looked like Ernest Hemingway, with maybe a little more of a Texas look. Or maybe it was John Wayne they looked like. The women didn't look like Hemingway at all. They were women who were obviously going to spend a few weeks at the hotel waiting. They were little, sweet, well-tended women, like secure mice; and as they passed I heard them speak of Neiman-Marcus in voices that seemed correct for Central Texas. They all sat down, and the women kept talking and the men began to speak in rumbling voices about things they ought to buy and people they had to see around the town. The room was full, and the waiters in red fezzes and white robes were slipping about among the tables. I could hear the shuffling sound of their bare feet above the talk of the safari party and the subdued voices of the English people. After a while the boy grew tired of waiting for the waiter and got up, went over to the buffet, and started piling a plate with cold cuts.

He was a manly looking boy, big for his age and healthy, a little heavy perhaps but not soft at all. There was a sort of aura of prepubic virility about him, partly built in, partly no doubt the result of a plan of his to be exactly like his father. The boy was a small big-game hunter beyond any doubt. He was probably going to be a good one. Maybe he already was good. There was an air of poise about the boy that made me feel this was not his first safari. My first thought, looking at him, was that he was a lucky boy. Not many boys have fathers who can give them an African safari for being good and manly.

I listened to the men talking seriously about the great game they were setting out to play, and I felt a little envious because no son of mine would probably ever go out on safari that way. But after thinking a while I was not so sure the boy was lucky. For his youth and a while afterward, he would have a solid thing to hold to—unless the Africans who are taking over their land should suddenly cut it off. But from the religious way the men were grooming him, they seemed to believe they were handing down some heritable asset for generations to come, like a good business or a wine cellar. What would be left of it when the boy would be his father's age? And how about the boys of the boy, I thought. What meaning would remain for them in the cult of the hunter?

46

Should We Treat the Symptoms
or the Disease?

Conflicts between scientists and practical men are of many different sorts. If there is a unity discernible in this variety, it probably resides in a difference in the "sightedness" of the two groups. Practical men, almost by definition, deal with the crisis of the moment, leaving the problems of tomorrow to take care of themselves. Scientists, by contrast, tend to be impatient of piecemeal solutions, and try to show us the larger picture into which the present crisis fits as only one piece of the jigsaw puzzle. A practical man, faced with silt in his streams, may propose building a catchment basin. Alan Gregg, a scientist, says that we had better think of our silted rivers as the telltale blood of a cancerous growth of population. Can we expect to cure a disease by treating only its symptoms?

Scientists are likely to refer to practical men as "short-sighted." Practical men return the compliment by calling scientists "visionary." We can do without the pejoratives, for we need both sorts of vision and action. Present crises often demand immediate action, even though it be only palliative. A symptom may be more than a symptom: it may become a cause if it serves as the stimulus or excuse for other evils. Short-sighted action is often required; but let us expect no more than short-term benefits from it.

Consider this report from the **Life** magazine of 14 June 1963:

Suddenly, across the U.S.—for reasons criminological, psychological or sociological but altogether shocking—there is an upsurge in discoveries of brutal cases of child beating.

Beyond doubt many cases never come to the attention of doctors. In those that do, the cause of injury is often written off as accidental. Even if the truth is suspected, it may be ignored because the doctors are unwilling either to believe the evidence or to get involved in legal complications. One problem is that only two states—California and Wyoming—require doctors to report battered child cases. Other states are now being urged to pass the necessary laws. "If we had the real figures," says Dr. Frederic N. Silverman, a Cincinnati radiologist, "the total could easily surpass auto accidents as a killer and maimer of children."

Parents who beat their children come from every economic level. They are usually immature and overly aggressive. Sometimes, it is believed, parents are repeating their own early mistreatment. But mostly, parents say they are just trying to get the child to behave.

Almost all of the victims are under 3 years of age. And one out of ten of them will die. Among those who survive, 15% suffer permanent brain damage. . . .

What should we do about such abominations? Pass laws? Inflict punishment? Probably we should. But we should expect no more of these actions than that they may serve as negative feedbacks to keep the amount of cruelty within limits. If we are to get at causes, rather than symptoms, we must seek a larger view of the problem. The following report by John Calhoun suggests some ideas that should be insinuated into the minds of all prophets of the American "Bigger and Better" version of the Idea of Progress.

47

Population Density and Social Pathology

John B. Calhoun
1917–

Scientific American, **206**(2):139 ff.

1962

In the celebrated thesis of Thomas Malthus, vice and misery impose the ultimate natural limit on the growth of populations. Students of the subject have given most of their attention to misery, that is, to predation, disease and food supply as forces that operate to adjust the size of a population to its environment. But what of vice? Setting aside the moral burden of this word, what are the effects of the social behavior of a species on population growth—and of population density on social behavior?

Some years ago I attempted to submit this question to experimental inquiry. I confined a population of wild Norway rats in a quarter-acre enclosure. With an abundance of food and places to live and with predation and disease eliminated or minimized, only the animals' behavior with respect to one another remained as a factor that might affect the increase in their number. There could be no escape from the behavioral consequences of rising population density. By the end of 27 months the population had become stabilized at 150 adults. Yet adult mortality was so low that 5,000 adults might have been expected from the observed reproductive rate. The reason this larger population did not materialize was that infant mortality was extremely high. Even with only 150 adults in the enclosure, stress from social interaction led to such disruption of maternal behavior that few young survived.

With this background in mind I turned to observation of a domesticated albino strain of the Norway rat under more controlled circumstances indoors. The data for the present discussion come from the histories of six different populations. Each was permitted to increase to approximately twice the number that my experience had indicated could occupy the available space with only moderate stress from social interaction. In each case my associates and I maintained close surveillance of the colonies for 16 months in order to obtain detailed records of the modifications of behavior induced by population density.

The consequences of the behavioral pathology we observed were most apparent among the females. Many were unable to carry pregnancy to full term or to survive delivery of their litters if they did. An even greater number, after successfully giving birth, fell short in their maternal functions. Among the males the behavior disturbances ranged from sexual deviation to cannibalism and from frenetic overactivity to a pathological withdrawal from which individuals would emerge to eat, drink and move about only when other members of the community were asleep. The social organization of the animals showed equal disruption. Each of the experimental populations divided itself into several groups, in each of which the sex ratios were drastically modified. One group might consist of six or seven females and one male, whereas another would have 20 males and only 10 females.

The common source of these disturbances became most dramatically apparent in the populations of our first series of three experiments, in which we observed the development of what we called a behavioral sink. The animals would crowd together in greatest number in one of the four interconnecting pens in which the colony was maintained. As many as 60 of the 80 rats in each experimental population would assemble in one pen during periods of feeding. Individual rats would rarely eat except in the company of other rats. As a result extreme population densities developed in the pen adopted for eating, leaving the others with sparse populations.

Eating and other biological activities were thereby transformed into social activities in which the principal satisfaction was interaction with other rats. In the case of eating, this transformation of behavior did not keep the animals from securing adequate nutrition. But the same pathological "togetherness" tended to disrupt the ordered sequences of activity involved in other vital modes of behavior such as the courting of sex partners, the building of nests and the nursing and care of the young. In the experiments in which the behavioral sink developed, infant mortality ran as high as 96 per cent among the most disoriented groups in the population. . . .

Females that lived in the densely populated middle pens became progressively less adept at building adequate nests and eventually stopped building nests at all. Normally rats of both sexes build nests, but females do so most vigorously around the time of parturition. It is an undertaking that involves repeated periods of sustained activity, searching out appropriate materials (in our experiments strips of paper supplied an abundance), transporting them bit by bit to the nest and there arranging them to form a cuplike depression, frequently sheltered by a hood. In a crowded middle pen, however, the ability of females to persist in this biologically essential activity became markedly impaired. The first sign of disruption was a failure to build the nest to normal specifications. These females simply piled the strips of paper in a heap, sometimes trampling them into a pad that showed little sign of cup formation. Later in the experiment they would bring fewer and fewer strips to the nesting site. In the midst of transporting a bit of material they would drop it to engage in some other activity occasioned by contact and interaction with other individuals met on the way. In the extreme disruption of their behavior during the later months of the population's history they would build no nests at all but would bear the litters on the sawdust in the burrows bottom.

The middle-pen females similarly lost the ability to transport their litters from one place to another. They would move only part of their litters and would scatter them by depositing the infants in different places or simply dropping them on the floor of the pen. The infants thus abandoned throughout the pen were seldom nursed. They would die where they were dropped and were thereupon generally eaten by the adults.

The social stresses that brought about this disorganization in the behavior of the middle-pen females were imposed with special weight on them when they came into heat. An estrous female would be pursued relentlessly by a pack of males, unable to escape from their soon unwanted attentions. Even when she retired to a burrow, some males would follow her. Among these females there was a correspondingly high rate of mortality from disorders in pregnancy and parturition. . . .

The aggressive, dominant animals were the most normal males in our populations. They seldom bothered either the females or the juveniles.

Yet even they exhibited occasional signs of pathology, going berserk, attacking females, juveniles and the less active males, and showing a particular predilection—which rats do not normally display—for biting other animals on the tail.

Below the dominant males both on the status scale and in their level of activity were the homosexuals—a group perhaps better described as pansexual. These animals apparently could not discriminate between appropriate and inappropriate sex partners. They made sexual advances to males, juveniles and females that were not in estrous. The males, including the dominants as well as the others of the pansexuals' own group, usually accepted their attentions. The general level of activity of these animals was only moderate. They were frequently attacked by their dominant associates, but they very rarely contended for status.

Two other types of male emerged, both of which had resigned entirely from the struggle for dominance. They were, however, at exactly opposite poles as far as their levels of activity were concerned. The first were completely passive and moved through the community like somnambulists. They ignored all the other rats of both sexes, and all the other rats ignored them. Even when the females were in estrous, these passive animals made no advances to them. And only very rarely did other males attack them or approach them for any kind of play. To the casual observer the passive animals would have appeared to be the healthiest and most attractive members of the community. They were fat and sleek, and their fur showed none of the breaks and bare spots left by the fighting in which males usually engage. But their social disorientation was nearly complete.

Perhaps the strangest of all the types that emerged among the males was the group I have called the probers. These animals, which always lived in the middle pens, took no part at all in the status struggle. Nevertheless, they were the most active of all the males in the experimental populations, and they persisted in their activity in spite of attacks by the dominant animals. In addition to being hyperactive, the probers were both hypersexual and homosexual, and in time many of them became cannibalistic. They were always on the alert for estrous females. If there were none in their own pens, they would lie in wait for long periods at the tops of the ramps that gave on the brood pens and peer down into them. They always turned and fled as soon as the territorial rat caught sight of them. Even if they did not manage to escape unhurt, they would soon return to their vantage point.

The probers conducted their pursuit of estrous females in an abnormal manner. Mating among rats usually involves a distinct courtship ritual. In the first phase of this ritual the male pursues the female. She thereupon retires for a while into the burrow, and the male lies quietly in wait outside, occasionally poking his head into the burrow for a moment but never entering it. (In the wild forms of the Norway rat this phase usually involves a courtship dance on the mound at the mouth of the burrow.) The female at last emerges from the burrow and accepts the male's advances. Even in the disordered community of the middle pens this pattern was observed by all the males who engaged in normal heterosexual behavior. But the probers would not tolerate even a short period of waiting at the burrows in the pens where accessible females lived. As soon as a female retired to a burrow, a prober would follow her inside. On these expeditions the probers often found dead young lying in the nests; as a result they tended to become cannibalistic in the later months of a population's history.

48
Migration as a Solution

George Kuriyan

From "The Population of India: A Geographical Analysis,"
Population Review, **6:**107–113

1962

Many people seem to think that the problem in India would easily be solved if the open spaces of Australia were thrown open for Indian settlement, but few realize the difficulties involved in a mass transfer of people from India to Australia, even if there were no political hurdles to be scaled. It must be remembered that if the emigration to Australia is to be successful, so as to give relief to the pressure at home, then at least a third of the population in India—approximately 150 millions—would have to leave the shores of India. This itself is a conservative figure because the population that is left over in the country would still be 300 millions, with an average per capita holding of one acre of cultivated land. Furthermore, the rate at which this emigration will have to be effected is also just as important; it has to be accomplished almost in the twinkle of an eye, as otherwise the relief created by the slow emigration is likely to be more than offset by a sudden spurt in the growth of population.

Few people realize how difficult and time-consuming it was for the Allied nations, with all their resources in ships and aeroplanes, to repatriate to their respective homes, the armed forces from the various theatres of war after their victory on V.J. Day. If 150 million Indians are to be transported, say within a year, the rate of transport would mount up to approximately 3 millions per week—a figure which may take up something more than the entire shipping facilities of the world. Surely, it will be foolhardy to imagine that all the nations of the world will remit their ships for transporting the poor Indians, in a succession of trips, across the Indian ocean from India to Australia. Even transporting 10 million people in a year would amount to 200,000 per week, a figure which may consume the entire shipping facilities of the Indian ocean as it exists at the present day. Emigration of 10 million people a year would not provide any relief whatever to the pressure at home and is therefore not to be encouraged, since it will only create problems with no compensating advantages.

49

The Demographic Open Door Policy

Emma Lazarus
1849–1887

From *The New Colossus*
(Lines inscribed on the Statue of Liberty; and, in part,
at Kennedy International Airport, New York)

1886

Give me your tired, your poor,
Your huddled masses yearning to breathe free,
The wretched refuse of your teeming shore,
Send these, the homeless, tempest-tossed, to me:
I lift my lamp beside the golden door.

50
World Population

Colin Clark
1905–

Nature, **181**:1235–1236

Most of the population controversy is waged between those who have thought about population and those who have not. There are, of course, exceptions. Among the more interesting of the thoughtful heretics in population matters is Colin Clark, an English economist of Roman Catholic persuasion.

1958

Prospects did not look good at the time when Malthus wrote. Real wages were low and did not rise until the middle of the nineteenth century. Nevertheless, the British courageously refused to listen to Malthus. Had they done so, Britain would have remained a small eighteenth-century-type agrarian community; and the United States and the British Commonwealth would never have developed. No great degree of industrialization would have been possible. The economics of large-scale industry demand large markets and a first-class transportation system, only obtainable with a large and growing population.

The country which did listen to Malthus was France, where size of family began to decline early in the nineteenth century. "If population limitation were the key to economic progress," as Prof. Sauvy said at the World Population Conference, "then France should be the wealthiest country in the world by now." France, which seemed to be on the point of dominating the world in 1798, has since seen her influence steadily decline; and the recurring inflations which France has suffered are an economic consequence of the excessive burden of pensions and other overhead costs which an ageing country has to carry.

When we look at the British in the seventeenth and eighteenth centuries, at the Greeks in the sixth century B.C., the Dutch in the seventeenth century, and the Japanese in the nineteenth century, we must conclude that the pressure of population upon limited agricultural resources provides a painful but ultimately beneficial stimulus, provoking unenterprising agrarian communities into greater efforts in the fields of industry, commerce, political leadership, colonization, science, and (sometimes but not always, judging from Victorian England) the arts.

But if a country fails to meet the challenge of population increase, it sinks into the condition known to economists as 'disguised unemployment' or rural overpopulation. The simpler forms of agriculture, using hand tools (as in China or Africa), can economically occupy 50 able-bodied men per sq. km. (246 acres), or 20 men per sq. km. using draught animals. A man working for a full year, using hand tools, produces at least two tons of grain-equivalent (expressing other products as grain at their local exchange values); twice that with draught animals. Minimum subsistence requirements can be estimated at 275 kilos of grain-equivalent per person per year (225 kilos of grain plus a few other woods and textile fibers). So one agricultural worker, even with hand tools, can produce subsistence for seven or eight people, that is to say, he can feed himself and his dependents at better than subsistence-level, and have some food to exchange for clothing, household goods, etc., so that an urban population can begin to grow up. (One Canadian grain grower, however, could feed 750 at subsistence-level.) Where, however, the densities of agricultural population exceed these limits, as in southern Italy, India, Egypt, etc., the marginal product of this additional labour is very low, and the consequence is that many men consume only a subsistence diet, are idle for a considerable part of their time, and have little surplus to exchange for industrial products. . . .

Countries the population of which has outrun their agricultural resources can industrialize, and exchange manufactures for imported food, as did Britain and Japan, and as India can—if they have a large population and a good transport system. Experience in both India and the U.S.S.R. has shown that, with modern engineering knowledge, capital requirements for establishing an industrial community are less than was previously supposed. This solution, however, is not open to the smaller and more isolated islands, away from the main channels of world trade. If they become overcrowded they must seek relief in emigration, which from an island such as Puerto Rico is as high as 2 per cent of the population per annum.

Some fear, however, that the agricultural resources of the world as a whole may soon be exhausted. The world's total land area (excluding ice and tundra) is 123 million sq. km., from which we exclude most of the 42½ million sq. km. of steppe or arid lands, discount anything up to half the area of certain cold or subhumid lands, but could double 10 million sq. km. of tropical land capable of bearing two crops per year. We conclude that the world possesses the equivalent of 77 million sq. km. of good temperate agricultural land. We may take as our standard that of the most productive farmers in Europe, the Dutch, who feed 385 people (at Dutch standards of diet, which give them one of the best health records in the world) per sq. km. of farm land, or 365 if we allow for the land required to produce their timber (in the most economic manner, in warm climates—pulp requirements can be obtained from sugar cane waste). Applying these standards throughout the world, as they could be with adequate skill and use of fertilizers, we find the world capable of supporting 28 billion people, or ten times its present population. This leaves us a very ample margin for land which we wish to set aside for recreation or other purposes. Even these high Dutch standards of productivity are improving at a rate of 2 per cent per annum. In the very distant future, if our descendants outrun the food-producing capacity of the Earth, and of the sea, they will by that time be sufficiently skilled and wealthy to build themselves artificial satellites to live on.

51

Population, Reality, and Escapist Literature

Is the earth the only world available to human populations or not? Plainly, our estimate of the seriousness of the population problem is significantly affected by our answer to this question. The question at issue is not whether earthly populations might send out a tiny inoculum of **Homo sapiens** to other heavenly bodies, but whether the impoverished millions of human beings can be shipped off at the rate of a hundred thousand or more a day to distances measured in millions of millions of miles. This is a problem of economics, in the broadest sense. The article that follows is an attempt to estimate the magnitude of this problem.

This paper had an interesting history. It was rejected by three scientific journals, although two of these had previously published writings of mine. The first editor said that the paper was superfluous because "everybody" knows that interstellar migration is impossible; the second said my article was polemic; and the third felt that his journal had already published too much on population. In answer to the first objection I can report that the proposal to ship off surplus population continues to crop up in the popular press, though not, I admit, in scientific journals. The second objection, that my writing was polemic, puzzles me. My dictionary tells me that polemic means "of the nature of, pertaining to, or involving controversy; controversial." This certainly describes **any** discussion of population problems. Could it be otherwise? However, the Greek word **polemikos** means warlike or aggressive; perhaps my rhetoric was too intemperate for the scientific journals of our day.

If I were to write this article over again I doubt that I would mute the tone, but I would alter a few details. My original analysis seems pessimistic to most worshippers of Progress; I would now make it even more so. When I originally evaluated the possibility of a trip to the planets of Alpha Centauri it had slipped my mind that this star is a triple star. From the laws of physics it is clear that a multiple star either has no planets at all or has planets whose orbits are so eccentric as to make improbable the maintenance of the equable temperature needed to sustain life. So Alpha Centauri won't do. The nearest single star is Barnard's Star, some 40 percent farther away. Whether this lukewarm giant has any planets of the right size at a suitable distance we do not know, but it is the best hope for terrestrial escapists. All in all, I think, my essay underestimates the difficulty of escape.

52

Interstellar Migration and the Population Problem

Garrett Hardin
1915–

Journal of Heredity, **50**:68–70

1959

Anyone who discusses population problems with lay audiences is, sooner or later, confronted with questions of this sort: "But why worry about overpopulation? Won't we soon be able to send our surplus population to other planets?" It is not only the audience that adopts this point of view; sometimes the lecturer does, as appears from an Associated Press dispatch of 6 June 1958. Monsignor Irving A. DeBlanc, director of the National Catholic Welfare Conference's Family Life Bureau is reported as favoring such mass migration, "deploring an often expressed idea that birth control is the only answer to problems created by a fast-growing world population."

Neither physicists nor professional demographers have, so far as I know, recommended extra-terrestrial migration as a solution to the population problem, but the idea appears to be gaining ground among the laity even without scientific support. The psychological reasons for embracing this idea are two. On the one hand, some Roman Catholics welcome it because it appears to offer an escape from the dilemma created by the Church's stand against "artificial" methods of birth control. On the other hand, citizens of all churches worship the new religion called Progress, of which Jules Verne is the prophet. In this religion all things are possible (except acceptance of the impossible). Who is to set limits to Science (with a capital S)? Yesterday, the telephone and the radio; today television and ICBM's; and tomorrow,—Space!—which will solve all our earthly problems, of course.

This is heady stuff. Strictly speaking, since it springs from an essentially religious feeling and is non-rational it cannot be answered by a rational argument. Nevertheless, for the sake of those bystanders whose minds are still open to a rational analysis it is worthwhile reviewing the facts and principles involved in the proposal to solve the population problem by inter-planetary travel.

The Cost of Space Travel

It now seems possible that, before the century is out, manned landings may be made on Venus or Mars, with the establishment of temporary quarters thereon. But all evidence points to the unsuitability of these, or any other planets of our sun, as abodes for *Homo sapiens*. We must, therefore, look beyond the solar system, to other stars for possible planets for colonization.

The nearest star is Alpha Centauri, which is 4.3 light-years away. How long would it take us to get there? The rockets that we are now planning to send to the moon will have a maximum velocity in the neighborhood of 10 kilometers per second, or about 19,000 miles per hour. This may sound fast. But a body traveling at such a speed towards Alpha Centauri (which is 4.07×10^{13} kilometers distant) would require 129,000 years to reach its destination. Surely no one believes that a fleet of space-

111

ships with so long a transit time would solve our explosive population problem. The question is, then, what is the probability of improvements in space travel that would significantly cut down the time required to make such an interstellar journey? In trying to answer this question I have relied on an analysis by L. R. Shepherd,[1] to which the interested reader is referred for technical details.

Shepherd presumes a technology in the release and utilization of nuclear energy that may take several centuries to achieve. To give the worshippers of Progress the maximum advantage we will assume that such an advance technology is available *now,* and see how long it would take to travel to the nearest star. Using fantastically optimistic assumptions, Shepherd calculates that it might be possible to make the transit in a mere 350 years. The average speed of the trip would be about 7,000,000 m.p.h., though the maximum speed would be somewhat more, since 50 years would be required for acceleration at the beginning of the trip and another 50 years for deceleration at the end. (In passing, it should be noted that acceleration is more of a limiting factor than is velocity.)

To evaluate interstellar migration as a population control measure we must examine its economics. Here the unknowns are obviously great, but from data assembled by A. V. Cleaver[2] it appears that the foreseeable cost of a rocket ship could hardly be as little as $50 a pound, assuming economies of mass production and allowing nothing for research and development costs. How many pounds of ship would be required per man? Since we have no data on such a spaceship, let us borrow from our knowledge of atomic submarines, which are perhaps not too dissimilar. A spaceship designed to be self-maintaining for 350 years could hardly be less complicated or less bulky than an underwater craft capable of operating away from its depots for only a month or two. According to a news release[3] the submarine *Seawolf* weighs 3,000 tons and carries 100 men, a burden of 60,000 lbs. per man. A spaceship of a similar design, at $50 a pound, would cost $3,000,000 per man travelling in it. Would this be a reasonable cost for solving the population problem? Those who propose such a solution presume, or even recommend, that we do not alter our present reproductive habits. What would it cost to keep the population of the United States fixed at its present level by shipping off the surplus in spaceships?

According to a recent estimate of the U. S. Bureau of the Census[4] our population is increasing by about 3,000,000 people per year. To ship this increase off to other planets would, on the above conservative assumptions, cost about 9,000 billion dollars per year. The Gross National Product is now nearly 450 billion dollars per year. In other words, to solve our national population problem by this means we would, then, have to spend 20 times as much as our entire income on this purpose alone, allowing nothing for any other use, not even for food. It would surely be unrealistic to suppose that we shall do this in the near future.

Another aspect of the population problem is worth commenting on. Many philanthropically minded citizens feel that it is an obligation of the United States to solve the population problems of the entire world, believing that we should use the riches produced by our technology to make up for the deficiencies in luck or foresight of other peoples. Let's examine the economics of so doing. According to a recent estimate[5] the population of the world is increasing at a rate of 123,000 per day. To remove one day's increment by the postulated spaceship would cost about 369 billion dollars. In other words, we Americans, by cutting our standard of living down to 18 percent of its present level, could in *one year's time* set aside enough capital to finance the exportation of *one day's increase* in the population of the entire world. Such a philanthropic desire to share the wealth may be judged noble in intent, but hardly in effect.

In passing, it should be noted that we have so far made no mention of certain assumptions that are of critical importance in the whole picture. We have assumed that our nearest star has planets; that at least one of these planets is suitable for human habitation; that this suitable planet is uninhabited—or, if inhabited, that the humanoids thereon will gracefully commit suicide when they find we need their planet for our *Lebensraum*. (The tender feelings that would make impossible the control of reproduction on earth would presumably not interfere with the destruction of life on other planets.) Should Alpha Centauri have no planet available for migratory earthlings, our expedition would presumably set out for an even more distant star, perhaps eventually becoming a latterday interstellar Flying Dutchman.

Paradoxes of Space Emigration

Cogent as the economic analysis of the problem is, it does not touch on issues that are of even greater importance. Consider the human situation on board this astronautical Mayflower. For 350 years the population would have to live under conditions of complete sociological stasis, the like of which has never been known before. No births would be permitted, except to replace the dead (whose substance would, of course, have to be returned to the common stores). Marriages would certainly have to be controlled, as would all other social interactions, and with an iron hand. In the spaceship, Progress would be unendurable. The social organization would have to persist unchanged for 10 generations' time, otherwise there

113

would be the risk that some of the descendants of the original crew might wish to change the plans. It would be as though the spaceship had to set sail, so to speak, under Captain John Smith and arrive at its goal under President Eisenhower, without the slightest change in ideas or ideals. Can we who have so recently seen how fragile and mutable a flower Education is suppose that we could set up so stable a system of indoctrination? Paradoxically, only a people who worship Progress would propose to launch such a craft, but such worshippers would be the worst possible passengers for it.

Those who seriously propose interstellar migration as a solution to overpopulation do so because they are unwilling to accept the necessity of consciously controlling population numbers by means already at hand. They are unwilling to live, or to admit living, in a closed universe. Yet—and here is the second paradox—that is precisely the sort of universe the interstellar migrants would be confined to, for some 10 generations. Since the present annual rate of growth of the world's population is about 1.7 percent,[6] by the time the first ship arrived at its destination, the whole fleet of spaceships en route would enclose a total population six times as large as that still present on the earth. That is, in attempting to escape the necessities of living in a closed universe, we would confine to the closed universes of spaceships a population six times as great as that of the earth.

Moreover, there would be a differential element in the emigration from the mother planet. The proposal to emigrate is made by those who, for religious or other reasons, are unwilling to curb the reproductive proclivities of mankind. But not for such as these is the kingdom of a spaceship. They must stay behind while the ship is manned by those whose temperament creates no need for emigration. The reproductively prudent would be exiled from a world made unbearably crowded by the imprudent—who would stay home to perpetuate the problem into the next generation. Whether the difference between the two groups is basically biological, or merely sociological, would not matter. In either case, natural selection would enter in. The end result of this selective emigration would be to create an earth peopled only by men and women unwilling to control their breeding, and unwilling, therefore, to make use of the very means they propose to escape the consequences.

The proposal to eliminate overpopulation by resort to interstellar migration is thus seen to yield not a rational solution at all. The proposal is favored only by men who have more faith in gadgetry than they do in rationality. Should men of this temper prevail, and should the gadgetry prove equal to the quantitative demands put upon it, the result would nevertheless be the ultimate production of a world in which the only remaining controls of population would be the "misery and vice" foreseen by Malthus 161 years ago.

[1] L. R. Shepherd, "The Distant Future," in L. J. Carter (ed.), *Realities of Space Travel*, London: Putnam, 1957.
[2] A. V. Cleaver, "The Development of Astronautics," in L. J. Carter, *op. cit.*, 1957.
[3] *Time* magazine, 1 August 1955, p. 13.
[4] *Science,* **127** (1958): 691.
[5] *Population Bulletin,* **13** (1957):133.
[6] *Science,* **127** (1958):1038.

53

The Economics of
the Coming Spaceship Earth

Kenneth E. Boulding
1910–

From *Environmental Quality in a Growing Economy*
Henry Jarrett, editor
Baltimore: Johns Hopkins Press

1966

The closed earth of the future requires economic principles which are somewhat different from those of the open earth of the past. For the sake of picturesqueness, I am tempted to call the open economy the "cowboy economy," the cowboy being symbolic of the illimitable plains and also associated with reckless, exploitative, romantic, and violent behavior, which is characteristic of open societies. The closed economy of the future might similarly be called the "spaceman" economy, in which the earth has become a single spaceship, without unlimited reservoirs of anything, either for extraction or for pollution, and in which, therefore, man must find his place in a cyclical ecological system which is capable of continuous reproduction of material form even though it cannot escape having inputs of energy. The difference between the two types of economy becomes most apparent in the attitude towards consumption. In the cowboy economy, consumption is regarded as a good thing and production likewise; and the success of the economy is measured by the amount of the throughput from the "factors of production," a part of which, at any rate, is extracted from the reservoirs of raw materials and noneconomic objects, and another part of which is output into the reservoirs of pollution. If there are infinite reservoirs from which material can be obtained and into which effluvia can be deposited, then the throughput is at least a plausible measure of the success of the economy. The gross national product is a rough measure of this total throughput. It should be possible, however, to distinguish that part of the GNP which is derived from exhaustible and that which is derived from re-producible resources, as well as that part of consumption which represents effluvia and that which represents input into the productive system again. Nobody, as far as I know, has ever attempted to break down the GNP in this way, although it would be an interesting and extremely important exercise, which is unfortunately beyond the scope of this paper.

By contrast, in the spaceman economy, throughput is by no means a desideratum, and is indeed to be regarded as something to be minimized rather than maximized. The essential measure of the success of the economy is not production and consumption at all, but the nature, extent, quality, and complexity of the total capital stock, including in this the state of the human bodies and minds included in the system. In the spaceman economy, what we are primarily concerned with is stock maintenance, and any tech-nological change which results in the maintenance of a given total stock with a lessened throughput (that is, less production and consumption) is clearly a gain. This idea that both production and consumption are bad things rather than good things is very strange to economists, who have been obsessed with the income-flow concepts to the exclusion, almost, of capital-stock concepts.

There are actually some very tricky and unsolved problems in-volved in the questions as to whether human welfare or well-being is to be regarded as a stock or a flow. Something of both these elements seems actually to be involved in it, and as far as I know there have been practically no studies directed towards identifying these two dimensions of human sat-isfaction. Is it, for instance, eating that is a good thing, or is it being well fed? Does economic welfare involve having nice clothes, fine houses, good equipment, and so on, or is it to be measured by the depreciation and the wearing out of these things? I am inclined myself to regard the stock con-cept as most fundamental, that is, to think of being well fed as more im-portant than eating, and to think even of so-called services as essentially involving the restoration of a depleting psychic capital. Thus I have argued that we go to a concert in order to restore a psychic condition which might be called "just having gone to a concert," which, once established, tends to depreciate. When it depreciates beyond a certain point, we go to another concert in order to restore it. If it depreciates rapidly, we go to a lot of concerts; if it depreciates slowly, we go to few. On this view, similarly, we eat primarily to restore bodily homeostasis, that is, to maintain a condition of being well fed, and so on. On this view, there is nothing desirable in consumption at all. The less consumption we can maintain a given state with, the better off we are. If we had clothes that did not wear out, houses that did not depreciate, and even if we could maintain our bodily condition without eating, we would clearly be much better off.

It is this last consideration, perhaps, which makes one pause. Would we, for instance, really want an operation that would enable us to restore all our bodily tissues by intravenous feeding while we slept? Is there not, that is to say, a certain virtue in throughput itself, in activity itself, in production and consumption itself, in raising food and in eating it? It would certainly be rash to exclude this possibility. Further interesting problems are raised by the demand for variety. We certainly do not want a constant state to be maintained; we want fluctuations in the state. Otherwise there would be no demand for variety in food, for variety in scene, as in travel, for variety in social contact, and so on. The demand for variety can, of course, be costly, and sometimes it seems to be too costly to be tolerated or at least legitimated, as in the case of marital partners, where the maintenance of a homeostatic state in the family is usually regarded as much more desirable than the variety and excessive throughput of the libertine. There are problems here which the economics profession has neglected with astonishing singlemindedness. My own attempts to call attention to some of them, for instance, in two articles,[1] as far as I can judge, produced no response whatever; and economists continue to think and act as if production, consumption, throughput, and the GNP were the sufficient and adequate measure of economic success.

It may be said, of course, why worry about all this when the spaceman economy is still a good way off (at least beyond the lifetimes of any now living), so let us eat, drink, spend, extract and pollute, and be as merry as we can, and let posterity worry about the spaceship earth. It is always a little hard to find a convincing answer to the man who says, "What has posterity ever done for me?" and the conservationist has always had to fall back on rather vague ethical principles postulating identity of the individual with some human community or society which extends not only back into the past but forward into the future. Unless the individual identifies with some community of this kind, conservation is obviously "irrational." Why should we not maximize the welfare of this generation at the cost of posterity? *"Après nous, le déluge"* has been the motto of not insignificant numbers of human societies. The only answer to this, as far as I can see, is to point out that the welfare of the individual depends on the extent to which he can identify himself with others, and that the most satisfactory individual identity is that which identifies not only with a community in space but also with a community extending over time from the past into the future. If this kind of identity is recognized as desirable, then posterity has a voice, even if it does not have a vote; and in a sense, if its voice can influence votes, it has votes too. This whole problem is linked up with the much larger one of the determinants of the morale, legitimacy, and "nerve" of a society, and there is a great deal of historical evidence to suggest that a society which loses its identity with posterity and which loses its positive image of the future loses also its capacity to deal with present problems, and soon falls apart.[2]

Even if we concede that posterity is relevant to our present problems, we still face the question of time-discounting and the closely related question of uncertainty-discounting. It is a well-known phenomenon that individuals discount the future, even in their own lives. The very existence of a positive rate of interest may be taken as at least strong supporting evidence of this hypothesis. It we discount our own future, it is certainly not unreasonable to discount posterity's future even more, even if we do give posterity a vote. If we discount this at 5 per cent per annum, posterity's vote or dollar halves every fourteen years as we look into the future, and after even a mere hundred years it is pretty small—only about 1½ cents on the dollar. If we add another 5 percent for uncertainty, even the vote of our grandchildren reduces almost to insignificance. We can argue, of course, that the ethical thing to do is not to discount the future at all, that time-discounting is mainly the result of myopia and perspective, and hence is an illusion which the moral man should not tolerate. It is a very popular illusion, however, and one that must certainly be taken into consideration in the formulation of policies. It explains, perhaps, why conservationist policies almost have to be sold under some other excuse which seems more urgent, and why, indeed, necessities which are visualized as urgent, such as defense, always seem to hold priority over those which involve the future.

All these considerations add some credence to the point of view which says that we should not worry about the spaceman economy at all, and that we should just go on increasing the GNP and indeed the gross world product, or GWP, in the expectation that the problems of the future can be left to the future, that when scarcities arise, whether this is of raw materials or of pollutable reservoirs, the needs of the then present will determine the solutions of the then present, and there is no use giving ourselves ulcers by worrying about problems that we really do not have to solve. There is even high ethical authority for this point of view in the New Testament, which advocates that we should take no thought for tomorrow and let the dead bury their dead. There has always been something rather refreshing in the view that we should live like the birds, and perhaps posterity is for the birds in more senses than one; so perhaps we should all call it a day and go out and pollute something cheerfully. As an old taker of thought for the morrow, however, I cannot quite accept this solution; and I would argue, furthermore, that tomorrow is not only very close, but in many respects it is already here. The shadow of the future spaceship, indeed, is already falling over our spendthrift merriment. Oddly enough, it seems to be in pollution rather than in exhaustion that the problem is first becoming salient. Los Angeles has run out of air, Lake Erie has become a cesspool, the oceans are getting full of lead and DDT, and the atmosphere may become man's major problem in another generation, at the rate at which we are filling it up with gunk. It is, of course, true that at least on a microscale, things have been worse at times in the past. The cities of today, with all their foul air and polluted waterways, are probably not as bad as the filthy cities of the pretechnical age. Nevertheless, that fouling of the nest which has been typical of man's activity in the past on a local scale now seems to be extending to the whole world society; and one certainly cannot view with equanimity the present rate of pollution of any of the natural reservoirs, whether the atmosphere, the lakes, or even the oceans.

---

[1] K. E. Boulding, "The Consumption Concept in Economic Theory," *American Economic Review,* **35** (May 1945):1–14; and "Income or Welfare?," *Review of Economic Studies,* **17** (1949–50):77–86.

[2] Fred L. Polak, *The Image of the Future,* Vols. I and II, translated by Elise Boulding, New York: Sythoff, Leyden and Oceana, 1961.

54

Population and Freedom

Joseph J. Spengler
1902–

Population Review, **6**(2):74–82

1962

Population growth makes average income less high than it otherwise would have been, and it thus makes man's range of choice less wide than it might have been and so reduces his freedom. First, population growth conduces to a less favorable age composition than emerges when a population is approximately stationary. The margin of inferiority depends upon how fast a population is growing, given that comparison is being made with a stationary population. Let us call the margin 10 percent; it may be greater or less. If a growing population includes 10 percent fewer persons of productive age, it includes 10 less potential workers per 100 inhabitants and its potential per capita output is therefore about 10 percent less. Were this population stationary, it could produce about 10 percent more per capita under roughly similar conditions, half of which might easily be saved. If this half (say 5 percent) were saved and well-invested, it would permit per capita income to rise 0.5 or more percent per year in countries that are relatively capital short.

Second, population growth slows down the formation of capital and the increase of capital per head. It reduces the saving rate in families with children though not in other agencies when savings flow. More importantly, the equipping of increments to a population absorbs capital; thus a population growing one percent per year absorbs capital amounting to something like 4 percent of national income and correspondingly larger amounts of capital are absorbed by populations growing 2 or 3 percent per year. This capital absorption extends also to education and the formation of personal capital in that, if a population is growing 2–3 percent per year, providing comparable education to persons of school age requires the services of about twice as large a fraction of the labor force as is required when the rate of population growth is much lower (say, around 0.5 percent).

The capital that population growth absorbs might otherwise be used to increase capital per head. For example, the capital absorbed by an annual population growth rate of 2 percent—around 8 percent of the national income—might otherwise enable capital per head to increase 2 percent per year and thereby enable per capita income to rise close to one-half or more percent per year. The actual overall advantage might be somewhat greater than this figure suggests; for much of the capital used to equip increments to the population is characterized by a relatively high capital-output ratio and may also be characterized by a relatively low marginal productivity.

My discussion of the unfavorable aspects of population growth has neglected its favorable aspects—the tendency of a growing population to be more flexible than a non-growing one, more favorable to technological and other important changes, less prone to unemployment, and so on. These aspects do not lend themselves readily to quantification. Moreover, they tend to be exaggerated, in that most of the difficulties implied arise only when a population is in transit from a relatively high to a relatively low rate of growth in a developed country; thereafter they subside. In underdeveloped countries the disadvantages of population growth are so very great that the benefits of their alleviation through a decline in gross reproduction swamp any adverse influences that might conceivably accompany transit.

Third, since population growth always takes place in a relatively finite environment, the more utilizable portions of which are eventually all brought under exploitation, increase in population density finally becomes relatively unfavorable to progress in per capita income. Such unfavorableness does not manifest itself at first, since economies associated with increasing division of labor and the fuller use of lumpy productive agents far out-weigh any disadvantages flowing from increasing pressure of numbers upon a fixed environment. Such unfavorableness may be very slow to manifest itself quite ostensibly, if a country is marked by a high rate of technological progress which makes possible economies and substitutions that in turn permit great savings in the use of particularly scarce elements in the physical environment. For then the cost of exploiting the physical environment will not seem to rise markedly (as one might have been led to expect), and less attention will be paid to the possibility that had population density been lower, this cost would have been even less. Unfortunately, technological progress of the sort that permits economy in the use of a population's physical environment is much less common to low-income, underdeveloped countries than it is to advanced ones, and they even seem less capable of realizing fully the advantages of the division of labor open to them. Underdeveloped countries therefore tend to feel the adverse effects of increase in population density earlier and more intensely than do advanced countries even as they feel more sharply capital shortages flowing out of population growth as such.

55

The Vulnerability of Civilization

Norbert Wiener
1894–1964

From *The Human Use of Human Beings*
Boston: Houghton Mifflin

1950

Thus in depending on the future of invention to extricate us from the situations into which the squandering of our natural resources has brought us we are manifesting our national love for gambling and our national worship of the gambler, but in circumstances under which no intelligent gambler would care to make a bet. Whatever skills your successful poker player must have, he must at the very least know the values of his hands. In this gamble on the future of inventions, nobody knows the value of a hand. . . .

If the food supply is falling short, or a new disease threatens us, inventions to relieve it must be made before famine and pestilence have done their work. Now, we are far nearer to famine and pestilence than we like to think. Let there be an interruption of the water supply of New York for six hours, and it will show in the death rate. Let the usual trains bringing supplies into the city be interrupted for forty-eight hours, and some people will die of hunger. Every engineer who has to deal with the administration of the public facilities of a great city has been struck with terror at the risks which people are willing to undergo and must undergo every day, and at the complacent ignorance of these risks on the part of his charges. . . .

The very increase of commerce and the unification of humanity render the risks of fluctuation ever mode deadly.

56
Famine—1975!

William and Paul Paddock
1921–
and 1907–

Boston: Little, Brown and Co.

1967

In a 1966 seminar I attended at the Hudson Institute one of the speakers said: "People who publish population figures are propagandists. They like the extreme projections. Everyone else believes population figures will decrease sharply within a generation."

Maybe so. I hope so. Yet even a generation is too short a lead time if—always that "if"—the population figures do, after all, "decrease sharply."

For the short, ten-year span from 1965 to 1975 United Nations projections for population growth show how much additional food will be required.[1]

Future Food Requirements of the Hungry World

	Population at Current Rates of Growth		Additional Food Production Needed Within Ten Years
	1965	*1975*	
East Asia	867 million	1.04 billion	20%
South Asia	975 million	1.25 billion	28%
Africa	311 million	404 million	30%
Latin America	248 million	335 million	35%
TOTAL	2.4 billion	3.0 billion	26%

Thus, simply to maintain today's inadequate dietary levels, the hungry nations must increase their production within a single decade by 26 percent.

123

For reasons covered in the next chapter, agricultural increases such as these cannot be attained by 1975. Since this is so then the diets of these nations must become considerably less than even today's level of malnutrition.

The end result for each of the affected nations will be the constant threat of catastrophe. Whenever there is too much or too little rain, whenever spring comes late or the harvest is wet, whenever civil unrest delays the plantings, whenever *anything* reduces the yield, then a portion of the population will slip over into the chasm of starvation.

"Famine isn't like a satellite count-down; you don't say, 'Three-two-one, it's here!' What happens is like the New York water shortage: it develops slowly; experts wring hands; public pays no attention; then, suddenly, it's headlined. That's what's happening in world food." [2] We cannot say precisely what it takes to starve a man to death. It is clear, however, that if the undeveloped world is not feeding itself today, it will feed itself even less well tomorrow.

The Swedish economist Gunnar Myrdal sees a "world calamity" in "five or ten years." [3]

Chester Bowles, Ambassador to India, says that the approaching world famine threatens to be "the most colossal catastrophe in history." [4]

Thomas M. Ware, testifying before a Senate committee, said, "Very few grasp the magnitude of the danger that confronts us." [5]

Dr. Raymond Ewell: "The world is on the threshold of the biggest famine in history. If present trends continue, it seems likely that famine will reach serious proportions in India, Pakistan and China in the early 1970's. . . . Such a famine will be of massive proportions affecting hundreds of millions." [6]

I agree with these forecasters, but I must be more specific—and in Chapter 5, I give reasons for choosing an actual year.

1975 will be a crucial year in the world, crucial because the world food shortage will then dominate the headlines and the results will be in full view. The present downward trends cannot be reversed, nor can they be dusted under the carpet. Those who say there are too many variables in the future to forecast food deficits ignore the present trends. . . .

The Thesis of "Triage"

"Triage" is a term used in military medicine. It is defined as the assigning of priority of treatment to the wounded brought to a battlefield hospital in a time of mass casualties and limited medical facilities. The wounded are divided on the basis of three classifications:

1. Those so seriously wounded they cannot survive regardless of the treatment given them; call these the "can't-be-saved."
2. Those who can survive without treatment regardless of the pain they may be suffering; call these the "walking wounded."
3. Those who can be saved by immediate medical care.

The practice of triage is put into effect when the flow of wounded fills the tents of the battlefield hospitals and when it becomes impossible for the available medical staff to give even rudimentary care to all. Furthermore, the number allowed to be sorted into the third group for immediate treatment must be limited by the number of doctors available. The marginal cases must then also be selected out into the other two groups.

It is a terrible chore for the doctors to classify the helpless wounded in this fashion, but it is the only way to save the maximum number of lives. To spend time with the less seriously wounded or with the dying would mean that many of those who might have lived will die. It would be a misuse of the available medical help.

Call triage cold-blooded, but it is derived from the hard experience of medical humaneness during a crisis. In fact, if there is time before the battle starts, the medical staff prepares in advance the facilities to sort out these three groups. . . .

At this point the Paddock brothers have an extended discussion of the actual application of the theory of triage to a number of illustrative cases, resulting in the following conclusion.

My own opinion as to the triage classification of these sample nations is:

Haiti	Can't-be-saved
Egypt	Can't-be-saved
The Gambia	Walking Wounded
Tunisia	Should Receive Food
Libya	Walking Wounded
India	Can't-be-saved
Pakistan	Should Receive Food

These examples seem to me to adhere closely to the basic triage divisions for the use of American *food* up to and during the Time of Famines. . . .

Here is the total list of 111 countries and dependencies that in 1965 received food from the United States under P.L. 480.[7] Where within the framework of triage does each belong?

125

Aden	Egypt	Lebanon	St. Vincent
Afghanistan	El Salvador	Libya	Senegal
Algeria	Ethiopia	Macao	Seychelles
Antigua	Fiji	Malagasy Rep.	Sierra Leone
Basutoland	France	Malawi	Singapore
Bolivia	Gabon	Malaysia	Somalia
Brazil	Gambia	Mali	Spain
British Guiana	Gaza	Malta	Sudan
British Honduras	Ghana	Martinique	Surinam
British Solomon	Greece	Mauritania	Swaziland
Islands	Grenada	Mauritius	Syria
Burma	Guadeloupe	Mexico	Tanzania
Burundi	Guatemala	Montserrat	Thailand
Cambodia	Guinea	Morocco	Togo
Cameroons	Haiti	Nicaragua	Tongo Islands
Central African	Honduras	Nigeria	Trieste
Republic	Hong Kong	Okinawa	Trinidad and
Ceylon	India	Pakistan	Tobago
Chad	Indonesia	Panama	Tunisia
Chile	Iran	Paraguay	Turkey
China (Taiwan)	Iraq	Peru	Turks and Caicos
Colombia	Israel	Philippine	Islands
Congo	Italy	Islands	Uganda
Costa Rica	Ivory Coast	Poland	Upper Volta
Cyprus	Jamaica	Portugal	Uruguay
Dahomey	Jordan	Rwanda	Venezuela
Dominica	Kenya	St. Helena	Vietnam
Dominican Rep.	Korea	St. Kitts	Yemen
Ecuador	Laos	St. Lucia	Yugoslavia

---

[1] Calculated from figures in Robert C. Cook's "World Population Projections, 1965–2000," *Population Bulletin,* October 1965, pp. 96–97.

[2] "Famine Is Here," *New Republic,* September 18, 1965.

[3] *Ibid.*

[4] *Ibid.*

[5] *Ibid.*

[6] Raymond Ewell, "Famine and Fertilizer," *Chemical Engineering News,* December 14, 1964, pp. 106–117.

[7] "The Annual Report of the President on Activities Carried Out under Public Law 480," 89th Congress, as amended, during the period January 1 through December 31, 1965, dated June 30, 1966.

57

Paying the Piper

Paul R. Ehrlich
1932–

New Scientist, **36**:652–655

1967

The battle to feed humanity is over. Unlike battles of military forces, it is possible to know the results of the population-food conflict while the armies are still "in the field." Sometime between 1970 and 1985 the world will undergo vast famines—hundreds of millions of people are going to starve to death. That is, they will starve to death unless plague, thermo-nuclear war, or some other agent kills them first. Many will starve to death in spite of any crash programmes we might embark upon now. And we are not embarking upon any crash programme. These are the harsh realities we face. . . .

The trends in both population growth and food production are clear. Only the US will be in a position to donate food to starving countries, and a catastrophic gap will appear soon between her supply and world demand. The United States Department of Agriculture has predicted that the curve representing possible exportable US grain surpluses will intersect the curve representing the food aid requirements of 66 developing countries in 1984. In an excellent book *Famine 1975* (Little, Brown; Boston, 1967), William and Paul Paddock argue cogently that the 1984 prediction is optimistic, and that calamity awaits us in the middle of the next decade. In either case it is too late to prevent the famines, and probably too late to do much to decrease their magnitude. . . .

For a moment, let us take the simplistic view that a solution involves only either increasing human food or limiting the human population. First let us look at the problem of increasing food supplies, either from the land or the sea. We rapidly can do away with what I have called the "Food from the sea myth." With very minor exceptions, man hunts the sea, he does not farm it or herd its animals. At the moment he cannot take advantage of its primary productivity, and so must feed at levels in the food chain at which much of the Sun's energy bound by photosynthesis has been lost in the inefficient transfers from producer to primary consumer to secondary consumer, and so forth. There already are disturbing signs that our relatively meagre present yield from the sea will be threatened by overexploitation of fisheries, as the world's protein shortage gets more acute. And what of farming the sea? The insignificant bit that we do now (much less than one tenth of one per cent of the yield) is done along the shoreline and is best viewed as an extension of terrestrial farming. No deep-sea farming is done now, even experimentally—and we lack the technical knowledge even if we wished to start. Some very optimistic people think that with colossal effort and strict international controls, we might conceivably almost double our yield from the sea in the next decade or so. But it should be obvious to all that such effort is not being made, and that such controls are not being developed. And our experience with attempting such controls in the international whaling industry gives us little hope that they would be effective if they were imposed. So from the point of view of the coming crisis, we can relegate the idea of saving mankind by tapping marine food supplies to the same fairyland as using hydroponics, synthesizing food from petroleum, and using desalination plants to make the deserts into vast granaries. None are practical in the short run—indeed, most would present serious difficulties even if we had a century instead of a decade in which to act. . . .

The United States, as the only world power with a prospect of food surpluses, should take immediate action in two areas. First, it must set an example for the world by establishing a crash programme to limit its own serious "population explosion." Then it must establish tough and realistic policies for dealing with the population crisis at the international level. We can hope that other Western countries will follow suit.

Some biologists feel that compulsory family regulation would be required to stabilize the population of the United States at a reasonable level—say 150 million people. Americans are unlikely to take kindly to the prospect, even though the alternative way of stopping their population growth may be thermonuclear war. I have proposed four less drastic steps which might get the job done, and which would at least make American intentions clear to the rest of the world. The steps are socially unpalatable and politically unrealistic, but, unfortunately, the time when sugar-coated solutions could be effective is now long gone.

The first step would be to establish a Federal Population Commission with a large budget for propaganda—propaganda which encourages reproductive responsibility. This Commission would be charged with making clear the connection between rising population and lowering quality of life. It would also be charged with the evaluation of environmental tinkering by other government agencies—with protecting the US from projects such as the Federal Aviation Agency's supersonic transports.

The second step would be to change American tax laws so that they discourage rather than encouarge reproduction. Those who impose the burden of children on society should, whenever they are able, be made to pay for the privilege. The income tax system should eliminate all deductions for children, and replace them with a graduated scale of increases. Luxury taxes should be placed on diapers, baby bottles and baby foods. It must be made clear to the American population that it is socially irresponsible to have large families. Creation of such a climate of opinion has played a large role in Japan's successful dealing with her population problem.

Third, the United States should pass federal laws which make instruction in birth control methods mandatory in all public schools. Federal legislation should also forbid state laws which limit the right of any woman to have an abortion which is approved by her physician.

Fourth, the pattern of federal support of biomedical research should be changed so that the majority of it goes into the broad areas of population regulation, environmental sciences, behavioural sciences and related areas, rather than into shortsighted programmes on death control. It is absurd to be preoccupied with the medical quality of life until and unless the problem of quantity of life is solved. Quantity is the first problem. If that one can be solved perhaps we will buy the time for scientists in fields such as biochemical genetics to solve some of the problems of quality. If the quantity problem is not solved, the quality problem will no longer bother us.

If the United States can attack the problem at home it will then be in a position to bring its prestige and power to bear on the world problem. Perhaps then the time of famines can be shortened. Even more important, perhaps the educational groundwork can be laid which will permit further cycles of outbreak and crash in the human population to be avoided. The United States should:

1. Announce that it will no longer ship food to countries such as India where dispassionate analysis indicates that the unbalance between food and population is hopeless. As suggested by the Paddocks, our insufficient aid should be reserved for those whom it may save.

2. Refuse all foreign aid to any country with an increasing population which we believe is not making a maximum effort to limit its population.

3. Make available to all countries extensive aid in the technology of population control.

4. Make available to all interested countries massive aid for in-

creasing the yield on land already under cultivation. The United States' most important export in this area should not be fertilizers, but teachers who understand not only agronomy, but ecology and sociology as well. Centres should be established in each developing country for the training of technicians who can promote the increase of yield while minimizing environmental deterioration.

5. The United States should use its power and prestige to bring extreme diplomatic and/or economic pressure on any country or organization impeding a solution to the world's most pressing problem. The US has gone against world opinion in other areas—why not in the most important area?

II

Evolution

58

The Unwelcoming of
Natural Selection

To the layman the word "evolution" calls forth images of monkeys, dinosaurs, and Darwin. In the mind of the professional biologist, by contrast, the immediate connection is more likely to be with Darwin and natural selection. The difference is important.

Morse Peckham, in reviewing the history of evolution—in the first sense given above—has remarked that

> Evolution may be considered as a fairly straightforward metaphysical theory with a long history which was not so much confirmed by the theory of natural selection as embarrassed by it. The difference between the two is indicated by the fact that Darwin himself did not use the word until the fifth edition of the **Origin** (1869), and then he appears to have used it with some hesitation, almost as if he did not quite know what he was talking about.[1]

Evolution as history—evolution as the idea that all living things are geneologically related as distant cousins are related to one another—is an old idea, embraced in whole or in part by many thinkers before Darwin: Buffon, Erasmus Darwin, Lamarck, and Robert Chambers were only a few of his more immediate predecessors. That the idea was in the air at the time of Darwin's great work is clearly shown by a passage from a letter by a seventeen-year-old university student, William Stanley Jevons (later to become a famous economist), written seven years before the publication of the **Origin of Species:**

> I have had several rather learned discussions with Harry about moral philosophy, from which it appears that I am decidedly a "dependent moralist," not believing that we have any "moral sense" altogether separate and of a different kind from our animal feelings. I have also had a talk about the origin of species, or the manner in which the innumerable races of animals have been produced. I, as far as I can understand at present, firmly believe that all animals have been transformed out of one primitive form by the continued influence, for thousands and perhaps millions of years, of climate, geography, etc.

Evolution as a consequence of natural selection was quite another matter. History is falsified very little when we say that the world was suddenly

133

introduced to this idea in 1858 and 1859 by the publications of Alfred Russel Wallace (1823–1913) and Charles Darwin. The gist of the idea can perhaps best be given in the summary form used by Wallace ten years later, in his **Natural Selection and Tropical Nature:**

A Demonstration of the Origin of Species by Natural Selection

Proved Facts	Necessary Consequences (afterwards taken as Proved Facts)
RAPID INCREASE OF ORGANISMS, pp. 23, 142 (*Origin of Species,* p. 75, 5th ed.) TOTAL NUMBER OF INDIVIDUALS STATIONARY, p. 23.	STRUGGLE FOR EXISTENCE, the deaths equaling the births on the average, p. 24 (*Origin of Species,* chap. iii.)
STRUGGLE FOR EXISTENCE. HEREDITY WITH VARIATION, or general likeness with individual differences of parents and offsprings, pp. 142, 156, 179 (*Origin of Species,* chaps. i. ii. v.)	SURVIVAL OF THE FITTEST, or Natural Selection; meaning, simply, that on the whole those die who are least fitted to maintain their existence (*Origin of Species,* chap. iv.)
SURVIVAL OF THE FITTEST. CHANGE OF EXTERNAL CONDITIONS, universal and unceasing.—See Lyell's *Principles of Geology.*	CHANGES OF ORGANIC FORMS, to keep them in harmony with the Changed Conditions; and as the changes of conditions are permanent changes, in the sense of not reverting back to identical previous conditions, the changes of organic forms must be in the same sense permanent, and thus originate SPECIES.

Acting in this way natural selection is often called "progressive selection" or "directional selection." This teleological naming sometimes leads to misunderstanding, which we need not go into here. Contrasted with this kind of selection is another kind called "stabilizing selection" (also "normalizing selection" and "centripetal selection"); the mechanism is precisely the same, only the consequences are different. Stabilizing selection maintains the statistical stability of the species (in a constant environment) in the face of unrelenting mutation pressure. Most of the time, in most species, it is stabilizing selection that rules the roost.

Only one person before Darwin can be said to have clearly understood the reality and significance of stabilizing selection: this was Edward Blyth (1808–1873), a competent but never famous naturalist. In two lengthy

134

papers in 1835 and 1837 he showed how stabilizing selection acted to conserve species characteristics. He never took the intellectual leap to directional selection. His work was almost unnoticed in his own time and after, until Loren Eiseley resurrected it in the centennial year of the **Origin**.[2]

That which was least original in the **Origin of Species**—the idea of evolution as history—gained the speediest assent. The idea of natural selection, by contrast, remained a continuing source of puzzlement, irritation, and outright rejection. A fair share of Darwin's critics denied it at a subconscious level; their overt discussions simply omitted the idea. This was, needless to say, distressing to the author. A paranoid historian of science could make a fair case for the submergence of the idea of natural selection by a professional conspiracy. I think this view could be defended only if one rigorously held to the barest etymological meaning of the word **con-spiracy**— that is, a "breathing together" (subconsciously), not a deliberate and conscious agreeing together (which is the usual connotation).

By the beginning of the twentieth century a widespread rumor was abroad that "Darwinism" (meaning natural selection) was on its deathbed. One writer spoke of "the softening of the brain of the Darwinians." Another suggested that we should pretend that Darwin "had never existed." Why the repulsion to what biologists now regard as one of the great foundation stones of biology? I think we can discern two reasons.

The first is a largely technical one. The progress of science is built on part-truths and their continual correction. It happened that around the turn of the century some new facts and ideas were available that **seemed** to undermine Darwinian theory. In the succeeding generation this impression was shown to be quite false. To make only the briefest allusion to technicalities, the work of G. H. Hardy and Wilhelm Weinberg in 1908, together with the subtle analysis of its significance by R. A. Fisher in 1930, showed that the idea of natural selection, far from being weakened by the more profound work of Darwin's successors, was made virtually impregnable thereby.

The other reason for the rejection of Darwinism can, I think, be called emotional; or equally well, esthetic. At every stage of the evolution of our picture of the world our thinking is subconsciously governed by something larger than our particular technical theses, something that an earlier generation of Germans called the **Weltanschauung,** and which more anthropologically minded commentators now refer to as the **myths** we live by. (The word "myth" is here to be taken in no invidious sense.) By the time a myth has become part of our world view it has become invested with beauty. The whole exists so much at a subconscious level that we may be unaware of this beauty until a new myth is offered as an alternative—and then we squeal like stuck pigs. No matter how great the intellectual rigor of a new idea, it doesn't have a chance of acceptance until it too has been invested with beauty. When we recognize this necessity we understand (and forgive) what otherwise would seem the unforgivable prolixity of so many of the great classics which mark the watersheds of man's intellectual development. A

135

great master is not merely trying to sell us an idea; he is trying to sell us a **picture.**

What is the picture of evolution by natural selection? This question is the burden of the present part of this book. And how, in detail, does the future of man fit into this picture? This will be one of the themes of Part III.

---

[1] Morse Peckham, *Victorian Studies,* **3:**19–40, 1959.

[2] Loren Eiseley, *Proceedings of the American Philosophical Society,* **103:**94–158, 1959.

59

The Economy of Nature

Aristotle
384–322 B.C.

From *On the Parts of Animals* (691 B, 4)

Nature never makes anything that is superfluous.

60

Elimination of the Unfit

Lucretius
ca. 99 B.C.–ca. 55 B.C.

It is generally held that the ideas expressed in Lucretius' **On the Nature of Things** are merely a poetic reworking of the views of the Greek philosopher Empedocles, who lived in the fifth century B.C. Attempting to analyze the complexities of this world in terms of simple components, Empedocles concluded that there were four elements—fire, air, water, and earth—and that these are acted upon by two elementary forces, love (a combining force) and hate (a disjoining force). In the evolution of the world, living things arose from nonliving by a random process of fusion of elementary, and then of compound, parts.

Hence, doubtless, Earth Prodigious forms at first
Engendered, of face and members most grotesque;
Monsters half-man, half-woman, not from each
Distant, yet neither total; shapes unsound,
Footless, and handless, void of mouth or eye,
Or from misjunction, maimed, of limb with limb:
To act all impotent, or flee from harm,
Or nurture take their loathsome days to extend.
    These sprang at first, and things alike uncouth;
Yet vainly; for abhorrent Nature quick
Checked their vile growths; . . . .
    Hence, doubtless, many a tribe has sunk suppressed,
Powerless its kind to breed. . . .
    Centaurs lived not; nor could shapes like these
Live ever.

61
Maud, the Eugenic Milkmaid

Thomas Robert Malthus
1766–1834

In the minds of both Darwin and Wallace, the stimulus that acted as the immediate releaser of the idea of natural selection was the reading of Malthus' **Essay on Population.** Did Malthus himself ever see the connection between the two ideas? There is only one suggestive passage, which occurs in Chapter 9 of the first edition. This passage, with its history, raises more questions than it answers. The "Bickerstaffs" referred to are fictional characters in the humorous and satirical "Tatler" papers of the early eighteenth century. Was Malthus taken in by the story of Maud, the milkmaid? Or was he, at the age of thirty-two, still young enough to enjoy a bit of fun at the expense of the reader? All we know is that Maud and the Bickerstaffs do not appear in subsequent editions, which are longer, more scholarly—and stuffier.

1798

The capacity of improvement in plants and animals, to a certain degree, no person can possibly doubt. A clear and decided progress has already been made, and yet, I think it appears that it would be highly absurd to say that this progress has no limits. In human life, though there are great variations from different causes, it may be doubted whether, since the world began, any organic improvement whatever in the human frame can be clearly ascertained. The foundations therefore, of which the organic perfectibility of man rest, are unusually weak, and can only be considered, as mere conjectures. It does not, however, by any means seem impossible, that by an attention to breed, a certain degree of improvement, similar to that among animals, might take place among men. Whether intellect could be communicated may be a matter of doubt: but size, strength, beauty, complexion, and perhaps even longevity are in a degree transmissible. The error does not seem to lie, in supposing a small degree of improvement possible, but in not discriminating between a small improvement, the limit of which is undefined, and an improvement really unlimited. As the human race however could not be improved in this way, without condemning all the bad specimens to celibacy, it is not probable, that an attention to breed should ever become general; indeed, I know of no well-directed attempts of this kind, except in the ancient family of the Bickerstaffs, who are said to have been very successful in whitening the skins, and increasing the height of their race by prudent marriages, particularly by that very judicious cross with Maud, the milkmaid, by which some capital defects in the constitution of the family were corrected.

62
Natural Theology

William Paley
1743–1805

Just ten days before the publication of the **Origin of Species** Darwin wrote: "I do not think I hardly ever admired a book more than Paley's 'Natural Theology.' I could almost formerly have said it by heart."— **Life and Letters,** vol. II, p. 15.

1802

Chapter I

In crossing a heath, suppose I pitched my foot against a *stone,* and were asked how the stone came to be there: I might possibly answer, that for any thing I knew to the contrary, it had lain there for ever: nor would it perhaps be very easy to shew the absurdity of this answer. But suppose I had found a *watch* upon the ground, and it should be inquired how the watch happened to be in that place; I should hardly think of the answer which I had before given, that, for any thing that I knew, the watch might have always been there. Yet why should not this answer serve for the watch as well as for the stone? Why is it not as admissible in the second case, as in the first? For this reason, and for no other, viz. that, when we come to inspect the watch, we perceive (what we could not discover in the stone) that its several parts are framed and put together for a purpose, e.g., that they are so formed and adjusted as to produce motion, and that motion so regulated as to point out the hour of the day; that, if the different parts had been differently shaped from what they are, of a different size from what they are, or placed after any other manner, or in any other order, than that in which they are placed, either no motion at all would have been carried on in the machine, or none which would have answered the use that is now served by it. To reckon up a few of the plainest of these parts, and of their offices, all tending to one result:—We see a cylindrical box containing a coiled elastic spring, which, by its endeavour to relax itself, turns round the box. We next observe a flexible chain (artificially wrought for the sake of flexure), communicating the action of the spring from the box to the fusee. We then find a series of wheels, the teeth of which catch in, and apply to each other, conducting the motion from the fusee to the balance, and from the balance to the pointer; and at the same time, by the size and shape of those wheels so regulating that motion, as to terminate in causing an index, by an equable and measured progression, to pass over a given space in a given time. We take notice that the wheels are made of brass in order to keep them from rust; the springs of steel, no other metal being so elastic; that over the face of the watch there is placed a glass, a material employed in no other part of the work, but in the room of which, if there had been any other than a transparent substance, the hour could not be seen without opening the case. This mechanism being observed (it requires indeed an examination of the instrument, and perhaps some previous knowledge of the subject, to perceive and understand it; but being once, as we have said, observed and understood), the inference, we think, is inevitable, that the watch must have had a maker; that there must have existed, at some time, and at some place or other, an artificer or artificers, who formed it for the purpose which we find it actually to answer; who comprehended its construction, and designed its use.

Chapter II

There cannot be a design without a designer; contrivance without a contriver; order without choice; arrangement without anything capable of arranging; subserviency and relation to a purpose, without that which could intend a purpose; means suitable to an end, and executing their office in accomplishing that end, without the end ever having been contemplated, or the means accommodated to it. Arrangement, disposition of parts, subserviency of means to an end, relation of instruments to a use, imply the presence of intelligence and mind.

Chapter III

Sturmius held, that the examination of the eye was a cure for atheism.

63

In Memoriam

Alfred Tennyson
1809–1892

Selections from LV and LVI

1849

Are God and Nature then at strife,
    That Nature lends such evil dreams?
    So careful of the type she seems,
So careless of the single life;

That I, considering everywhere
    Her secret meaning in her deeds,
    And finding that of fifty seeds
She often brings but one to bear, . . .

"So careful of the type?" but no.
    From scarped cliff and quarried stone
    She cries, "A thousand types are gone:
I care for nothing, all shall go.

"Thou makest thine appeal to me:
    I bring to life, I bring to death:
    The spirit does but mean the breath:
I know no more." And he, shall he,

Man, her last work, who seem'd so fair,
    Such splendid purpose in his eyes,
    Who roll'd the psalm to wintry skies,
Who built him fanes of fruitless prayer,

141

Who trusted God was love indeed
And love Creation's final law—
Tho' Nature, red in tooth and claw
With ravine, shrieked against his creed—

Who loved, who suffered countless ills,
Who battled for the True, the Just,
Be blown about the desert dust,
Or seal'd within the iron hills?

64
Did Adam Have a Navel?

During the first half of the nineteenth century the idea of evolution received more and more attention. That man should be related to the ape seemed, on various grounds, to be a plausible hypothesis. The clergy almost unanimously opposed such a view. In 1837 the Reverend Nicholas Wiseman— later made (in)famous as Robert Browning's "Bishop Blougram"—stated that "It is revolting to think that our noble nature should be nothing more than the perfecting of the ape's maliciousness." Revolting or not, this was precisely what people were called upon to think when Robert Chambers, in 1844, published his shocking **Vestiges of Creation.**

Chambers was a highly successful Edinburgh publisher who also wrote popularizations of science. **Vestiges** was published anonymously, no doubt in part to avoid hurting his publishing business (though we must remember that anonymous publications were a much commoner thing a century ago than now). Chambers' book was enormously successful: by the time of the **Origin** it was in its tenth edition. As a scientific work it was poorly regarded by biologists, but Darwin, always kind, years later wrote: "In my opinion it has done excellent service in this country in calling attention to the subject, in removing prejudice, and in thus preparing the ground for the reception of analogous views."

Although Chambers had proposed no plausible mechanism for evolution, his book had gained a wide following simply because, by this time, every educated man knew something about geology, and saw that the most plausible explanation of the succession of fossils in the rocks was a corresponding succession of different forms of life throughout time. This contradicted the literal interpretation of **Genesis,** of course. Many devout biologists were disturbed by this contradiction, and sought a way out. Among these was one Philip Henry Gosse, who contributed one of the most anguished chapters in the history of evolutionary theory. Philip Gosse (later to be the father of Edmund Gosse, who became a distinguished poet and critic) was born in England and emigrated to the New World, where he tried farming in Canada and teaching in Alabama before returning to England in 1839. He became a naturalist in the grand tradition; it was he, more than anyone else, who turned the attention of English naturalists toward the seashore and the microscope.

Like many a fine descriptive biologist, Philip Gosse was appalled by the growing popular acceptance of the theory of evolution. As a member of a conservative religious group, the Plymouth Brethren, he was moved to strike out vigorously against the growing heresy. He did so in a curious and now-forgotten book entitled **Omphalos.**

The Greek word "omphalos" means navel. To understand the title's appropriateness to Gosse's theme you should leaf through a collection of reproductions of Renaissance paintings of Adam and Eve. If you do, you may note the curious position of the "accidentally" disposed greenery. That it generally covers the pubic region of each of the original sinners is no surprise, but you should note that it also often covers the navel. This is not because any great titillation was associated with the sight of that modest structure; rather, the obscuring herbiage was designed to circumvent a difficult logical-theological point. If Adam was created from the dust, and Eve from Adam's rib, did the primeval pair possess navels? Some argued that since God creates nothing that is superfluous he would not have created navels in beings who were never nourished through umbilical cords. Opponents of this view held that the first humans were the type-specimens of all later humanity and must, therefore, have been blessed with typical navels. The umbilicus is normally evidence of a previous developmental history of the human body; but such cannot be true of the navels of Adam and Eve.

This was the metaphor that Gosse used for his book: that the fossils embedded in the rocks are like Adam's navel, structures formed there by God Himself, and having no developmental significance at all. Gosse was writing in a time when the conflict between science and theology was waxing ever fiercer; like many a man who stands in the middle, he was caught in a fire from both camps. The next selection, an excerpt from Gosse's book, is followed by the salvo of a man of religion, the Reverend Charles Kingsley (known to us for **Westward Ho!** and **Water Babies**). Gosse never recovered from the bitter reception given his book.

65

Omphalos: an Attempt to Untie the Geological Knot

Philip Henry Gosse
1810–1888

London: John Van Voorst

1857

It has been shown that, without a solitary exception, the whole of the vast vegetable and animal kingdoms were created,—mark! I do not say *may* have been, but **MUST** have been created—on this principle of a prochronic development, with distinctly traceable records. It was *the law of organic creation.*

It may be objected, that, to assume the world to have been created with fossil skeletons in its crust,—skeletons of animals that never really existed—is to charge the Creator with forming objects whose sole purpose was to deceive us. The reply is obvious. Were the concentric timber-rings of a created tree formed merely to deceive? Were the growth lines of a created shell intended to deceive? Was the navel of the created **Man** intended to deceive him into the persuasion that he had had a parent? . . .

Finally, the acceptance of the principles presented in this volume, even in their fullest extent, would not, in the least degree, affect the study of scientific geology. The character and order of the strata; their descriptions and displacements and injections; the successive floras and faunas; and all the other phenomena, would be *facts* still. They would still be, as now, legitimate subjects of examination and inquiry. I do not know that a single conclusion, now accepted, would need to be given up, except that of actual chronology. And even in respect of this, it would be rather a modification than a relinquishment of what is at present held; we might still speak of the inconceivably long duration of the processes in question, provided we understand *ideal* instead of *actual* time;—that the duration was projected in the mind of God, and not really existent.

66
Omphalos Scorned

Charles Kingsley
1819–1875

Letter to Philip Henry Gosse, 4 May 1858
From *The Life of Philip Henry Gosse*
London: Kegan Paul, Trench and Trubner, 1890

1858

Shall I tell you the truth? It is best. Your book is the first that ever made me doubt it [i.e., "the act of absolute creation"], and I fear it will make hundreds do so. Your book tends to prove this—that if we accept the fact of absolute creation, God becomes a *Deus quidem deceptor*. I do not mean merely in the case of fossils which *pretend* to be the bones of dead animals; but in the one single case of your newly created scars on the pandanus trunk, and your newly created Adam's navel, you make God tell a lie. It is not my reason, but my *conscience* which revolts here; which makes me say, 'Come what will, disbelieve what I may, I cannot believe this of a God of truth, of Him who is Light and no darkness at all, of Him who formed the intellectual man after His own Image, that he might understand and glory in His Father's works.' I ought to feel this I say, of the single Adam's navel, but I can hush up my conscience at the single instance; at the great sum total, the worthlessness of all geologic instruction, I cannot. I cannot give up the painful and slow conclusion of five and twenty years' study of geology, and believe that God has written on the rocks one enormous and superfluous lie for all mankind. . . .

To this painful dilemma you have brought me, and will, I fear, bring hundreds. It will not make me throw away my Bible. I trust and hope. I know in whom I have believed, and can trust Him to bring my faith safe through this puzzle, as He has through others; but for the young I do fear. I would not for a thousand pounds put your book into my children's hands. . . .

I *do* fear, with the editor of this month's *Geologist,* that you have given the 'vestiges of creation theory' the best shove forward which it has ever had. I have a special dislike to that book; but, honestly, I felt my heart melting toward it as I read *Omphalos.*

67
Autobiography

Charles Darwin
1809–1882

The autobiography of Charles Darwin is surely unique. He said that he wrote it for his children, that they might know what sort of man he was. At first sight, such a statement seems incredible. As an art form, autobiography is inherently—almost by definition—narcissistic; the larger world is so patently the audience the writer poses for. Yet when we read Darwin's autobiography—word by word, line by line, and between the lines—we end with the surprising conclusion that it really was written only for his family. Incredible, but true. The author is not posing for his picture; rather he is looking at himself with the same evaluative gaze he previously focused on pigeons, orchids, and earthworms. It is a scientific document. It is also warmly human.

It is painful to select only part of the **Autobiography** when it is so much of a piece. What is here reprinted is just the minimal amount needed to understand the origins of Darwin's greatest work. If you are dissatisfied with this small selection and are stimulated to seek out the whole, so much the better.

1876

After my return to England it appeared to me that by following the example of Lyell in Geology, and by collecting all facts which bore in any way on the variation of animals and plants under domestication and nature, some light might perhaps be thrown on the whole subject. My first note-book was opened in July 1837. I worked on true Baconian principles, and without any theory collected facts on a wholesale scale, more especially with respect to domesticated productions, by printed enquiries, by conversation with skilful breeders and gardeners, and by extensive reading. When I see the list of books of all kinds which I read and abstracted, including whole series of Journals and Transactions, I am surprised at my industry. I soon perceived that selection was the keystone of man's success in making useful races of animals and plants. But how selection could be applied to organisms living in a state of nature remained for some time a mystery to me.

146

In October 1838, that is, fifteen months after I had begun my systematic enquiry, I happened to read for amusement 'Malthus on Population,' and being well prepared to appreciate the struggle for existence which everywhere goes on from long-continued observation of the habits of animals and plants, it at once struck me that under these circumstances favourable variations would tend to be preserved, and unfavourable ones to be destroyed. The result of this would be the formation of new species. Here then I had at last got a theory by which to work; but I was so anxious to avoid prejudice, that I determined not for some time to write even the briefest sketch of it. In June 1842 I first allowed myself the satisfaction of writing a very brief abstract of my theory in pencil in 35 pages; and this was enlarged during the summer of 1844 into one of 230 pages, which I had fairly copied out and still possess.

But at that time I overlooked one problem of great importance; and it is astonishing to me, except on the principle of Columbus and his egg, how I could have overlooked it and its solution. This problem is the tendency in organic beings descended from the same stock to diverge in character as they become modified. That they have diverged greatly is obvious from the manner in which species of all kinds can be classed under genera, genera under families, families under sub-orders and so forth; and I can remember the very spot in the road, whilst in my carriage, when to my joy the solution occurred to me; and this was long after I had come to Down. The solution, as I believe, is that the modified offspring of all dominant and increasing forms tend to become adapted to many and highly diversified places in the economy of nature.

Early in 1856 Lyell advised me to write out my views pretty fully, and I began at once to do so on a scale three or four times as extensive as that which was afterwards followed in my 'Origin of Species;' yet it was only an abstract of the materials which I had collected, and I got through about half the work on this scale. But my plans were overthrown, for early in the summer of 1858 Mr. Wallace, who was then in the Malay archipelago, sent me an essay "On the Tendency of Varieties to depart indefinitely from the Original Type;" and this essay contained exactly the same theory as mine. Mr. Wallace expressed the wish that if I thought well of his essay, I should send it to Lyell for perusal.

The circumstances under which I consented at the request of Lyell and Hooker to allow of an abstract from my MS., together with a letter to Asa Gray, dated September 5, 1857, to be published at the same time with Wallace's Essay, are given in the 'Journal of the Proceedings of the Linnean Society,' 1858, p. 45. I was at first very unwilling to consent, as I thought Mr. Wallace might consider my doing so unjustifiable, for I did not then know how generous and noble was his disposition. The extract from my MS. and the letter to Asa Gray had neither been intended for publication, and were badly written. Mr. Wallace's essay, on the other hand, was admirably expressed and quite clear. Nevertheless, our joint productions excited very little attention, and the only published notice of them which I can remember was by Professor Haughton of Dublin, whose verdict was that all that was new in them was false, and what was true was old. This shows how necessary it is that any new view should be explained at considerable length in order to arouse public attention.

In September 1858 I set to work by the strong advice of Lyell and Hooker to prepare a volume on the transmutation of species, but was often interrupted by ill-health, and short visits to Dr. Lane's delightful hydropathic establishment at Moor Park. I abstracted the MS. begun on a much larger scale in 1856, and completed the volume on the same reduced scale. It cost me thirteen months and ten days' hard labour. It was published under the title of the 'Origin of Species,' in November 1859. Though considerably added to and corrected in the later editions, it has remained substantially the same book.

It is no doubt the chief work of my life. It was from the first highly successful. The first small edition of 1250 copies was sold on the day of publication, and a second edition of 3000 copies soon afterwards. Sixteen thousand copies have now (1876) been sold in England; and considering how stiff a book it is, this is a large sale. It has been translated into almost very European tongue, even into such languages as Spanish, Bohemian, Polish, and Russian. . . .

The success of the 'Origin' may, I think, be attributed in large part to my having long before written two condensed sketches, and to my having finally abstracted a much larger manuscript, which was itself an abstract. By this means I was enabled to select the more striking facts and conclusions. I had, also during many years followed a golden rule, namely, that whenever a published fact, a new observation or thought came across me, which was opposed to my general results, to make a memorandum of it without fail and at once; for I had found by experience that such facts and thoughts were far more apt to escape from the memory than favourable ones. Owing to this habit, very few objections were raised against my views which I had not at least noticed and attempted to answer.

It has sometimes been said that the success of the 'Origin' proved "that the subject was in the air," or "that men's minds were prepared for it." I do not think that this is strictly true, for I occasionally sounded not a few naturalists, and never happened to come across a single one who seemed to doubt about the permanence of species. Even Lyell and Hooker, though they would listen with interest to me, never seemed to agree. I tried once or twice to explain to able men what I meant by Natural Selection, but signally failed. What I believe was strictly true is that innumerable well-observed facts were stored in the minds of naturalists ready to take their proper places as soon as any theory which would receive them was sufficiently explained. Another element in the success of the book was its moderate size; and this I owe to the appearance of Mr. Wallace's essay; had I published on the scale in which I began to write in 1856, the book would have been four or five times as large as the 'Origin,' and very few would have had the patience to read it.

I gained much by my delay in publishing from about 1839, when the theory was clearly conceived, to 1859; and I lost nothing by it, for I cared very little whether men attributed most originality to me or Wallace; and his essay no doubt aided in the reception of the theory. I was forestalled in only one important point, which my vanity has always made me regret, namely, the explanation by means of the Glacial period of the presence of the same species of plants and of some few animals on distant mountain summits and in the arctic regions. This view pleased me so much that I wrote it out in extenso, and I believe that it was read by Hooker some years before E. Forbes published his celebrated memoir on the subject. In the very few points in which we differed, I still think that I was in the right. I have never, of course, alluded in print to my having independently worked out this view.

Hardly any point gave me so much satisfaction when I was at work on the 'Origin,' as the explanation of the wide difference in many classes between the embryo and the adult animal, and of the close resemblance of the embryos within the same class. No notice of this point was taken, as far as I remember, in the early reviews of the 'Origin,' and I recollect expressing my surprise on this head in a letter to Asa Gray. Within late years several reviewers have given the whole credit to Fritz Müller and Häckel, who undoubtedly have worked it out much more fully, and in some respects more correctly than I did. I had materials for a whole chapter on the subject, and I ought to have made the discussion longer; for it is clear that I failed to impress my readers; and he who succeeds in doing so deserves, in my opinion, all the credit.

This leads me to remark that I have almost always been treated honestly by my reviewers, passing over those without scientific knowledge as not worthy of notice. My views have often been grossly misrepresented, bitterly opposed and ridiculed, but this has been generally done, as I believe, in good faith. On the whole I do not doubt that my works have been over and over again greatly overpraised. I rejoice that I have avoided controversies, and this I owe to Lyell, who many years ago, in reference to my geological works, strongly advised me never to get entangled in a controversy, as it rarely did any good and caused a miserable loss of time and temper.

Whenever I have found out that I have blundered, or that my work has been imperfect, and when I have been contemptuously criticised, and even when I have been overpraised, so that I have felt mortified, it has been my greatest comfort to say hundreds of times to myself that "I have worked as hard and as well as I could, and no man can do more than this." I remember when in Good Success Bay, in Tierra del Fuego, thinking (and, I believe, that I wrote home to the effect) that I could not employ my life better than in adding a little to Natural Science. This I have done to the best of my abilities, and critics may say what they like, but they cannot destroy this conviction. . . .

68

Letter to Asa Gray

Charles Darwin
1809–1882

The 1858 presentation of Darwin's and Wallace's papers before the Linnaean Society included an abstract of a letter to the American botanist Asa Gray, which is reproduced below. Darwin's close friend, Joseph Hooker, reported that the interest at the meeting was intense. Nevertheless, the President of the Society, summing up at the end of the year, expressed his disappointment that 1858 had "not been marked by any of those striking discoveries which at once revolutionize, so to speak, the department of science on which they bear." In the popular and scholarly press of the day there is no critical reaction to contradict this judgment.

One recalls, and is haunted by, Brueghel's great painting, "The Fall of Icarus."

1858

1. It is wonderful what the principle of selection by man, that is the picking out of individuals with any desired quality, and breeding from them, and again picking out, can do. Even breeders have been astounded at their own results. They can act on differences inappreciable to an un-

educated eye. Selection has been *methodically* followed in *Europe* for only the last half century; but it was occasionally, and even in some degree methodically, followed in the most ancient times. There must have been also a kind of unconscious selection from a remote period, namely in the preservation of the individual animals (without any thought of their off-spring) most useful to each race of man in his particular circumstances. The "roguing," as nurserymen call the destroying of varieties which depart from their type, is a kind of selection. I am convinced that intentional and occasional selection has been the main agent in the production of our domestic races; but however this may be, its great power of modification has been indisputably shown in later times. Selection acts only by the accumulation of slight or greater variations, caused by external conditions, or by the mere fact that in generation the child is not absolutely similar to its parent. Man, by this power of accumulating variations, adapts living beings to his wants —may be said to make the wool of one sheep good for carpets, of another for cloth, &c.

2. Now suppose there were a being who did not judge by mere external appearances, but who could study the whole internal organization, who was never capricious, and should go on selecting for one object during millions of generations; who will say what he might not effect? In nature we have some *slight* variation occasionally in all parts; and I think it can be shown that changed conditions of existence is the main cause of the child not exactly resembling its parents; and in nature geology shows us what changes have taken place, and are taking place. We have almost unlimited time; no one but a practical geologist can fully appreciate this. Think of the Glacial period, during the whole of which the same species at least of shells have existed; there must have been during this period millions on millions of generations.

3. I think it can be shown that there is such an unerring power at work in *Natural Selection* (the title of my book), which selects exclusively for the good of each organic being. The elder De Candolle, W. Herbert, and Lyell have written excellently on the struggle for life; but even they have not written strongly enough. Reflect that every being (even the elephant) breeds at such a rate, that in a few years, or at most a few centuries, the surface of the earth would not hold the progeny of one pair. I have found it hard constantly to bear in mind that the increase of every single species is checked during some part of its life, or during some shortly recurrent generation. Only a few of those annually born can live to propagate their kind. What a trifling difference must often determine which shall survive, and which perish!

4. Now take the case of a country undergoing some change. This will tend to cause some of its inhabitants to vary slightly—not but that I believe most beings vary at all times enough for selection to act on them.

Some of its inhabitants will be exterminated; and the remainder will be exposed to the mutual action of a different set of inhabitants, which I believe to be far more important to the life of each being than mere climate. Considering the infinitely various methods which living beings follow to obtain food by struggling with other organisms, to escape danger at various times of life, to have their eggs or seeds disseminated &c. &c., I cannot doubt that during millions of generations individuals of a species will be occasionally born with some slight variation, profitable to some part of their economy. Such individuals will have a better chance of surviving, and of propagating their new and slightly different structure; and the modification may be slowly increased by the accumulative action of natural selection to any profitable extent. The variety thus formed will either coexist with, or, more commonly, will exterminate its parent form. An organic being, like the woodpecker or mistletoe, may thus come to be adapted to a score of contingencies—natural selection accumulating those slight variations in all parts of its structure, which are in any way useful to it during any part of its life.

5. Multiform difficulties will occur to every one, with respect to this theory. Many can, I think, be satisfactorily answered. *Natura non facit saltum* answers some of the most obvious. The slowness of the change, and only a very few individuals undergoing change at any one time, answers others. The extreme imperfection of our geological records answers others.

6. Another principle, which may be called the principle of divergence, plays, I believe, an important part in the origin of species. The same spot will support more life if occupied by very diverse forms. We see this in the many generic forms in a square yard of turf, and in the plants or insects on any little uniform islet, belonging almost invariably to as many genera and families as species. We can understand the meaning of this fact amongst the higher animals, whose habits we understand. We know that it has been experimentally shown that a plot of land will yield a greater weight if sown with several species and genera of grasses, than if sown with only two or three species. Now, every organic being, by propagating so rapidly, may be said to be striving its utmost to increase in numbers. So it will be with the offspring of any species after it has become diversified into varieties, or sub-species, or true species. And it follows, I think, from the foregoing facts, that the varying offspring of each species will try (only few will succeed) to seize on as many and as diverse places in the economy of nature as possible. Each new variety or species, when formed, will generally take the place of, and thus exterminate its less well-fitted parent. This I believe to be the origin of the classification and affinities of organic beings at all times; for organic beings always *seem* to branch and sub-branch like the limbs of a tree from a

common trunk, the flourishing and diverging twigs destroying the less vigorous—the dead and lost branches rudely representing extinct genera and families.

This sketch is *most* imperfect; but in so short a space I cannot make it better. Your imagination must fill up very wide blanks.

69
The Origin of Species

Charles Darwin
1809–1882

That Wallace had a fair idea of the contents of Darwin's impending great work before 1858 is clear from the published correspondence of the two men. For example, there is that famous letter of 22 December 1857—the letter in which Darwin said, "I am a firm believer that without speculation there is no good and original observation," thus repudiating the rigid Baconian view of science so worshipped by William Whewell of Cambridge and other philosophers of the day. Toward the end of this letter, Darwin said to Wallace: "You ask whether I shall discuss 'man.' I think I shall avoid the whole subject, as so surrounded with prejudices; though I fully admit that it is the highest and most interesting problem for the naturalist."

Darwin stuck to this intention. The following passage, which concludes the **Origin of Species,** includes the **only** reference to man in the entire work.

1859

In the distant future I see open fields for far more important researches. Psychology will be based on a new foundation, that of the necessary acquirement of each mental power and capacity by gradation. Light will be thrown on the origin of man and his history.

Authors of the highest eminence seem to be fully satisfied with the view that each species has been independently created. To my mind it accords better with what we know of the laws impressed on matter by the Creator, that the production and extinction of the past and present inhabitants of the world should have been due to secondary causes, like those determining the birth and death of the individual. When I view all beings not as special creations, but as the lineal descendants of some few beings which lived long before the first bed of the Silurian system was deposited, they seem to me to become enobled. Judging from the past, we may safely infer that not one living species will transmit its unaltered likeness to a distant futurity. And of the species now living very few will transmit progeny of any kind to a far distant futurity; for the manner in which all organic beings are grouped shows that the greater number of species of each genus, and all the species of many genera, have left no descendants, but have become utterly extinct. We can so far take a prophetic glance into futurity as to foretell that it will be the common and widely-spread species, belonging to the larger and dominant groups, which will ultimately prevail and procreate new and dominant species. As all the living forms of life are the lineal descendants of those which lived long before the Silurian epoch, we may feel certain that the ordinary succession by generation has never once been broken, and that no cataclysm has desolated the whole world. Hence we may look with some confidence to a secure future of equally inappreciable length. And as natural selection works solely by and for the good of each being, all corporeal and mental endowments will tend to progress towards perfection.

It is interesting to contemplate an entangled bank, clothed with many plants of many kinds, with birds singing on the bushes, with various insects flitting about, and with worms crawling through the damp earth, and to reflect that these elaborately constructed forms, so different from each other, and dependent on each other in so complex a manner, have all been produced by laws acting around us. These laws, taken in the largest sense, being Growth with Reproduction; Inheritance which is almost implied by reproduction; Variability from the indirect and direct action of the external conditions of life, and from use and disuse; a Ratio of Increase so high as to lead to a Struggle for Life, and as a consequence to Natural Selection, entailing Divergence of Character and the Extinction of less-improved forms. Thus, from the war of nature, from famine and death, the most exalted object which we are capable of conceiving, namely, the production of the higher animals, directly follows. There is grandeur in this view of life, with its several powers, having been originally breathed into a few forms or into one; and that, while this planet has gone cycling on according to the fixed laws of gravity, from so simple a beginning endless forms most beautiful and most wonderful have been, and are being, evolved.

The Huxley-Wilberforce Debate

Thomas Henry Huxley
1825–1895

Nature, **172**(1953):920

Every history of Darwinism delightedly recounts the famous Huxley-Wilberforce debate, the principal historical source being the **Life and Letters of T. H. Huxley.** In 1953, almost a century after the event, a new document was uncovered. It was published in a short article by D. J. Foskett, "Wilberforce and Huxley on Evolution," reproduced here in its entirety.

1860

It was a famous moment in the history of science when, during the discussion of Darwin's theory of evolution at the British Association meeting at Oxford in 1860, Bishop Wilberforce turned to T. H. Huxley and asked him whether he claimed descent from an ape on his father's or his mother's side.

The actual words of Huxley's reply are not known; in the excitement, members of the audience noted different points, and two or three versions appear in the biographies and histories. The main source of our information, his son Leonard Huxley, wrote "most unluckily, no contemporary account of his own exists of the encounter." [1]

Such an account does, however, exist in a letter written to Dr. Dyster within a few months of the meeting, on September 9, 1860, and now preserved in the collection of Huxley Papers at the Imperial College of Science and Technology, London. The style of the quotation has the authentic tone: the putting his opponent in the wrong from the start, the use of antithesis, the long complex build-up to a dramatic pause, and then final swift and decisive swoop. Considering also the accuracy with which Huxley was able to recall the details of what he had once formulated in his mind, it seems likely that this letter contains as nearly correct a record as we shall ever possess.

> When I got up I spoke pretty much to the effect—that I had listened with great attention to the Lord Bishop's speech but had been unable to discover either a new fact or a new argument in it—except indeed

the question raised as to my personal predilections in the matter of ancestry—That it would not have occurred to me to bring forward such a topic as that for discussion myself, but that I was quite ready to meet the Right Rev. prelate even on that ground. If then, said I, the question is put to me would I rather have a miserable ape for a grandfather or a man highly endowed by nature and possessing great means and influence and yet who employs those faculties and that influence for the mere purpose of introducing ridicule into a grave scientific discussion—I unhesitatingly affirm my preference for the ape.

Whereupon there was unextinguishable laughter among the people, and they listened to the rest of my argument with the greatest attention . . . I happened to be in very good condition and said my say with perfect good temper and politeness—I assure you of this because all sorts of reports [have] been spread about e.g. that I had said I would rather be an ape than a bishop, etc.[2]

I am indebted to the Governors of the Imperial College for permission to publish this extract.

---

[1] Huxley, Leonard, *The Life and Letters of T. H. Huxley* (vol. 1), New York: Macmillan, 1903, p. 259.
[2] Imperial College, "The Huxley Papers," 15:117–118.

71
An Alternative to Paley

Charles Kingsley
1819–1875

The following passage is taken from **More Letters of Charles Darwin** (vol. I, p. 225), edited by F. Darwin and A. C. Seward.

1862

Kingsley's letter to Huxley, dated Dec. 20th, 1862, contains a story or parable of a heathen Khan in Tartary who was visited by a pair of proselytising Moollahs. The first Moollah said: "Oh! Khan, worship my God. He is so wise that he made all things." But Moollah No. 2 won the day by pointing out that his God is "so wise that he makes all things make themselves."

The Art of Publishing Obscurely

As a feast attracts jackals, so fame attracts fortune seekers. As soon as the **Origin of Species** was published various critics hastened to assert that the book was no more than Lamarck or Erasmus Darwin reborn; moreover, there was Buffon. All these men had some claim to the idea of evolution. As for natural selection, a claimant to this appeared in less than half a year after the **Origin** was published. In the **Gardeners' Chronicle** for 7 April 1860, one Patrick Matthew claimed the idea as his on the basis of some remarks he had published in 1831, quoting the passages in question. Replying two weeks later Darwin said: "I freely acknowledge that Mr. Matthew has anticipated by many years the explanation which I have offered of the origin of species, under the name of natural selection. I think that no one will be surprised that neither I, nor apparently any other naturalist, had heard of Mr. Matthew's views, considering how briefly they are given, and that they appeared in the appendix to a work on Naval Timber and Arboriculture." Which is, one must admit, a curious place to publish so monumental an idea.

In later editions of the **Origin** Darwin included some words of credit to Matthew; but Matthew regarded them as insufficient and continued to push his claim. No one took him seriously; he was just annoying. The irritation was brought to an end in 1865 when, as Darwin wrote to his friend J. D. Hooker: "A Yankee has called my attention to a paper attached to Dr. Wells' famous 'Essay on Dew,' which was read in 1813 to the Royal Soc., but not [then] printed, in which he applies most distinctly the principle of Natural Selection to the Races of Man. So poor old Patrick Matthew is not the first, and he cannot, or ought not, any longer to put on his title-pages, 'Discoverer of the principle of Natural Selection'!"

Though "read" in 1813, this contribution of the physician William Charles Wells (1757–1817) was not published until the year after his death. The title of this book was even more curious than Mr. Matthew's, being: **Two Essays: Single Vision with Two Eyes; Dew.** Let's see what Dr. Wells had to say:

Amongst men, as well as among other animals, varieties of a greater or less magnitude are constantly occurring. In a civilized country . . . those varieties, for the most part, quickly disappear, from the intermarriages of different families. . . . In districts, however, of very small extent, and having little intercourse with other countries, an accidental difference in the appearance of the inhabitants will often descend to their late posterity. . . . Again, those who attend to the improvement of domestic animals, when they find individuals possessing . . . the qualities they desire, couple a male and female of these together, then take the best of their offering as a new stock, and in this way proceed till they approach as near the point in view as the nature of things will permit. But, what is here done by art, seems to be done with equal efficacy, though more slowly, by nature, in the formation of varieties of mankind, fitted for the country which they inhabit. Of the accidental varieties of man, which would occur among the first few and scattered inhabitants of Africa, some would be better fitted than the others to bear the diseases of the country. This race would subsequently multiply, while the others would decrease, not only from their inability to sustain the attacks of disease, but from their incapacity of contending with their more vigorous neighbors.

A lawyer could make a good case out of this, and yet scientists blithely ignore Wells' claim to credit. Why? To an outsider such action may look like some sort of conspiracy designed to sequester all the credit within a clique. Scientists have a different explanation; they agree with the philosopher Alfred North Whitehead, who said: "We give credit not to the first man to have an idea but to the first one to take it seriously." If we accept this as a moral directive there is no question about assigning the credit for the idea of natural selection. In hundreds of pages and with scores upon scores of examples blanketing the entire field of biology, Darwin took the idea most seriously. Today, a century later, we take it even more seriously.

Why did Matthew and Wells fail to capitalize on their idea? Not knowing, it is safest for us to suppose no more than that they failed to recognize their diamond in the rough. This is a safe explanation, but—emboldened by Freud—can we not suggest another possibility? "Forgetting," we have learned, is seldom a mere negative act; we **will** to forget. Thus, failure may signify more than lack of ability; failure also may be the result of willing. All of us show great ingenuity in failing to see things which threaten our established system of values. The human implications of the idea of selection are so upsetting that even today most people, including many biologists, cannot see the most threatening of them. To see truly one needs to be free; but no one is truly free. And we are often not free enough.

Did Matthew and Wells dimly see some of these disturbing implications and "pull their punches"? We shall probably never know, so we certainly should not take very seriously this unprovable hypothesis. Yet I cannot forbear pointing to certain suggestive evidence—the very titles of the works in which they presented the idea of natural selection: **Single Vision with Two Eyes** and **Naval Timber and Arboriculture**. The most elaborate indexing apparatus available to scientists today would fail to index the idea of natural selection in either of these books if they were freshly published and sent to **Biological Abstracts**. Could it be that their authors did not want the idea to be noticed?

It is no answer to point out that they must have wanted some notice to be taken, or else they would not have said anything at all. We all understand the ambivalence of human desires; it is possible to wish, and not wish, at the same time. In the theory of speech pathology such ambivalance is recognized as the primary cause of stuttering; the speaker wants to say something but fears disapproval by some significant Other, and so he "chooses" a way of saying, and not saying, at the same time. Some of the maneuvers of academic scholars stem from the same pathology: the relegation of important ideas to footnotes or tailnotes, for example, where there is a fair chance that the significant Other will not notice them, but where they are memorialized to be later pointed to if events prove the author was right (which makes him then willing to claim the credit). One of the most capable geneticists of the twentieth century made life miserable for his colleagues by his all too frequent use of the Ploy of the Significant Footnote.

It is not provable, of course, but is it not at least possible that Wells and Matthew did not want to be heard when they announced the idea of natural selection? If so, the burial of the idea in treatises on binocular vision and naval timbers becomes understandable.

73

On the Importance of Words

Charles Darwin
1809–1882

Letter to Alfred Russel Wallace, 5 July 1866
From *Life and Letters*

1866

My Dear Wallace,—I have been much interested by your letter, which is as clear as daylight. I fully agree with all that you say on the advantages of H. Spencer's excellent expression of 'the survival of the fittest.' [1] This, however, had not occurred to me till reading your letter. It is, however, a great objection to this term that it cannot be used as a substantive governing a verb; and that this is a real objection I infer from H. Spencer continually using the words, natural selection. I formerly thought, probably in an exaggerated degree, that it was a great advantage to bring into connection natural and artificial selection; this indeed led me to use a term in common, and I still think it some advantage. I wish I had received your letter two months ago, for I would have worked in 'the survival, &c.,' often in the new edition of the 'Origin,' which is now almost printed off, and of which I will of course send you a copy. I will use the term in my next book on Domestic animals, &c., from which, by the way, I plainly see that you expect much, too much. The term Natural Selection has now been so largely used abroad and at home, that I doubt whether it could be given up, and with all its faults I should be sorry to see the attempt made. Whether it will be rejected must now depend 'on the survival of the fittest.' As in time the term must grow intelligible the objections to its use will grow weaker and weaker. I doubt whether the use of any term would have made the subject intelligible to some minds, clear as it is to others; for do we not see even to the present day Malthus on Population absurdly misunderstood? This reflection about Malthus has often comforted me when I have been vexed at the misstatement of my views.

---

[1] Extract from a letter of Mr. Wallace's, July 2, 1866: "The term 'survival of the fittest' is the plain expression of the fact; 'natural selection' is a metaphorical expression of it, and to a certain degree indirect and incorrect, since . . . Nature . . . does not so much select special varieties as exterminate the most unfavourable ones."

74

Darwin Refuted

Anonymous

Review of a Work on Evolution
Athenaeum, **2102** (8 February 1867):217

1867

In the theory with which we have to deal, Absolute Ignorance is the artificer; so that we may enunciate as the fundamental principle of the whole system, that, IN ORDER TO MAKE A PERFECT AND BEAUTIFUL MACHINE, IT IS NOT REQUISITE TO KNOW HOW TO MAKE IT. This proposition will be found, on careful examination, to express, in a condensed form, the essential purport of the theory, and to express in a few words all Mr. Darwin's meaning; who, by a strange inversion of reasoning, seems to think Absolute Ignorance fully qualified to take the place of Absolute Wisdom in all the achievements of creative skill.

75

Dover Beach

Matthew Arnold
1822–1888

1867

The sea is calm to-night.
The tide is full, the moon lies fair
Upon the straits;—on the French coast the light
Gleams and is gone; the cliffs of England stand
Glimmering and vast, out in the tranquil bay.

Come to the window, sweet is the night-air!
Only, from the long line of spray
Where the sea meets the moon-blanch'd land,
Listen! you hear the grating roar
Of pebbles which the waves draw back, and fling.
At their return, up the high strand,
Begin, and cease, and then again begin,
With tremulous cadence slow, and bring
The eternal note of sadness in.

Sophocles long ago
Heard it on the Ægean, and it brought
Into his mind the turbid ebb and flow,
Of human misery; we

Find also in the sound a thought,
Hearing it by this distant northern sea.

The Sea of Faith
Was once, too, at the full, and round earth's shore
Lay like the folds of a bright girdle furl'd.
But now I only hear
Its melancholy, long, withdrawing roar,
Retreating, to the breath
Of the night-wind, down the vast edges drear
And naked shingles of the world.

Ah, love, let us be true
To one another! for the world, which seems
To lie before us like a land of dreams,
So various, so beautiful, so new,
Hath really neither joy, nor love, nor light,
Nor certitude, nor peace, nor help for pain;
And we are here as on a darkling plain
Swept with confused alarms of struggle and flight,
Where ignorant armies clash by night.

76

Liberation From Paley

Francis Galton
1822–1911

The following letter to Galton's cousin, Charles Darwin, is taken from C. P. Blacker. **Eugenics: Galton and After,** 1952, p. 83.

My Dear Darwin,

It would be idle to speak of the delight your letter has given me, for there is no one in the world whose approbation in these matters can have the same weight as yours. Neither is there anyone whose approbation I prize more highly, on purely personal grounds, because I always think of you in the same way as converts from barbarism think of the teacher who first relieved them from the intolerable burden of superstition. I used to be wretched under the weight of the old-fashioned arguments from design, of which I felt, though I was unable to prove to myself, the worthlessness. Consequently, the appearance of your *Origin of Species* formed a real crisis in my life; your book drove away the constraint of my old superstition as if it had been a nightmare and was the first to give me freedom of thought.

77

The History of Materialism

Frederick Albert Lange
1828–1875

New York: Harcourt Brace. Third ed. (First ed., 1866)

In his biographical notes, Ernest Chester Thomas, the translator of the following work, has this to report of the German philosopher and historian, F. A. Lange: "His heart beat for the lot of the masses, and he felt that the question of labour would be the great problem of the coming time, as it was the question that decided the fall of the ancient world. The core of this problem he believed to be 'the struggle against the struggle for existence,' which is identified with man's spiritual destiny."

1877

All teleology has its root in the view that the builder of the universe acts in such a way that man must, on the analogy of human reason, call his action purposeful. . . . It can now, however, be no longer doubted that nature proceeds in a way which has no similarity with human purposefulness; nay, that her most essential means is such that, measured by the standard of human understanding, it can only be compared with the blindest chance. On this point we need wait for no future proof; the facts speak so plainly and in the most various provinces of nature so unani-

163

mously, that no view of things is henceforth admissible which contradicts these facts and their necessary meaning.

If a man, in order to shoot a hare, were to discharge thousands of guns on the great moor in all possible directions; if, in order to get into a locked-up room, he were to buy ten thousand casual keys, and try them all; if, in order to have a house, he were to build a town, and leave all the other houses to wind and weather,—assuredly no one would call such proceedings purposeful, and still less would any one conjecture behind these proceedings a higher wisdom, unrevealed reasons, and superior prudence. But whoever will study the modern scientific laws of the conservation and propagation of species, even of those species the purpose of which we cannot see, as, e.g., the intestinal worms, will everywhere find an enormous waste of vital germs. From the pollen of the plant to the fertilised seed, from the seed to the germinating plant, from this to the full-grown plant bearing seed in its turn, we constantly see repeated the mechanism which, through thousandfold production for immediate destruction, and through the casual coincidence of favourable conditions, maintains life, so far as we see it maintained in the existing state of things. The perishing of vital germs, the abortion of the process begun, is the rule; the "natural" development is a special case among thousands; it is the exception, and this exception is the result of that Nature whose purposeful self-conservation the teleologist shortsightedly admires. "We behold the face of nature," says Darwin, "bright with gladness; we often see superabundance of food; we do not see, or we forget, that the birds which are idly singing round us mostly live on insects or seeds, and are thus constantly destroying life; or we forget how largely these songsters, or their eggs, or their nestlings, are destroyed by birds and beasts of prey; we do not always bear in mind that although food may be now superabundant, it is not so at all seasons of each recurring year." The struggle for a spot of earth, success or nonsuccess in the persecution and extermination of other life, determines the propagation of plants and animals. Millions of spermatozoa, eggs, young creatures, hover between life and death that single individuals may develop themselves. Human reason knows no other ideal than the presence and perfection, as far as may be, of the life that has begun, combined with the limitation of births and deaths. To Nature luxuriant propagation and painful destruction are only two oppositely working forces which seek an equilibrium. Even for the "civilised" world political economy has revealed the sad law that misery and famine are the great regulators of the increase of population. Nay, even in the intellectual sphere it seems to be the method of Nature that she flings a thousand equally gifted and aspiring spirits into wretchedness and despair in order to form a single genius, which owes its development to the favour of circumstances. Sympathy, the fairest flower of earthly organisms, breaks forth only at isolated points, and is even in the life of humanity more an ideal than one of its ordinary motives.

What we call Chance in the development of species is, of course, no chance in the sense of the universal laws of Nature, whose mighty activity calls forth all these effects; but it is, in the strictest sense of the word, chance, if we regard this expression in opposition to the results of a humanly calculating intelligence. Where, however, we find adaptation in the organs of animals or plants, there we may assume that in the eternal slaughter of the weak countless less adapted forms were destroyed, so that here too that which maintains itself is only the favourable special case in the ocean of birth and death. This, then, would be, in fact, a fragment of the much-reviled philosophy of Empedokles, confirmed by the endless materials which only the last decades of exact research have brought to light.

78

The Darwinian Theory and the Argument from Design

Alvar Ellegård
Lychnos (1956):173–192.

1956

Now the theory of Natural Selection was the only feature that distinguished Darwin from the earlier evolutionists, of whom Lamarck may be considered as the chief spokesman. We therefore have the paradoxical situation that ten years after Darwin had published, almost everybody who was at all in a position to judge had been converted to Evolution, not in Darwin's form, but in the version which the same people, a few years earlier, had declared wholly untenable and unscientific. The Natural Selection theory clearly met with incomparably stronger resistance than the Evolution theory as such. This circumstance in itself would justify the assertion that Natural Selection touched the ideology of the age at a more vital point than did the Evolution theory pure and simple.

The evidence leaves no doubt as to what the point was. The theory of Natural Selection was seen to cut away the ground from under the Design argument. . . . It was difficult to regard as simple, lucid, and beautiful a process which gave rise to a thousand times more waste products than finished articles. This feeling was expressed in a review in the [London] *Times* [31 January 1867, p. 5] of an anti-Darwinian treatise: "Natural selection . . . is adaptation by chance, and therefore not, by design. . . . It is . . . a theory of waste . . . and in that it does violence to nature, of which economy is a fundamental law. . . ."

Darwin himself had, however, reckoned with the painful readjustment that his theory would necessitate, and he diligently sought to soften the shock. By so doing he certainly succeeded in gaining a more sympathetic hearing. . . . At the same time, by his concessions to the religious feelings of the public Darwin indubitably made it more difficult for his readers to understand his theory. The way the Natural Selection theory was misrepresented in the press was, as Darwin often complains in his correspondence, simply amazing. It is obvious that the critics did not wish to understand, and to some extent Darwin himself encouraged their wishful thinking. . . .

At the present day there is hardly any doubt that the basic process underlying variation is a random one. But it has taken a long time to establish this experimentally, and it is interesting to observe that each time some experiment has appeared to contradict this assumption, it has been seized upon and advertized by metaphysically minded biologists and laymen as an indication of predetermined evolution. It is significant that among novelists and poets—in fact, among non-scientists generally— it is this kind of evolutionism that has always been predominant.

166

79

In Praise of Waste

Garrett Hardin
1915–

From *Nature and Man's Fate*
New York: Rinehart

1959

Darwin changed our views of the origin of living things, but more important still, he changed our attitude toward waste. Before Darwin, the adaptedness of species was explained by William Paley as an example of "design in nature"—a design that existed in the mind of a Creator Who then fashioned nature in accordance with His blueprint; only so, said Paley, could such a marvelously adapted structure as the eye have been produced.

Not at all, said Darwin. It is not necessary that there exist in some mind the idea of a beautifully adapted machine in order that this machine may come into existence. It is enough if nature be permitted to try countless experiments—"mutations" we now call them—among which a tiny percentage produces good results. Each such successful experiment is saved by natural selection and used as a base for further experimentation and natural selection. Mutation occurs at random and entails enormous waste, but natural selection acts like a ratchet to preserve each tiny element of progress; thus do nature's beautifully adapted machines come into being. There need be no blueprint for design to emerge; trial and error suffice. Something of this sort must have been meant by the poet William Blake who said, "To be an error and to be cast out is a part of God's design."

Design can emerge from blind waste. How old is this thought? Who can trace the earliest embryological stages of so tenuous an entity as an idea? Perhaps it is centuries old, but certainly its form was not unambiguously clear until Robert Malthus wrote his *Essay on Population* in 1798. This much-misunderstood work, yearly buried by liberal critics and yearly resurrected by its own vigor, has, entangled in its many errors, a correct view of stability achieved through waste—the Malthusian dynamic scheme of population. From the superabundant vitality of nature comes the ever-present threat of geometric increase, but this is opposed by the limitations set by the environment. The result is an equilibrium achieved through waste, an equilibrium that may, it is true, be subject to temporal shifts, but an equilibrium nonetheless. Forethought, planning and charity are either of secondary importance or are self-defeating in such a system.

This mode of thought met with immediate favor when it was put forward by Malthus, but within a very few years it was vigorously opposed by another idea of independent birth and apparently contradictory implications—the idea of cruelty, *i.e.,* the idea that cruelty is something to be abhorred rather than enjoyed. Strange as it may seem, this idea is a rather young idea as far as the bulk of mankind is concerned. In the distant past, the gentle Jesus was a conspicuous exception among men. It is only within comparatively recent times that many Christians have become Christian.

The Christianization of Christians was made possible by a change in perspective. In the Middle Ages it was common for the population of a city to be lowered as much as 10 per cent in a single year by disease or famine; even a 25 per cent loss was not unknown. In a world so filled with suffering not caused by humans, it would seem to some rather out of perspective to complain of a little human fun—like the Spanish Inquisition, say. As suffering and death from seemingly divinely caused diseases decreased—as it did even before Pasteur and bacteriology—man's view of his own cruelties changed, perhaps because they loomed proportionately larger. Cruel fate was becoming reformed; cruel man now looked crueler. Tenderminded poets and novelists were determined that he, too, should reform, and quickly.

Into this world of tender intensions burst Malthus, asserting that suffering was inevitable, simply because population had the capability of increasing more rapidly than the means of subsistence. A reasonable balance between population and subsistence—a decent scale of living for some—could be maintained only if others suffered from insufficient means of subsistence. Nor would it be a true solution for the haves to divide their means with the have-nots—this would merely encourage the production of more have-nots. Such a sentiment provoked a storm of protest from the literati, who were now making the cause of the poor and the unfortunate their cause. The wealthy Percy Shelley saw a great social threat in "sophisms like those of Mr. Malthus, calculated to lull the oppressors of mankind into a security of everlasting triumph." The poet's friend William Hazlitt asserted that "Mr. Malthus' gospel is preached only to the poor."

This is not the place to examine Malthus' thesis—or rather, his theses, for there were several. We need only point out that the early decades of the nineteenth century saw an establishment of sharp lines of battle between—shall we say—humanitarians and analysts; it is difficult to name the factions without arousing prejudice. It must not be supposed that men like

Malthus were inhumane; in his personal relations with family and friends, Malthus was the kindest and most considerate of men. But in his public statements he insisted on the primacy of analysis in the attack on social problems, whereas his opponents insisted on the humanitarian treatment of all existing people—particularly the poor and unfortunate—in the hope, or belief, that future generations would present no problem. The here and now is much more real than the there and tomorrow. The humanitarians won the minds of common men—who are, in the nature of things, the majority.

What Malthus was trying to get at in his bumbling way, and all-unconscious of what he was doing, was what we now call the impotence principles of science and logic. The trisection of an angle with ruler and compass alone is impossible—this is an impotence principle. So also is the principle of the conservation of matter and mass, and the finite velocity of the speed of light. Impotence principles tell us what cannot be done and for that reason are inacceptable to immature minds. Angle trisectors, circle squarers, and inventors of perpetual-motion machines we will always have with us. What these men fail to realize is that impotence principles are not only restrictive but also permissive. Only if some things are impossible can other things be. The second law of thermodynamics not only tells us to stop looking for a perpetual-motion machine but also tells us how to improve the machines already invented.

One of the impotence principles of biology is this—waste is inevitable. Waste, in the Darwinian scheme, not only produces progress but also conserves the advances already made. There is no heredity without its tax of mutation; most mutations are bad; their production and elimination are a kind of waste. The sentimentalist who seeks to eliminate the waste in a species by preserving all mutants and breeding equally of all genetic types ultimately brings about the extinction of the entire species. It is a throwing of good money after bad. It is the saving of pawns and losing the game.

One of the most surprising things about science is the way it begins as common sense, and ends up with most uncommonsensical statements to which, nevertheless, common sense must give its assent once it has examined the evidence. The curvature of space is such an idea in astronomy. In biology we have the astonishing conclusion of the Haldane-Muller principle which says: In a state of nature, all bad mutations are, in their cumulative, ultimate effects, equally bad. How can this be true? To say that a gene that is only mildly harmful to the individual is just as harmful to the race as is one that is completely lethal to the individual seems to be flying in the face of reason. But it is true.

When we say, "Gene A is not as bad as gene B," what do we mean? How do we measure "badness" in nature? The only acceptable way, in an

169

evolutionary sense, is by the gene's effect on success in leaving progeny. The "worse" the gene is, the greater the diminution in progeny it causes in early generations; and consequently, the sooner the gene is completely eliminated. A gene that causes only slight damage in each generation does so for many generations. These two factors—damage in one generation, and the number of generations sustaining damage—bear a reciprocal relation to each other. As a result, the total damage of a gene, over all generations, is a fixed quantity, the same for all deleterious genes.

The preceding discussion presupposes a species living "in a state of nature." The meaning and the reason for the qualification should be fairly clear—the principle applies directly only to organisms other than man, organisms that do not consciously control their breeding. Man, if he controls his breeding, may be said, in some sense, not to be living in a state of nature—in which case the losses exacted by mutation need to be examined all over again. Can man alter these losses?

Certainly he can increase them. In fact, he is increasing them now deliberately, though not intentionally, by increasing the general radiation level through medical X rays, atomic bombs and atomic-energy installations. How much he is increasing the mutational losses through his present actions we do not yet know; nor do we know how much he will increase the general radiation level in the future. We play with atoms because we believe there are benefits to be gained from our play. We know there are losses. Ethics is not so well-developed a science that it can tell us how to balance possible profits and certain losses. At the present time, unavoidable mutations cause the production of about 2,000,000 defective babies per year throughout the world. Suppose we increase radiation to such a level that it brings about an ultimate increase in the number of defective babies produced each year by 200,000. Is this a trivial addition or not? Is it small in comparison to the gains brought by atomic energy? How can we say? It is a small wonder that men of equal intelligence and Christianity come up with opposing answers.

Another of the impotence principles of biology, and of sociology, is this—competition is inescapable. The form of competition and the participants may change; but it is always with us. A species that is not numerous competes principally against other species; as it increases in number, the situation changes. The "successful" species end by becoming its own principal competitor. So it is with man, now. The world, in spite of comic-strip science, is a limited one. Man, freed of the population-controlling factors of predators and disease organisms, must—willy-nilly, like it or not—control his own numbers by competition with his own kind. By taking thought, he can elect the kind of competition he employs; but he cannot escape all kinds. This is not to imply that the election is a trivial matter. Surely there are few who would not prefer the endemic celibacy of the Irish to the ritual blood sacrifices of the Aztecs, who, at the dedication of the temple of Huit-zilopochtli in 1486, slaughtered at least 20,000 victims—by the most conservative accounts—tearing the hearts out of the living bodies. There surely can be no serious question as to which behavior is preferable, but we should note that, though both practices have a religious "reason," both are, in the eyes of a biologist, competitive techniques associated with the threat of overpopulation, however unconscious of that threat the practitioners may be. The question is not whether competitive techniques shall be employed, but what techniques and by whom.

The game must go on; that is nature's command. But it is up to man to determine the ground rules and the teams. The determination of the rules is principally the responsibility of the specialist in ethics. The delineation of the teams—well, that is a task for which many disciplines are needed. It may be that no synthesis, of all the relevant considerations is yet possible. But such a synthesis is one that we must work toward. The biologist, with the wisdom gained from a century's preoccupation with evolution, has some things to say about the choosing of the teams.

Any species that becomes one big melting pot of genes puts—to mix metaphors—all its eggs in one basket. If circumstances change rapidly, it may be unable to adapt, and so will perish. Conspicuous success in evolution, as in human affairs, is all too likely to be the prelude to extinction. That the dinosaurs should have become extinct at the end of the Mesozoic Era is no cause for wonder; what needs explaining is how such highly successful forms lasted so long.

It is not that the relatively unsuccessful have a better chance of survival because of their deficiencies. Rather, their advantage comes when their lack of success results in the species' being broken up into many separate breeding populations, among which there is very little interchange of genes. Under these conditions, there is a great increase in variety within the species, each isolated population necessarily differentiating into a different race; how different will depend on many factors, including the extent of environmental differences. With a greater variety of harmonious genotypes in existence, the species is better adapted to face a varying and unpredictable future. Not all of its breeding populations may survive a change; but the chance that at least some will is greater than the chance of survival of a single, large population. And those races that survive a change can then repopulate regions left vacant by those that have succumbed.

Such is the picture presented to us by a spelling out of the consequences of biological inheritance. But man is subject also to a kind of inheritance that we may call cultural. Will this alter the picture? We don't know. The Gregor Mendel of cultural inheritance has not yet appeared.

But there are strong intuitive reasons for believing that the mechanism of cultural inheritance will, if anything, merely increase the contrast in the picture. The loss of adaptability of a species is the result of the inevitable tendency of a breeding population to become genetically uniform. Surely we have seen enough of social power to realize that the pressure toward uniformity is even greater in the cultural realm than in the biological.

To the biologist it is clear that the best chances for man's long-time survival depend on the fragmentation of the species into well-separated populations. But it would be foolhardy to say what form the separation should take. It might be a matter of nations, as we know them; or some sort of caste system that would permit genetic isolation with geographic unity; or—far more likely—some new kind of communities: neither nation nor caste nor anything yet conceived.

In postulating a new world are we adding but one more "utopia" to library shelves that are already too well stocked with these childish wish fulfillments? I think not, for what we have just suggested differs in significant ways from the classical utopias. These dream worlds, however much they vary, agree in two characteristics. The societies they sketch have a high degree of rigidity and finality; and they seek to eliminate all waste, which is variously conceived in terms of economic waste, human suffering or moral turpitude. The student of biological evolution cannot accept a utopia that embodies either of these features. Evolution is an unending process, in which waste plays an indispensable role. Until proof to the contrary is forthcoming, the evolutionist must assume that man is a part of nature. The biologist sees no end-state for man and his society, which must continue evolving until the day of his extinction. No one has conceived any substitute for the mechanism of evolution (whether biological or social) that does not necessarily involve variation and selection—that is to say, waste. Man, the slender reed that thinks, can alter the force and direction of natural forces somewhat, but only within limits. The wisdom of so doing is always questionable. Who is so wise as to descry the lineaments of man 1000 millenniums from now, using these visions as guides for consciously warping the course of human evolution? And as for waste, the more we try to eliminate it, the more we are impressed with its protean changeability and elusiveness. The time-study man who saves 1000 man-hours by altering work procedures, may be astonished to find himself faced with a sitdown strike that costs 1,000,000 man-hours. Reducing the waste of walking to work by inventing horseless carriages may ultimately double the time wasted in transportation by making possible the modern city and its congestion. And so it goes. We do not yet have a scientific theory of waste, but all men of experience recognize its ubiquity and its inevitability. We can often exchange one kind of waste for another; and we can sometimes—

though not as often as we like—decrease it somewhat in amount. But always we must live with it. If we are wise, we even make waste work for us a bit.

But though we may never be able to get rid of waste entirely, it is only natural—or rather, human—that we should try to diminish it as much as possible. Spontaneous mutations entail waste; can we do anything about this? In one sense we cannot. The Haldane-Muller principle tells us that each gene mutation must be paid for by one gene elimination—"genetic death," Muller calls it. Genetic death—which is not really death—is a subdivisible quantity; it may occur by degrees and over many generations. A lethal gene kills at one fell stroke—this is death as we ordinarily conceive it. But a gene that has a selective worth of only 90 per cent (as compared with a normal gene) diminishes the reproductivity of every individual in which it shows by 10 per cent. If we multiply the fraction of the population that suffers this loss by the amount of loss each individual suffers, we come out with the number 1, no matter what the selective worth. This means that each new, bad mutation is ultimately eliminated completely, and that it "kills" a total of one individual, which it may do by "killing" fractions of several individuals. But it does not follow from this that there is nothing that can be done to diminish the loss to human beings. To say that nothing can be done is to assert that death is the only form of human waste, a thesis that surely few would hold. The sublethal gene does not merely diminish the reproductivity of its possessor, it also diminishes his vigor, his health, his *joie de vivre*. We would be little concerned if genetic death were the only consequence of Huntington's chorea, Mongolism, phenylketonuria, pyloric stenosis, or fibrocystic disease of the pancreas. But these conditions cause other losses that we state in terms of human suffering. These losses can be reduced.

Until very recent times, the only method of attacking the problem of suffering was by medicine. Medicine is surely one of the glories of mankind, but we are now perceiving its limitations. For a disease in which it is accurate to say that the hereditary component is negligible—say, for smallpox—medicine has been an unalloyed blessing. But where the hereditary component is great—for instance, in hemophilia—we have our doubts. In such conditions recourse to somatic medicine only delays genetic death while increasing human suffering. Hemophiliacs are now kept alive by frequent, sometimes daily, blood transfusions. We can, if we wish, encourage them to have children. Suppose we saw to it that hemophiliacs had, on the average, precisely as many children as normal people: what would be the result? Genetic death would thus be completely eliminated, but the cost in suffering would be established as a perpetual and continuing cost, a kind of overhead of misery. However small the cost might be per generation, it would increase without limit as time went on. Every bad mutation is a sort of fine levied against mankind. We can either pay the fine promptly or we can delay or avoid payment altogether—by paying in another way.

We are in the position of the traffic violator who either can pay a fifty-dollar fine once in court or can pay one-dollar hush money every week to a dishonest officer to keep from having the violation reported. In the long run, even the cheapest blackmail charge mounts up to more than the most expensive fine. In the long run, unobstructed genetic death is the cheapest way to pay for the unavoidable misfortune of mutation.

Mutation is a form of waste which, manage it though we will, we must in some sense accept. It is inevitable. It is the stuff from which are fashioned new adaptations to the world. In this realization we are brought back to an insight that is old, very old; much older than the theory of evolution. When we come to think of it, we realize that what we call charity owes its origin at least in part to a subconscious realization of the value of waste. Most interesting of early prescriptions for charity is the Jewish "law of the corner," which is given thus in Leviticus 19:9–10: "And when ye reap the harvest of your land, thou shalt not wholly reap the corners of thy field, neither shalt thou gather the gleanings of thy harvest. And thou shalt not glean thy vineyard, neither shalt thou gather every grape of thy vineyard; thou shalt leave them for the poor and stranger. . . ." Such a directive sprang, no doubt, in part from a tender heart; but it may also have indicated an embryonic recognition of the danger of an unmodified competition in human affairs—a recognition that if competition were pure and unbridled, the more efficient man (the landowner) would starve out him who was less so (the poor and the stranger). Coupled with this was a surmise that perhaps complete efficiency might not always be best or right.

In Deuteronomy 24:19, there is a further injunction: "When thou cuttest down thine harvest in thy field, and hast forgot a sheaf in the field, thou shalt not go again to fetch it: it shall be for the stranger, for the fatherless, and for the widow. . . ." Thus there came into being that curious entity of Jewish practice known as "that-which-is-left-through-forgetfulness," which belongs to the poor. The devout were urged always to see to it that something was left through forgetfulness. It is certainly difficult to remember to forget. It is no wonder that the principle of the deliberate tithe—one tenth of one's income given to charity—later replaced so operationally difficult a procedure as deliberate forgetfulness.

Recent developments of the theory of evolution by Sewall Wright and R. A. Fisher have shown us that evolution also proceeds most effectively when the competitive process is somewhat interfered with. It is highly probable that the same principle applies to the social evolution of man. Countries that have been fully populated for long periods of time—for example, classical China—have produced a negligible amount of science. The reason is not difficult to find. Science—pure science—is, in its inception, pure waste. An item of information in pure science "pays off" in a practical way only after it has long been in existence and has been combined with other items of pure science. We are reminded of the new mutation, which is almost always bad, but which—if protected somewhat—may eventually be able to combine with other and similarly "wasteful" genes to produce a new and superior constellation of genes. Prosperity is the great protector of novel thought. A people whose nose is constantly to the grindstone of poverty cannot look up to see the world as it is; all that exists is the nose and the grindstone. A people living under completely Malthusian conditions cannot discover even so much as the Malthusian principle. Science is not produced by eternally busy, wretched people. The flowering of science in the western world in the last four centuries paralleled the increase in prosperity. Cause? Effect? Both. However the new science got started—prosperity was only a necessary condition, not a sufficient one—once started, it produced more prosperity as an effect which fed back into the system as a cause. Science and technology make a circular system that produces wealth and material progress.

Can this system go on forever? Who can say? It is not without its enemies, and among the most important of these today we must count the ever-increasing population of mankind and the "other-directed" men that crowding produces. An other-directed man—to use David Riesman's phrase—is an animal who tends to be intolerant of the independence of thought that is indispensable for the advancement of science.

There is need for the spirit of science to move into fields not now called science, into fields where tradition still holds court. We can hardly expect a committee to acquiesce in the dethronement of tradition. Only an individual can do that, an individual who is not responsible to the mob. Now that the truly independent man of wealth has disappeared, now that the independence of the academic man is fast disappearing, where are we to find the conditions of partial alienation and irresponsibility needed for the highest creativity?

If we solve this problem, we can expect progress to be made in fields more important to man's welfare than is science as presently conceived. Social inheritance will be based on new foundations, and ways will be found to secure the blessings of nonmaterial inheritance without nullifying the implications of genetic recombination. Light will be thrown on the problem of the value of life.

Authors of the greatest persuasiveness seem to be convinced that tomorrow is the world of the other-directed man. Perhaps they are right. No one sees how this eventuality may be easily avoided in a Pasteurian world.

However, no fate may ever be said to be an inevitable one for man, for merely saying so may alter the truth. (Here is a mode of truth, undreamed of and unallowed for in what we now call science. Here is a problem that requires its own Bolyai and Lobachevsky.) Even other-directed men may be rational, and if rational, may be convinced of the necessity of cherishing those not of their own kind. The inner-directed man, he who is answerable only to his own conscience, is always a thorny tablemate, doubly so when Nature's board is crowded. To ask that all men be inner-directed would be quixotic in the extreme; but it is not unreasonable to ask that other-directed men add the care and nurture of a small corps of inner-directed men to their tithing duties. It is not planning that is needed here, and certainly not organization. It is, rather, a systematic allowance for waste, for heterodoxy for the unforeseeable. It is perhaps not even understanding that is demanded —that would be asking too much of other-directed man—but something in the nature of faith. Faith in the future, and faith in the fruitfulness of waste, properly allowed for.

Those who have painted pictures of an organized heaven have, implicitly or otherwise, appealed to the esthetic sense in man to try to gain assent to their plans. We know now that a completely planned heaven is either impossible or unbearable. We know that it is not true that design can come only out of planning. Out of luxuriant waste, winnowed by selection, come designs more beautiful and in greater variety than ever man could plan. This is the lesson of Nature that Darwin has spelled out for us. Man, now that he makes himself, cannot do better than to emulate Nature's example in allowing for waste and encouraging novelty. There is grandeur in this view of life as a complex of cybernetic systems that produce adaptedness without foresight, design without planning, and progress without dictation. From the simplest means, man, now master of his own fate, may evolve societies of a variety and novelty—yes, and even of a beauty— that no man living can now foresee.

III

Birth Control

The Ancient and Honorable History of Contraception

No longer under a taboo, the subject of birth control can at last be freely discussed and its implications explored. It is about time.

In the United States the taboo was given legal sanction by that most fascinating character, Anthony Comstock, who headed the Society for the Suppression of Vice. He was obsessed by sex. As a result of his activities, Congress in 1873 passed the notorious "Comstock Law," which made it a criminal offense not only to import, mail, or transport in interstate commerce "any article of medicine for the prevention of conception or for causing abortion," but made it equally criminal to import, mail or transport in interstate commerce "obscene literature." Obscene literature from the very first was interpreted to include not only the unexpurgated edition of **The Arabian Nights,** but also all descriptions of contraceptive devices and methods. Not even doctors could exchange such knowledge among themselves using the means of interstate commerce. The taboo was locked into the legal system. As late as 1960, the leading publisher of case abstracts for the legal profession did not include in the index of its digests the heading of "Birth Control." Cases involving this subject had to be sought under the headings of Obscenity, Abortion, Statutes, Constitutional Law, and Post Office.

Though the law lagged behind, Comstockery was pretty well brought to an end in the first half of the twentieth century. Better methods of birth control were developed, and knowledge of them was disseminated by a host of courageous workers, of whom the nurse Margaret Sanger in this country and the botanist Marie Stopes in England deserve special notice. Laws and customs restricting the broadcasting of information were eroded away. However, because the subject had been so long under a taboo, the lack of literature led to a general impression that birth control was essentially a modern thing—a belief that served the ends of those who opposed it, for it is always easy to equate modernism with sinfulness. All historical support for this belief was removed in 1936 by Norman E. Himes' **Medical History of Contraception** (Baltimore: Williams & Wilkins). The title of this work is itself significant; the book is much broader in scope than its title and should perhaps have been called a "Social History of Contraception." The adjective **medical** was probably chosen to get the book through the mails.

In addition to Himes' book, we now have another excellent history by John T. Noonan, Jr., namely **Contraception,** published in 1965 by the

Harvard University Press, and republished in paperback in 1967 by the New American Library. The subtitle of Noonan's book reads: "A History of Its Treatment by the Catholic Theologians and Canonists." Like Himes' book, the coverage is broader than the title page would indicate. As both histories show, knowledge of contraception is found in numerous papyruses from Egypt dating back at least to 1900 B.C. Although public discussion of contraception may be a new thing, interest in the subject is not. As Himes put the matter: "Men and women have always longed for both fertility and sterility, each at its appointed time and in its chosen circumstances. **This has been a universal aim, whether people have always been conscious of it or not.**"

81

Be Fruitful and Multiply

The Bible
Genesis 1:26–28 (King James version)

And God said, Let us make man in our image, after our likeness: and let them have dominion over the fish of the sea, and over the fowl of the air, and over the cattle, and over the earth, and over every creeping thing that creepeth upon the earth.

So God created man in his own image, in the image of God created he him; male and female created he them.

And God blessed them, and God said unto them, Be fruitful, and multiply, and replenish the earth, and subdue it: and have dominion over the fish of the sea, and over the fowl of the air, and over every living thing that moveth upon the earth.

"Nature" as Norm in Tertullian

Arthur O. Lovejoy
1874–1963

The traditional Roman Catholic argument against the licitness of contraception is based on the idea that chemicals and devices are "unnatural," and on an identification of "unnatural" with evil. The basis for this argument is found in the writings of the third-century jurist and theologian, Tertullian (ca. 160–ca. 230), as further modified and interpreted by Thomas Aquinas. An analysis of Aquinas' works is presented in a later selection. Here we take up Tertullian's ideas as analyzed by Arthur Lovejoy, a famous historian of ideas at Johns Hopkins University for many years. This selection is taken from his **Essays in the History of Ideas** (Baltimore: Johns Hopkins Press, 1948).

1948

But while the enjoyment of man of whatever is "natural" is good, indulgence in what is not "natural" is evil; and Tertullian's notion of what is contrary to nature is undeniably far-reaching. It forbids any alteration of things from the character which God has chosen to give to them; it extends by implication to everything artificial, though Tertullian does not carry the implication through consistently; if he had, he would have been (what we have seen that he was not) a cultural primitivist of the most extreme sort. "What God was unwilling to produce ought not to be produced [by men]. Those things therefore are not best by nature which are not from God, the Author of nature. Consequently, they must be understood to be from the Devil, the disturber of nature; for what is not God's must necessarily be his rival's." One specific moral which Tertullian draws from this premise is that dyed fabrics should not be used for clothing. The materials of garments should be left in their natural colors, since "that which he has not himself produced is not pleasing to God." It cannot be supposed that "he was unable to command sheep to be born with purple or sky-blue fleeces." But if he was able to do so, but has not, "then plainly he was unwilling." [1] The specific moral here strikes us now as trivial and silly; but other deductions from the same premise were recurrently to be heard throughout history, and may still be heard today, in arguments against one or another exercise of human "art"—of man's intelligence and skill—to add to or amend what is supposed to be the "natural" order of things. It had not occurred to Tertullian—though Democritus had made the observation before Shakespeare[2]—that "That art which you say adds to nature is an art which nature makes; . . . the art itself is nature."

From similar premises Tertullian derives a proof of the immorality of the pagan practice of wearing crowns of flowers on the head. *Major efficitur ratio christianarum observationum, cum illas etiam natura defendit, quae prima omnium disciplina est:* "the argument for Christian observances becomes stronger when even Nature, which is the first of all teaching, supports them." How then is the teaching of Nature with respect to the propriety of wearing floral chaplets to be known? By observing that, while Nature—or "our God, who is the God of nature"—evidently intended us to enjoy "the pleasures afforded by his other creatures," since he provided us with various sense-organs of which the exercise is naturally pleasurable, there is no such *natural* pleasure in wearing a wreath of flowers on the head. For the sensible pleasures attached to flowers are those of sight and smell. "With sight and smell, then, make use of flowers, for these are the senses by which they were meant to be enjoyed." But you can neither see the color nor smell the fragrance of flowers on top of your head. *Ergo:*

> It is as much against nature to crave a flower with the head as to crave food with the ear or sound with the nostril. But everything which is against nature is deservedly known amongst all men as a monstrous thing; but still more among us it is condemned as a sacrilege against God who is the Lord and Author of Nature.[3]

The invocation of "nature" as a norm in this fashion could thus, with a little ingenuity, serve as a rhetorical device for damning almost any custom of the pagans which differed from those of Christians.

But the crucial and difficult issue for Tertullian arose when, holding that everything *proprie naturale* is good and designed for man's use and enjoyment, he was compelled to face the fact that human beings are endowed with sex. The glorification of virginity and the feeling of something inherently evil in sex had by the early third century become widely prevalent, and probably almost universal, in the Christian moral temper and teaching—however limited its application in practice. And with this temper Tertullian clearly was sympathetic. Yet it could not well be denied that sex and the pleasures attaching to it are "natural"; certainly God had "produced" it; and in view of the premises to which Tertullian was committed, he could not escape the question to which Pope was to give the most pointed expression in the eighteenth century:

> Can that offend great Nature's God
> Which Nature's self inspires?

And the answer which the premises required seemed evident: to reject or despise this gift of Nature could be no less than sacrilege against the Author of Nature. Scripture, moreover, taught that procreation is a duty laid upon mankind by the divine command in Eden. Logic, and the weight of biblical authority, thus pressed Tertullian towards one view on the highly practical question whether celibacy or marriage should be the rule—or at least the ideal—for Christians; the sentiment of his fellow-believers, which he shared, and an already potent tradition, pressed him towards the opposite view; and his utterances on the subject make evident the inner conflict which resulted.

In a few passages his piety towards "nature" leads him to a reverential glorification of marriage and of the sexual act, and to the praise of maternity, not virginity, as sacred. His scorn of the contrary attitude is expressed in a sharp epigram which deserves to have been remembered: *natura veneranda est, non erubescenda.*

DE ANIMA

> Nature is to be reverenced, not blushed at.[4] It is lust, not the act itself, that makes sexual union shameful; it is excess, not the [marital] state as such, that is unchaste; for the state itself has been blessed by God: "Be ye fruitful and multiply." Upon excess, indeed, he has laid a curse—adulteries and fornications and the frequenting of brothels. Now in this usual function of the sexes which brings male and female together—I mean, in ordinary intercourse—we know that the soul and the body both take part: the soul through the desire, the body through its realization, the soul through the impulse, the body through the act.[5]

His own marital experience, moreover, moved Tertullian to eulogize in the highest terms the union of believers—a union involving both flesh and spirit. In a writing addressed to his wife he exclaims: "How can we sufficiently describe the happiness of that marriage which the Church approves, which the offering confirms, and the benediction signs and seals; which the angels report to Heaven, and the Father accepts as valid! . . . what kind of 'yoke' is that of two believers who share in one hope, one desire, one discipline, and the same service? Both are brethren, both fellow-servants, with no separation of spirit or of flesh—nay, rather, they are 'two in one flesh,' and where the flesh is one, so is the spirit also." [6] It was not in this tone that Paul had written—still less, that Augustine was to write—of marriage.

Nor, in truth, is it in this tone that Tertullian always or usually writes. His most frequent passages on the subject express a violent effort to reconcile the *veneratio naturae* which he had extolled, and a deference to the divine injunction in Genesis, with the feeling, which he evidently could not repress, that virginity is after all the better state. Even in the *Ad uxorem* he exhorts his wife, if she should survive him, not to marry again. To marry once is lawful, since "the union of man and woman . . . was blest by God as the *seminarium generis humani* and devised by him for the replenishing of the earth and the furnishing of the world." Nowhere in Scripture is marriage prohibited; it is recognized as a "good thing." But "what is better than this good thing we learn from the Apostle, who permits marriage but prefers abstinence." Most to be praised, then, are those who from the moment of their baptism practise continence, and those wedded pairs "who by mutual consent cancel the debt of matrimony—voluntary eunuchs for the sake of their desire for the kingdom of heaven." [7] Second marriage, however, is positively immoral; it is a kind of adultery. Tertullian assails the Marcionites for rejecting marriage altogether. "The law of nature," though it is "opposed to lechery . . . does not forbid connubial intercourse"; it condemns "concupiscence" only in the sense of "extravagant, unnatural and enormous sins." Yet Tertullian at once proceeds to assert "the superiority of the other and higher sanctity, preferring continence to marriage, but by no means prohibiting the latter. For my hostility is directed against those who are for destroying the God of marriage, not those who follow after chastity." "We do not reject marriage but only avoid it, we do not prescribe celibacy (*sanctitas*) but only urge it—keeping it as a good and, indeed, the better state, if each man seeks after it in so far as he has the strength to do so; yet openly defending marriage when hostile attacks are made upon it as a filthy thing, to the disparagement of the Creator." [8]

Yet Tertullian himself is here manifestly rejecting "the God of marriage" and "the God of nature," since, if celibacy is the more perfect state, it must be the state in which the Creator intended and desires human beings to live. At best marriage could only be regarded as a concession to the weakness of fallen man—a venial sin, perhaps, but nevertheless a sin. The attempt of Tertullian to reconcile his two positions by means of a distinction between marriage as "good" and virginity as "better" only makes the incongruity of the two strains in his teaching the more evident. For it could not well be held to be morally approvable knowingly to choose "the good" rather than "the better." Tertullian himself is constrained to admit that "what is [merely] permitted is not 'good,' " and that "a thing is not 'good' merely because it is not evil." [9]

Finally, in some writings of Tertullian's latest period, the *Exhortatio castitatis* and the *De pudicitia,* the ascetic strain becomes wholly dominant, and the *veneratio naturae,* so far as sex is concerned, is quite forgotten. "Flesh" *is* now represented as at war with "soul," and all sexual indulgence is condemned: "let us renounce fleshly things, in order that we may finally bring forth fruits of the spirit"; "those who wish to be received into Paradise ought to cease from that thing from which Paradise is intact." [10] Not only second marriages but even first marriages are nothing but a species of fornication, for "the latter also consist of that which is defiling" (*et ipsae constant ex eo quod est stuprum*); only virginity has no *affinitas stupri* at all. Tertullian too has in the end come to "blush at nature." He still, it is true, feels some obligation to reconcile his present position with the biblical command, "Increase and multiply"; for this purpose he falls back upon the theory of progress in the revelation of religious and moral truth. What was legitimate or even obligatory under the Old Dispensation is not necessarily legitimate under the New. Marriage is not to be condemned as *always* evil, because, for those living in the former age, it was not blameworthy. You do not "condemn" a tree when the time has come to cut it down; nevertheless you cut it down. "So also the marital state requires the hook and sickle of celibacy, not as an evil thing, but as one ripe to be abolished."

---

[1] *De cultu feminarum,* I, 8. The injunction against wearing dyed fabrics is here addressed to women, but it obviously applied to both sexes. Among other things which Tertullian held, apparently for the same reason, to be against nature, were play-acting and the shows of the circus, in which the faces and forms of men and women were disfigured—and shaving. "Will God be pleased with one who applies the razor to himself and completely changes his features?" (*De spectaculis* 23). This practice had similarly been condemned by the Cynic moralists as "contrary to nature."

[2] Cf. *Primitivism in Antiquty,* 207–8.

[3] *De corona* 5.

[4] For the Latin reader there was a possible double meaning here. One of the senses of *natura* was "the genitalia"; and the word is used in this sense by Tertullian in *De anima* 46. In the text, below, "usual function" is probably the better rendering of *solemne officium,* which, however, may possibly mean "sacred duty."

[5] Cf. also *De carne Christi* 4: The Marcionites look upon the phenomena of parturition as disgusting; in doing so they "spit upon the *veneratio naturae*"; childbirth is in truth to be regarded as *pro natura religiosum.* So *Adv. Marcionem* III, 11: *Age iam, perora illa sanctissima et reveranda opera naturae;* the particular works of nature here characterized as "most sacred and deserving of veneration" are gestation and birth.

[6] *Ad uxorem* II, 8.

[7] *Adv. Marcionem,* I, 29; *De Monogamia,* 3.

[8] *Adv. Marcionem,* I, 29.

[9] *Ad uxorem* I, 4.

[10] *Exhortatio castitatis* 10, 13.

83

On Sex, Love, and Contraception

Thomas Robert Malthus
1766–1834

The two passages below from Malthus' **Essay** show that he was not unaware of the human element in the population problem. The obscure first passage is traditionally held to have reference to the condom, or, as it was commonly known to the English of his time, the "French letter."

1798

Chapter VIII

Mr. Condorcet, however, goes on to say that should the period which he conceives to be so distant ever arrive, the human race, and the advocates [of] the perfectibility of man, need not be alarmed at it. He then proceeds to remove the difficulty in a manner which I profess not to understand. Having observed, that the ridiculous prejudices of superstition would by that time have ceased to throw over morals a corrupt and degrading austerity, he alludes either to a promiscuous concubinage, which would prevent breeding, or to something else as unnatural. To remove the difficulty in this way will, surely, in the opinion of most men, be to destroy that virtue and purity of manners, which the advocates of equality, and of the perfectibility of man profess to be the end and object of their views.

Chapter IX

We have supposed Mr. Godwin's system of society once completely established. But it is supposing an impossibility. The same causes in nature which would destroy it so rapidly, were it once established, would prevent the possibility of its establishment. And upon what grounds we can presume a change in these natural causes, I am utterly at a loss to conjecture. No move towards the extinction of the passion between the sexes has taken place in the five or six thousand years that the world has existed. Men in the decline of life have in all ages declaimed a passion which they have ceased to feel, but with as little reason as success. Those who from coldness

186

of constitutional temperament have never felt what love is, will surely be allowed to be very incompetent judges with regard to the power of this passion to contribute to the sum of pleasurable sensations in life. Those who have spent their youth in criminal excesses and have prepared for themselves, as the comforts of their age, corporal debility and mental remorse may well inveigh against such pleasures as vain and futile, and unproductive of lasting satisfaction. But the pleasures of pure love will bear the contemplation of the most improved reason, and the most exalted virtue. Perhaps there is scarcely a man who has once experienced the genuine delight of virtuous love, however great his intellectual pleasures may have been, that does not look back to the period as the sunny spot in his whole life, where his imagination loves to bask, which he recollects and contemplates with the fondest regrets, and which he would most wish to live over again. The superiority of intellectual to sensual pleasures consists rather in their filling up more time, in their having a larger range, and in their being less liable to satiety, than in their being more real and essential.

Intemperance in every enjoyment defeats its own purpose. A walk in the finest day through the most beautiful country, if pursued too far, ends in pain and fatigue. The most wholesome and invigorating food, eaten with an unrestrained appetite, produces weakness instead of strength. Even intellectual pleasures, though certainly less liable than others to satiety, pursued with too little intermission, debilitate the body, and impair the vigour of the mind. To argue against the reality of these pleasures from their abuse seems to be hardly just. Morality, according to Mr. Godwin, is a calculation of consequences, or, as Archdeacon Paley very justly expresses it, the will of God, as collected from general expediency. According to either of these definitions, a sensual pleasure not attended with the probability of unhappy consequences does not offend against the laws of morality, and if it be pursued with such a degree of temperance, as to leave the most ample room for intellectual attainments, it must undoubtedly add to the sum of pleasurable sensations in life. Virtuous love, exalted by friendship, seems to be that sort of mixture of sensual and intellectual enjoyment particularly suited to the nature of man, and most powerfully calculated to awaken the sympathies of the soul, and produce the most exquisite gratifications.

Mr. Godwin says, in order to shew the evident inferiority of the pleasures of sense, "Strip the commerce of the sexes of all its attendant circumstances, and it would be generally despised." He might as well say to a man who admired trees: strip them of their spreading branches and lovely foliage, and what beauty can you see in a bare pole? But it was the tree with the branches and foliage, and not without them, that excited admiration. One feature of an object, may be as distinct, and excite as different emotions, from the aggregate, as any two things the most remote, as a beautiful woman, and a map of Madagascar. It is "the symmetry of person, the vivacity, the voluptuous softness of temper, the affectionate kindness of feelings, the imagination and the wit" of a woman that excite the passion of love, and not the mere distinction of her being a female.

84

Conscience and Courage: The Life of Francis Place

Shortly after Malthus' essay was published (1798), William Godwin wrote Malthus to suggest that there was an escape from the dismal consequence of the population principle—an escape made possible by man's conscious rationality. Man did not have to couple like an unthinking animal; he could, if he wished, restrain himself.

Of long-continued restraint, Malthus had little hope. But he admitted to Godwin that if marriage could be delayed until a man was financially able to support a family; and if before his marriage a man was strictly continent; and if all men would live by this rule, then the unfortunate consequences of population could be averted. Malthus called living by such a rule "moral restraint," a discussion of which he introduced into the second edition (1803) of his **Essay.** Malthus was adamant in insisting that sexual behavior within marriage must not be impeded by unnatural devices. On page 512 of the appendix to the fifth edition of his **Essay** (1817), he wrote:

> I should always particularly reprobate any artificial and unnatural modes of checking population, both on account of their immorality and their tendency to remove a necessary stimulus to industry. If it were possible for each married couple to limit by a wish the number of their children, there is certainly reason to fear that the indolence of the human race would be very greatly increased, and that neither the population of individual countries nor of the whole earth would ever reach its natural and proper extent. But the restraints which I have recommended are quite of a different character. They are not only pointed out by reason and sanctioned by religion, but tend in the most marked manner to stimulate industry.

To his total population theory this new addition of Malthus gave a rather curious turn. In 1798 he had said that only misery and vice could keep population under control. In 1803 he had added "moral restraint" to the acceptable corrective feedbacks, though he seemed dubious of its effectiveness. Now, in 1817, he decided that even if a truly effective and painless corrective feedback were to be found it should not be used because men need the misery of overpopulation to make them industrious! He never stated his new position as blatantly as this, of course, but his relegation of this statement to an appendix is evidence that forces of psychological denial were at work.

In the light of all this it is rather curious that the birth-control movement that arose in the nineteenth century should have been called "neomalthusianism," an identification that must surely have made Malthus turn in his grave. Only one country now lives by malthusian ethics, and that is Ireland, where delayed marriage (with, apparently, continence outside of marriage) is the principal check to population growth.

The contramalthusian approach to population problems was taken by a slightly younger contemporary of Malthus, one Francis Place. Both for what he did and for his extraordinarily courageous character, this man deserves to be more widely remembered. Unlike Malthus, a well-to-do gentleman who knew of poverty only by public report, Place knew it from the most intimate personal experience. His father was a scoundrel, governed, as Place tells us, "almost wholly by his passions and animal sensations. . . . He never spoke to any of his children in the way of conversation; the boys never ventured to ask him a question, since the only answer which could be anticipated was a blow. If he were coming along a passage or any narrow place such as a doorway, and was met by either me or my brother, he always made a blow at us with his fist for coming in his way. If we attempted to retreat he would make us come forward, and as certainly as we came forward he would knock us down." Respite from this treatment came only on those frequent occasions when his father deserted the home for several months, leaving the mother to support the family by her needlework.

At fourteen, Francis was apprenticed to a leather-breeches maker. His life was filled with work and the pandemonium of a London street-life that Hogarth had earlier depicted in his **Gin Lane.** Though apparently participating fully in this life, he was saved from its worst consequences by two influences: a schoolteacher who interested him in books, and the love of a good wife, whom he married when he was twenty.

Immensely industrious and canny, Place, by the time he was thirty, had worked his way to prosperity, becoming the owner of a fashionable men's shop in Charing Cross. Unlike many self-made men, he never lost his sympathy for the underdog. From beginning to end he was a leader in labor organizations, which were then regarded by the vested interests as little short of criminal conspiracies. He led a double life in Charing Cross. In the front of the shop he was a modest and seemingly uneducated servant of gentlemen and fops; in his quarters at the rear, after hours, he read from his excellent personal library or held conversations with labor leaders and men of influence in Parliament. A friend of James Mill and an admirer of Bentham, he sought to bring reason into the regulation of public affairs.

Place had 15 children, of whom 5 died in infancy—probably the normal survival rate of the time. He himself could support such a family, but he knew that ordinary laborers could not, and that the bargaining power of laborers was immensely weakened by their acute poverty. Only by controlling their numbers could laborers expect to achieve freedom and power, Place believed. How was this to be achieved? By malthusian "moral restraint"? Place, who had inherited the vigor of his father, had no confidence in this line of action. Writing to his friend George Ensor, he spoke bitterly of "moral restraint, which has served so well in the instances of you & I—and Mill, and Wakefield—mustering among us no less I believe than 36 children—rare fellows we to teach moral restraint."

What was to be done? Talking this over together, Place and his close friend James Mill agreed that propaganda of some sort was necessary. Mill was the first to broach the matter in public, in his article on "Colony" for the **Encyclopaedia Britannica** Supplement published in 1818. There, in discussing the best means of checking population, Mill introduced these guarded remarks:

> And yet, if the superstitions of the nursery were discarded, and the principle of utility kept steadily in view, a solution might not be very difficult to be found; and the means of drying up one of the most copious sources of human evil . . . might be seen to be neither doubtful nor difficult to be applied.

Three years later Mill returned to the subject in his **Elements of Political Economy** where he spoke of "prudence; by which, either marriages are sparingly contracted, or care is taken that children, beyond a certain number, shall not be the fruit." The sentiment was clear, but the writing could hardly be said to constitute a "How to do it" manual.

Place felt that more explicit directions were called for, but was dissuaded by his friends from taking any radical action. His friends rightly pointed out that any overt action in this field would likely cause him to lose the influential position he enjoyed in other matters of reform. Finally, after several years of hesitation, Francis Place took the calculated risk. In the year 1822, he caused to be distributed two handbills: "To the Married of Both Sexes," and "To the Married of Both Sexes in Genteel Life"; and one four-page pamphlet entitled "To the Married of Both Sexes of the Working People." The size of the latter, 3 by 5¾ inches, suggests that it was designed for the pocket, to be disseminated inconspicuously. The text of this pamphlet is reproduced in the next reading.

Place's friends proved to be good prophets. Many of his acquaintances shunned him on the street thereafter, and his political influence was much diminished. He did not complain. Apparently he felt his prestige had been well spent. He continued to be active in public affairs for another two decades, but when he died the obituaries spoke of him as a man largely forgotten. The **Spectator** said: "Few men have done more of the world's work with so little external sign. . . . He was essentially a public man, but his work usually lay behind the curtain. . . . He loved quiet power for the purpose of promoting good ends."

The obscurity that enveloped him and his promotion of birth control steadily deepened during the Victorian era. When his life was written up in the standard British reference work, the **Dictionary of National Biography,** only a single mention was made of his "neomalthusian propaganda." This biography was published in 1896, at which time the shocking subject could be mentioned only in terms of this ironical euphemism. Even as late as 1967, the account of Place's life in the **Encyclopaedia Britannica** included no mention whatever of his birth control activities.

How influential was Place's propaganda? Unfortunately, the conspiracy of silence that blanketed the propaganda also prevented a recording of its effects. How widely distributed was his little pamphlet? How effective was the curious method proposed therein? Why didn't Place propose the use of the condom? The answer to the last question may lie in economics. The vulcanization of rubber had not yet been invented, and the best condoms available—sheep caeca—may have been too expensive for the working class. Or perhaps Place felt that a contraceptive method that depended on the female for its use, rather than the male, was more likely to be used, since it is on the woman that the greatest horrors of overfertility fall. These are only a few of the unanswered questions we have regarding Place's work and its effects.

He who is interested in sociological biology cannot but be irritated with the lacunae in our historical records. The French naturalist J. H. Fabre has said: "History celebrates the battlefields whereon we meet our death, but scorns to speak of the plowed fields whereby we thrive." It is equally silent about the bedrooms wherein the virtues of a people are not only practiced, but also generated. As Malthus pointed out: "Like the commodities in a market, those virtues will be produced in the greatest quantity for which there is the greatest demand." A world filled to overflowing with humanity will not live by the liberal code of ethics that is possible to the people who know the joys of abundance. Freedom and overpopulation can never be bedmates. This tragic truth is apparently not known to those who view with equanimity the burgeoning of our population.

85

To the Married of Both Sexes
of the Working People

Francis Place
1771–1854

1822

This paper is addressed to the reasonable and considerate among you, the most numerous and most useful class of society.

It is not intended to produce vice and debauchery, but to destroy vice, and put an end to debauchery.

It is a great truth, often told and never denied, that when there are too many working people in any trade or manufacture, they are worse paid than they ought to be paid, and are compelled to work more hours than they ought to work.

When the number of working people in any trade or manufacture, has for some years been too great, wages are reduced very low, and the working people become little better than slaves.

When wages have thus been reduced to a very small sum, working people can no longer maintain their children as all good and respectable people wish to maintain their children, but are compelled to neglect them; —to send them to different employments;—to Mills and Manufactories, at a very early age.

The misery of these poor children cannot be described, and need not be described to you, who witness them and deplore them every day of your lives.

Many indeed among you are compelled for a bare subsistence to labour incessantly from the moment you rise in the morning to the moment you lie down again at night, without even the hope of ever being better off.

The sickness of yourselves and your children, the privation and pain and premature death of those you love but cannot cherish as you wish, need only be alluded to. You know all these evils too well.

And, what, you will ask is the remedy?

How are we to avoid these miseries?

The answer is short and plain: the means are easy. Do as other people do, to avoid having more children than they wish to have, and can easily maintain.

What is done by other people is this. A piece of soft sponge is tied by a bobbin or penny ribbon, and inserted just before the sexual intercourse takes place, and is withdrawn again as soon as it has taken place. Many tie a piece of sponge to each end of the ribbon, and they take care not to use the same sponge again until it has been washed.

If the sponge be large enough, that is, as large as a green walnut, or a small apple, it will prevent conception, and thus, without diminishing the pleasures of married life, or doing the least injury to the health of the most delicate woman, both the woman and her husband will be saved from all the miseries which having too many children produces.

By limiting the number of children, the wages both of children and of grown up persons will rise; the hours of working will be no more than they ought to be; you will have some time for recreation, some means of enjoying yourselves rationally, some means as well as some time for your own and your children's moral and religious instruction.

At present, every respectable mother trembles for the fate of her daughters as they grow up. Debauchery is always feared. This fear makes many good mothers unhappy. The evil when it comes makes them miserable.

And why is there so much debauchery? Why such sad consequences?

Why? But, because many young men, who fear the consequences which a large family produces, turn to debauchery, and destroy their own happiness as well as the happiness of the unfortunate girls with whom they connect themselves.

Other young men, whose moral and religious feelings deter them from this vicious course, marry early and produce large families, which they are utterly unable to maintain. These are the causes of the wretchedness which afflicts you.

But when it has become the custom here as elsewhere, to limit the number of children, so that none need have more than they wish to have, no man will fear to take a wife, all will be married while young—debauchery will diminish—while good morals, and religious duties will be promoted.

You cannot fail to see that this address is intended solely for your good. It is quite impossible that those who address you can receive any benefit from it, beyond the satisfaction which every benevolent person, every true Christian, must feel, at seeing you comfortable, healthy, and happy.

86

Disguised Infanticide

William L. Langer
1896–

From "Europe's Initial Population Explosion"
American Historical Review, **69**:1–17

1963

For Malthus "the whole train of common diseases and epidemics, wars, plague and famine" were all closely linked to "misery and vice" as positive checks to population growth. But misery and vice also included "extreme poverty, bad nursing of children, excesses of all kinds."

In this context it may be said that in Europe conditions of life among both the rural and urban lower classes—that is, of the vast majority of the population—can rarely have been as bad as they were in the early nineteenth century. Overworked, atrociously housed, undernourished, disease-ridden, the masses lived in a misery that defies the modern imagination. This situation in itself should have drastically influenced the population pattern, but two items in particular must have had a really significant bearing. First, drunkenness: this period must surely have been the golden age of inebriation, especially in the northern countries. The per capita consumption of spirits, on the increase since the sixteenth century, reached unprecedented figures. In Sweden, perhaps the worst-afflicted country, it was estimated at ten gallons of *branvin* and *akvavit* per annum. Everywhere ginshops abounded. London alone counted 447 taverns and 8,659 ginshops in 1836, some of which at least were visited by as many as 5,000–6,000 men, women, and children in a single day.[1]

So grave was the problem of intemperance in 1830 that European rulers welcomed emissaries of the American temperance movement and gave full support to their efforts to organize the fight against the liquor menace. To what extent drunkenness may have affected the life expectancy of its addicts, we can only conjecture. At the very least the excessive use of strong liquor is known to enhance susceptibility to respiratory infections and is often the determining factor in cirrhosis of the liver.[2]

Of even greater and more obvious bearing was what Malthus euphemistically called "bad nursing of children" and what in honesty must be termed disguised infanticide. It was certainly prevalent in the late eighteenth and nineteenth centuries and seems to have been constantly on the increase.[3]

In the cities it was common practice to confide babies to old women nurses or caretakers. The least offense of these "Angelmakers," as they were called in Berlin, was to give the children gin to keep them quiet. For the rest we have the following testimony from Benjamin Disraeli's novel *Sybil* (1845), for which he drew on a large fund of sociological data: "Laudanum and treacle, administered in the shape of some popular elixir, affords these innocents a brief taste of the sweets of existence and, keeping them quiet, prepares them for the silence of their impending grave." "Infanticide," he adds, "is practised as extensively and as legally in England as it is on the banks of the Ganges; a circumstance which apparently has not yet engaged the attention of the Society for the Propagation of the Gospel in Foreign Parts."

It was also customary in these years to send babies into the country to be nursed by peasant women. The well-to-do made their own arrangements, while the lower classes turned their offspring over to charitable nursing bureaus or left them at the foundling hospitals or orphanages that existed in all large cities. Of the operation of these foundling hospitals a good deal is known, and from this knowledge it is possible to infer the fate of thousands of babies that were sent to the provinces for care.[4]

The middle and late eighteenth century was marked by a startling rise in the rate of illegitimacy, the reasons for which have little bearing on the present argument. But so many of the unwanted babies were being abandoned, smothered, or otherwise disposed of that Napoleon in 1811 decreed that the foundling hospitals should be provided with a turntable device, so that babies could be left at these institutions without the parent being recognized or subjected to embarrassing questions. This convenient arrangement was imitated in many countries and was taken full advantage of by the mothers in question. In many cities the authorities complained that unmarried mothers from far and wide were coming to town to deposit their unwanted babies in the accommodating foundling hospitals. The statistics show that of the thousands of children thus abandoned, more than half were the offspring of married couples.

There is good reason to suppose that those in charge of these institutions did the best they could with what soon became an unmanageable problem. Very few of the children could be cared for in the hospitals themselves. The great majority was sent to peasant nurses in the provinces. In any case, most of these children died within a short time, either of malnutrition or neglect or from the long, rough journey to the country.

The figures for this traffic, available for many cities, are truly shocking. In all of France fully 127,507 children were abandoned in the

195

year 1833. Anywhere from 20 to 30 percent of all children born were left to their fate. The figures for Paris suggest that in the years 1817–1820 the "foundlings" comprised fully 36 percent of all births. In some of the Italian hospitals the mortality (under one year of age) ran to 80 or 90 percent. In Paris the *Maison de la Couche* reported that of 4,779 babies admitted in 1818, 2,370 died in the first three months and another 956 within the first year.[5]

The operation of this system was well known at the time, though largely forgotten in the days of birth control. Many contemporaries denounced it as legalized infanticide, and one at least suggested that the foundling hospitals post a sign reading "Children killed at Government expense." Malthus himself, after visting the hospitals at St. Petersburg and Moscow, lavishly endowed by the imperial family and the aristocracy, could not refrain from speaking out:

> Considering the extraordinary mortality which occurs in these institutions, and the habits of licentiousness which they have an evident tendency to create, it may parhaps be truly said that, if a person wished to check population, and were not solicitous about the means, he could not propose a more effective measure than the establishment of a sufficient number of foundling hospitals, unlimited as to their reception of children.

In the light of the available data one is almost forced to admit that the proposal, seriously advanced at the time, that unwanted babies be painlessly asphyxiated in small gas chambers, was definitely humanitarian.[6] Certainly the entire problem of infanticide in the days before widespread practice of contraception deserves further attention and study. It was undoubtedly a major factor in holding down the population, strangely enough in the very period when the tide of population was so rapidly rising.

---

[1] James S. Buckingham, *History and Progress of the Temperance Reformation* (London, 1854), 28 ff.; Adolf Baer, *Der Alcoholismus* (Berlin, 1878), 196, 203 ff.

[2] On the liquor problem, see P. S. White and H. R. Pleasants, *The War of Four Thousand Years* (Philadelphia, 1846), 240 ff.; P. T. Winskill, *The Temperance Movement and Its Workers* (4 vols., London, 1891–92), I, Chap. IV; John C. Woolley and William E. Johnson, *Temperance Progress of the Century* (Philadelphia, 1905), Chap. XV; Johann Bergmann, *Geschichte der anti-Alkoholbestrebungen* (Hamburg, 1907), Chap. XII.

[3] Alexander von Öttingen, *Die Moralstatistik* (3d ed., Erlangen, 1882), 236 ff.

[4] In the years 1804–1814 the average annual number of births in Paris was about 19,500. Of these newcomers, roughly 4,700 were sent to the country by the *Bureau des Nourrices,* and another 4,000 were sent by the foundling hospital (*Maison de la Couche*). With the addition of children privately sent, it appears that a total of about

13,500 babies were involved. (Louis Benoiston de Chateauneuf, *Recherches sur les consommations . . . de la Ville de Paris* [Paris, 1821], 37.)

⁵ Léon Lallemand, *Histoire des enfants abandonnés et delaissés* (Paris, 1885), 207, 276. Among contemporary commentators, see Johnston, *Public Charity in France,* 319 ff.; Frederic von Raumer, *Italy and the Italians* (2 vols., London, 1840), I, 180 ff., 266; II, 80, 284; Richard Ford, *Gleanings from Spain* (London, 1846), Chap. XVII; and among later stddies F. S. Hügel, *Die Findelhäuser und das Findelwesen Europas* (Vienna, 1863), 137 ff.; Arthur Keller and C. J. Klumper, *Säuglingsfürsorge und Kinderschutz in den europäischen Staaten* (2 vols., Berlin, 1912), I, 441 ff.; Joseph J. Spengler, *France Faces Depopulation* (Durham, N. C., 1938), 45 ff.; Roger Mols, *Introduction à la démographie historique des villes d'Europe du XIVᵉ au XVIIIᵉ siècle* (3 vols., Louvain, 1954–56), II, 303 ff.; Krause, "Recent Work in Historical Demography," 164–88; Hélène Bergues, *La prévention des naissances dans la famille* (Paris, 1960), 17 ff.

⁶ "Marcus" (pseudo.), *Essay on Populousness and on the Possibility of Limiting Populousness* (London, 1838). The quotation for Malthus is in the last edition of his *Essay* (6th ed., London, 1826), reprinted by G. T. Bettany (London and New York, 1890), 172.

87

On Woman's Place in Nature

The Rev. William John Knox Little
1839–1918

One can hardly understand the opposition to birth control without knowing something of the attitude toward women that prevailed for many centuries. The following passage is taken from pp. 151–152 of Eugene A. Hecker, **A Short History of Women's Rights,** New York: Putnam, 1910; it states explicitly that which was probably the unconscious attitude of most men in the western world.

1880

God made himself to be born of a woman to sanctify the virtue of endurance; loving submission is an attribute of a woman; men are logical, but women, lacking this quality, have an intricacy of thought. There are those who think women can be taught logic; this is a mistake. They can never by any power of education arrive at the same mental status as

197

that enjoyed by men, but they have a quickness of apprehension, which is usually called leaping at conclusions, that is astonishing. There, then, we have distinctive traits of a woman, namely, endurance, loving submission, and quickness of apprehension. Wifehood is the crowning glory of a woman. In it she is bound for all time. To her husband she owes the duty of unqualified obedience. There is no crime which a man can commit which justifies his wife in leaving him or applying for that monstrous thing, divorce. It is her duty to subject herself to him always, and no crime that he can commit can justify her lack of obedience. If he be a bad or wicked man, she may gently remonstrate with him, but refuse him never. Let divorce be anathema; curse it; curse this accursed thing, divorce; curse it, curse it! Think of the blessedness of having children. I am the father of many children and there have been those who have ventured to pity me. "Keep your pity for yourself," I have replied, "they never cost me a single pang." In this matter let women exercise that endurance and loving submission which, with intricacy of thought, are their only characteristics.

88

The First Five Lives of Annie Besant

Arthur H. Nethercot
1895–

Chicago: University of Chicago Press

The birth control movement Francis Place launched in 1822 did not really get under way until 1877, when an ardent feminist, Annie Besant (1847–1933), and a liberal politician, Charles Bradlaugh (1833–1891), joined in publishing a "How to do it" pamphlet written by an American physician, Dr. Charles Knowlton. This pamphlet, quaintly titled **Fruits of Philosophy,** had caused the jailing of its author in America a generation earlier. Besant and Bradlaugh proposed to test English law. Let's follow their trials and tribulations.

1960

The large new edition of the Knowlton pamphlet had been printed in preparation for its imminent sale and stored in the Bradlaughs' home.

Bradlaugh was away in Scotland, and the three women, resolute but filled with feminine trepidation, were left alone. Mrs. Besant's fear of the possibility of a police raid and seizure of the books finally reached such a pitch that she persuaded the girls to help her wrap them up in waterproof parcels and hide them in every conceivable place. Some were buried in her garden at night, some hidden behind the cistern, and others put under a loosened board in the floor. When Bradlaugh was informed of this female cleverness, he was greatly annoyed and sent word that there was to be no more hiding. Fully aware that a raid was perfectly possible, he had no wish to appear ridiculous; and as soon as he returned he initiated the reverse process, but found that the women had done their secreting so well that it was some time before even they could rediscover all their "treasure."

Bradlaugh came back from Scotland on March 22, in order to direct the opening of the sales campaign the next day. First, he dispatched a copy of the new *Fruits* to the Chief Clerk of the Magistrates at the Guildhall, accompanied by a formal notice that the book would be sold in Stonecutter Street the following day, Saturday, from four to five. A similar notice was sent to the Detective Department, with a polite request asking that they arrest him at some hour convenient to them both; the officer in charge replied in the same spirit. A third notice was delivered to the City Solicitor, J. T. Nelson, who was expected to lead the prosecution, but did not do so.

On Saturday, Bradlaugh and Mrs. Besant, accompanied by his daughters and Mr. and Mrs. Parris, marched on Stonecutter Street at the appointed hour. They found a crowd jamming the narrow way, though there had been no advertising of the sale anywhere except in the *National Reformer*. Two policemen were calmly patrolling the area and keeping traffic moving. Once inside, the girls eagerly wrapped up copies of the book at sixpence each, singly or in packets, and counted out the change; but their father would let no one but himself and Mrs. Besant actually make the sales. Five hundred copies passed over the counter in the first twenty minutes. Among the purchasers were several detectives, one of whom bought two copies from Bradlaugh, gracefully retired, and then, in a second role, returned to buy another from Mrs. Besant. Members of the Dialectical Society, in whose discussions and debates she had recently been distinguishing herself and which was now scheduling debates on topics like "Physiology and Morality," dropped in to offer bail if necessary. A rival bookseller was angry when charged full price; but one of Watts's sons came in and was allowed to buy seven copies at the trade price, while the sales force speculated about whether Watts intended to resell. By six o'clock about eight hundred copies had been sold, and many parcels had been wrapped to be mailed to the rest of the country. Yet, to the great disappointment of the participants, no one was arrested.

The largest crowd in years turned out at the Hall of Science on Sunday to hear their heroine lecture on "The Prison and the Crown," with their hero in the chair; and his concluding statement on the Knowlton affair was received with "vehement cheering" and assurances of support. Watts was not present at this meeting, but the following Sunday he defended his position before a divided audience.

No arrests having been made by the beginning of the next week, the two lawbreakers again notified the police that they would be in their shop to be arrested on Thursday. Upstairs they held a "bright party" of a few insiders, including Dr. Drysdale; and a group of some "twenty gentlemen" filled the shop downstairs. But the law would not be hurried, so Annie and Bradlaugh impatiently took a cab to the Old Jewry to see what was amiss. There they were told very courteously that the papers would be ready early the next week and that the Home Office had received a delegation of two from the Christian Evidence Society and another unidentified deputation asking that the Lord Chancellor himself take up the matter. Pleased with the nature of their opposition, they passed the intervening time printing a new defense fund notice and congratulating themselves on the attention the affair was arousing in both the city and the provincial press. They were deluged with news clippings and letters; five thousand copies had been sold, and many orders had to be left temporarily unfilled. The population question was now being widely discussed everywhere. . . .

Finally, one warm, sunny morning in the middle of April, after Bradlaugh had again helpfully notified the police that he and Mrs. Besant would be at their office from ten to eleven, the officers appeared. Hypatia had been previously instructed by her father that when this happened she was to rush home and fetch his volumes of Russell's *On Crime and Misdemeanours,* while the older but less aggressive Alice was to stay with him for any other errands. So Hypatia dashed off to St. John's Wood, picked up the three bulky tomes of Russell, and ran to catch the next train back to the city. Hot and anxious, but feeling with nineteen-year-old innocence that she had the golden key to all legal problems in the three slippery volumes, she was the object of considerable curiosity and amusement from the other passengers. But when she and her sister reached the police court in the Guildhall, they found that their elders had not yet been arraigned. So they sat in shuddering disgust while "some of the lowest specimens of London low life" were tried for drunkenness or assault in the very dock which their father and Mrs. Besant were to occupy.

In the meantime, as Mrs. Besant recounted with proud but ironical relish in her lengthy running accounts of the affair in the *National Reformer,* the detectives had taken them in the friendliest fashion to the nearest police office, where they were examined, searched, measured, and generally put on the criminal records. Then, guarded by some sergeants, they were conducted to the Guildhall, where they were kept waiting for two and a half hours in separate jail cells, through the gratings of which they could dimly see each other. They passed the time by joking, reading the *Secular Review,* and correcting proofs for the next *Reformer,* shoving the sheets through the bars to each other. Finally they were taken to the dock before Alderman Figgins, "a nice, kindly old gentleman, robed in marvellous, but not uncomely, garments of black velvet, purple, and dark fur." Everyone was smiling and civil to everyone else, the testimony of the detectives was taken, there were many laughs in the testimony, subpoenas were issued for many witnesses, bail and recognizances were accepted, and, to partisan cheering, the case was adjourned until April 17. Afterward, they all went home to talk over their next strategy.

At the next hearing, reported verbatim in the *Reformer,* with additional comments by Mrs. Besant, Alderman Figgins was joined by two or three other aldermen, who had been instructed by the City Solicitor. Everybody was very fair, very polite, and mutually complimentary. When Bradlaugh began his defense of himself and Mrs. Besant, some of the officials wanted to exclude women from the room, since the testimony might prove embarrassing to them; but Figgins ruled they might remain if they insisted. The girls stayed the first day, but later waited outside.

Through a series of hearing and adjournments, Bradlaugh argued his case in his usual masterful manner, citing Malthus, Fawcett, and Mill, among others, but especially Acton. He inquired into the meaning of "obscene" under the terms of Lord Campbell's Act, examined the drawings and illustrations in other medical handbooks, and discussed "prudential checks" both before and after marriage. Mrs. Besant then took the stand to make her own statement and defense and impressed everyone by her self-control and grasp of the subject. In fact, her speech was printed in full in both the *Evening Standard* and the *Daily Telegraph* and was translated and telegraphed to Germany the same night. Figgins then adjourned the case until the Central Criminal Court's sessions of May 7.

This gave Bradlaugh his chance to show his mastery of the intricacies and opportunities of the law. He submitted an application to have the case transferred by a writ of certiorari to the Queen's Bench and heard by a special judge and jury. Lord Chief Justice Cockburn and Mr. Justice Mellor were both present at the hearing, and after examining all the records and affidavits, Cockburn decided that the case was of the type and importance to deserve this treatment. It was a tremendous triumph for Bradlaugh, and for Annie, too, since she was allowed merely to affirm and not to take the Christian oath on the Bible before the Commissioner, who could hardly

201

believe that she did not have "a little private deity" of her own, "somewhere out of sight." . . .

The post office . . . was making new trouble. Even though the sale of the new edition of the *Fruits* had now passed five thousand copies (and another printer had struck off a fraudulent imitation with a similar cover and top title), Bradlaugh charged in public letters that not only was his correspondence being opened, but copies of the *Fruits* and the *Text-Book* sent through the mails were being seized and impounded. The Postmaster General at first professed ignorance, but Bradlaugh finally forced him to a bland admission of the truth, as stated in the *Times* for May 15. . . .

The big news in London to Bradlaugh and Mrs. Besant was that the great Lord Chief Justice Cockburn had decided that their case had become of such national consequence that he would hear it himself. The Knowlton pamphlet had now sold over 133,000 copies of a printing of twice that number, the newspapers were full of the issues involved, and the preachers and public speakers could not keep it out of their addresses. Mrs. Besant started a new section in the *National Reformer* entitled "Prosecution Varieties," written in a light, jesting tone which continued to mark her commentaries and which suggested that at first she might not have realized the full gravity of the dangerous situation she had helped to create.

She declared that on the whole the press had been very fair, but that in a few quarters its treatment had been "foul and coarse." So great was the anticipated public interest that the *Reformer* announced a series of "Special Trial Numbers" to supplement the regular issues with a verbatim report of the trial—except for purely physiological details. This series continued to come out with inexorable thoroughness for several weeks after the trial was ended, so determined were the editors to get every scrap of the testimony before their eager readers. New "very handsome" cabinet photographs and less expensive *cartes de visite* of the two principals were prepared for sale.

In spite of the overpowering battery of official legal talent arrayed against them, the intrepid pair insisted that they would conduct their own case. The news that Mrs. Besant would again plead in person aroused many shocked protests against her unwomanliness.

Leading up to the opening of the trial in the Court of Queen's Bench on June 18, there were various hearings and legal preliminaries. Attempts to subpoena several prominent authorities like Charles Darwin and Henry Fawcett, M.P., professor of political economy, resulted in a courteous excuse in the one case and a rude rebuff in the other. Stewart Headlam, like other lesser notables, was happy to testify, even though he knew he would get into trouble with his bishop and his vicar if he did.

Annie, who had burrowed into Bradlaugh's library with her usual zealous thoroughness and had mined some rich veins there, was the first to be called. For two days she spoke fluently on the social and national problem of limiting population; and the special jury and the learned justices hung on her every word, with only Cockburn and Bradlaugh infrequently interrupting for a question or a comment. Her final sentence, "I ask you to give me a verdict of 'Not Guilty,' and to send me home unstained," was directed with such shrewd femininity at masculine hearts that the court officers had to suppress the applause. Then Charles Bradlaugh took over, with a defense which was almost an attack. He also spoke for almost two days, interrupted only by Cockburn and the Solicitor General, Sir Hardinge Giffard. Drysdale testified, too. Then Cockburn delivered his summing-up. It was judicious, unbiased, and often flattering, praising the defendants for their honesty, integrity, and courage, as well as their service to society, and reprimanding Giffard for his unprecedentedly ill-advised and injudicious proceedings. Everything looked delightfully auspicious to the defendants. They could not have had a fairer trial, Mrs. Besant wrote; the jury had been attentive and intelligent, the judges courteous and helpful, and only the Solicitor General had sometimes used "coarsely vicious" language.

When the jury went out, even the Bradlaugh girls were hopeful. Dressed in black because of the recent death of their mother and frightened for the possible fate of their elders, they had gone to Westminster every day. They had deferred to public opinion and stayed out of the courtroom, pacing up and down the great hall outside. Now their father summoned them in to join him for the verdict. The four, with their other friends, settled back happily to listen.

After an hour and thirty-five minutes of unexpected delay, the foreman delivered the decision: "We are unanimously of opinion that the book in question is calculated to deprave public morals, but at the same time we entirely exonerate the defendants from any corrupt motive in publishing it." As Mrs. Besant commented ironically, this amounted to saying, "Not guilty, but don't do it again."

Cockburn looked perplexed and confused, but stated that he would have to interpret the verdict as meaning "Guilty" and pass judgment accordingly.

Like so many historic occurrences, the Besant-Bradlaugh affair petered out in a splutter of anticlimaxes. The verdict, which was satisfactory to neither party, was eventually set aside on a legal technicality—which was also unsatisfactory. Nevertheless, the principal aim of the birth controllers had been achieved—publicity. Their success is evidenced in the numerous cries of anguish proceeding from what we would now call the Establishment. The Lord

Chief Justice, for example, in his summing up spoke of "the mischievous effect of this prosecution"—bringing the topic of contraception out of its hiding place into the full light of public consideration, where it has since remained.

89

Fighters Against Comstockery

Peter Fryer
1927–

From *The Birth Controllers*
London: Secker & Warburg

1965

For forty-two years Anthony Comstock's violent and unshakable prejudices stood between the American people and the free dissemination of contraceptive knowledge. Comstock believed that advocates of contraception were doing the devil's work, in the most literal sense. He could not imagine anyone sincerely proposing birth control as a solution to the social and medical problems of over-large families. His hatred of the physicians who tried to give advice on family limitation, and of the radicals who championed their right to do so, was not lessened by the close links which existed, in America as in Britain, between the birth control and freethought movements. Infidelity (i.e. atheism) and obscenity occupied the same bed, he declared in a characteristic metaphor. As for dealers in contraceptives, he called them 'abortionists'. And for abortionists he had no pity whatever.

One of his victims who was in fact a professional abortionist, 67-year-old Ann Lohman—better known as Madame Restell—cut her throat with a carving-knife the night before she was due to appear in court. 'A bloody ending to a bloody life', was Comstock's comment.[1] Another 'abortionist', so-called, was a dealer in rubber goods named Kendall, who was induced by one of Comstock's cleverly written decoy letters to send him a vaginal syringe through the post. For this crime Kendall spent six months in prison. From its foundation in 1873 to the end of 1882, Comstock's New York Society for the Suppression of Vice was responsible for

700 arrests, 333 sentences of imprisonment totalling 155 years and 13 days, fines totalling 65,256 dollars, and the seizure of 27,856 lb. of 'obscene' books and 64,836 'articles for immoral use, of rubber, etc.' And Comstock, as special inspector for the Post Office Department, had travelled 190,098 miles outside New York City—or nearly 60 miles *a day* for nine years.[2]

Not that he was always successful. In 1878 he arrested Dr. Sara B. Chase for having sold two vaginal syringes, such as might have been bought at any chemist's shop. Comstock had posed as a 'Mr Farnsworth', husband of a woman who had allegedly attended some lectures by Dr Chase on family limitation. Unwisely he described her as a rival of Madame Restell; a juryman asked him if he meant to drive her to suicide too; the jury found her not guilty.

To lesser men this might have been a mortifying defeat. But Comstock was nothing if not thick-skinned. He did not even mind admitting, before a spellbound court-room, that he and four other vice-hunters had gone to a brothel and hired three young women—the charge was fourteen dollars and fifty cents—to parade naked before them so that he might arrest them for indecent exposure. Another of his exploits was a raid on the premises of the U.S.A.'s leading art school, the arrest of its woman secretary, and the seizure of 5,000 copies of its magazine—all because of an issue which contained a few nude studies. And when the Reverend Mabel McCoy published a periodical called *The Cradle,* advocating perfect chastity for both sexes, he excluded it from the mails on the ground that the subject was unfit for discussion.

Comstock was not at all embarrassed by a revelation about the president of his very own Vice Society, the soap manufacturer Samuel Colgate. The revelation was made by De Robigne Mortimer Bennett (1818–82), a leader of the agnostic National Liberal League and editor of *The Truth Seeker* (founded 1873). Bennett gleefully told his readers that in a pamphlet issued by the house of Colgate to advertise the vaseline it sold as agent of the Chesebrough Manufacturing Company, directions were given for the use of that substance, blended with salicylic acid, as a contraceptive (which it is not).[3] The Colgate pamphlet was withdrawn like greased lightning. But Comstock had his revenge. Soon afterwards, Bennett was fined 300 dollars and imprisoned for thirteen months with hard labour for posting *Cupid's Yokes: or The Binding Forces of Conjugal Life* (1876). Written by the Massachusetts freethinker Ezra Hervey Heywood (1829–93), *Cupid's Yokes* was 'an essay to consider some moral and physiological phases of Love and Marriage'; it asserted 'the natural right and necessity of Sexual Self-Government'. Comstock objected to it for several reasons: not least because it described him as 'a *religio-monomaniac,* whom the mistaken will of Congress and the lascivious fanaticism of the Young Men's Christian Association have empowered to use the Federal courts to suppress free inquiry'.[4]

Heywood himself had been arrested by Comstock in 1877 for sending *Cupid's Yokes* and Trall's *Sexual Physiology* through the post. Comstock has left a vivid description of the arrest, which took place in Boston, at a conference of the New England Free Love League (which had discarded A.D. in favour of Y.L.—'Year of Love'):

> I took a seat without being recognized. The address was made up of abuse of myself and disgusting arguments for their cause. I looked over the audience of about 250 men and boys. I could see lust in every face. After a little the wife of the president (the person I was after) took the stand, and delivered the foulest address I ever heard. She seemed lost to all shame. The audience cheered and applauded. It was too vile; I had to go out.

He returned with a carriage, which he left waiting at the entrance while he went back inside. Heywood was presiding 'with great self-complacency. You would have thought he was the champion of some majestic cause instead of a mob of free-lusters.' At length Heywood went into an anteroom; Comstock followed and arrested him. Fearing a rescue attempt by Heywood's supporters once they were told about the arrest, he refused to let his prisoner go back into the hall, even to get his coat, and hustled him downstairs.

> We got part way down the top flight, and I heard a tremendous yell. Then came . . . a rush of many feet, pell-mell over benches and seats, in their scramble to see who would get out and down first. I took my man by the nape of the neck and we went down the next flight rather lively, and into the carriage. Before the first one of the audience touched the sidewalk, we were half a block away. . . . Thus, reader, the devil's trapper was trapped.[5]

Brought to trial in January 1878, Heywood was treated with great prejudice by the judge, who would not allow his witnesses to testify. After retiring for twenty hours, the jury found him guilty. He was sentenced to two years' hard labour; but his friend Laura Cuppy Smith, the advocate of women's rights, persuaded President Hayes to pardon him on the ground that his health was bad and imprisonment was endangering his life. Harried by Comstock, he lived another fifteen years. He was tried once more at Boston in 1883. The first two counts in the indictment were dismissed: publishing *Cupid's Yokes* and two poems by Whitman ('To a Common

Prostitute' and 'A Woman Waits for Me', which includes the scarcely pro-contraception line, 'I dare not withdraw till I deposit what has so long accumulated within me'). And the jury, after listening to him for four and a half hours, found him not guilty on the third and fourth counts, relating to an advertisement in his journal *The Word* (1872–93) for what the advertiser irreverently styled the 'Comstock Syringe'.[6] Heywood's supporters pointed out that, judging by the size of their families, well-to-do Fifth Avenue churchgoers were using the knowledge they were paying Comstock 4,000 dollars a year to suppress. At yet another trial, Heywood was convicted and sent to prison for two years.

Comstock was more consistently successful in his persecution of the birth control and sexual reform advocate Moses Harman (1830–1910), editor of *Lucifer, the Light-Bearer* (1880–1907) and later of the *American Journal of Eugenics* (1907–10). In 1890 Harman was sentenced to five years in the penitentiary and fined 300 dollars for using the mails to circulate 'obscene' literature: a plainly-worded protest against a husband's assault on his wife while she was under treatment after a serious operation. In 1906, at the age of seventy-five, he went to prison for another year, this time for publishing an article by a grandmother pleading the cause of voluntary parenthood. The old man had to break stones for nine hours a day in all weathers, and was refused medical attention. A prison officer told him brutally that he could do nothing better than die. Harman shared a cell with two men, one of whom was in an advanced stage of pulmonary consumption and coughed and spat incessantly; the other was a violent man, imprisoned for murder. Till the day before his death, at the age of eighty, Harman worked hard to keep his journal going, seeing it through the press, addressing wrappers, not knowing whether he could afford the stamps to post the next issue.

Many of Comstock's victories were unspectacular, consisting in forcing would-be birth control educators to omit from their books, as Edward Bliss Foote had had to do, all practical details of contraceptive methods. Thus the Boston physician Sydney Barrington Elliot, though devoting over thirty pages of his *Ædœology: A Treatise on Generative Life* (1892) to family limitation, was prevented—to his great surprise—from including a chapter on methods. His protest against the Comstock law led to the formation in March 1895 of the short-lived National Scientific Family Culture Institute, with the Reverend Mary T. Whitney, a Universalist preacher, as president and Dr Flora S. Russell as secretary. The Institute, which published *Family Culture* (1896–97), was

> the first organization, not strictly radical in its nature, initiated by a
> member of the regular medical profession in good standing, and sup-

ported by physicians, members of the clergy and other highly respected citizens, unconcealedly and on grounds of the highest human interests upholding the principle of the limitation of offspring.[7]

Dr William Josephus Robinson (1867–1936) was the first to demand that contraceptive knowledge be taught to medical students; he edited the *Medico-Pharmaceutical Critic and Guide* (1898–1915), afterwards the *Medical Critic and Guide* (1916–36), which hammered away month after month at the need to free physicians from legal interference. He left five blank pages in his book *Fewer and Better Babies; or, The Limitation of Offspring by the Prevention of Conception; the Enormous Benefits of the Practice to the Individual, Society and the Race Pointed Out and All Objections Answered* (1915). These blank pages were in place of two chapters, entitled 'The Best, Safest and Most Harmless Means for the Prevention of Conception' and 'Means for the Prevention of Conception Which Are Disagreeable, Uncertain or Injurious', omitted because of Comstock's law, but promised for the first edition of the work to be published after these 'brutal laws' were removed from the statute books.

> The further discussion of this subject [Dr Robinson wrote] has been completely eliminated by our censorship, which . . . is . . . as real and as terrifying as any that ever existed in darkest Russia. In fact in this respect the Russian censorship is more liberal than ours. Our censorship hangs like a Damocles' sword over the head of every honest radical writer. . . . Not only are we not permitted to mention the safe and harmless means, we cannot even discuss the unsafe and injurious means and methods. And this we call Freedom of the Press!

These two chapters, he added, in an afterword to the eighth edition, were the most eloquent in the book; a judge and a state governor had told him it was those blank pages, more than anything else, that made them see the absurdity of the laws and induced them to work quietly for their abrogation.[8]

---

[1] Broun and Leech, *Anthony Comstock* (1928), p. 168.

[2] Comstock, *Traps for the Young* (1883), p. 137.

[3] *The Truth Seeker*, May 18, 1878, as quoted by Bennett, *Champions of the Church* (1878), p. 1076. The National Secular Society and the Malthusian League gave a joint reception in Bennett's honor when he visited Britain in 1880 (see *The Malthusian*, no. 23, pp. 179–80, December 1880.

[4] As quoted by Broun and Leech, *op. cit.*, p. 185.

[5] Comstock, *op. cit.*, pp. 163–6.

[6] Cf. Herrick, *Michigan Medical News*, vol. v (1882), p. 9.

[7] Morton, *Medical Critic and Guide,* July 1917, p. 260.

[8] Robinson, *Fewer and Better Babies* (11th ed., 1917), pp. 136 n., 140 n., 247.

90

An Autobiography

Margaret Sanger
1883–1966

New York: W. W. Norton

Though they suffered much from the Comstock Law, physicians did little to combat it, settling instead for "peace in our time." It was left to a nurse, Margaret Sanger, the mother of three children, to lead the fight against Comstock and the laws he had inspired. How she happened to take up the fight for "birth control"—the phrase is her coinage—is told in the following passage.

1938

One stifling mid-July day of 1912 I was summoned to a Grand Street tenement. My patient was a small, slight Russian Jewess, about twenty-eight years old, of the special cast of feature to which suffering lends a madonna-like expression. The cramped three-room apartment was in a sorry state of turmoil. Jake Sachs, a truck driver scarcely older than his wife, had come home to find the three children crying and her unconscious from the effects of a self-induced abortion. He had called the nearest doctor, who in turn had sent for me. Jake's earnings were trifling, and most of them had gone to keep the none-too-strong children clean and properly fed. But his wife's ingenuity had helped them to save a little, and this he was glad to spend on a nurse rather than have her go to a hospital.

The doctor and I settled ourselves to the task of fighting the septicemia. Never had I worked so fast, never so concentratedly. The sultry days and nights were melted into a torpid inferno. It did not seem possible there could be such heat, and every bit of food, ice, and drugs had to be carried up three flights of stairs.

Jake was more kind and thoughtful than many of the husbands I had encountered. He loved his children, and had always helped his wife wash and dress them. He had brought water up and carried garbage down before he left in the morning, and did as much as he could for me while he anxiously watched her progress.

After a fortnight Mrs. Sachs' recovery was in sight. Neighbors, ordinarily fatalistic as to the results of abortion, were genuinely pleased that she had survived. She smiled wanly at all who came to see her and thanked them gently, but she could not respond to their hearty congratulations. She appeared to be more despondent and anxious than she should have been, and spent too much time in meditation.

At the end of three weeks, as I was preparing to leave the fragile patient to take up her difficult life once more, she finally voiced her fears, "Another baby will finish me, I suppose?"

"It's too early to talk about that," I temporized.

But when the doctor came to make his last call, I drew him aside. "Mrs. Sachs is terribly worried about having another baby."

"She well may be," replied the doctor, and then he stood before her and said, "Any more such capers, young woman, and there'll be no need to send for me."

"I know, doctor," she replied timidly, "but," and she hesitated as though it took all her courage to say it, "what can I do to prevent it?"

The doctor was a kindly man, and he had worked hard to save her, but such incidents had become so familiar to him that he had long since lost whatever delicacy he might once have had. He laughed goodnaturedly. "You want to have your cake and eat it too, do you? Well, it can't be done."

Then picking up his hat and bag to depart he said, "Tell Jake to sleep on the roof."

I glanced quickly at Mrs. Sachs. Even through my sudden tears I could see stamped on her face an expression of absolute despair. We simply looked at each other, saying no word until the door had closed behind the doctor. Then she lifted her thin, blue-veined hands and clasped them beseechingly. "He can't understand. He's only a man. But you do, don't you? Please tell me the secret, and I'll never breathe it to a soul. *Please!*"

What was I to do? I could not speak the conventionally comforting phrases which would be of no comfort. Instead, I made her as physically easy as I could and promised to come back in a few days to talk with her again. A little later, when she slept, I tiptoed away.

Night after night the wistful image of Mrs. Sachs appeared before me. I made all sorts of excuses to myself for not going back. I was busy on other cases; I really did not know what to say to her or how to convince her of my own ignorance; I was helpless to avert such monstrous atrocities. Time rolled by and I did nothing.

The telephone rang one evening three months later, and Jake Sachs' agitated voice begged me to come at once; his wife was sick again and from the same cause. For a wild moment I thought of sending someone else, but actually, of course, I hurried into my uniform, caught up my bag, and started out. All the way I longed for a subway wreck, an explosion, anything to keep me from having to enter that home again. But nothing happened, even to delay me. I turned into the dingy doorway and climbed the familiar stairs once more. The children were there, young little things.

Mrs. Sachs was in a coma and died within ten minutes. I folded her still hands across her breast, remembering how they had pleaded with me, begging so humbly for the knowledge which was her right. I drew a sheet over her pallid face. Jake was sobbing, running his hands through his hair and pulling it out like an insane person. Over and over again he wailed, "My God! My God! My God!"

91

Birth Control and the Christian Churches

Flann Campbell

Population Studies, **14**(2):131–147

1960

The attitude of the Christian Churches towards population policies and movements is a subject of growing social and political importance throughout the world. The Churches' concern at current demographic trends is shown by a series of solemn pronouncements from Rome, Lambeth, Geneva and other guiding centres of the Christian faith; while scientists, eugenists and social planners—who in the past may not generally have felt called upon to intervene in doctrinal disputes about the nature of sex and sin—increasingly find themselves involved in debates about marriage principles and family planning practices which raise issues as much theological as sociological. At international population conferences there are frequent clashes of opinion between delegates of different religious (or agnostic) views which cut across national and professional boundaries and which discuss matters that formerly might have been considered to lie outside the scope of demography. The work of the World Health Organization, for example, has been seriously hampered in some fields because of failure by members to agree as to desirability of certain methods of family limitation. In the U.S.A. birth control, which a generation ago no respectable politician would have dared mention, was raised as a sensational issue in the presidential election campaign.

During such a period, when the area of public controversy widens and the problems raised become more acute because of new chemical and biological discoveries, it will be useful to outline the history of the Christian Churches' teachings on contraception.

For centuries the Christian doctrine regarding deliberate family limitation was clear-cut and unambiguous. The primary (some Fathers of the Church claimed the *only*) aim of sexual intercourse in marriage was the procreation of children. Secondary aims such as mutual help between husband and wife or the alleviation of concupiscence were much less important in the marriage relationship. Any artificial interference with the natural processes of coitus and conception was contrary to the laws of God, and must be condemned as gravely sinful. St. Augustine of Hippo wrote: "Sexual intercourse even with a lawful wife is unlawful and shameful, if the offspring of children is prevented. This is what Onan, the son of Juda, did, and on that account God put him to death." For priests or laymen to query these eternal and immutable laws as laid down by St. Augustine in the fourth century, and elaborated by St. Thomas Aquinas in the thirteenth century, was not merely presumptuous but possibly heretical. Even the coming of the Reformation and all it represented in the way of challenge to the dogmas of the mediaeval Catholic Church had no apparent influence on Christian doctrine concerning birth control. Protestant divines were as much in agreement on this point as they were in disagreement about others. During the nineteenth century, in spite of the warnings of Malthus, and the reforming zeal of Place, Knowlton, Bradlaugh, Besant and others, the policy of the Churches—with very rare exceptions—was publicly to say as little as possible about such a disagreeable subject, and privately, if any warning was needed, to repeat the traditional condemnation by the Church.

In striking contrast to the centuries of relatively inflexible dogma reinforced by a policy of secrecy and silence, the last fifty years have been remarkable for an almost complete reversal of traditional doctrine on birth control by the Protestant Churches, and serious modifications by the Roman Catholic Church. Simultaneously, there has been an outpouring of literature on the whole subject of marriage in all its aspects—medical, social and spiritual. Once the floodgates of discussion were open the

Church authorities realised that they must try and direct the dangerous waters of controversy into clerically-approved channels.

The volume of this published work, particularly during the last two or three decades, is impressive, as is also the skilful way in which presentation of doctrine is adapted to audiences of widely differing levels of culture and environment. This is especially true of Roman Catholic publications which range from serious, scholarly works designed for the clergy and theologians down to popular works written for the mass of the Roman Catholic population. At the highest level there are the Papal Encyclicals such as the celebrated Encyclical *Casti Conubii* issued by Pope Pius XI in 1930. These documents are addressed to the faithful all over the world, are translated into numerous languages, and contain the definitive teachings of the Church on a variety of subjects related to married life. They are binding on all members of the Church.

Roman Catholic priests are supplied with manuals of pastoral theology giving detailed instructions how to deal in the confessional with sexual as well as other problems.[1] Medical textbooks are also available in both Britain and the U.S.A. in which most aspects of sexual and obstetrical practice are discussed from the Roman Catholic viewpoint. Some of these are written for doctors and midwives rather than priests or laymen, and to non-Roman Catholics the curious mixture of theology and gynaecology may appear somewhat gruesome—not to say comic!

For the less educated but none the less faithful masses of the population there are nowadays many cheap and simply written booklets and pamphlets usually available at the Church door or nearby religious bookshop. Even in the Republic of Ireland, where a strict literary censorship operates and where the Roman Catholic hierarchy are almost Manichaean in their hostility towards discussion about sex, it is now possible to buy for a few shillings a booklet giving the most precise details how to avoid conception after coitus by means of the "safe period."

Some of these popular writings may seem naive, over-censorious, or even absurdly puritanical in theme, but their continued publication (and some pamphlets run into dozens of editions) suggest that the hierarchy regard them as serving a useful purpose, and their readers welcome them as guides to behaviour.

The Anglican and Nonconformist literature on the subject is less abundant, and appears to be written more for the "middlebrow" Protestant minister or layman than for theologian on the one hand or the semi-literate masses on the other. The appearance of *The Family in Contemporary Society*[2] shortly before the last Lambeth Conference was a landmark in the history of Church of England publications about marriage, for several reasons. The volume is a remarkable document—well-written, refreshingly free from moralising and censoriousness, sharply aware of modern world demographic problems, and having among its authors a group of distinguished social scientists. The most recent and comprehensive statement of the Protestant position is contained in *The Population Explosion and Christian Responsibility* written by the American demographer and churchman, Dr. Richard M. Fagley, on behalf of the World Council of Churches.[3]

The first public support by a Christian minister in Britain of the view that other means of family limitation, apart from continence or the use of the "safe period," might be justifiable under certain circumstances came shortly after the Bradlaugh-Besant trial. Preaching at the South Place Chapel, London, in 1878, the prominent American radical clergyman, Moncure Conway, denounced the police persecution of the publishers of birth control literature, and afterwards expressed sympathy with some of the aims of the Malthusian League.[4] Seven years later the Christian Socialist parson, Stewart Headlam, speaking at a meeting of the Junior Clergy Society in London at which a paper was read on "Marriage and Neo-Malthusianism" said he could find nothing anti-Christian "in the use of the checks recommended by Mrs. Besant." [5]

However, the advanced liberal views of Conway and Headlam were not by any means representative of prevailing Christian opinion during this period, and it was among the Nonconformist Churches that a more broadly-based movement developed in favour of birth control. This was hardly surprising in view of the more liberal theology of these Churches, their greater emphasis on freedom of individual conscience, and also their wider representation among the lower middle classes among whom there was the strongest economic pressure to limit the size of families.

In 1893 a Nonconformist weekly journal, *The Christian World* published a letter from a Methodist minister's wife which expressed many of the anxieties so typical of the harassed and economically struggling professional family of that time—too many children and too little money, physical exhaustion resulting from too frequent childbearing, lack of opportunity for outside interests or recreation, endless household chores, the selfishness of husbands. Immediately there was a flood of letters to the editor sympathising with the minister's wife, and asking what could be done to help those many Godly and long-suffering wives ("hundreds of thousands of them," according to one correspondent) bearing similar burdens.

The reply of *The Christian World* was guarded and cautious (due to the "delicacy of the subject") but was none the less forthright. "The conditions are assuredly wrong which bring one member of the marriage partnership into a bondage so cruel," said the editor. "There was a time when any idea of voluntary limitation was regarded by pious people as interfering with Providence. We are beyond that now and have become capable of recognising that Providence works through the commonsense of individual brains. We limit population just as much by deferring marriage for prudential motives as by any action that may be taken after it. . . . It would obviously be impossible for us to enter into the details of such a topic, but this much may, at least be said, that, apart from certain methods of limitation, the morality of which is gravely questioned by many, there are certain easily understood physiological laws of the subject the failure to know and to observe which is inexcusable on the part either of men or women in these circumstances." [6]

Twenty years later, the Rev. W. F. Lofthouse, a spokesman of the Methodist Church, giving evidence at the National Birth Rate Commission,[7] said that the Protestant Churches had been too reticent, both publicly and privately, in expressing their views about contraception. Cross-examined as to the attitude of the Free Church Council on the subject, he thought that as there were so many economic, social and medical issues involved, Church ministers could not be expected to lay down the law on so "difficult and delicate" a matter as family limitation. Asked if in his opinion, where moral restraint was not possible, he would allow mechanical means of contraception, he replied unequivocally "Yes."

The contemporary Nonconformist attitude broadly speaking is that so long as the aims of birth control are not merely selfishness or un-restricted sensuality, and the techniques used are not unhealthy or aesthet-ically objectionable, then the methods themselves are not important. The decision should be a matter for the individual conscience.[8]

The Church of England was slower to face the challenge pre-sented by new social conditions—particularly the growing demand for women's emancipation—and was more reluctant to change its traditional doctrine about sex, marriage and the family. There was, for example, no mention at all of contraception during the Lambeth Conferences of 1867 and 1897, and the first official Anglican statement on the subject did not appear until 1908 when the Lambeth Conference produced a long report on what was described as "Restriction of Population." Regret was expressed at the decline of the birth rate among English-speaking peoples, especially the upper and middle classes, and it was suggested that many physical and mental diseases might be a direct consequence of the use of contraceptives.[9] The bishops,[10] having denounced birth control as "preventive abortion," recommended that all contraceptive appliances and drugs be prohibited by law and their advocates prosecuted.

The theme that sexual pleasure, even in marriage, was sinful if indulged in for its own sake, and that large families were to be preferred to material comforts, was again emphasised in a memorandum presented to the National Birth Rate Commission which first met in October, 1913, in London.[11] Chastity in married people "may be exceedingly hard but it is entirely consistent with health," said this report. Christian men and women "must bear the Cross and keep themselves in purity and temperance." Women "should not shrink from the heavy burthens which marriage may entail for them. . . ." Large families were "admirable schools of vigorous, dutiful and unselfish character" and husbands and wives must avoid a "love of pleasure and comfort, and a standard of expenditure on dress, furniture or holidays higher than the family means reasonably allow." The bishop of Southwark gave it as his own personal opinion that sexual intercourse was only justified if the procreation of children was intended (otherwise it was "mere gratification"), and that continence might have to be practised even if it meant the break up of the marriage.[12]

At the next Lambeth Conference, despite the shattering impact of the first World War upon accepted patterns of social behaviour, and the emergence of a much more tolerant attitude towards family planning in many communities, the episcopal language was almost as vehement and condemnation equally strong. The bishops by this time were thoroughly alarmed at what they considered to be the spread of sexual immorality (which they believed to be partly fostered by easier methods of birth control) and the freer way in which sex was generally discussed.

"The temptations of sexual sin are probably the most universal in the world," stated one Conference report,[13] while Resolution 68, which was adopted without opposition, declared unequivocally:

> The Conference, while declining to lay down rules which will meet the needs of every abnormal case, regards with grave concern the spread of theories and practices hostile to the family. We utter an emphatic warning against the use of unnatural means for the avoidance of conception, together with the grave dangers—physical, moral and religious —thereby incurred, and against the evils with which the extension of such use threatens the race. In opposition to the teaching, which under the name of science and religion, encourages married people in the deliberate cultivation of sexual union as an end in itself, we steadfastly uphold what must always be regarded as the governing considerations of Christian marriage. One is the primary purpose for which marriage exists, namely the continuation of the race through the gift and heritage of children; the other is the paramount importance in married life of deliberate and thoughtful self-control.

By 1930, however, a significant shift had occurred in the Church's attitude, and there had emerged a strong group of Anglicans, at first a minority, but before many years had elapsed a majority, with a more liberal viewpoint on the subject. The Lambeth Conference of that year produced a long report entitled "Marriage and Sex" which again warned about the dangers of sexual license and fornication but admitted that sexual desire had its own value and importance in the Christian home and must be recognised as a "God-given factor." [14] On this occasion the Conference was deeply divided on the permissibility of birth control, and after much debate the following resolution was carried by 193 to 67 votes:

> Where there is a clearly felt moral obligation to limit or avoid parenthood, the method must be decided on Christian principles. The primary and obvious method is complete abstinence from intercourse (as far as may be necessary) in a life of discipline and self-control lived in the power of the Holy Spirit. Nevertheless, in those cases where there is such a clearly felt moral obligation to limit or avoid parenthood, and where there is a morally sound reason for avoiding complete abstinence, the Conference agrees that other methods may be used, provided that this is done in the light of the same Christian principles. The Conference records its strong condemnation of the use of any methods of conception control from motives of selfishness, luxury, or mere convenience.

Further to emphasize the cleavage of opinion among Anglicans, this Conference was soon followed by the publication of *Marriage and Birth Control* which collected in one volume the conflicting points of view on contraception. The Bishop of St. Albans persisted in the traditional viewpoint that contraception was intrinsically sinful and contrary to God's law. He admitted that sexual abstinence might be difficult and even cause neurosis, but it was, as he expressed it, the "heroic way." "I have a strong instinctive feeling that the whole thing (birth control) is repellent, degrading and wrong," he concluded.[15] The Bishop of Liverpool believed that previously the bishops' minds were too much set upon the dangers and evils of sex, and that the sex-impulse was instituted by God not merely for ensuring the continuance of the human race, but also for fostering the mutual love of husband and wife.[16] Abstinance from sex relations within marriage would be a severe strain, possibly with harmful results. He criticised the viewpoint of the minority at the Conference, which included some "bishops without experience of married life" who implied that sexual intercourse even in marriage was a regrettable necessity, and stressed new social developments such as the emancipation of women, advances in medicine and psychology, and the threat of overpopulation (though he did not sharply emphasise the latter point).

Thus for nearly thirty years—the 1948 Lambeth Conference did not discuss the topic—the Anglican layman was presented with two alternative viewpoints, and he (or she) could choose between them according to conscience.

The Lambeth Conference of 1958 which was attended by 310 bishops from 46 countries, was held in an atmosphere very different from that prevailing during previous conferences. The traditionalists were by this time thoroughly routed, and no delegate spoke in complete condemnation of birth control. On this occasion, instead of repeated warnings about the possible dangers of unbridled sexuality, there was far more emphasis on the broader social aspects of family life. A remarkable feature of the conference and the reports which followed it was the concentration upon social and economic trends, housing, factory conditions, urbanisation, and living standards in different countries. At all stages of debate there was refreshing evidence that the Church authorities were by now fully aware of current demographic trends in Christian and non-Christian countries alike. On this occasion, at least, it was a case of the bishops quoting more from the blue books and less from the Bible.

Finally, the following resolution[17] was passed without a single dissentient:

> The Conference believes that the responsibility for deciding upon the number and frequency of children has been laid by God upon the conscience of parents everywhere; that this planning, in such ways as are mutually acceptable to husband and wife in Christian conscience, is a right and important factor in Christian family life and should be the result of positive choice before God. Such responsible parenthood built on obedience to all the duties of marriage, requires a wise stewardship of the resources and abilities of the family as well as a thoughtful consideration of the varying population needs and problems of society and the claims of future generations.

Since then there has been growing interest among all the Protestant denominations in the problems of marriage, parenthood and population culminating in a meeting of a study group of the World Council of Churches[18] at Oxford in April, 1959, and followed by the publication of *The Population Explosion and Christian Responsibility* a year later.

The development of the Roman Catholic Church's doctrine on contraception provides an even more striking example of the way in which a dogmatic theology may be forced to respond to changed social, scientific and medical circumstances.

Traditionally, the Vatican's teachings on this point had always been quite explicit—not even acute poverty, overcrowding, serious ill health, the possibility of bringing diseased children into the world or immediate danger to the wife through pregnancy could be accepted as excuses for artificial means of birth control.[19] If husband and wife for any reason whatsoever wished to avoid having children (and the Church's strongly held view was that children were the supreme blessing of a happy marriage) then the only alternative was the strictest sexual continence. If such abstention from normal married relations proved difficult, then God's grace would help the suffering people. This simple, easily understood and unchanging doctrine of the Church had been accepted throughout the ages and was expected to be obeyed by the faithful in all lands and among all societies in which the Church had members.

Generally, during the latter half of the nineteenth century there was little need—except possibly in France where the birth rate had fallen substantially—for the Church to become involved in public controversy about birth control. Roman Catholic husbands and wives might not always be as strict in their marriage practices (especially about *coitus interruptus*) as their priests would have liked, but there was little serious questioning of the basic principles of the Church's teaching on this point. The danger of contamination by freethinkers or Protestants was also not nearly so serious as it became later.

Nevertheless, by the outbreak of the first World War the problem had grown acute enough in Britain for the Catholic hierarchy to feel it necessary to restate and amplify their views. The Rev. Monsignor Brown, Vicar-General of the Diocese of Southwark, gave to the National Birth Rate Commission a lengthy exposition of his Church's attitude towards family limitation, concluding with the usual warning against the "grave sin of Onanism." [20]

During the 1920's the situation from the Church's point of view rapidly deteriorated—propaganda in favour of contraception became more widespread, birth control clinics were opened in several countries, the danger of Catholics being led astray became more obvious—and the Pope found it advisable in 1930 to issue a special encyclical on the duties and responsibilities of Christian marriage.[21] This celebrated encyclical was a lengthy document covering a wide range of related subjects such as divorce, abortion, euthanasia, and sterilisation, but its main theme was on the question of birth control, and on this point the Pope's words were forceful and unambiguous. Artifical contraception was "shameful and intrinsically immoral," "criminal abuse," "an unspeakable crime," and so forth. The sharpness of the language and the detailed manner in which the Pope developed his arguments were clearly meant as a solemn warning to actual or potential backsliders in the Church; and before long all the resources of the Vatican, from the proudest Cardinal to the humblest parish priest, and drawing in Catholic physicians, lay workers and publicists, were mobilized in the campaign. In those countries where Roman Catholics were in a majority, the hierarchy made every effort to ensure that legislation already in force prohibiting the sale of contraceptives (e.g. France,

Italy and Belgium) should be continued, or new legislation introduced (as in the Irish Free State). For this policy they usually had the enthusiastic support of the pro-natalist groups (including some non-Catholics) which wanted larger populations for nationalistic or militarist reasons.[22]

In countries such as the U.S.A. or Britain where Roman Catholics are in a minority, they advised that all possible pressure should be brought to bear upon the faithful to prevent them from following the example of their non-Catholic fellow citizens.[23]

However, the important—and from the long-term point of view, revolutionary—development in Church doctrine during this period was not that the Pope reaffirmed a viewpoint which was already well known, but the new medical discoveries relating to the alleged "safe period" in the ovulation cycle of women. The fact that there are certain times of the month when women appear less likely to conceive after normal coitus had long been suspected, but the physiological reasons for it were obscure. It was commonly suspected that conception in women was most likely to occur during or near menstruation.[24] Many biologists and gynaecologists denied the existence of a "safe period" altogether,[25] and as late as 1924 such an eminent authority as Dr. Marie Stopes could write: ". . . the ordinary working-class healthy woman has no safe period at all." [26]

It was the publication in 1930 of the results of two independently conducted research investigations by the distinguished Japanese gynaecologist, Dr. K. Ogino, and Prof. H. Knaus of the University of Prague, that gave scientific validity to the "safe-period" theory. Ogino concluded that ovulation in women takes place 12–16 days before menstruation, and that the ovum only survived (if not fertilised) for 3–12 hours.[27] The male spermatozoa, in his opinion, might live for up to three days after coitus. Knaus suggested that ovulation takes place 14–16 days before menstruation, that the ovum survived "only a few hours after it leaves the Graafian follicle," and that the male spermatozoa might live for two days.[28]

If these theories are true—and most informed medical opinion now supports them[29]—then it necessarily followed that for only a comparatively short time during the monthly cycle would it be possible for the normal woman to conceive. Sexual intercourse outside this period would inevitably be sterile. The difficulty, of course, was how to calculate accurately the fertile and infertile phases.[30]

The increasing number of Roman Catholic theologians who were becoming keenly aware of the conflict between what was described as the "irresistible pressure of society in favour of contraception" and the "immovable condemnation of the Church" [31] warmly welcomed the discoveries of Ogino and Knaus. The use of the "safe period," as has already been pointed out, had been approved as early as the mid-nineteenth century in

France, and Monsignor Brown, a spokesman of the English hierarchy, giving evidence to the National Birth Rate Commission during the first World War, stated: "Where all other deterrents fail, married couples may be allowed to limit intercourse to the intermenstrual period, sometimes called *tempus agenesos*." [32] It was the work of Ogino and Knaus, however, which provided a more scientific basis for the theory, while it was the American gynaecologist, Latz, who popularized the new ideas in his book *The Rhythm*[33] which sold over 200,000 copies (mostly in the U.S.A.) between 1932 and 1939.

Nevertheless, though Latz's book was given semi-official approval by American ecclesiastics, the more conservative[34] elements in the Church, steeped in the old traditions about sex and birth control, persisted in their distaste for the whole subject, and only a few years ago a priest writing in a widely-circulated marriage manual (containing the *Imprimatur* of the Vicar-General) made this very plain when replying to a question about the right of husband and wife to limit their family if they had a small income, poor health, and were living in overcrowded conditions. "The right thing is to live a normal married life," he wrote. "Leave the number of children to God. He is the Creator. We do not dictate a number to him . . . no priest and no pope give a calendar or chart to couples to follow. . . . Rhythm frequently leads to denying one another, birth prevention, drunkenness and divorce." [35]

On the other hand, Keenan and Ryan in their officially-approved and widely circulated book, *Marriage: A Medical and Sacramental Study*[36] say that the temporary use of the "safe period" would be justified in cases of minor illness or disease, after a recent pregnancy, too great frequency of pregnancies, economic difficulties, or for fostering mutual concord between husband and wife who agree over intercourse but not over a fresh pregnancy in the near future. The persistent use of the "safe period" would be justified only in cases in which there was grave danger to the mother from a further pregnancy, the impossibility of supporting or educating further children, incurable hereditary disease, or the prevention of perversion if this were likely in one partner because the other refused the use of the infertile period.

But the final word, as always in the Roman Catholic Church, rests with the Pope, and the most recent statements from the Vatican make it quite clear that the "safe period" method may be quite legitimately used to limit the number of children in marriage.

Speaking in 1951, Pope Pius XII said:[37]

> . . . the Church knows how to consider with sympathy and understanding the real difficulties of the married state in our day. Therefore, in our late allocution on conjugal morality, we affirmed the legitimacy

and, at the same time, the limits—in truth very wide—of a regulation of offspring, which, unlike so-called "birth control," is compatible with the law of God. One may even hope (but in this matter the Church naturally leaves the judgment to medical science) that science will succeed in providing this licit method with a sufficiently secure basis, and the most recent information seems to confirm such a hope.

The Pope was speaking before the recent experiments with an oral contraceptive pill, and it is possible that ultimately this method may provide the "sufficiently secure basis" to which the Pope referred. If the chemists produce a pill which can, without harmful side effects, regulate the ovulatory cycle with a high degree of accuracy then the theologians may have to reconsider their views about what are "artificial" and what are "natural" methods of family limitation. The complicated charts and elaborate calculations which must be used at present by the good Catholic wife who wishes to estimate her "safe period" with any hope of success are in many ways more artificial than conventional mechanical methods of birth control, and the Church authorities have already shown in the case of Ogino-Knaus that they would welcome new scientific methods which would make for greater accuracy and effectiveness. In this aspect, as in so many other aspects of the problem, the progress of science continually presents the theologians with new difficulties.[38]

The Christian Churches, with their varying historical backgrounds, doctrines, and forms of organisation, reacted, as we have seen, in different ways and with different degrees of urgency to the challenge presented by the spread of birth control throughout the world, but the external forces which compelled them to modify their traditional dogma have been broadly similar—namely, the rapid increase in population in certain territories, the advances in medical science, and the failure of the Churches to enforce discipline among their own flocks.

The Churches can no longer ignore the fact that world population is increasing at the rate of fifty millions a year, and that—if present trends continue—in the year 2000 there may be twice as many people on the earth as there are to-day. Even the most unworldly bishop or cloistered cardinal can hardly fail to appreciate the significance in terms of food supply, living standards, race relations and political conflict, of the extraordinarily rapid multiplication of the peoples of China, India, Japan, South-East Asia, Brazil, Egypt and Central America. One of the most striking sections of *The Family in Contemporary Society* is the contribution of the Anglican bishops of India who show a very keen awareness of the demographic problems of that country. Dr. Richard Fagley as an official spokesman for the World Council of Churches devotes over one-third of his book *The Population*

Explosion and Christian Responsibility to the broader economic and technological aspects of population growth. Roman Catholic demographers, both clerical and lay, are also becoming increasingly concerned at the need for a social programme which will be practical and realistic as well as in conformity with traditional philosophy in a period of rapid population expansion. Such authorities as Gibbons and Burch in the U.S.A., Lestapis in France, Zeegers in Holland, and Fogarty in Britain have written with sympathy and understanding of the threatened population crisis in those regions of the world already suffering from poor nutrition, lack of capital and low labour productivity.[39] In 1957 the journal *Social Compass* published by the Catholic Institute of Social Research in Geneva offered a prize of $5,000 for an essay on the population problems of under-developed countries. The Church's spokesmen do not all agree as to what is the best social policy to adopt (it is perhaps significant that so far the judges in the essay contest have not announced the award of the $5,000 prize), but there is a general consensus of opinion that the more intensive cultivation of the earth's surface would produce a much larger food supply.[40] Colin Clark, the Oxford economist, states in a recent article, for example, that the agricultural resources of the world would suffice for ten times the present world population.[41] It is doubtful whether other Catholic experts would support such a claim.

The second powerful reason for the evolution of religious doctrine is the immense progress in medical science and psychology since the beginning of the century. Sixty years ago gynaecology was in a fairly primitive state and comparatively little was known about reliable birth control techniques. The physiology of the human male and female reproductive systems was understood only in general terms, and there was no exact knowledge about the length of life of the human sperm and ova. Such contraceptives as were available were generally crude, unreliable, expensive and difficult to obtain, and regular birth control (apart from *coitus interruptus*) was the practice of only a relatively small minority, mostly from the upper and middle classes. Marie Stopes and Margaret Sanger were schoolgirls, while Havelock Ellis was an obscure figure on the edge of respectable medicine and being harried by the police. Freud's revolutionary discoveries about the nature of human sexuality were still being treated, outside a small group of devotees, with contempt or ridicule. In these circumstances it was not surprising that the Church authorities should either ignore, or else condemn outright, any suggestion of birth control.

But in modern industrial communities (at least among those where Protestants predominate) with a better educated and less subservient population, with cheap manuals of sexual technique available in many book stores and condoms sold in most chemist's shops, a simple policy of silence or disapproval is not enough. Social realities must be faced, arguments met and answered, new formulae invented. Can we imagine, for example, Cardinal Manning debating birth control before a nation-wide audience as the Roman Catholic Bishop of Salford did on a television programme in 1959?

A related aspect of this problem is the way in which the Christian Churches generally have faced up to the whole problem of sex in the modern world. Nowadays probably only a minority of obscurantist and puritanical clergymen (as in Spain or Ireland) still regard the sexual instinct as "nasty" and debased, and there is much wider appreciation by all Churches that there may be secondary (some claim equal) aims in marriage apart from the procreation of children.[42] "Sex is a God-given factor in the life of mankind, and its functions are therefore essentially noble and creative," says a report of the 1930 Lambeth Conference.[43] "Sexual intercourse (in marriage) . . . is lawful, honourable, morally good and may be meritorious," writes the Jesuit Father Davis.[44]

Freud may still be an unpleasant word for some theologians (in all the extensive Roman Catholic literature read by the present writer on sex, birth control and the family, Freud's name was hardly ever mentioned) but there can be no doubt that his influence on certain aspects of religious teaching has been considerable. What could be more steeped in Freudianisms, for example, than the following extract from a book on Christian marriage by the Jesuit Father J. Leycester King?

> Sex and its implications are indeed of all-pervading importance and significance to society and the individual human personality, and failure to recognise this can only lead to error and disaster. Sex is not, as it were, a separable aspect of human nature, rather is it the case that sex is in some way relevant to every aspect of human nature, and that scarcely any single facet of man's complexity can be adequately understood without it.[45]

The third important factor encouraging a new approach to the problem by Church authorities is the gradual realisation by those most closely in touch with the realities of family life, and not merely living a cloistered life with their exegesis of the Bible[46] and texts of the Fathers of the Church, that social and environmental pressures were proving stronger than episcopal edicts so far as contraception is concerned. "The birth control movement has established itself with little regard for ecclesiastical pronouncement," admit the authors of *The Family in Contemporary Society*,[47] while Father Alan Keenan, O.F.M., in his Preface to a widely circulated booklet on family limitation, speaks of a "crisis" in the Church because "the Church condemns birth control and some Catholics use contraceptives."[48] In the U.S.A. the Jesuit Father Reiner speaks of the

224

"heresy" of contraception having made "terrifying advances" which bring "danger of disruption" to the Roman Catholic Church.[49]

The extent to which this "heresy" has spread naturally depends upon the strictness of the particular Church's rules, the powers—clerical or lay—which the Church may have to enforce its edicts, and the kind of society in which the Church operates. Thus, among the Protestant communities of Britain, U.S.A. or northern Europe the problem may only be an issue for a devout minority, and even for them the doctrine may be so loose or vague as to allow wide individual interpretation, whereas in Spain, Italy or the Republic of Ireland the combined influence of Church and state may be very powerful indeed.[50] Clearly also, the problem would be very different in, say, a simple village community in Portugal as compared with an urbanised cosmopolitan population in New York or London.[51]

That there is good reason for the authorities of the Roman Catholic Church to be alarmed may be seen in the evidence—direct and indirect—from widely differing communities.

In three southern European countries the birth rate declined as follows during the last thirty years:

Birth rate in Italy, Spain and Portugal

Year	Italy	Spain	Portugal
1920–4	30.1	30.0	33.0
1930–4	24.5	27.5	29.3
1956	18.1	20.7	22.9

In the Republic of Ireland the higher professional classes are restricting their families much more than the working classes, as may be seen in the following table:

Number of children born per 100 married women (aged 20–34 at marriage) in the Republic of Ireland, 1946 [52]

Social group (non-agricultural)	Number
Higher professional	286
Lower professional	358
Employers and managers	343
Skilled wage earners	401
General labourers	434

This evidence, of course, is only indirect—it might be that in these countries or among certain occupations the birth rate varies for other

225

reasons apart from birth control—but there is more direct proof that Roman Catholics are practising contraception in increasing numbers. For example, in Britain the official *Report on Family Limitation*[53] estimates the following percentages of Roman Catholics as using contraceptive devices:

Date of marriage	Percentage of Roman Catholic women in sample using birth control methods
1900–9	0
1910–9	21
1925–9	32
1935–9	46
1940 and later	39

Dr. Eustace Chesser in his survey of the marital relationships of English women found that 47% of his sample of married Roman Catholic women used birth control, and that 39% of single Roman Catholic women thought they should use it.[54] Slater and Woodside in their study of urban working-class marriage concluded: ". . . the evidence in nearly every case suggests that where contraception is concerned, the Roman Catholic Church, at least in an urban area, is fighting a losing battle." [55]

In the U.S.A. in the 1930's Himes found that about one-quarter of the patients in birth control clinics in Baltimore, Cleveland, and Newark were Roman Catholics, though the latter only comprised between one-third and one-half the population of those cities.[56] Latz quotes figures to show that between 1921–28 in New York and Chicago birth control clinics 36% of the users were Roman Catholics. ". . . we Catholics are furnishing more than our quota of clients," he laments.[57] More recently, an investigation of the contraceptive practices of a representative cross-section of white married women aged 18–39 years showed that even among those Catholic wives who were regular churchgoers 26% were using birth control methods condemned as gravely sinful by their Church.[58]

In view of these figures it is not surprising that the prominent American Roman Catholic publicist, Father John A. O'Brien,[59] could write: ". . . a large proportion, if not the great majority (of Catholics) are probably practising birth control already, salving their conscience with the plea that the Catholic law as understood by them is morally impossible of observance," or that Father Andrew Beck[60] (now Roman Catholic Bishop of Salford) can say: ". . . among Catholics, though in a lesser degree than among non-Catholics, there has been a marked decline in fertility, and there seems little doubt that in one form or another family limitation is being adopted as a policy."

In the past the Christian Churches have faced other crises brought about by the progress of science, but in some ways the problems which then arose proved simpler for the theologians to handle because they concerned (at least to begin with) the theory rather than the practical application of scientific discovery, and they involved the beliefs of an educated minority rather than those of the majority of the population. Presumably, the average man in the street of sixteenth-century Italy did not worry overmuch whether the sun went round the earth or *vice versa,* and most people in nineteenth-century England did not lose much sleep over the argument whether they were descended from apes or angels. These were points for experts to debate, and they certainly did not involve, except for a few individuals, grave and immediate issues of ethics and morality. Eventually, the Christian Churches—with the exception of the fundamentalists—came to terms with such "heretics" as Galileo and Darwin; and the new astronomy and the new evolution are now encompassed in the wide folds of modern Christian theology.

But when scientific discovery touches intimately the lives of ordinary families, and when everyday standards of human conduct and behaviour are involved then the dilemma from the Churches' point of view is much more acute. Particularly is this true of any discussion of sexual morality, surrounded as the subject is with so much emotion, hedged in with so many traditional beliefs, and laden historically with such a burden of anxiety and guilt. In the strange borderland where sex and metaphysics meet, it is not surprising to find that sociologists and theologians often disagree—they must travel a good deal further before they meet on common ground.

---

[1] These manuals are normally written in English (or other vernacular) but those sections which deal with the more physical aspects of sexual behaviour are usually written in Latin.

[2] *The Family in Contemporary Society* (S.P.C.K., 1958).

[3] *The Population Explosion and Christian Responsibility* by Richard M. Fagley. (Oxford University Press, New York, 1960.)

[4] *Liberty and Morality:* A Discourse given at the South Place Chapel, Finsbury, by Moncure D. Conway, M.A. (Freethought Publishing Co., 1878.)

[5] *The Malthusian.* June, 1885.

[6] *The Christian World.* Editorial entitled "A Marriage Problem." June 15, 1893.

[7] *Report of the National Birth Rate Commission.* Evidence of the Rev. W. F. Lofthouse, pp. 374–380. (Chapman & Hall, 1916.)

[8] *Man and Wife Together* by Kenneth G. Greet. (Epworth Press, 1958.)

[9] "Mental and moral vigour may become impaired, and the question has been asked whether the increase of insanity may not be closely connected with the habits of restriction." *The Six Lambeth Conferences* 1867–1920, p. 401 by Lord Davidson of Lambeth, Archbishop of Canterbury, 1903–28 (S.P.C.K., 1929.)

[10] The fact that many of the laity and clergy differed from their bishops on this point is evident from the report given to the National Birth Rate Commission a few

years later. "In the absence of any recognised authoritative teaching, there are wide differences of opinion among the Anglican clergy on this subject (of birth control)," said this Report. "The objections formerly felt by almost all of them to family limitation have grown decidedly weaker since the beginning of the century; but their condemnation of mechanical and chemical devices is still almost unanimous. Among conscientious and high-minded laymen and women in the Anglican Church there are many who openly justify the use of preventives, and this attitude has become far more common during the last few years." *Report of the National Birth Rate Commission,* pp. 64–65 (Chapman & Hall, 1916).

[11] *Report of the National Birth Rate Commission,* pp. 383–387 (Chapman & Hall, 1916).

[12] *Report of the National Birth Rate Commission,* pp. 436–450. Evidence of the Bishop of Southwark.

[13] *The Six Lambeth Conferences,* 1867–1920, p. 107 by Lord Davidson of Lambeth, Archbishop of Canterbury, 1903–28. (S.P.C.K., 1929.)

[14] "Sex is a God-given factor in the life of mankind, and its functions are therefore essentially noble and creative . . . a new day has dawned, in which sex and sex matters are emerging from the mists of suspicion and even shame, in which for centuries they have been enveloped into the clear atmosphere of candour, honesty and truth." Resolution from the 1930 Lambeth Conference, *Marriage and Birth Control,* p. 10 by Rt. Rev. A. A. David, Bishop of Liverpool and Rt. Rev. M. B. Furse, Bishop of St. Albans (James Nisbet, c. 1930).

[15] *Marriage and Birth Control,* p. 27 by the Rt. Rev. A. A. David and the Rt. Rev. M. B. Furse (James Nisbet, c. 1930).

[16] The words of the marriage ceremony in the Revised Prayer Book had recently been altered to include this second aspect of marriage.

[17] *The Lambeth Conference,* 1958, p. 57 (S.P.C.K., 1958).

[18] The report of this group was published in the *Ecumenical Review,* Geneva, October 1959. Dr. Fagley points out in his book that during the last ten years the following churches have issued statements which are in broad agreement with the Lambeth thesis on family planning: the Church of Sweden, the Presbyterian Church of Ireland, the Calvinist Church of Holland, United Lutheran Church of America, Methodist Church of the U.S.A., Reformed Church of France, Lutheran Church of Finland, Baptist Union of Denmark, and the United Presbyterian Church of the U.S.A.

[19] ". . . if God sends another mouth to fill, he will find means to fill it." *Birth Control and Ethics,* p. 53 by Henry J. Davis (Burns Oates & Washbourne, 1927).

[20] *Report of the National Birth Rate Commission.* Evidence of the Right Rev. W. F. Brown, Vicar-General of the Diocese of Southwark, pp. 392–393 (Chapman & Hall, 1916). For the Church's attitude towards the use of the "safe period," see later pages.

[21] *Encyclical Letter on Christian Marriage* (Casti Conubii) by Pope Pius XI (new translation by Canon G. D. Smith, Catholic Truth Society, 1951).

[22] For account of the pro-natalist movement see *Population Policies and Movements in Europe* by D. V. Glass (O.U.P., 1940).

[23] For an account of a particularly violent campaign against the suggested opening of birth control clinics in Massachusetts (a state with many inhabitants of Irish or Italian descent) during 1942 and 1947 see *Freedom and Catholic Power* by Paul Blanshard (Secker & Warburg, 1951).

[24] "It used to be thought that ovulation coincided with menstruation, and according to this erroneous view, it was believed that the women would conceive most

readily just before or just after the period." *Reports of the Biological and Medical Committee,* p. 42. Vol. IV. Papers of the Royal Commission on Population. (H.M.S.O., 1950).

The American demographers Freedman, Whelpton and Campbell quote the following query about the "safe-period" addressed by some French Roman Catholics to the Sacred Penitentiary in Rome in 1880. "In the judgment of learned physicians and physiologists, women for the most part are not permanently able to conceive, but only periodically able, that is, from the time at which the menstrual flow begins to the fourth day after it has ceased; in the rest of the month they are usually sterile. They assert that this theory has been verified in 94 per cent of the women observed.

Having learned of this, Doctor L. thought that a remedy might therein be found to prevent many serious sins, by persuading spouses who turn to onanism from fear of conception, to abstain from relations at that time at which conception is possible, and to have relations in the proper way at the time at which conception does not usually take place. . . . Doctor L. has asked of the Sacred Penitentiary: (1) Whether spouses can so act without mortal or venial sin; (2) Whether a confessor may urge this way of acting on a wife who detests the onanism of her husband but is unable to correct it, or on either spouse who wishes to avoid too many children; (3) Whether the danger of a reduction in the number of offspring must be provided against or whether this must be considered of secondary importance to the profit realised from avoidance of sin and peace of conscience."

In reply the Sacred Penitentiary stated: "Spouses using marriage in the aforesaid way should not be disturbed, and a confessor may suggest, but cautiously, the opinion under discussion to those spouses whom he has vainly tried by another method to lead away from the detestable crime of Onan." The same reply had been given to a similar question addressed by the Bishop of Amiens to Rome in 1853. *Family Planning, Sterility and Population Growth.* Appendix A, p. 416. By Ronald Freedman, Pascal K. Whelpton and Arthur A. Campbell. (McGraw Hill. New York. 1959).

[25] "Up till about 1930 it was generally believed that women could conceive at any time during the menstrual cycle. This theory remains a cardinal point in the classical theory of the physiology of human reproduction," p. 67, *The Rhythm of Sterility and Fertility in Women* by Leo J. Latz (Latz Foundation, Chicago, 1939).

[26] *Contraception,* p. 89, by Marie Carmichael Stopes (Health Promotions Ltd., 1924).

[27] *Conception Period of Women* by Dr. Kyusaka Ogino (translated into English, Medical Arts Publishing Co., Harrisburg, U.S.A., 1934). Dr. Ogino's work was published in Japan several years earlier, and in Germany in 1930—the same year as the publication of Dr. Knaus's work.

[28] *The Rhythm of Sterility and Fertility in Women,* p. 24 by Leo J. Latz (Latz Foundation, Chicago, 1939).

[29] "Evidence has now accumulated to show that ovulation takes place, as a general rule, 13–15 days before the onset of menstruation, and that the fertile phase lies therefore in mid-cycle. It is thought that the ovum remains fertilisable for only about one day after ovulation, and that sperms retain their powers of fertilising an ovum for not more than three days." *Reports of the Biological and Medical Committee,* p. 42, vol. IV, Papers of the Royal Commission on Population (H.M.S.O., 1950).

[30] It is well known that the menstrual cycle may be affected by a large number

229

of factors such as pregnancy, miscarriage, illness, emotional disturbances, etc. Moreover, if the "safe period" method is to be used regularly with any hope of success the woman concerned must record her menstrual flows systematically, be given competent medical advice, and have an unusual capacity for self-control in her sexual relationships. In view of this, how safe is the "safe period"? Roman Catholic physicians claim a high degree of reliability if the proper precautions are taken, but non-Catholics generally regard it as a relatively ineffective method of birth control. For example, Dr. C. P. Blacker expresses grave doubts as to its efficacy when tried among a backward and largely uneducated population (Eugenics Review, July, 1955 and October, 1955. "The Rhythm Method: Two Indian Experiments").

[31] *Family Limitation*, p. 9, by John Ryan, with a Foreword by Alan Keenan, O.F.M. (Sheed & Ward, 1957).

[32] *Report of the National Birth Rate Commission*, p. 393. Evidence of the Right Rev. W. F. Brown, Vicar-General of the Diocese of Southwark (Chapman & Hall, 1916).

[33] *The Rhythm of Sterility and Fertility in Women*, by Leo J. Latz (6th edition, Latz Foundation, Chicago, 1939) has a Foreword by the Jesuit Father Joseph Reiner, and is described as being published with "ecclesiastical approbation."

[34] In a Church so dogmatic in theology and monolithic in organisation as the Roman Catholic, it is probably unwise to contrast too sharply the differences between "conservative" and "liberal," "traditionalist" or "modernist" viewpoints. Nevertheless, on questions of sexual relationships and birth control there would appear to be marked differences of approach by various groups within the Church. Dr. Richard Fagley examines this problem in some detail in his book, distinguishing between what he describes as the "pro-fertility" and "responsible parenthood" factions among Roman Catholics. He claims that the former group has tended to re-establish its ascendancy during recent years. (*The Population Explosion and Christian Responsibility*, pp. 184–7, by Richard M. Fagley, O.U.P., New York, 1960).

[35] *The Catholic Book of Marriage*, pp. 84, 94, 96 by the Rev. P. C. M. Kelly (Longmans, 1952).

[36] *Marriage: A Medical and Sacramental Study* by Alan Keenan, O.F.M., and John Ryan (Sheed and Ward, 1955). This book has the *Imprimatur* of the Archbishop of Boston.

[37] "Morality in Marriage, A Pronouncement by Pius XII." Original text in Italian, *Acta Apostolicae Sedis*. Dec. 20th, 1951.

[38] Problems of greater complexity may arise for all the Christian Churches as chemists and biologists produce ever more refined methods of contraception. At what precise moment, for example, does conception occur—at the moment when the egg is fertilised or when nidation in the wall of the womb takes place? The distinction between contraception and abortion may present theologians with as much difficulty during the second half of the twentieth century as the debate over the question when the soul entered the body did in mediaeval Europe.

[39] *Population and World Resources*, a statement by Prof. M. P. Fogarty presented to the International Union of Social Studies, 1953.

La Limitation des Naissances by S. de Lestapis, S.J. (Spes, Paris, 1959).

Over-Population—Is Birth Control the Answer? by the Rev. Arthur MacCormack (Catholic Truth Society, 1960).

[40] Catholics agree with Communists in this respect!

[41] "Over-Population—Is Birth Control the Answer?" by Colin Clark. (Review article in *Family Planning*, April, 1960.)

[42] Both the Protestant and Roman Catholic Churches show remarkably similar

developments in doctrine in this respect. Traditionally, the view was that sexual pleasure within marriage was somewhat sinful (even if venially so) and that the sole aim of marriage was begetting children. The more recent view is that "mutual help" (a wide phrase covering a multitude of ways in which husbands and wives may help and please each other) is also an essential part of the marriage contract. The newest Roman Catholic manuals on marriage insist that a happy and mutually satisfying sexual relationship may be an important factor in keeping husbands and wives together and thus preventing divorce.

[43] *Marriage and Birth Control,* p. 10, by the Rt. Rev. A. A. David and the Rt. Rev. M. B. Furse (James Nisbet, c. 1930).

[44] *Moral and Pastoral Theology,* vol. IV, p. 243, by Rev. Henry Davis, S.J. (Sheed & Ward, 1948).

[45] *Two in One Flesh: An Introduction to Sex and Marriage,* p. XIII, by the Rev. E. C. Messenger. (Sands, 1948).

[46] For example, the debate whether Onan was punished for "spilling his seed upon the ground" or for failing to obey the levirate law of the Old Testament Jews.

[47] *The Family in Contemporary Society,* p. 13 (S.P.C.K., 1958).

[48] *Family Limitation,* p. 8, by John Ryan, M.B., B.S., F.R.C.S., F.I.C.S. with a Preface by Alan Keenan, O.F.M. (Sheed & Ward, 1957).

[49] *The Rhythm of Sterility and Fertility in Women* by Leo J. Latz (Latz Foundation, Chicago, 1939). Preface by Joseph Reiner, S.J.

[50] Not only, as previously explained, may the sale of contraceptives be forbidden by law, but local priests will try to ensure that their warnings are not being ignored by, for example, descreet enquiries to young married couples, if childless, why they are not beginning a family.

[51] Roman Catholic priests are particularly concerned at the danger of contamination of their flocks in mixed Protestant-Catholic communities. For example, Father Keenan in his Foreword to *Family Limitation* points out that Roman Catholics in Britain and the U.S.A. are only a minority of the population living in a society built largely on principles contrary to what they believe. "But they must breathe its air," he says, "share its life, seek its rewards, accept its responsibilities, endure its social pressures and accept its outlook. As sharers in this society, they are relentlessly moulded by its mass media of communication. Like other citizens, they have the same wish to conform to the group, to be good Englishmen or good Americans, never deviants as far as they can be from accepted social practice." *Family Limitation,* p. 6, by John Ryan, M.B., B.S., F.R.C.S., F.I.C.S.; foreword by Alan Keenan, O.F.M.

[52] *Report of the Commission on Emigration and Other Population Problems.* 1948–54, p. 96 (Stationery Office, Dublin).

In Britain the Royal Commission on Population, *Report,* para. 72 (H.M.S.O., 1949) comments: ". . . Roman Catholics of different occupational groups seem to differ in average family size in very much the same way as non-Catholics."

[53] *Papers of the Royal Commission on Population,* vol. I, p. 81 (H.M.S.O., 1949).

[54] *The Sexual, Marital and Family Relationships of the English Women* by Dr. Eustace Chesser, Joan Maizels, Leonard Jones and Brian Emmet (Hutchinson, 1956).

[55] *Patterns of Marriage: A Study of Marriage Relationships in the Urban Working Classes,* p. 210, by Eliot Slater and Moya Woodside (Cassell, 1951).

[56] *Medical History of Contraception,* by Norman E. Himes, p. 415 (Allen & Unwin, 1936).

[57] *The Rhythm of Sterility and Fertility in Women,* by Leo J. Latz, p. 149 (Latz Foundation, Chicago, 1939).

[58] *Family Planning, Sterility and Population Growth,* p. 174 by Ronald Freedman, Pascal K. Whelpton and Arthur A. Campbell (McGraw Hill, New York, 1959).

[59] *Homiletic and Pastoral Review,* May, 1933. "Birth Control and Catholic Leakage," by John A. O'Brien.

[60] *The Family and the Future,* p. 37 by Andrew Beck (Catholic Social Guild, Oxford, 1948).

92

Resistance to Birth Control Within the Medical Profession

For many decades, the proponents of birth control had to fight the spokesman for organized religion. It would be nice to report that the birth controllers were supported in this by organized medicine, but they were not. Some individual physicians showed considerable heroism, but organized medicine was either neutral or antagonistic until quite recently. At every epoch there were doctors whose attitudes were indistinguishable from the attitudes of the more conservative religious men of their day. One Isaac Peirce, M.D., wrote in 1888:

> Every man knows the horrors of illicit love and the suffering of misguided though patient and confiding women; no man is insensible to the lifelong shame of a child thrown upon the world without knowing a father; and no man denies the wickedness of criminal abortion. No medical man doubts the suffering, and in many cases permanent injury, of the woman who practices abortion that she may escape the shame of her own wickedness, sinning doubly that she may shield herself and her destroyer from the condemnation of the world. No, it takes no one to tell us this; we all know it too well; the poor creatures come to us almost every day, broken down in health, asking for treatment, asking that their secret be protected, and are willing to undergo anything to relieve their physical suffering and escape the consequences of their error. There are others known to us who are in a worse condition, those who yield to the seducer's embrace, bear their children, and, losing all respect for self, plunge into the depths of misery and disease, becoming of those to whom Mr. Lecky thus alludes in his **History of Morals in Europe:** "That unhappy being whose very name is a shame to speak, who counterfeits, with a cold heart, the transports of affection; scorned and insulted as the vilest of her sex, and doomed, for the most part, to abject wretchedness and an early grave, she is in every age the perpetual symbol of the

degeneration and sinfulness of man; she remains while creeds and civilizations rise and fall, the eternal priestess of humanity blasted for the sins of the people."

Now, knowing the state of things as the members of the medical profession do, and having exerted every effort toward a remedy, is there a possibility of bettering these conditions by preventing conception . . . ? I say No! I think it can be made plain to every man that we would but bring about a worse state of affairs, if it is possible to imagine anything worse. It is true we may prevent criminal abortion, we may lessen suffering, pauperism, and neglect among children the issue of illicit love; but we do more, and we should look at this side of the question. Is it the woman, who in the hour of her fall thinks of conception? Does a preventive suggest itself to her? Does she dream that this act will crown the love and trust she has given her seducer before the hour of its perpetration? Or is it the man, who, knowing his vows of love and marriage to be false, plans her fall and studies the question of a preventive? In eight cases out of ten, I think it is the man; and, with a sure preventive in his hands, how much stronger will be his argument, how much oftener will his persuasion meet compliance, and we all know how the falsity of his promise of marriage will increase. In the other two cases, it will require no offer of marriage, no vows of love; the desire and the preventive will be all that is required to carry them from the arms of one lover to those of another.

If . . . a man is not culpable before the laws of God and man who interferes to prevent gestation **before** conception has occurred, as I see it, he will institute a new moral law which will be entirely different from that taught by any period of the world's history. . . . I think I have ground for my fear when I shudder at what would be the result of the promiscuous prevention of conception, even with the idea of stopping criminal abortion, pauperism, and suffering of illegitimate children. I believe that if we put into the hands of men a ready and sure means of preventing conception, there will be more prostitutes, fewer marriages, and more disease amongst women. . . .

Let it become generally known that the medical profession countenances a preventive even in a few cases, and there is reason to fear this will be stretched to a license which will work much mischief to women who are already experimenting in this direction, who have no reason why they should not fulfill the God-given function which makes happy homes, and who are now only held in check by the judgment of the world.[1]

The history of Margaret Sanger's encounter with the medical profession shows that thirty years later the attitude of Dr. Peirce was a common one among physicians; and it did not disappear entirely even in another thirty years.

This attitude toward the practice of medicine interfered also with medical investigation. In 1918, Dr. William A. Cary devised one of the first contraceptive jellies, but he found that he could not publish the formula in medical journals.[2] Many of his colleagues shunned him. Like most gynecologists he was interested in both increasing and decreasing fertility, according to the individual needs and desires of the patients. But so great was the discouragement of research in reproduction that when he came to write a review of infertility in the early 30's he could uncover only 55 citations in the entire literature in four languages in sixty years.

In 1937, after two decades of prodding by Margaret Sanger, the American Medical Association gave a guarded endorsement of birth control. By this time the most important court battles had been won. Many doctors simply did not want to think about such matters. When Dr. Alan Guttmacher conducted a mail poll of physicians in 1944, seeking to determine their attitudes toward birth control, more than 75 percent did not reply.

Personal contact would have elicited more replies, of course. But as late as 1957, using this approach the National Opinion Research Center (University of Chicago) found that nine percent of the non-Catholic and 19 percent of the Catholic physicians refused to cooperate. As one would expect, older Catholics were less cooperative than younger. Regardless of religion, the sort of medical service such noncooperating doctors were administering to their female patients can be easily (though not pleasantly) imagined.

A doctor is not only a man who has been technically trained; he is also the aggregation of a lifetime of psychological experiences, traumas, and enduring threats with which he has somehow made his peace. The conditions of this unwritten peace may prejudice the way in which he practices medicine. Lawrence Kubie, a psychiatrist of wide experience, has written:

> As an example of the role of unconscious residues of childhood's battles, I would cite the gynecologist whose ancient and infantile curiosities were not to be satisfied by the justified activities of his profession, and who was plagued by an insatiable compulsion to visit burlesque shows. One could hardly ask for a better experimental demonstration of the fact that unconscious needs cannot be gratified by conscious fulfillment. A comparable example is found in the X-ray man whose choice of a career was determined predominantly by his unconscious curiosity about the internal structure of his mother's body. In all innocence both men dedicated their lives to the service of childhood cravings which were buried in guilt and fear.[3]

Perhaps the proportion of physicians who suffer from improperly resolved guilt and fear is only a minority of the whole—at least I hope so. But it is in the nature of things that fearful, guilt-ridden men are disproportionately influential in shaping human organizations, including medical organizations. It is the consequences of their dominance that account for the pessimistic view of society expressed by W. B. Yeats:

> The best lack all conviction, while the worst
> Are full of passionate intensity.

The best, by definition, are those who use reason to lead them to the truth. Having used reason thus far they are generally inclined to trust it further to shape their actions. In the short run they may lose out to men whose unresolved fears evoke instant action. But in the long run . . . ? Does not the history of man's real progression toward dignity in human reproduction give us grounds for optimism?

[1] *Medical and Surgical Reporter,* **59** (1888):614–616.
[2] *Fertility and Sterility,* **4** (1953):109.
[3] Maurice R. Stein, Arthur J. Vidich, and David Manning White (eds.), *Identity and Anxiety,* Glencoe, Ill.: Free Press, 1960, p. 248.

References

Peel, John. 1964. "Contraception and the medical profession." *Population Studies,* **18:**133–145.

Spirack, S. S. 1963. *Doctors and Family Planning.* New York: National Committee on Maternal Health, Pub. No. 19.

93

Birth Control and Catholic Doctrine

Alvah W. Sulloway
1915–

Boston: Beacon Press

1959

Granting that the immorality of contraception may have been a doctrine of the Church before 1920, still it differed from certain other better known doctrines in one notable respect. The Trinity and the Resurrection, for example, are preached year in and year out, regardless of whether the members of the Church are concerned about them at a particular time or place. The sinfulness of contraception, on the other hand, had little significance as a doctrine of the Church until the discovery of efficient contraceptives in the nineteenth century gave it a reason for existence. It must be assumed that earlier and usually oblique references to contraception in the writings of Aquinas, Augustine, and others did not refer, whatever they may have meant, to contraceptive techniques as they are known today. Nor did these writers have within their range of observation social and economic conditions comparable to those of the present time.

Catholic publications show the remarkable evolution undergone by the Church's doctrines on birth control in the twentieth century. Significantly, the *Catholic Encyclopedia,* published in 1907, does not even list the subject of birth control although it does contain a long article on theories of population. This article was written by Reverend John A. Ryan, who later became one of the most forceful Catholic opponents of the birth control movement. After a historical review of population theories and a long exposition of Malthus, Ryan proceeds to criticize the Malthusian theory, devoting several paragraphs to a discussion of the Neo-Malthusianism, the then current name for birth control. He points out that the practices of Neo-Malthusianism are "intrinsically immoral, implying as they do either foeticide, or the perversion of natural faculties and functions." From a social standpoint, he says, a small family is harmful both to the members of the family and to the nation for it "fosters a degree of egotism and enervating self-indulgence which in turn diminishes the incentive to labour and reduces industrial production." The rising standard of living contemplated by Neo-Malthusianism will, we are told, create a lower rather than a higher plane of life, "not more genuine culture or lofty morals, but more abundant physical enjoyments and a more refined materialism."

This article in the *Catholic Encyclopedia* is especially noteworthy because it treats birth control as only one aspect of the population problem. Ryan's critique is that of the economist, sociologist, or moralist and not that of the churchman. He never mentions specifically any ecclesiastical prohibitions against Neo-Malthusianism. He states no ecclesiastical doctrines. He does not discuss theology and, while he refers to a "perversion of natural faculties," he does not develop the natural law thesis which the Church subsequently elaborated as the root of its opposition to birth control. Whereas the same writer in 1930, during the course of an article on St. Thomas Aquinas for the *Encyclopaedia of the Social Sciences,* refers to the Angelic Doctor's pronouncement that birth control is against nature and therefore morally wrong, he does not in 1907 attempt to reinforce his critique of Neo-Malthusianism by a reference to St. Thomas nor does he cite other available authorities or precedents for his opinion.

This omission is even more significant when one considers the exhaustive treatment given by the *Catholic Encyclopedia* to such an allied subject as usury. Usury was condemned by the medieval Church because among other reasons the lending of money at interest contravened natural law. Although an important ingredient of the sin was the advantage taken by the lender of necessitous men, the metaphysical idea, first expressed by Aristotle, that money is by nature sterile underlies almost all ecclesiastical discussions of usury and gives the Church's attitude its philosophical basis. From these discussions we learn that the natural and proper end of money is considered to be exchange. If it feeds on itself as it does when it is loaned at interest, the lender is said to be guilty of frustrating its natural end, an idea strikingly similar to the Church's later arguments against contraception. By 1907 usury had long ceased to be a subject of controversy. The Church had modified its original position which prohibited all loans at interest regardless of whether or not the rate was excessive, thereby demonstrating that seemingly unchangeable doctrines of natural law are subject to interpretation and change. The interesting point is that notwithstanding the currently academic status of the usury issue in the twentieth century the *Catholic Encyclopedia* nevertheless took the opportunity to show that usury was still a subject of great concern to the Church. It supported this view by a citation of authorities and conciliar decisions. But since natural law prohibitions against birth control are, according to Catholics, as ancient as the prohibitions against usury—in fact more ancient if we date them back to Onan—the dissimilarity of the treatment of the two subjects in the *Catholic Encyclopedia* of 1907 would indicate that Catholic doctrines on birth control are, for all practical purposes, of more recent innovation than Catholic writers after 1914 would lead their readers to believe.

The *Catholic Encyclopedia Supplement* published in 1922 also discusses birth control under the title of "Population." While the word *Neo-Malthusianism* is retained throughout the article, the term *Birth Control* appears in its proper alphabetical order with the reference: "See *Population*." Unlike the earlier treatment of population theories by Ryan, this unsigned article does not even pretend to be concerned with the general problems of population. Indeed, it is devoted entirely to an exposition of the errors of Neo-Malthusianism and the evils attendant upon its practice. In the first sentence it states, "Fresh interest has been developed the past ten years in the Malthus theories on over-population and the consequent necessity of controlling or limiting the number of births, not by continence or the practice of self-restraint, as he came to counsel in his later works, but by various prohibitions, physical or chemical, for the use rather of the woman than of the man." By this indirect reference to the rise of the birth control movement, the article prepares its readers for the lurid counterattack which, in contrast to the restrained and dignified prose of Ryan in 1907,

237

it is about to launch against the proponents of contraception. Their motive is said to be "an apparent quest for lucre." The article charges that the "unnatural and immoral principles" of the movement will cause "grave physical and moral disorders," fibroid tumors, sterility instead of pregnancy, neurasthenia, loss of mutual self-respect, infidelity, separation, and divorce. The woman who practices contraception accepts "the conditions of a prostitute for those of married life."

In order to destroy the very foundation of Neo-Malthusianism the article next directs its attack against the Malthusian thesis that population will soon outstrip food supply. This thesis is refuted by arguing that an increase in population will lead to an increase and improvement in the means of production, an argument not substantiated by the facts of population growth and food supply during the next thirty-five years. To clinch this argument, the article refers to the catastrophies of famine, volcano, and earthquake which, in spite of all human skill and effort, will occur to kill off population. Any excess overlooked by nature will be removed by man.

> What nature may not do, human beings themselves will do, as did Greece two hundred years before Christ, anticipating as they did the counsels of Malthus, living in luxury, controlling, that is to say, avoiding pregnancy, and decaying as a consequence, as did their conquerors, the Romans, who in turn imitated these vices, and since then notably the Mohammedan and other peoples who, to indulge in lust, have ignored the command to increase and multiply.

This is one of the rare occasions in Catholic literature on contraception when nature, in either its human or its nonhuman capacity, has been invoked as an agent of population control. Moreover, the violent and unrestrained tone of the article suggests, which was of course the fact, that since the publication of the *Catholic Encyclopedia* in 1907 birth control had ceased to be a theoretical issue which could be quietly discussed in books of reference and learned periodicals.

94

Birth Control and Dogma

Various

An exchange of Letters to the Editor;
reprinted in their entirety
Science, **131:**1010 ff.

1960

George Calingaert

LETTER

The comments of J. K. O'Loane [*Science* **130,** 1302 (1959)] on M. E. Davis' review of Sulloway's *Birth Control and Catholic Doctrine* [*Science* **130,** 559 (1959)] deserve notice because they illustrate strikingly the dual intellectual attitude of the Catholic scientist. O'Loane is quite correct, of course, in his description of the distinction which the Catholic Church makes between its doctrine and its opinion. As a scientist he will no doubt understand that for a non-Catholic what matters is what the church claims and does, and not whether, inside the Church, one particular claim is based on doctrine, or on personal taste, or on scientific evidence. It must have been small consolation to Bruno and Galileo that their torments were caused by the then prevalent opinion of the Church and not by a point of immutable doctrine.

As regards the important subject of controlling the size of our population, scientists are glad to learn from O'Loane that Catholic *doctrine* is not against artificial birth control; this justifies the hope that on this point also the Catholic Church will someday change its opinion, even if —as in the case of the heliocentric system—it takes three centuries to do so.

Robert Hoffman

LETTER

In a recent letter J. Kenneth O'Loane reproved M. Edward Davis for accepting Sulloway's view that the Catholic Church has made an official pronouncement against contraception. O'Loane contended, *au contraire,*

239

that although some Catholic writers have adopted the position alleged by Sulloway to be the Church's, the Church itself "never has taken a doctrinal stand that 'separation of intercourse and parenthood' is wrong." In this dispute I side with Davis and Sulloway and should like to provide the Papal text that supports their position and to comment briefly upon the issue.

In the encyclical *Casti connubii,* dated 31 December 1930, Pius XI declared the following with regard to contraception: "Since, therefore, openly departing from the uninterrupted Christian tradition, some recently have judged it possible solemnly to declare another doctrine regarding this question, *the Catholic Church,* to whom God has entrusted the teaching and defense of the integrity and purity of morals, standing erect in the midst of the moral ruin which surrounds her, in order that she may preserve the chastity of nuptial union from being defiled by this foul stain, *raises her voice in token of her divine ambassadorship and through Our mouth proclaims anew: any use whatsoever of matrimony exercised in such a way that the act is deliberately frustrated in its natural power to generate life is an offense against the law of God and of nature, and those who indulge in such are branded with the guilt of grace sin"* (italics added).[1] This quotation reproduces section 56 of the encyclical in its entirety. The three sections immediately preceding it should also be consulted, for they make manifest the full intensity of the Papal condemnation.

O'Loane emphasized that "the Church is considered to have taken a doctrinal stand in a matter when she has (i) made an infallible pronouncement by the head of the Church; (ii) defined by an Ecumenical Council; (iii) authoritatively proposed some creed, formula of belief, or matter of moral behavior." Although O'Loane did not so indicate by placing the word *or* between the second and third of the criteria, each of them is a sufficient condition. Clearly, the second is not applicable to the case in point. Let us, therefore, consider the first. According to the canons of the Vatican Council of 1870, the Roman Pontiff is infallible when he speaks ex cathedra—that is, when he speaks "in discharge of the office of pastor and doctor of all Christians (*sic*)."[2] Referring to the text quoted above and keeping in mind that the encyclical was addressed to all the faithful, one is logically entitled to conclude that Pius XI was speaking ex cathedra. Moreover, it would be difficult to deny that the portion of the text reading "the Catholic Church . . . raises her voice in token of her divine ambassadorship and through Our mouth proclaims . . ." fulfills the third of O'Loane's criteria.

Perhaps, then, neither Sulloway nor Davis is as "deficient in philosophical and theological background" as O'Loane would have us think.

Alan Rhodes

LETTER

In a recent issue O'Loane presents a Catholic criticism of *Science's* review of the book *Birth Control and Catholic Doctrine.* O'Loane does not like the review and says that the editors of *Science* should "insist on the same objectivity in presentation of the position of the Catholic Church that they would on any strictly scientific matter."

O'Loane then proceeds to draw a fine legalistic type of distinction between the actions and views of the Catholic Church that are backed up by a "doctrinal stand" and those that are not. He tells us that the Catholic Church has taken no doctrinal stand on birth control and cites as a parallel case the dispute over an earth-centered versus a sun-centered solar system. He says that no doctrinal stand was taken on either of these matters, and he therefore implies that discussion of either of these matters is irrelevant. Apparently it is also irrelevant that Galileo was condemned for his views, that the sentence was ratified by the Pope, and that his works were placed on the *Index,* where they remained for 200 years. Is a victim of an undeclared war any less dead than the victim of a declared war?

In contrast, the doctrine of the Assumption is cited as an infallible article of doctrine because of the statement of the Pope on 1 November, 1950. Therefore scientist O'Loane must be certain that the Virgin Mary ascended bodily to heaven, flesh, skin, bones, hair, toenails, and all.

The only way a scientist can accommodate this sort of thinking is to have a bicompartmented mind—one compartment for logical reasoning, the other compartment for matters of faith. In a scientific discussion logic is not allowed to enter the sphere of faith, or at least is allowed to enter only on a subordinate basis. That is why the Catholic logician is always subordinate to the Catholic theologian. The theologian is the dogma-maker, and the logician fits his logic to the dogma, or if he can't make it fit, he is required to suspend judgment.

A scientist who discards scientific objectivity as soon as the thought process arrives in the forbidden area of dogma and doctrine is only a part-time scientist. Indeed it would be more wholesome if such a scientist would base himself squarely on faith and make no pretense to a scientific apology for doctrinal belief.

As to the tremendous import of the population bomb, which is the essential message of Sulloway's book, I would that some Amos or Isaiah could wake up the sleeping minds of our Catholic brethren.

J. Kenneth O'Loane

In my earlier letter (p. 1364) I said: "The Catholic Church . . . believes the end does not justify the means, and the use of bad means for a good end makes [an] act morally bad . . . the means, artificial birth control, are always wrong." Apparently it was not clear to some that this is equivalent to saying that it is a *doctrine* of the Catholic Church that artificial birth control is always morally wrong. My reply will be confined to attempting to clear up some errors of fact and to answering the charge of "the dual intellectual attitude of the Catholic scientist."

When a married couple wishes to limit the number of their children, there are, omitting any consideration of sterilization, four methods they can use: they are (i) refrain from using their marital rights; (ii) make use of their marital rights in the proper manner, but at a time when conception cannot normally take place; (iii) make use of some method of artificial birth control; (iv) resort to abortion.

The term *proper manner* means that the marital act is performed so that the male organ deposits semen in the vagina of the female. The term *artificial birth control* means interference with the proper manner of performing the marital act by withdrawal or by some chemical, mechanical, or other artificial means designed to prevent conception.

Regarding the four methods of limiting the size of the family the doctrine of the Catholic Church is as follows: (i) abstinence is permissible under certain circumstances; (ii) marital rights may, under certain circumstances, be used in the proper manner at a time when conception cannot normally take place; (iii) artificial birth control is *always* morally wrong; (iv) therapeutic abortion is regarded as murder.

Methods (ii) and (iii) are both means for separating intercourse and parenthood. Intercourse and parenthood are also separated when the partners are sterile by virtue either of natural defect or of age. Sulloway is undoubtedly correct in saying there were Catholic *authors* who, as Davis[3] puts it, "attributed . . . dire consequences to the separation of intercourse and parenthood." From this Davis and Sulloway erroneously concluded that the Catholic *Church* had taken a stand against the "separation of intercourse and parenthood." Sulloway did not (and cannot) prove this.

Apparently Sulloway fell into this error because he did not understand the relationship between what a Catholic writer may say and what the Church teaches. Since Catholic authors can be on either or both sides of a disputed question, one must not attribute to the Church the views of some particular author. This error is, unfortunately, quite common among non-Catholics and formed the basis for a considerable number of additional errors made by an Episcopalian bishop in a recent issue of *Life* magazine.

This was why I used the dual illustration of the Copernican theory and the dogma of the Assumption. The first illustrates the case in which, although Catholic writers were on both sides of a question for many decades, the Church took no doctrinal stand. This was obviously not parallel to the case of birth control.

Copernicus,[4] who died some 20 years before Galileo was born, was one of a growing number of churchmen-scientists who realized that the idea, then current among theologians, that the Bible gave detailed information on astronomy and geology was wrong. James B. Conant[5] has pointed out that a new scientific idea takes hold slowly even among scientists. So it was in this case. Eventually it was realized that Copernicus was correct in his scientific theory and in the idea, not original with him, as to the relation of the Bible and astronomy.

The Church never took a doctrinal stand one way or the other. It took *disciplinary* action against Galileo—he was never tortured—because he violated a gentleman's agreement of 1616 which allowed him to teach Copernicus' theory as a scientific hypothesis but not as a fact.[6]

The second example, that of the doctrine of the Assumption, illustrates a dispute concerning an apostolic tradition commonly accepted by the Eastern Orthodox and Catholic churches for many centuries[7] but not formally defined as a doctrine. Since it was not formally defined, further discussion was permissible, and Catholic writers were found on both sides until the Church finally crystallized its stand in an irrevocable doctrinal decision in 1950.

With respect to the position of the Church on separation of intercourse and parenthood, the facts are that it has repeatedly condemned method (iii), artificial birth control, but never method (ii).

In 1823 the Sacred Penitentiary declared the prevention of conception by artificial means contrary to the natural moral law. In 1851 the Holy Office said that the onanistic use (Gen. 38:9) of marriage was opposed to the natural moral law.[8] The latest condemnation is that quoted by Hoffman from Pius XI's encyclical on "Christian Marriage."

The legitimacy of the so-called rhythm method is mentioned in the same encyclical: "Nor are those considered as acting against nature who in the married state use their right in the proper manner, although on account of natural reasons, either *of time* or of natural defects, new life cannot be brought forth" (italics added).[9] Because, as I said in my earlier letter, the Church had never condemned the separation of intercourse and parenthood, no shift in its position was necessary when the rhythm method became

243

known. Davis' and Sulloway's allegation that the Church shifted its position is but another of their many errors.

Although Hoffman wrongly understood his quotation from the encyclical as condemning the separation of intercourse and parenthood, and although he is also mistaken in thinking that the encyclical satisfies the conditions for an ex cathedra pronouncement,[10] he is correct in concluding that the condemnation of artificial birth control has a doctrinal basis in the Catholic Church.

There remains the question of whether, as Sulloway, Davis, and Calingaert hope, the Catholic Church will change its opinion, even if it takes a few centuries to do so. This hope has been expressed repeatedly in the past several years by members of the Planned Parenthood Federation, various demographers, and even Protestant clergymen, who, in some cases, have asserted that the Catholic Church must or will change its mind. Perhaps the worst feature of Sulloway's very unfortunate book[11] will be its effect in helping to foster this delusion.

This vain hope arises because these critics do not understand that the Church's ban on artificial birth control is not a disciplinary matter, as are, for example, Friday abstinence, the observance of Sunday instead of the Sabbath, and the celibacy of the clergy. In the case of birth control the Church is interpreting both the natural moral law and Sacred Scripture. When she does this, she acts only as a teacher, not as a lawmaker. Since God, not the Church, is the author of the law, the Church cannot change it.

As I said previously, "an *essential* claim of the Catholic Church is that when it *does* take a definite doctrinal stand it cannot be in error." The Catholic Church would collapse if it ever changed in essence one of its doctrines. However, "over a period of 20 centuries the Church has never made an essential change in any of its doctrines," and it never will.

Since the purpose of the first letter was to correct serious misstatements appearing in a review, it was not *ad rem* to discuss the problem of control of population. However, since Calingaert and Rhodes have mentioned it, I shall make just two remarks. If there is a population control problem in some parts of the world, the duty of the individual Catholic is not solved by pointing out the moral law. Catholics, as well as others, are bound to aid in its solution by using all *moral* means.[12]

It is not surprising that Calingaert and Rhodes, having missed the main points of my letter, should be in difficulty in assessing the situation where other, more subtle, factors, such as evaluation of the intellectual attitude of a whole age, are involved. Passing over their various fantasies and implications, unwarranted either in logic or fact, I come to the problem of the supposed dual intellectual attitude of the Catholic scientist.

In the short space of a letter to the editor all I can hope to do is outline the situation briefly. Neither in my earlier letter nor in this one am I presenting any apologia for doctrinal belief, either scientific or philosophical. I am only [trying to clear] up errors of fact and sketching a position in outline.[13] A good starting point is to consider what the non-Catholic scientist would have to investigate if he wished really to understand Catholicism.

Many scientists today are materialistic monists in metaphysics and positivists in epistemology. The first thing one has to be willing to do is to subject these conclusions to methodic doubt. If at the end of this preliminary investigation one is still convinced that these are valid positions, there is no use going any further. If, however, one comes to the conclusion that the universe is best explained metaphysically by a material and spiritual dualism and that true and certain knowledge can be obtained by other means in addition to the complex vaguely called the "scientific method," the really basic question is whether or not there exists an intelligent, supreme being.

Careful, reflective thinking is necessary at this point. The few scraps of philosophical knowledge picked up in an education often markedly deficient in the liberal arts, and a materialist and positivist bias absorbed from teachers, will not be adequate and proper.[14]

If one concludes that there is no God, he will remain a speculative atheist; if he concludes that we cannot know, he is an agnostic. However, if there does exist a supreme, personal, spiritual being, the second question is, has he ever had any formal, public contacts with the human race. Of all the literature on this subject only the books of the Old and New Testament can satisfactorily pass the required tests as valid historical documents. While an Orthodox Jew will reject the New Testament, he can certainly accept everything else up to this point.

The New Testament reveals a person who claimed, and proved himself to be, both God and man. Some Unitarians will drop out here, but most Christians will remain. It also shows that he founded a Church which cannot err in matters of faith or morals. Obviously most Protestants will not believe their church is infallible in faith and morals, although they will be able to accept the rest. However, if one is morally certain on the last five points, it is eminently rational to believe whatever such a church proposes for belief in the sphere in which it is competent.

When there is added to this the reasonable conclusion that truth in science cannot clash with truth in philosophy and theology, and vice versa, the problem of the supposed dualism as formulated by Calingaert and Rhodes simply does not arise. Apparent differences between science and theology are due to an incomplete understanding of the one or the other and will certainly be resolved on further study, though this, just as with purely scientific questions, may take years of effort. Theologians, being human, will occasionally make errors in scientific fields, as they did in the case of

Galileo and Darwin. Scientists, at least as human, will make errors in the fields of philosophy and theology.

In my own experience, what has usually happened is that people who pride themselves on being very scientific will reject a priori, on what are actually philosophical, not scientific grounds, some religious belief. This is what Rhodes has done, in rather offensive terms, with respect to the doctrine of the Assumption.[13] He is quite mistaken in saying that "scientist O'Loane is certain" on this point. *Scientist* O'Loane says nothing about this point for the reason that *science* says nothing pro or con. As I said earlier, it is a matter of an apostolic tradition, which is morally certain and accepted both by Eastern Orthodox churches and by the Catholic Church.

The experience of two thousand years confirms the conclusion of a rational faith: there has never been *anything* in Catholic doctrine contrary to scientific fact, nor can there be in the future.

---

[1] Pope Pius XI, *"Casti connubii,"* reprinted in T. P. McLaughlin (ed.), *The Church and the Reconstruction of the Modern World* (Image Books, Garden City, N.Y., 1957), p. 136.

[2] "First Dogmatic Constitution on the Church of Christ," chap. iv, reprinted in G. MacGregor, *The Vatican Revolution* (Beacon, Boston, 1957), p. 195.

[3] M. E. Davis, *Science* **130,** 559 (1959).

[4] W. M. Agar, *Catholicism and the Progress of Science* (Macmillan, New York, 1940), pp. 32–40.

[5] J. B. Conant, *On Understanding Science* (Yale Univ. Press, New Haven, Conn., 1947); *Science and Common Sense* (Yale Univ. Press, New Haven, Conn., 1951).

[6] C. S. Slichter, *Am. Scientist* **31,** 168 (1943) (one of the fairer treatments by a non-Catholic mathematician).

[7] P. F. Palmer, *Mary in the Documents of the Church* (Newman, Westminster, Md., 1952), pp. 59–61; quotation from St. John Damascene's sermon, "On the falling asleep of the Mother of God" (8th century).

[8] D. Pruemmer, *Birth Control* (Paulist Press, New York, 1933), p. 5.

[9] *Four Great Encyclicals* (Paulist Press, New York), p. 92. The paragraph referred to is the third following the quotation given by Hoffman.

[10] J. M. O'Neill, *Catholicism and American Freedom* (Harper, New York, 1952), p. 160.

[11] J. R. Connery, *America* **101,** 250, 252 (1959); D. J. Bradley, *Catholic World* **189,** 250 (1959).

[12] Editorial, *The Commonweal* **60,** 333 (1954); A. M. Churchill, *ibid.* **60,** 344 (1954); D. Lyons, *ibid.* **60,** 438 (1954); W. J. Grace, *Catholic World* **183,** 406 (1956); R. H. Amundson, *ibid.* **185,** 352 (1957).

[13] Those who wish to know more of the reasons behind the Catholic Church's position on birth control may see J. L. Thomas, *Daedalus* **88,** 444 (1959); *Ave Maria* **91,** 5, 24 (1960); T. J. O'Donnell, *Morals in Medicine* (Newman, Westminster, Md., 1959).

[14] J. H. Ryan, *An Introduction to Philosophy* (Macmillan, New York, 1924); J. Maritain, *An Introduction to Philosophy* (Sheed and Ward, New York); D. J.

Sullivan, *An Introduction to Philosophy* (Bruce, Milwaukee, 1957); F. J. Sheed, *Theology and Sanity* (Sheed and Ward, New York, 1946).

[13] For the positions of various schools of Catholic thought on the condition of the body after resurrection, see George G. Smith (Ed.), *The Teaching of the Catholic Church* (Macmillan, New York, 1950), vol. 2, pp. 1232–1247.

95

How Good Is the Rhythm Method?

During the 1940's Catholic spokesmen waged a strong campaign for the rhythm method of birth control. Many of them maintained that it was at least as good as contraception, and almost all of them insisted that it was the only moral method. The second assertion led to some trouble in international affairs. When the government of India, in 1951, asked the World Health Organization for help in reducing its population growth, Catholic countries threatened to resign from the international organization if it advocated any but the rhythm method. Faced with this ultimatum, WHO capitulated and did its best to make the rhythm method work in Indian villages. The result was an abysmal failure.

The rhythm method, though it looks cheap because it involves no expensive supplies, can hardly be the method of choice among illiterate or undisciplined people, which the impoverished of the world generally are. The user of the method must at least be able to count and keep track of days if she is to make it work. And we should not be very optimistic about persuading the impoverished to use it unless we offer them other amusements to replace the one we propose so much to deprive them of. These other amusements— radios, television, automobiles, what have you—cost money, so it is hardly conceivable that the rhythm method will be the most economical method to export to what we euphemistically call the "underdeveloped nations." If all costs are considered, the rhythm method is probably the most expensive of the lot.

Given ideal conditions, does the rhythm method work? Fortunately we have a statistically sound study[1] that answers this question. The statistic utilized is the "number of conceptions per 100 woman-years exposure"—that is, exposure to copulation. By way of background: if no birth control methods at all are used (not even the rhythm method), the number is 90 or a bit higher. It is less than 100 because some couples are naturally sterile; the percentage varies from one population to another, but in the United States sterility affects about 10 percent of all married couples.

As of the mid-twentieth century, the medical profession regarded the diaphragm and contraceptive jelly as the best method of contraception. This method decreases the conception rate to about 6.5 per 100 woman years exposure. This sounds good, though one cannot but ask: Why is the figure not zero? No definitive answer is available in the literature, but there is **no** reason to distrust the spermicidal quality of the jelly or the impermeability of the rubber. Taboos against the discussion of sexual matters are still not wholly at an end in the medical profession. The reported failure rate of 6.5 is undoubtedly due to undiscussed psychological matters; and we will just have to accept this rather high figure as the control rate against which we must compare the efficacy of other methods.

In evaluating the rhythm method, Tietze, Poliakoff, and Rock first sorted out their women patients into those with and those without regular rhythms. **The latter, approximately one-sixth of the population, were eliminated from the study.** The rhythmic women were so identified only after the completion of three regular cycles during which they (and their husbands) voluntarily abstained from coitus. (Is this a random sample?) These rhythmic women were then carefully indoctrinated in the method. Their records were supervised throughout the study. It was assumed that "the fertile period extends from and includes the nineteenth day before the **earliest** likely menstruation up to and including the ninth day before the latest likely menstruation." Stated more simply, and approximately: in terms of a presumptive standard 28-day menstrual cycle this means no intercourse from day 9 to day 19. If we add to these days of continence the (approximately) 6 days of menstrual flow, we find that this "natural" method of birth control requires continence during 57 percent of the days of cohabitation.

Among the 387 women cooperating in the subject 57 "accidental" pregnancies were reported. When the time involved was reckoned in, this indicated a conception rate of about 9.4 per 100 woman-years. This is only about 50% higher than the diaphragm-jelly rate, which seems not bad. Had the authors been as unscientific as many of their predecessors they no doubt would have reported this figure, and stopped. But they noticed that a number of their subjects had dropped out of the study. Drop-outs always occur in any voluntary study, of course; but one should never assume that they are a random sample of the total population. When the authors flushed the dropouts from hiding they found that there had been a total of 87 accidental pregnancies, yielding a final conception rate of 14.4 ± 1.5 per 100 woman-years exposure, using the rhythm method. Why were the dropouts a nonrandom sample? Were they ashamed at having "let the doctor down"? Were they disillusioned with science? Interesting questions, these; but clearly minor.

What does the inferiority of the rhythm method mean in the emotional life of the couple practicing it? No one need be any longer in ignorance of the answer. As a result of changes in the Church set in train by Pope John before he died (1963), Roman Catholics, both clergy and laity, have been speaking out with increasing vigour and clarity during the sixties, questioning and even attacking various church doctrines. The Church's stand on birth control has been particularly singled out for attention. From a very large literature indeed, two examples will suffice to give the flavor of the attacks.

The first comment is from a Catholic husband, Bruce Cooper:

> If a mechanical appliance is used, the couple using it are offending the natural law. But the natural law has never been satisfactorily explained. What is the law of my nature? At one level it is to express affection towards my wife regardless of any consequence. If I believe this affection might lead to the conception of another child I have two choices, to stifle that affection or to use some device that will allow the expression of affection but will not result in conception. As a Catholic, if I do not wish to increase my family, I must choose the former, and by careful consultation of calendars, almanacks, thermometers and gynometers, in a manner faintly reminiscent of a stud farm, try to manufacture my affection during the safe period. This period is only partly safe and depends upon the regularity of the menstrual cycle, which can be put out of gear by illness or even emotional upset. This method is allowable, though not really encouraged. It is sometimes known as the rhythm method, but a method so manufactured and artificial has only the rhythm of a machine, not of two loving human beings whose emotions are unpredictable.[2]

The second comment is from a Catholic wife, Rosemary Ruether:

> Psychologically, rhythm is the most negative of all methods of family limitation because it hangs constantly over your head. Every day you must take your temperature, test your glucose, and fit the data into the calculations of the ever-present chart. The man and woman using rhythm live beneath the overarching tyranny of the "safe period" and the "dangerous period." The nagging question intrudes itself into every act of love, "Did we calculate right?" Every time the menstrual period is late or the daily tests show something that seems to diverge from the previous forecast, there is a period of panic. I consider this among the most inhuman tyrannies over the self and the natural creative instincts that has ever been devised. I find it, to be blunt, a sexual version of the Chinese water torture. Because it is a constant concern, rhythm tends to intrude into all the normal feelings of the husband and wife toward each other; the question is obsessive: "Have we kept from getting pregnant this month? Have we kept from getting pregnant this month?" Some who have not experienced these matters may impatiently retort, "Nonsense! It's all in your mind." This is precisely the point. The method forces you to keep it constantly in mind and thus, by its nature, creates an obsessive situation.
>
> I submit both from my experience with rhythm and my experience with the birth control pills that the latter represent an enormous psychological gain over the former. With rhythm you helplessly as-

sume that you can't keep from having children, and all your energies are expended on keeping from having a dozen. The negative dominates. In the second case you know that you are the master of the situation, that you can choose to have a child as a free act of maternal desire. Psychologically there is an enormous gain when a child is not an accident, but is wanted. The obsessive negativeness of the rhythm method, despite the best intentions of the couple, tends to carry over to the child himself. The couple tends to assume, and the rest of society concurs in reinforcing the assumption, that the Catholic's children are forced upon him. The repressed hostility created by this situation can scarcely help being carried over to the child in some form, just because the parents grow tired of having children in spite of themselves instead of because of themselves. I have too often heard a Catholic father make disgusted hostile remarks about his expected child, and watched the silent face of the mother concur in his joylessness.[3]

[1] Tietze, C., S. R. Poliakoff, and J. Rock, 1951, "The Clinical Effectiveness of the Rhythm Method of Contraception," *Fertility and Sterility,* **1:**444–450.
[2] Leo Pyle (ed.), *The Pill and Birth Regulation,* London: Darton, Longman and Todd, 1964, p. 49.
[3] William Birmingham (ed.), *What Modern Catholics Think About Birth Control,* New York: New American Library, 1964, p. 238.

96
Catholic Opinion of Rock's Book

Daniel S. Greenberg
1931–

Science, **140:**791–792

1963

Catholic reviewers, lay and clerical, have now had an opportunity to say their piece on John Rock's recently published book, *The Time Has Come: A Catholic Doctor's Proposals To End the Battle over Birth Control* (Knopf, New York, 1963, 204 pp.).

Their reactions are as interesting as the book, which is indeed an interesting one, and provide some illuminating examples of the intellectual ferment which exists in the supposedly monolithic Church.

Rock, who organized the field trials for the now widely used progesterone oral contraceptive, retired as clinical professor of gynecology in 1956 after a 34-year association with Harvard Medical School. Now, at age 73, he is director of the Rock Reproductive Clinic and one of the most active and articulate public campaigners for family planning.

Rock's thesis, briefly, is that Catholics and non-Catholics are fundamentally in agreement on the usefulness of limiting family size; the difference occurs on the question of method. To resolve this difference, he suggests, ample funds should be made available for research that would provide more certainty for all methods, including the rhythm method, which is alone acceptable to Catholics; at the same time, public funds should be made available for providing birth control counseling acceptable to all faiths. Catholics, for example, would be counseled exclusively on the rhythm method.

As for the pill, Rock concedes that it is not now acceptable to the Church, but he contends that Church leaders should reconsider their position. When progesterone is naturally secreted, he argues, it induces the "safe" period of the rhythm method, and, during pregnancy, it protects the fertilized ovum against a competing conception.

If it is theologically acceptable to utilize this naturally induced sterility to avoid conception, he writes, why would it not be equally acceptable to utilize a sterility that is rationally decided upon and produced by a duplicate of the natural agent—namely, the pill?

The most influential answer was provided by Richard Cardinal Cushing, Archbishop of Boston, in a review published in the Boston *Pilot*. The Cardinal first rapped Rock's knuckles lightly for having failed to abide by the Church law that, as Cushing put it, "requires every Catholic who writes on a subject pertaining to faith or morality [to] submit his manuscript to Church authority for a so-called 'imprimatur'." (Rock explained at a press conference in Washington last week that he was unaware of this requirement.)

The Cardinal then went on to say that "In this book there is much that is good. . . . [Rock] has clearly demonstrated that the Church is not opposed to birth control as such but to the artificial means to control births. . . . He presents many cogent arguments for the formation of a public policy on birth control, and some of his suggestions could contribute to the establishment of domestic peace in our pluralistic society. With reason, he calls to task those who are unwilling to face the implications of the much publicized population explosion. He also makes an eloquent, and much needed, plea, for Federal grants to perfect the so-called Rhythm

251

System so that it might become a means of controlling births which is not only morally acceptable but also scientifically accurate."

The reviewer then made it clear, however, that he felt that Rock's theology was not up to his medicine. The book, he said, "contains several statements which are theologically incorrect and certainly misleading. When he [Rock] speaks on the formation of the Catholic conscience, he fails to take into consideration the true complexity of this problem and so commits in the field of theology the same mistake he urges against the theologians in the field of reproductive physiology. . . . In his defense of the 'natural' and, to his mind, 'lawful' use of the progestational steroids as contraceptive devices, Dr. Rock does not meet the incisive arguments against his position which have been continually voiced by Catholic moral theologians," the Cardinal concluded, "must recognize the competence of Dr. Rock in the field of reproductive physiology but he must recognize their competence in the field of Catholic moral teaching. Fair-minded people will appreciate that such cooperation in no way curtails the doctor's scientific freedom. It would rather aid him in his dedicated pursuit of the ultimate truth in this matter, the defense and formulation of which in theological terms is not the task of the individual but that of the whole teaching Church."

A more critical attitude toward the Rock thesis was offered by the Right Reverend Monsignor John Knott, director of the family life bureau of the National Catholic Welfare Conference, in a review in the Washington *Post*. "The cause of honest discussion would be better served," Father Knott wrote, "if Dr. Rock and all Americans were to face the reality of the Catholic position on contraceptives. It has not changed and will not change. This may be an unpalatable fact of life to many people, but it serves no purpose to ignore or obfuscate it."

Finally, *Commonweal,* a liberal Catholic journal, noted editorially that the debate stirred by Rock's book was less a testimonial to the book's virtues than a reflection of the Church's reluctance to accept a re-examination of its position on birth control. "Is it any wonder, then, that a book as inadequate as Dr. Rock's should receive publicity out of all proportion to its merits and soundness. Where most Catholics tread with muffled shoes and theologians keep their doubts to themselves, anyone who speaks frankly is bound to be made a hero or a villain. . . . The time has come—not to praise Dr. Rock's book, but for the Church and its theologians to confront anew the issues which he raises."

97

Natural Law

Frederick E. Flynn
1912–

The Catholic Messenger, **78**(30):6

The argument in Dr. John Rock's book **The Time Has Come** leans significantly on an analysis of "natural law" made by Dr. Frederick E. Flynn, professor of ethics and philosophy at the College of St. Thomas in St. Paul, Minnesota. This paper was first given (15 May 1960) as an address in Los Angeles to the Catholic Physicians' Guild of California.

1960

The term "natural law" itself is ambiguous. There are three quite different meanings. 1. When the physical scientist speaks of "laws of nature" he may refer to those determined regularities observable in inanimate nature which he records in a formula. Here the "law of nature" is formulized observation itself: Boyle's Law, for example. 2. Or again, the scientist may also speak of "laws of nature" in referring to those dynamic tendencies which he sees operating in the world about him. Thus, he may speak of the laws of growth, the law of the survival of the fittest as applying to organisms as laws of nature. 3. The moral and political philosophers speak of the natural law by which man is guided to his natural good.

Now most of the confusions about natural law stem from identifying natural law as taken in the second and third senses. That is, we often confuse the natural law which represents the primitive, spontaneous urges of all living things with the natural law which represents the rules of human conduct. All living things, through an inherent dynamism toward their respective goods, live according to nature. Thus, the tropisms in plants and the reflexes in animals and men are but natural mechanisms whose purpose is self-preservation, the spontaneous drive of all living things. Thus, to preserve his life reasonably, to satisfy his desires for sexual love reasonably, to live in society reasonably, to do all that he does reasonably are what we mean by fortitude, temperance, justice and prudence. These are the unchangeable and eternal necessities by which man attains his human good, natural happiness.

Nature and reason: these are the twin dynamisms in man, at times in partnership, at times in conflict. These are the law of the members and the law of the mind of which St. Paul speaks. Nature, the spontaneous, the blind: reason, the controlled vision. Is man bid to live only according to nature? Hardly, else he would go through life naked, eating uncooked hay, and sleeping in the forest. Live according to reason? Obviously, else why does man clothe himself with an artificial skin of wool, sit in a chair artificially fortified with vitamins.

Does morality bid man live according to nature? Hardly; nature is neither kind nor cruel, neither benevolent nor malevolent. To speak so is to speak only figuratively. Anthropomorphically. Nature is blind, irrational, capricious. This is why it is blasphemous to identify God and nature, the supreme Intelligent Creator and His dumb creature. With unseeing and impartial fury the floods and famines, the storms and stresses of nature beat alike upon the virtuous and the vicious. Look to nature for moral norms? Hardly. We cannot look to the rabbit or the mink for lessons in the morality of sex, or answers to the population problem. Nor can our wives—thank God for us men—take lessons in maternal duty from the behavior of the queen bee who destroys her mate as soon as he performs his conjugal duty. Nature is prolific when we do not want her to be—and so we have mosquito control. Nature is barren when we do not want her to be—and so we irrigate deserts.

This leads us to an important point: *frustration of nature far from being immoral is man's vocation.* If the march of physical science and technology means anything it means the progressively rational control of nature *by* man and *for* man. Man has always frustrated nature from the time he invented the first tool and will continue to do so until on his last day on earth he lays down his latest invention. And every canal and every dam that man has built are monumental frustrations of nature's even flow. Fundamentalists, of course, will always greet each new tool with the cry "Violation of nature" just as they did, for example, when drugs were introduced to lessen the pains of childbirth. When nature is deficient in doing what it should for human welfare, human art makes up for that deficiency. If this be frustration of nature the human cry is "Give us more of it." When nature is excessively generous in producing its bounties human art controls that generosity. In short, frustration of nature is often necessary for man's very survival.

98

The Ghost of Authority

Garrett Hardin
1915–

Perspectives in Biology and Medicine, **9**:289–297

1966

The controversy over the propriety of contraception which has raged for almost a century seems on the verge of being settled. Propaganda in favor of contraception was begun by Francis Place in 1822,[1] but discussion of this tabooed idea was muted until the subject was brought into the open in 1877 by the trial of Charles Bradlaugh and Annie Besant.[2] Thereafter, decade by decade, the volume of disputatious literature increased, the rate of production reaching a climax in the late 1950's as it became clear that birth control is not only a private matter but is also an issue in which population growth has created an inescapable public interest.

Two recent collections of materials written by Roman Catholics[3, 4] suggest an imminent settling of the dispute in a way that will be reasonably satisfactory to both Catholics and non-Catholics. Once resolved, a controversy ceases to be of keen interest per se; but since it is certain that comparable differences of opinion on other issues will appear in the future it is of more than antiquarian interest to identify the factors involved in the resolution of past difficulties. In the sexual sphere alone we see several issues that threaten public peace: abortion, sterilization, and artificial insemination, to mention only the more obvious. What can we learn from the course of the birth-control controversy that may help in resolving the disputes ahead of us?

Dipping into the rather large literature on this subject I have been forcibly struck by the remarkable and (to me) unexpected change that has taken place in the attitude of practicing Roman Catholics toward the concept of authority. For the most part the change is no more than implicit in the discussions; but once the reader has become sensitive to it he finds it all pervasive. Because quotable, explicit statements are so few, there is a danger that the remarkable developments in this area will be entirely lost from sight in a short time and hence will fail to serve the valuable pedagogic function of history. We like to believe that "history teaches," but, as Thomas Kuhn has demonstrated, in the evolution of science at least,[5] there are self-healing processes in the recording of history which tend to cover the wounds of each resolved controversy, leaving visible only the final conclusions, thus depriving posterity of useful insights into the processes by which controversies are brought to an end. The recording of history by even the best intentioned of people is uncomfortably reminiscent of that depicted in George Orwell's *1984*.

I. Contraception and the Re-examination of Authority

What we may call the classical attitude toward authority is displayed in the following quotation from Patrick J. Ward:[6] "The Catholic Church teaches that the artificial prevention of conception by mechanical, chemical or other means is intrinsically evil. Since this is the universal moral law, it applies with equal force to Catholic and non-Catholic." Notice that this statement not only asserts a particular doctrine about contraception but also asserts the authority of the Catholic Church to settle questions of right and wrong. Implicit, but just as real, is the assertion that authority exists— that there are documents, men, or institutions whose pronouncements determine or define the truth. Is this true? Does authority exist?

It should be clear that the word "authority" in this context has quite a different meaning from its use in scientific literature. When we say "Smith, 1961, found that . . ." we are not establishing the subsequent statement as true but merely assigning Smith the responsibility for correctly reporting the evidence. In principle, science is built on indefinitely repeatable observations; but in practice, as a matter of economy, we do not establish from the ground up every observation on which a particular conclusion is based. He who doubts a particular fact can repeat the work himself. "If it isn't true, don't blame me, blame Smith"—this is the meaning of authority in science.

The authority theologians confront us with is quite a different thing. This authority validates, proves, establishes or defines truth. It is somehow prior to, or superior to, observation and reason; and it is certainly not to be questioned. Every Western religion—if one excepts borderline institutions like the Unitarian Church—assumes the validity of authority. The greatest and most powerful church of all asserts its authority most explicitly, particularly since the Vatican decree of 1870 which established as apparently inescapable orthodoxy a belief in the infallibility of the Pope.[7] Because of this belief, consequences of great moment were set in train by the encyclical *Casti connubii,* which Pope Pius XI published on the last day of 1930. In it he said:[8] "Any use whatsoever of matrimony exercised in such a way that the act is deliberately frustrated in its natural power to generate life is an offence against the law of God and of nature, and those who indulge in such are branded with the guilt of a grave sin."

One might expect that such a solid statement would put an end to dissension and aberrant practice within the church; but it did not. Public opinion surveys during the next thirty years showed that an increasing number of Roman Catholics were using methods of birth control that had been condemned by papal authority.[9]

How did the communicants justify their sin (as defined by the Pope)? No doubt in many different ways, but their rationalizations were almost all made in private, and hence it would be hazardous to discuss them. The ordeal of conscientious members of the church finally came out into the open with the publication[10] of *The Time Has Come* by John Rock, a Catholic physician who had played an important part in the development of the contraceptive progesterone pill. Dr. Rock argued that "the pill" should be licit for Catholics. An important part of his argument revolved around the meaning of "Natural Law," a concept which (in spite of its name) does not lie in the realm of the natural sciences but is, rather, a theological invention. This aspect of Rock's book will be bypassed here in order to plunge directly to the heart of the problem of authority. Rock does not devote much space to this matter, but (significantly) he places his remarks at the very beginning of his story. In the preface he recalls a day from his childhood. He was a shy boy of fourteen, and Father Finnick, a curate of his parish, had invited him to come on a visit to the Poor Farm.

> I shall never forget the short slow ride in the small buggy down East Main Street to the Sudbury road. . . .
>
> I don't remember how the conversation started, if you could even call it that. We did not interrupt Father in class, as he gently but firmly expounded Catholic doctrine to us: now also, I listened intently. I noticed, as we jogged along, the big Walcott house set back behind a wide lawn on the right side of East Main Street about halfway to our turnoff at the Sudbury road.
>
> It was just then that he said, "John, always stick to your conscience. Never let anyone else keep it for you." And, after but a moment's pause, he added, "And I mean *anyone* else."

When Father Finnick said, "Never let anyone else keep it for you," did he have any mental reservations? From the following sentence it is surely clear that he made no exceptions. From John Rock's remembrance and repetition of the story one presumes that Rock also makes no exceptions.

257

That neither of them has been more explicit is understandable; perhaps those of us who are bystanders should decently join them in this reticence.

A few years after Rock's book, an even more astonishing document came from England, from a Roman Catholic convert, the mother of seven children, a physician who had opened up a birth-control clinic. The author, Dr. Anne Biezanek, was led to her unusual position by painful personal experience. She tells us:[11]

> Suspicion dawned that a domestic crisis was approaching. Our house went with my job. I could see for myself and quite clearly that I could not continue to hold this, or any other job, if I continued to give birth to children with such regularity. . . . I explained the danger I felt I was in to the Roman Catholic chaplain at the hospital where I worked, and he seemed to understand for he had doubtless come across problems like this before. He advised that I should procure the services of an able spiritual director, and he then recommended one to me by name. He also explained to me that for spiritual direction to work in accordance with the whole Roman Catholic spiritual theory one must place oneself in a position of total submission to the advice of the director, and orientate oneself to this opinion as though it were the Lord in person giving it. . . . In the course of the next eighteen months, as total physical and emotional collapse assailed me (I had my fifth child and a miscarriage in this period), I repeatedly queried it. On each occasion I received the same answer: I was not free to abandon my profession. I was accused at the time, by colleagues and relations, of acting irresponsibly in thus allowing myself to reach a dangerous point of exhaustion. My defense to them was: "I was acting under obedience." I see now of course that this is no defense. The responsibility for putting myself under a director was mine. If my director considered any of the responsibility his, he has certainly kept marvellously quiet about it, and has done so to this day.

It is interesting to note the closely parallel experience of another convert to Roman Catholicism in the last century, St. George Mivart (1827–1900). The material issues were different, but the conclusion was the same. As his biographer[12] tells the story: "By the end of his life, he had thrown off the last and strongest external authority to which he had been subject. In the midst of his last great controversy, he announced to his archbishop and through him to his Church: 'All of us, however submissive to authority, must in the last resort, rest upon the judgment of our individual reason. How otherwise could we know that authority had spoken at all or what it had said?' "

In the light of these factual accounts, it is interesting to note that the dramatist George Bernard Shaw deduced that Joan of Arc must have traveled the same intellectual path in the fifteenth century. In Scene VI of *St. Joan* we see the young heretic—it would be antihistorical to call her a saint at this point—chained by the ankles, submitting to questioning about her "voices."

> LADVENU: Good. That means, does it not, that you are subject to our Lord the Pope, to the cardinals, the archbishops, and the bishops for whom his lordship stands here today?
>
> JOAN: God must be served first.
>
> D'ESTIVET: Then your voices command you not to submit yourself to the Church Militant?
>
> JOAN: My voices do not tell me to disobey The Church; but God must be served first.
>
> CAUCHON: And you, and not the Church, are to be the judge?
>
> JOAN: What other judgment can I judge by but my own?
>
> THE ASSESSORS (*scandalized*): Oh! (*They cannot find words.*)

II. The Rejection of Authority

The conclusion to be derived from all these witnesses is surely obvious. Put bluntly it is this: *Authority does not exist*—not in the sense that is meant by those who would have us govern our lives by Authority with a capital *A*. If I accept authority, says Biezanek, the responsibility for acceptance is mine. "What other judgment can I judge by but my own?" asks Joan. "All of us," says Mivart, "however submissive to authority, must in the last resort, rest upon the judgment of our individual reason." The external agent referred to is an illusion. Whether one calls the internal agent "conscience" or "reason" is perhaps only a matter of taste. But it is clear that, from an operational point of view,[13] "authority" is empty of content since it is a redundant word for "conscience." The operational meaning of *this* word is not easy to establish, but we make no progress by introducing "authority" as a mere synonym for it. It would be naïve to argue that one word is as good as another, for the very reasons for preferring the word "authority" are the reasons why it should not be used. If I justify my actions by reference to authority, I thereby announce my intention of rejecting reason and its demands for rigorous honesty. Acceptance of personal responsibility necessarily requires the rejection of authority.

III. The Uses of Authority

Authority is a ghost. Why is this truth not more widely advertised? The error of believing in this holy ghost is shared by millions. An error so

259

widespread and so persistent must serve important psychological and sociological functions. These are not difficult to discover.

In the first place, if I cite authority as the reason for my actions, it may well be because I have a sneaking suspicion that I cannot justify them by reason. Authority, by definition, is unexaminable; reason is always subject to scrutiny. Acceptance of authority arises naturally from the facts of individual psychological development. Normal development necessarily begins with a childhood phase in which authority resides in *other* persons: the child is not competent to assume control. The complete life cycle, however, includes also an adult phase in which the individual is now his own authority; he does not try to foist responsibility for his actions and beliefs onto others. Needless to say, a considerable, and sometimes dangerously large proportion, of the legally adult population is not psychologically adult.

Whether or not I personally accept authority, I may urge others to do so for reasons of personal aggrandizement. Each of us, to a greater or lesser extent, wants to control others. *I* want to control *you.* How can I do so? One of the first things each of us learns is the feebleness of naked power. If I tell you to do something, you instinctively ask "Why?" If I then say, "Because I say so," I make no progress in furthering my will to power. But if I can first insinuate into your mind the idea that there exists a being or spirit who is always right—say the Zoroastrian god Mazda, to take a non-provocative example—and if I then say you should do thus and so because Mazda says so, I may then succeed in controlling you. If I am successful, it is because I have succeeded in putting Mazda in the psychological locus formerly occupied by your parents (hence the term "father figure") without your catching on to the fact that Mazda is really *me*. In general, the more distant in time and space, the less questionable authority is, hence the more authoritative. As an ambitious, aggressive individual, it is to my interest to maintain in you the illusion that authority exists.

The on-going associations of individuals that we call institutions have an equally strong interest in maintaining the fiction of authority. It is not unreasonable to ask if the most successful institution ever devised by man, the Church of Rome, has to any extent suppressed (or at any rate failed to publicize) thoughtful discussions of authority. One might suspect that some of the church's most profound thinkers in the past may have reached a conclusion similar to that of Shaw's fictional St. Joan.

I have not found it easy to document this suspicion. I thought that I might be led to relevant passages by the syntopicon volumes[14] of the Great Books of the Western world, but I found them more wonderful than useful. The *Syntopicon* subsumes all knowledge under the headings of "102 Great Ideas." It is hardly to be expected that any two persons would agree on the 102 most seminal ideas of the Western world, but it seems rather odd that the list established by Mortimer J. Adler and William

Gorman should omit both *conscience* and *authority* while including such relative trivia as *monarchy, eternity,* and *angel.*

At one time I had thought to canvass the writings of the most revered of Catholic writers, St. Thomas Aquinas (1225–74). I found this task too great for one not disciplined in the Thomistic idiom, and so I can do no better than present a paraphrase of Aquinas made by Eric D'Arcy.[15]

> The proper object of the will is not the good as it exists objectively, or as it is known to some moral genius with a skill and an insight superior to one's own: it is the good as apprehended and presented to a man by the judgment of his own reason. Of course, one of the elements of the decision which one's reason ultimately makes will be the guidance of authoritative and skilled moralists whose standing we accept; but it has to be the individual's judgment of conscience that this *is* an authority which we may safely accept.

If we grant the accuracy of D'Arcy's paraphrase, we are justified in saying that St. Thomas Aquinas anticipated the discoveries of St. George Mivart, John Rock, Anne Biezanek, and George Bernard Shaw. There is no evidence that any of these people drew on the wisdom of "the angelic doctor" in reaching their conclusions. Neither is there any sign that this aspect of St. Thomas' thought has been, or is being given, unduly wide publicity by the church of his affiliation.

IV. Truth versus Tact

The conclusion that authority does not exist comes as no surprise to scientists, whose working life is built on this premise. The Royal Society of London has as its motto *Nullius in verba,* which may be colloquially translated as "We don't take anybody's word for it." Can other phases of human effort be infected with this attitude?

There is little question but that this infection is already proceeding, and with some success (from a scientist's point of view!). However, every cluster of human beliefs is a homeostatic system with immense powers of repair in the face of logical attack. Put another way, each truth that is contrary to a well-established system seems to have a very short half-life; such truth has to be discovered over and over again, each new statement of it being speedily transmuted into innocuous intellectual isotopes by the internal forces of Freudian denial.

The decay of truth is aided by kindly and practical men. An incident from Victorian history will serve as an illustrative example. When anesthesia was introduced into England, it was forcibly resisted on the grounds that it was unnatural and hence contrary to God's will. This argument might have been countered by a general discussion of the nature of evidence and authority—though probably without much effect. A wiser approach (at least in the short run) was that of the physician James Y. Simpson, who played the game of authority by arguing[16] that the users of chloroform were but following the example set by the Lord, who, intent upon extracting one of Adam's ribs for the fabrication of Eve, considerately "caused a deep sleep to fall upon Adam" before beginning the operation (according to Gen. 2:21). Most written authorities are sufficiently prolix, inconsistent, and ambiguous to make this method of counterattack effective in the hands of kindly and witty men. Playing the game of authority, Simpson won his particular point by implicitly reassuring his audience that he would not tackle the more general issue of authority itself. Tact paid off. The welcome given to tact is part of the homeostatic mechanism of tradition.

Because tactful victories are limited in scope, each new problem must be attacked *de novo,* as if nothing of its sort had ever been seen before. Thus, in our own time, we witness literally hundreds of fine Catholic minds wrestling with the meaning of "natural" as concerns contraception, because few will face the logically simpler issue of authority. It now seems likely that the theologians will soon find a suitable key to contraception. But the insight that authority is a ghost would be more in the nature of a skeleton key that would open many doors. In this day of an accelerating rate of appearance of new ethical problems, we stand sorely in need of more general, more powerful methods of analyzing them. Progress would occur much faster if we could persuade the common man that authority is a ghost.

Is this persuasion possible? I think this question is not answerable by armchair research. To determine how one can replace one homeostatic epistemology by another requires, I think, nothing less than experimental work with human beings. If a label is needed, such an activity might be called experimental anthropology. It can be argued with some degree of plausibility that the development of this science is essential for the survival of mankind.

---

[1] N. E. Himes, *Medical History of Contraception,* Baltimore: Williams & Wilkins, 1936.

[2] A. H. Nethercot, *The First Five Lives of Annie Besant,* Chicago: University of Chicago Press, 1960.

[3] L. Pyle, *The Pill and Birth Regulation,* London: Darton, Longman and Todd, 1964.

[4] W. Birmingham, *What Modern Catholics Think About Birth Control,* New York: Signet Books, New American Library, 1964.

[5] T. S. Kuhn, *The Structure of Scientific Revolutions* (Chap. xi), Chicago: University of Chicago Press, 1962.

[6] P. J. Ward, *New Republic,* May 29, 1929, p. 35.

[7] G. MacGregor, *The Vatican Revolution,* Boston: Beacon Press, 1957.

[8] A. Freemantle, *The Papal Encyclicals,* New York: Mentor Books New American Library, 1956, p. 239.

[9] F. Campbell, *Pop. Studies,* **14:**13, 1960.

[10] J. Rock. *The Time Has Come.* New York: Knopf, 1963.

[11] A. C. Biezanek, *All Things New,* New York: Harper & Row, 1964, pp. 45–47.

[12] J. W. Gruber, *A Conscience in Conflict,* New York: Columbia University Press, 1960, p. 227.

[13] P. W. Bridgman, *The Logic of Modern Physics,* New York: Macmillan, 1927.

[14] M. J. Adler and W. Gorman (eds.), *The Great Ideas: A Syntopicon of Great Books of the Western World,* Chicago: Encyclopaedia Britannica, Inc., 1952.

[15] E. D'Arcy, *Conscience and Its Right to Freedom,* New York: Sheed & Ward, 1961, pp. 215–216.

[16] H. L. Gordon, *Sir James Young Simpson and Chloroform,* London: Unwin, 1897.

99

Anguish after John

Vatican Papers
From reports of the Papal Study Commission (1966)
and *Humanae Vitae* (1968)

At the death of Pope John XXIII in 1963, Paul VI succeeded to the Papacy. As of that date the prospects of the Church's eventually accepting some form of contraception looked good. Pope John had repeatedly emphasized the primacy of individual conscience. "Every human being has the right to honor God according to the dictates of an upright conscience," he had said on one occasion, and many devout Catholics took this as a license to go beyond traditional thinking. Canon Janssens of Louvain had denounced the rhythm method because it destroyed the "total, mutual abandon" that should characterize the sexual act. Catholic clergy in the Netherlands openly recommended contraceptives to their parishioners. The Church seemed on the brink of change.

With the succession of Pope Paul, however, it soon became apparent that institutional reforms started during the reign of his predecessor would be pushed with something less than precipitate haste. As the population of the world continued to double every 35 years, the Vatican approached the birth control problem with glacial deliberateness. A Papal Study Commission was appointed, and later augmented. On 26 June 1966 it made its report to the Pontiff.

More than nine months passed without a word from Rome. During this time the population of the world increased by 54 million—somewhat more than the population of Italy. Then the report "leaked." Unofficial translations from the Latin were prepared, and published first in the western hemisphere in the **National Catholic Reporter,** a lay publication in Kansas City. Significant excerpts are presented in I and II below.

The Pontiff kept silent for fifteen more months. During this time world population increased by another 100 million—approximately the population of Japan. On 29 July 1968 Pope Paul released an encyclical entitled **Humanae Vitae** ("Of Human Life"). Portions of this are reprinted in III below. With this statement the Pope sought to return the Church to the position of 1930, before Rock, before the Pill, and before John.

Since Pope Paul's statement on 29 July 1968 the population of the world has increased by . . . .

I. From the Majority Report, Papal Commission, 1966

In fulfillment of its mission, the church must propose obligatory norms of human and Christian life from the deposit of faith in an open dialogue with the world. But since moral obligations can never be detailed in all their concrete particularities, the personal responsibility of each individual must always be called into play. This is even clearer today because of the complexity of modern life; the concrete moral norms to be followed must not be pushed to the extreme.

THE FUNDAMENTAL VALUES OF MARRIAGE

A couple ought to be considered above all a community of persons which has in itself the beginning of new human life. Therefore those things that strengthen and make more profound the union of persons within this community must never be separated from the procreative finality which specifies the conjugal community.

God created man male and female so that, joined together in the bonds of life, they might perfect one another through a mutual, corporal and spiritual giving and that they might carefully prepare their children, the fruit of this love, for a truly human life.

RESPONSIBLE PARENTHOOD AND THE REGULATION OF CONCEPTION

Responsible parenthood—through which married persons intend to observe and cultivate the essential values of matrimony with a view to the good of persons (the good of the child to be educated, of the couples themselves and of the whole of human society)—is one of the conditions and expressions of a true conjugal chastity. For genuine love, rooted in faith, hope and charity, ought to inform the whole life and action of a couple. By the strength of this chastity the couple tend to the actuation of that true love precisely inasmuch as it is conjugal and fruitful. They accept generously and prudently their task with all its values, combining them in the best way possible according to the particular circumstances of their life and in spite of difficulties.

The regulation of conception appears necessary to many couples who wish to achieve a responsible, open and reasonable parenthood in today's circumstances. If they are to observe and cultivate all the essential values of marriage, married people need decent and human means for the regulation of conception. They should be able to expect the collaboration of all, especially from men of learning and science, in order that they can have at their disposal means agreeable and worthy of man in the fulfilling of his responsible parenthood.

The morality of sexual acts between married people takes its meaning first of all and specifically from the ordering of their actions in a fruitful married life, that is, one which is practiced with responsible, generous and prudent parenthood. It does not depend upon the direct fecundity of each and every particular act.

II. From the Minority Report, Papal Commission, 1966

Contraception is understood by the church as any use of the marriage right in the exercise of which the act is deprived of its natural power for the procreation of life through the industry of man. Contraceptive sterilization may be defined theologically as any physical intervention in the generative process (opus naturae) which, before or after the proper placing of generative acts (opus hominis), cause these acts to be deprived of their natural power for the procreation of life by the industry of man.

It must be noted that the Holy See between 1816 and 1829, through the Roman Curia, answered questions in this matter 19 times. Since then it has spoken almost as many times. In the responses given, it was at least implicitly supposed that contraception was always seriously evil.

History provides fullest evidence that the answer of the church has always and everywhere been the same. The theological history of contraception is sufficiently simple, at least with regard to the central question: Is contraception always seriously evil? For in answer to this question there has never been any variation and scarcely any evolution in teaching. The ways of formulating and explaining this teaching have evolved, but not the doctrine itself.

Similarly they have not said that contraception is evil because God has said 'Increase and multiply,' but because they have considered it in some way analogous to homicide. In every age it is clearly evident that contraception essentially offends against the negative precept: "One may not deprive the conjugal act of its natural power for the procreation of new life."

WHY CANNOT THE CHURCH CHANGE HER ANSWER?

The Church cannot change her answer *because this answer is true.* Whatever may pertain to a more perfect formulation of the teaching or its possible genuine development, the teaching itself cannot not be substantially true. It is true because the Catholic Church, instituted by Christ to show men a secure way to eternal life, could not have so wrongly erred during all those centuries of its history. The Church cannot substantially err in teaching doctrine which is most serious in its import for faith and morals, throughout all centuries or even one century, if it has been constantly and forcefully proposed as necessarily to be followed in order to obtain eternal salvation. The Church could not have erred through so many centuries, even through one century, by imposing under serious obligation very grave burdens in the name of Jesus Christ, if Jesus Christ did not actually impose these burdens. The Catholic Church could not have furnished in the name of Jesus Christ to so many of the faithful everywhere in the world, through so many centuries, the occasion for formal sin and spiritual ruin, because of a false doctrine promulgated in the name of Jesus Christ.

If the Church could err in such a way, the authority of the ordinary magisterium in moral matters would be thrown into question. The faithful could not put their trust in the magisterium's presentation of moral teaching, especially in sexual matters.

III. *From Pope Paul's* Humanae Vitae, *1968*

These acts, by which husband and wife are united in chaste intimacy and by means of which human life is transmitted, are, as the council recalled, "noble and worthy," and they do not cease to be lawful if, for causes independent of the will of husband and wife, they are foreseen to be infecund, since they always remain ordained toward expressing and consolidating their union. In fact, as experience bears witness, not every conjugal act is followed by a new life. God has wisely disposed natural laws and rhythms of fecundity which, of themselves, cause a separation in the succession of births. Nonetheless the Church, calling men back to the observance of the norms of the natural law, as interpreted by her constant doctrine, teaches that each and every marriage act ("quilibet matrimonii usus"), must remain open to the transmission of life.

We must once again declare that the direct interruption of the generative process already begun, and, above all, directly willed and procured abortion, even if for therapeutic reasons, are to be absolutely excluded as licit means of regulating birth.

Equally to be excluded, as the teaching authority of the Church has frequently declared, is direct sterilization, whether perpetual or temporary, whether of the man or of the woman. Similarly excluded is every action which, either in anticipation of the conjugal act or in its accomplishment, or in the development of its natural consequences, proposes, whether as an end or as a means, to render procreation impossible.

To justify conjugal acts made intentionally infecund, one cannot invoke as valid reasons the lesser evil, or the fact that such acts would constitute a whole together with the fecund acts already performed or to follow later, and hence would share in one and the same moral goodness. In truth, if it is sometimes licit to tolerate a lesser evil in order to avoid a greater evil or to promote a greater good, it is not licit, even for the gravest reasons, to do evil so that good may follow therefrom; that is, to make into the object of a positive act of the will something which is intrinsically disorder and hence unworthy of the human person, even when the intention is to safeguard or promote individual, family or social well-being.

Consequently it is an error to think that a conjugal act which is deliberately made infecund and so is intrinsically dishonest could be made honest and right by the ensemble of a fecund conjugal life.

If . . . there are serious motives to space out births, which derive from the physical or psychological conditions of husband and wife, or from external conditions, the Church teaches that it is then licit to take into account the natural rhythms immanent in the generative functions, for the use of marriage in the infecund periods only, and this way to regulate birth without offending the moral principles which have been recalled earlier.

The Church is coherent with herself when she considers recourse to the infecund periods to be licit, while at the same time condemning, as being always illicit, the use of means directly contrary to fecundation, even if such use is inspired by reasons which may appear honest and serious. In reality, there are essential differences between the two cases: in the former, the married couple make legitimate use of a natural disposition; in the latter, they impede the development of natural processes. It is true that, in the one and the other case, the married couple are concordant in the positive will of avoiding children for plausible reasons, seeking the certainty that offspring will not arrive; but it is also true that only in the former case are they able to renounce the use of marriage in the fecund periods when, for just motives, procreation is not desirable, while making

267

use of it during infecund periods to manifest their affection and to safeguard their mutual fidelity. By so doing, they give proof of a truly and integrally honest love.

GRAVE CONSEQUENCES OF METHODS OF ARTIFICIAL BIRTH CONTROL

Upright men can even better convince themselves of the solid grounds on which the teaching of the church in this field is based, if they care to reflect upon the consequences of methods of artificial birth control. Let them consider, first of all, how wide and easy a road would thus be opened up toward conjugal infidelity and the general lowering of morality. Not much experience is needed in order to know human weakness, and to understand that men—especially the young, who are so vulnerable on this point—have need of encouragement to be faithful to the moral law, so that they must not be offered some easy means of eluding its observance. It is also to be feared that the man growing used to the employment of anti-conceptive practices, may finally lose respect for the woman and, no longer caring for her physical and psychological equilibrium, may come to the point of considering her as a mere instrument of selfish enjoyment, and no longer as his respected and beloved companion.

Let it be considered also that a dangerous weapon would thus be placed in the hands of those public authorities who take no heed of moral exigencies. Who could blame a government for applying to the solution of the problems of the community those means acknowledged to be licit for married couples in the solution of a family problem? Who will stop rulers from favoring, from even imposing upon their peoples, if they were to consider it necessary, the method of contraception which they judge to be most efficacious? In such a way men, wishing to avoid individual, family or social difficulties encountered in the observance of the divine law, would reach the point of placing at the mercy of the intervention of public authorities the most personal and most reserved sector of conjugal intimacy.

CREATING AN ATMOSPHERE FAVORABLE TO CHASTITY

On this occasion, we wish to draw the attention of educators, and of all who perform duties of responsibility in regard to the common good of human society, to the need of creating an atmosphere favorable to education in chastity, that is, to the triumph of healthy liberty over license by means of respect for the moral order.

To rulers, who are those principally responsible for the common good, and who can do so much to safeguard moral customs, we say: Do not allow the morality of your peoples to be degraded; do not permit that by legal means practices contrary to the natural and divine law be introduced into that fundamental cell, the family. Quite other is the way in which public authorities can and must contribute to the solution of the demographic problem: namely, the way of a provident policy for the family, of a wise education of peoples in respect of the moral law and the liberty of citizens.

100

Japan's Population

David Cushman Coyle
1887–

Population Bulletin, **15**(7):119–136

1959

Defeat took the heart out of the policy of expansion. It was clear that the Japanese people had no place to go, and in addition some 3.5 million who had been living abroad in Japanese-controlled areas were thrown back into the home country to look for jobs among the millions of returning soldiers. Moreover, the raw materials and markets that Japan desperately needed were henceforth to be under foreign control and subject to competition in world trade. Conservatives still clung to their dislike of a policy of birth control, but the majority of the people could see that their own circumstances called for smaller families than had been customary in the past. After the normal postwar baby boom, fertility fell off rapidly.

The American Occupation was not in a position to take a positive attitude on Japanese population policy. American tradition in this field is conservative, resting mainly on the prohibition of abortion and restriction of birth-control facilities, with some slight gestures toward subsidizing children. Even though Japanese imperialism had been recognized as an effect of population pressure, the Americans, with their background, could hardly be expected to prescribe a treatment to reduce the rate of population growth.

But the Americans could not avoid studying the economic problems of the country which they had undertaken to govern. The Economic and Scientific Section of SCAP (Supreme Commander Allied Powers) made estimates of the future population, and the National Resources Section analyzed future requirements in the light of the population projections. In its report, the National Resources Section came to the natural conclusion that the discrepancies between population and resources could hardly be met in any "humane" way except by a reduction of the birth rate.

Under protest from the Catholic Women's Club of Tokyo-Yokohama, SCAP recalled the report, cut out the offending sentences, and gave the book to a private concern for publication. The Japanese got the point that Americans in general favored birth control as a means of economic protection for the family. They did not fail to observe that personally most Americans were evidently limiting their families, and under far less economic pressure than was felt by the Japanese. The whole episode was probably salutary, particularly the suppression of the report, by which the Occupation avoided an official policy that might have backfired as attempted genocide. It is evident that advice to any group on how to limit its numbers comes with best grace from within the membership. . . .

Before 1948 the law forbade abortion except in cases of medical emergency. But in 1948 the Diet passed the Eugenic Protection Law, which stated as its objective the protection of women whose health would be endangered by childbirth, and also the prevention of inferior progeny that might be expected if children where born to unhealthy mothers. There was no outward recognition of the need for limiting population growth, though some members of the Diet regarded the law as likely to operate in that way.

The Eugenic Protection Law also permitted the extension of birth-control facilities, and allowed sterilization for health reasons in certain cases. In 1949 the law was amended to allow a doctor to take economic factors into consideration as indicating that a woman's health might be endangered by further childbearing.

The 1948 law and its later modifications were definitely centered on health rather than on population control. Abortions had to be performed by a physician, and originally most of them required the approval of a local Eugenic Protection Committee. As revised in 1952, the law allows certain approved doctors to perform an abortion without consultation, requiring only the consent of the two persons chiefly concerned. Nominally the operation must be justified on grounds of health, but the inclusion of economic considerations leaves wide latitude for discretion.

Sterilization was allowed under the original 1948 law only for certain specified reasons, such as infectious leprosy or a known hereditary disease. Later amendments relaxed these specifications, but the health standard was maintained by still requiring the authorization of an approved physician. In the same way assistance in birth control was kept in the hands of technically trained people—doctors and later licensed midwives and nurses.

The effects of the American Occupation were generally favorable to family limitation. The land redistribution, by relieving rural distress, might have made room for the production of more children, other things being equal—which they were not. The abolition of primogeniture, equal rights for women, wider education, and in particular the contacts with Americans and their movies and other productions, tended to encourage birth control.

A number of studies made in the early 1950's showed positive evidence of the widespread use of contraceptives. In 1950 a survey found that nearly one in five couples reported that they were practicing birth control and nearly half as many more had used it at some time. By 1955 more than a third reported the current use of birth control and 52 percent had used it. A remarkable feature was the rapid increase of birth control in the country districts, where some experience with contraceptives was reported by about one-quarter of the couples in 1950 and by over 50 percent in 1955. Even among farmers and fishermen, by 1955 more than a quarter were currently using some form of birth control, and another fifth had done so at some time in the past.

In 1952 the Institute of Public Health began active promotion of birth control as a means of reducing the number of abortions and in less than two years 36,000 contraception workers had been trained.

Another indication of the drift of public opinion was that in 1955 nearly two-thirds of the people interviewed were in favor of family limitation, and 43 percent of the couples with two children said they wanted no more; only one couple in five wanted as many as four children.

The fact that abortions are permitted under a fairly wide range of conditions, and the Japanese habit of collecting statistics, have resulted in the production of official reports on legal abortions which shed some light on the prevalence of this practice. The number of induced abortions was reported as 246,000 in 1949, and as 1,170,000 in 1955.[1] It is estimated that the total number actually performed may have been about twice the number reported, amounting to more than half of all the pregnancies. An important feature has been the introduction of penicillin, which has greatly

271

reduced the danger of the operation. To a large extent it seems that more and more people are relying on birth control, with abortion as a backstop in case of a failure.

Sterilization of 42,000 women was reported for 1955; it is commonly believed that the unreported cases were about ten times as many. Often these represent the failure of attempts at contraception and the desire to avoid further abortions. The Japanese choose more readily than we do between contraception and abortion, since abortion is an old custom and is relatively cheap and easily accessible. But even in Japan abortion often means concealment as something "not quite proper," and it involves pain and inconvenience, and some danger. Contraception, on the other hand, has its inconveniences, including the purchase of supplies and the risks of failure. More and more people, after having a couple of children, and in view of the present low death rates and small danger of being left childless, are resorting to sterilization as a permanent solution to their problem.

---

[1] The number of abortions is given by M. Muramatsu (*Family Planning,* Vol. 7, No. 3, October 1958) as 1.2 million in 1956 and 1.1 million in 1957. (Note added by Editor of the *Population Bulletin.*)

101

Abortion Reform Spreads in U. S.

News Reports

Newsletter
Association for the Study of Abortion, 3(2):1–4

1968

Abortion bills were introduced in 16 of the 29 states which have not recently adopted more liberal abortion laws and which did have legislative sessions this year.

In two of those states, Georgia and Maryland, bills with provisions similar to the Model Penal Code of the American Law Institute were passed.

In two of the states, New Jersey and Virginia, bills establishing abortion law study commissions were passed. In addition, the Legislative

Council of the State of Indiana established such a study commission. The New York Governor's Abortion Review Commission has issued its report (see story in this section).

In Arizona, Delaware, Hawaii, Kentucky, Massachusetts, Missouri, New York, Ohio, Oklahoma, Pennsylvania, and Rhode Island bills based generally on the provisions of the ALI Model Penal Code were introduced. In addition, a bill to repeal the sections of the law relating to the crime of abortion was introduced in Virginia. In Tennessee, a bill providing for abortions to preserve the woman's life or in cases of pregnancy by rape or incest was introduced.

New Laws in Georgia and Maryland

In February and March of this year the Georgia and Maryland legislatures passed abortion reform bills. Governor Maddox allowed the Georgia bill to become law without his signature and on May 7th Govenor Agnew signed the Maryland bill.

Each of the new laws provides for authorizing an abortion to preserve the woman's life, in cases of pregnancy by forcible rape, and in cases in which there is likelihood of fetal damage. The Georgia statute provides for authorizing an abortion if the woman's health is endangered by the pregnancy; the Maryland statute specifies "physical or mental health." The Georgia statute provides that abortions may be performed in cases of pregnancy by statutory rape.

There is no residency requirement in the Maryland law and applications can be passed on by a "hospital abortion review authority." Georgia's new statute requires that the woman and her physician swear that she is a resident and that the physician apply to a hospital committee after being joined in the application by two consulting physicians.

California Not a Haven For Out-of-State Abortion Patients

During the first two months the new California abortion law was in effect, 254 women received legal abortions. All but four of those women were California residents.

A survey of all the accredited hospitals of the state indicated that in the last two months of 1967 there were 214 abortions done to preserve the woman's mental health, 15 were done to preserve her physical health, 18 were done in cases of pregnancy engendered by rape, and 7 in incest cases. Ages of the pregnant women ranged from 12 to 45.

This study was undertaken by the California Medical Association, the State Department of Public Health, and the California Hospital Association. The study estimated that the number of clandestine, out-of-hospital abortions in California each year could range from 20,000 to 120,000.

A.C.L.U. Sees Abortion Choice As Civil Right

"The American Civil Liberties Union asserts that a woman has a right to have an abortion—that is, a termination of pregnancy prior to the viability of the fetus—and that a licensed physician has a right to perform an abortion, without the threat of criminal sanctions." Thus, the A.C.L.U. proposed that legislatures abolish all laws imposing criminal penalties for abortions performed by licensed physicians, no matter what the reason.

This proposal was made after 18 months of study by the A.C.L.U.'s due-process committee and its board of directors. The conclusion reached was that anything short of complete repeal of the abortion laws "deprives women of the liberty to decide whether and when their bodies are to be used for procreation, without due process of law."

The abortion laws, which the group terms "unconstitutionally vague" are also objected to because "They deny to women in the lower economic groups the equal protection of the laws guaranteed by the Fourteenth Amendment, since abortions are now freely available to the rich but unobtainable by the poor."

The A.C.L.U. further argued that the abortion statutes "infringe upon the right to decide whether and when to have a child, as well as the marital right of privacy."

A final violation by these laws of civil liberties is found in the fact that "They impair the right of physicians to practice in accordance with their professional obligations in that they require doctors not to perform a necessary medical procedure." The policy statement notes, ironically, that "In many cases their failure to perform this medical procedure because of the statutory prohibitions on abortion, would amount to malpractice" in the absence of those prohibitions.

The Physicians Forum recently took a similar stand, declaring, "We believe that abortion is a medical concern and urge the repeal of all laws which accept the premise that abortion is a criminal act. Such laws restrict the physician's ability to render the highest level of medical care. Thus these laws deprive the pregnant woman of her right to health."

New York Governor's Study Commission Report

Recommendations for liberalizing New York's abortion law in greater measure than any bill yet considered by the legislature were made by Governor Rockefeller's Abortion Law Review Commission and, with one exception, endorsed by the Governor.

The following grounds for abortion were included in the statute proposed by the commission:

(a) such [abortion] is necessary to preserve the life of such female; or

(b) continuance of the pregnancy would gravely impair the physical or mental health of such female; or

(c) such female has a permanent physical or mental condition which would render her incapable of caring for the child, if born; or

(d) there is a substantial risk that the child, if born, would be so grossly malformed or would have such serious physical or mental abnormalities as to be permanently incapable of caring for himself; or

(e) the pregnancy resulted from an act of rape in the first degree, as defined in the penal law; or

(f) the pregnancy resulted from an act of incest, as defined in the penal law; or

(g) the pregnancy commenced while the female was unmarried and under sixteen years of age, and is still unmarried; or

(h) where the female already has 4 living children . . .

The commission, which consisted of 4 Catholic and 7 non-Catholic members, agreed unanimously on condition (a) (to save the woman's life); 9 members agreed on condition (e) (rape); 8 members agreed on condition (b) (health), (c) (incapacity to care for the child), (d) (deformed child), (f) (incest), and (g) (unmarried girl under 16); and 7 members agreed on condition (h) (over four children). It was this final condition that was not included in the Governor's recommendation to the legislature.

"Shocking and appalling" was the comment of Charles J. Tobin, Jr. He is secretary of the New York State Catholic Committee which represents the state's eight Roman Catholic dioceses, and which has strongly opposed change in the abortion law.

Mr. Tobin said, "The proposals of the Governor's committee go beyond the laws of every other country of the western world. It takes every effort to attempt to react in a calm and unemotional way to [such a] bald proposal to legalize the destruction of innocent life."

The report stated that the members of the majority had given thoughtful consideration to the views of those not in agreement with their conclusions, but that, "it should here be noted that our recommendations require no woman to seek an abortion, and no physician, no hospital or staff member to participate in one. Each is entirely free conscientiously to act or not to act within the framework of our recommendations."

The minority report, signed by Robert M. Byrn, Esq., John Grant Harrison, M.D., and Monsignor William F. McManus, argued "1. That by modern secular standards, the fetus is at all times a human child. 2. That as a human child, his life is sacred. 3. That in the mainstream of modern American Law, the human child *in utero* is regarded as being possessed of fundamental legal rights." The majority report labelled this stand as "clearly fallacious."

Arguments in favor of a more permissive abortion statute were summarized by the report as follows:

"1. The deaths, sterility and harm to physical and mental health resulting from the large number of illegal abortions each year could largely be prevented if such abortions were performed by competent physicians in proper hospital surroundings, within the framework of reasonable legislation.

"2. The wide disparity between the statutory law and actual practice encourages a disrespect for the law, and places the conscientious physician in an intolerable conflict between his medical duty to his patient and his duty as a citizen to uphold the law.

"3. The present law places an unfair discrimination on the poor, in that persons with money may obtain safe abortions either by traveling to other jurisdictions, by going to high-priced, competent though illegal abortionists, or by obtaining legal abortions here based on 'sophisticated' psychiatric indication."

With respect to procedural requirements, the aim of the committee recommendations was "a) to discourage circumvention of the law, b) to provide an opportunity for supervision and review of all abortions performed, not only within individual hospitals, but also by the State Department of Health, and c) to avoid the red tape pitfall which has plagued Scandinavian efforts to implement liberalized abortion regulations." On the basis of these aims, then, the commission recommended that the establishment of hospital abortion boards not be required.

Abortion Reform Dies in New York Assembly

Assemblyman Albert H. Blumenthal's abortion reform bill was rejected after five hours of emotional debate on the Assembly floor this year. Last year it was killed in committee.

Mr. Blumenthal, vowing to try again next year, noted that "The pressures were just too great in an election year. We had four votes we needed and they backed out." Asked to identify the pressure, Mr. Blumenthal said he had "noticed Mr. Tobin sitting in the back with a roll-call sheet." Charles J. Tobin represents the state's eight Roman Catholic dioceses.

The twelve legislators who spoke against the bill were Roman Catholics who charged that it would legalize the "murder of innocent children."

Charles Rangel, one of the 18 Assemblymen who spoke in favor of the bill, said of his colleagues, "Those who have placed so high a value on the life of the unborn child have not shown so much regard for the civil rights of the living. They talk of bringing back the electric chair and have voted against medical care for 30 percent of families earning under $10,000. Those who would now protect life have done nothing when the mortality rate of black mothers is four times higher than of whites; when the Negro infant mortality rate is 58 percent higher and when the death rate within one month is three times as high."

Clergy Committee Urges Abolition of Abortion Law

"Deep disappointment" with the proposals of the New York Governor's Abortion Review Committee was expressed by the Clergy Consultation Service on Abortion which said those proposals would be of "little help" to thousands of women seeking legal abortions.

In face of what it considered to be inadequate recommendations, the ministers' group advocated complete abolition of the present law.

Drinan Opposes Easing Abortion Laws

"Birth control of the poor" is the way the Rev. Dr. Robert F. Drinan, S.J. characterizes the effect of repealing all laws against abortion.

At a conference on ethics sponsored by Rice University in Houston, Father Drinan, according to the *New York Times,* said that doctors, philosophers, clergymen and others in a position to influence public opinion in behalf of easier abortions must consider whether abortions would come to be viewed in the United States by the white majority as a means of controlling over-crowding in Negro ghettos.

102

Abortion in
Anthropological Perspective

Suddenly in the 1960's the word **abortion** was spread across the pages of American newspapers, repeatedly. In earlier decades the word had seldom been seen. Style books of many newspapers specified that only its euphemism "illegal operation" was to be printed. Now all was changed. Newspapers, popular magazines, radio and television returned to the topic repeatedly. The occasional articles that appeared in popular magazines before 1960 discussed abortion only in horrified terms. By the second half of the decade, the most respectable magazines were carrying articles that recommended legalizing the practice (balanced by other articles that did not). Even magazines written for teen-age girls discussed the issue openly and objectively. Ten years earlier no one had dreamed that such a sudden shift in public attitude could take place. What had happened?

Two bits of intelligence that appeared in the 50's prepared the way, I think, for the apparently sudden change in the succeeding decade. First there was the news of the massive use of abortion as a method of birth control in Japan. We had known, of course, that abortion had been legal in the Scandinavian countries since the 30's; but it was also pretty well understood that the practice was marginal. A woman had to plead and fight to get a legal abortion there; it was not so different from the U. S. But Japan! Suddenly, we found that the Japanese were using abortion as casually as other methods of birth control. Women were not being ruined. The family was not dissolving. The state was not collapsing. . . . It made one stop and think.

In 1954 the Planned Parenthood Federation of America decided the time had come to hold a conference on abortion. Forty-three men and women, mostly M.D.'s, were assembled at Arden House in New York for two lengthy conferences in 1955; the results, edited by Dr. Mary Steichen Calderone, were published in 1958.[1] The conference was a scientific and dramatic triumph. For the first time the true facts about modern abortion were made clear to the medical profession with a clarity that put them beyond dispute. They were resisted, of course. One of the most dramatic events of the conference was the confrontation of a retired professional illegal abortionist, G. Lotrell Timanus, M.D., with his more legal and less daring colleagues. Even in cold print, the electric atmosphere of this meeting can be sensed. It was one of those rare confrontations of adversaries in which accused and accusor exchange places. It was worthy of a Zola. . . . Dr. Timanus has since appeared on a television documentary, where it was obvious that he is everybody's kindly grandfather. This is not the way we used to think of an "abortionist." It shakes one's faith in black-and-white morality. If you can't believe in a stereotype, what can you believe in?

The publication of Calderone's **Abortion in the United States** was greeted with an almost absolute critical silence. A search of book review indexes made by Fred Dietrich has failed to reveal a single review of this book in either the medical or the popular literature; among the semipopular magazines, only one reviewed it, namely **Scientific America.** The January 1959 issue carried a long and sympathetic account by James R. Newman. I think many students of family planning trace their interest in abortion to a reading of Newman's review; I know I do.

Japan's adoption of abortion and the publication of the proceedings of the Arden House conference in the 50's undoubtedly contributed to the breaking of the taboo against discussing abortion in the 60's. As the taboo disappeared, twelve basic (and surprising) facts about abortion became visible:

1. Abortion is a method of birth control. This, by definition; but more importantly the definition springs naturally from the attitude of women who have undergone abortions. For them, abortion is the backstop method of birth control to be used when other methods have failed. (It is a mistake to contrast abortion and birth control, as is often done. The proper contrast is between abortion and contraception, one being the killing of live cells after fertilization, the other the killing of live cells before fertilization.)

2. Most of the women who are aborted are married women.[2] It may be titillating to think of promiscuous unmarried girls as the principal patrons of abortionists, but it isn't true, neither in the United States nor in any other country studied.

3. Even a small contraceptive failure rate produces an absolutely large need for a backstop method.[3] In a population the size of ours, a "one percent" failure rate—i.e., one pregnancy per 100 woman-years exposure to the risk of pregnancy—would produce a quarter of a million unwanted babies each year. One percent failure is probably the best the pill can do. Older methods have a failure rate five or more times greater. In the light of these facts the rate of illegal abortions estimated at the Arden House conference (200,000 to 1,200,000 per year in the U. S.) seems not out of line.

4. Abortion has been employed as a method of birth control by 99 percent of all societies studied by anthropologists.[4]

5. Abortion is the most widely used **single** method of birth control in the world today.[5]

6. A properly performed abortion is much less dangerous than a normal childbirth.[6] The most recent experience indicates that surgical abortion ("D and C"—dilatation and curettage), as carried out legally in eastern Europe, is only one-eighth as dangerous as a **normal** childbirth in the United States (with complicated childbirths the contrast is even greater). A vacuum

279

method of early abortion, first developed in Russia and now being used in England and America, will undoubtedly prove even safer.

7. Abortion does not produce sterility.[7] An incompetently performed one can, of course.

8. Abortion, when legal, need not be expensive. In Roumania, it costs less than $2.00.[8] We should not expect such a bargain in the United States, but $25.00 would perhaps be a reasonable fee by American standards. The essential thing is to perform the abortion early (before the 12th week). If it is performed early there is no need for a hospital; a clinic or a doctor's office will do. (You can't get in and out of an American hospital for less than two hundred dollars.)

9. Abortion, **per se,** causes no psychological damage.[9] Psychological analysis shows that where guilt is felt, it has been interjected into the woman by a disapproving society. In a culture that approves it, abortion is psychologically no more traumatic than a tooth extraction.

10. Unwanted pregnancies occur most often in women least fitted for motherhood: the underaged, the overaged, and the psychologically disturbed.[10] Successful prevention of all wanted pregnancies would increase the proportion of children being raised by resentful mothers.

11. Illegal abortion discriminates against the poor.[11] In addition to out-and-out illegal and expensive abortionists, there are the legitimate doctors who are much more amenable to bending the rules for well-to-do women (who may be their friends) than they are for poor women, who are strangers to them. Besides, there's always Japan for those who can afford the fare.

12. Unwanted children increase the tax burden, because they increase the load on mental health, welfare, and penal services.[12]

These facts are now crystal clear and undeniable. How could we have been so long unaware of them? Principally because of the taboo, of course. Taboo is far more effective than censorship. A censor is an external agent, who seeks to prevent overt, public expression. We can still think about those things the censor forbids us to write about; and we delight in outwitting him. But taboo, the internalized equivalent of the censor, is **myself** indeed. How can I think of outwitting myself? Taboo not only prevents overt expression; it prevents thinking itself. If the much overused word "unthinkable" has any meaning at all, it refers to those subjects that are under taboo. Abortion was unthinkable to a large proportion of the population in the western world until only a few years ago.

To how large a proportion? For a long time I assumed that the great majority of our people were incapable of thinking about abortion—until my eyes were suddenly opened to an anthropological fact I had not been aware of. My education began when a middle aged woman was telling me about getting an abortion in Spain, where she had been living at the time.

"And what did your husband think of it?" I asked.

"My husband?" she said in some surprise. "You don't think I told him, do you? It was none of his business."

I was amused, but thought no more of the matter until a few weeks later when I was told of a strikingly similar event that took place in Italy.

"And what did you tell your husband?" I asked the woman.

"Nothing," she replied calmly. "He's much too immature to think about such things."

Suddenly I remembered something I had read about the Rif tribes of northern Africa.[13] Among these people abortion is a very serious offence. If a husband were certain that his wife had had one he would, at the least, divorce her; and he might kill her, with the approval of his friends. Does this mean that abortions do not occur among the Rifs? Not at all! In addition to the general market, the women have a market place of their own to which men are forbidden to come. The women's market specializes in the needs of women, including contraceptives and abortions. Since men can never enter, they can never really know what goes on. No doubt they have their suspicions, but they probably learn not to voice them. Even in a primitive society whose women are in a very subservient role wives still have means of enforcing a minimum of civility among their menfolk. They can always put more pepper in the soup, if nothing else.

In other words, the intolerable laws promulgated by men in this society were tolerated simply because women lived in a different culture—or more exactly, subculture. The Rif situation shows this up particularly well; but, once seen, the same arrangement can be recognized all over the world. In Europe, for many centuries, the specifically female needs of women were taken care of by other women—mothers, mothers-in-law, grandmothers, and midwives (female). Methods of contraception—often not very good, it is true —were passed down from mother to daughter, from midwife to wife. Abortions were performed by midwives, with husbands ("too immature," or its medieval equivalent) generally left out of the confidence. The separation of the two subcultures permitted an oceanic separation of theory and practice.

Consider Italy. A Roman Catholic country, its official face is set solidly against all abortions; but it is generally estimated that the abortion rate is equal to the live birth rate,[14] which makes Italian abortions four times as common as American. Italian men write the laws of Italy, and men write books on theology; women have the abortions and the children, with scarcely a glance at the literature of the other subculture. For a long time the male subculture has been literate and theoretical, the female subculture nonliterate and practical. The written analysis of sexual problems has been carried out by males who certainly never had the experience of having children; many of them did not even have the experience of living and sharing with the childbearing subculture. With such a separation of experience and theory-construction it is scarcely to be wondered at if male theories often bore little relationship to reality. Those who are trained in the sciences know how essential it is to keep theorizers close to the growing edge of experience. It is hard for scientists to take seriously the vast bulk of theological writings on motherhood. Women have children, and men write books on theology. . . . When men take over the bearing and day-to-day raising of children, perhaps

281

then women, seeking the ineffable they have lost, will take to theologizing. (That will be the day!)

In the meantime we are in trouble because the centuries-old separation of the two subcultures is breaking down. Women have become literate and are taking up men's occupations. Women midwives are disappearing in Europe (and are almost nonexistent in America). Their place is being taken by men physicians who try to enforce the mores of the male subculture, seldom realizing that there is any other. Women, the rising but subservient class, tend to adopt the standards of the class they are rising into. This is orthodox sociology; ambitious Negroes adopt the standards of the white class they seek to join. In reaction to this, some Negroes have recently pushed for greater psychological and sociological separation under the banner of "Black Power." Perhaps the revolutionaries are wise. Perhaps we also need a Woman Power movement to preserve the traditional moral standards of the female subculture in the face of repressive male power.

---

[1] *Abortion in the United States,* New York: Harper-Hoeber, 1958.

[2] *Ibid.,* p. 60.

[3] Garrett Hardin, "Blueprints, DNA, and Abortion: A Scientific and Ethical Analysis," *Medical Opinion and Review,* 3 (1967):74–85, and "A Scientist's Case for Abortion," *Redbook,* May 1967, p. 62.

[4] George Devereux, *A Study of Abortion in Primitive Societies,* New York: Julian, 1955.

[5] Ronald Freedman, "News Report," *Eugenics Review,* 57 (1965):157.

[6] Christopher Tietze and Hans Lehfeldt, "Legal Abortion in Eastern Europe," *Journal of the American Medical Association,* 175 (1961):1149–1154, and Christopher Tietze, "Induced Abortion and Sterilization as Methods of Fertility Control," *Journal of Chronic Diseases,* 18 (1965):1161–1171.

[7] Calderone, *op. cit.,* p. 61, and Paul H. Gebhard, Wardell B. Pomeroy, Clyde E. Martin, and Cornelia V. Christenson, *Pregnancy, Birth and Abortion,* New York: Harper-Hoeber, 1958, p. 203.

[8] K. H. Mehlan, "Legal Abortion in Roumania," *Journal of Sex Research,* 1 (1965):31–38.

[9] Gebhard et al., *op. cit.,* p. 208, and Family Planning Association, *Abortion in Britain,* London: Pitman, 1966, pp. 70, 90.

[10] Hans Lehfelt, "Willful Exposure to Unwanted Pregnancy (WEUP)," *American Journal of Obstetrics & Gynecology,* 78 (1959):661–665.

[11] H. L. Packer and R. J. Gampell, "Therapeutic Abortion: A Problem in Law and Medicine," *Stanford Law Review,* 11 (1959):417–455.

[12] Hans Forssman and Inga Thuwe, "One Hundred and Twenty Children Born after Application for Therapeutic Abortion Refused," *Acta Psychiatrica Scandinavica,* 42 (1966):71–88.

[13] Carleton S. Coon, *Tribes of the Rif,* Cambridge, Mass.: Peabody Museum, 1931.

[14] Livio Zanetti, "The Shame of Italy," *Atlas,* August 1966, p. 18.

103
The Right to Life

Norman St. John-Stevas
1929–

London: Hodder and Stoughton;
New York: Holt, Rinehart and Winston

Norman St. John-Stevas, English barrister, television personality, and member of Parliament, brilliantly led the Catholics in their opposition to the reform of the English abortion laws. (They lost.) A master of clear exposition, he is unquestionably the most eloquent spokesman for the official position of the male subculture of the Roman Catholic world.

1963

Rejection of abortion seems to result from the nature of man himself. The Hippocratic oath, which dates back to the fifth century B.C., contains an explicit repudiation of abortion. Roman law punished abortionists by sending them to the mines or into exile. If death resulted from an abortion the death penalty was enforced.

With the coming of Christianity condemnation of abortion was reinforced and became absolute. The fathers of the Church were never in any doubt on the issue. Tertullian, at the end of the second century, writes: "But to us, manslaying having once been forbidden, it is not lawful to undo even what is conceived in the womb, while the blood is as yet undetermined to form a man. Prevention of birth is a precipitation of murder: nor doth it matter whether one takes away a life when formed or drive it away while forming. He also is a man, who is about to be one." The Church was vigorous in condemning the practice of abortion as well as child exposure, which still survived amongst the pagans. The Council of Elvira denounced abortion in A.D. 306 and the Sixth Oecumenical Council did the same in 680–681. Canon law from the time of Gratian imposed penalties on abortionists. These penalties altered from time to time, but the condemnation was always maintained. Today the canon law of the Catholic Church punishes all who "effectively" procure abortion with an excommunication reserved to the bishop (canon 2350). The Church of

England makes no canonical condemnation of abortion, but its moral condemnation in all save extreme cases of necessity is clear.

Christianity equated abortion with murder because of its conviction of the presence in the foetus of the soul. The soul, according to traditional Christian teaching is directly created by God, but how can one tell when the soul and therefore the essential principle of life is first present? There was much confusion on this point. At the beginning of the Christian era, contemporary medical science drew a distinction between the "formed" and the "unformed" foetus. It was held that there was no rational soul present in the foetus for a considerable time after conception—a period which came to be fixed at forty days in the case of the male and eighty in that of the female. This theory had antiquity but little else to recommend it. Aristotle accepted it and taught that a miscarriage could be legitimately induced before the foetus became animated (see Aristotle's *Politics,* Book VII). St. Augustine also accepted the theory and hence concluded that while the abortion of the embryo *informatus* should be punished with only a fine, destruction of the embryo *formatus* was murder and should be punishable with death. The distinction found its way into Gratian's codification of canon law, which was published about the year 1140. It influenced the English common law, and from the time of Bracton life was taken to be present in the embryo not when it was conceived but when some movement occurred in the womb. "Life," wrote Blackstone in the first book of his Commentaries, is the immediate gift of God, a right inherent by nature in every individual and it "begins in contemplation of law as soon as the infant is able to stir in the mother's womb."

Innocent III gave official recognition to the distinction between the two types of foetus in his canonical legislation of 1211. It recurs in canon law but was finally abandoned by Pius IX in a constitution of 1869. The point is of rather more than academic importance, since most abortions occur in the early days of pregnancy before the foetus has in fact "quickened," and were the distinction to be valid today the moral difficulties occasioned by abortion would be greatly reduced. The distinction, however, is a false one, the error being biological rather than theological, the theological deduction as to the moment of the infusion of the soul being perfectly reasonable given the biological premise. Today, and indeed for a very considerable period, it has been accepted by biologists that there is no qualitative difference between the embryo at the moment of conception and at the moment of quickening. Life is fully present from the moment of conception. It follows that if there be a soul it too must be present from the time of conception.

An aspect of this problem that has aroused more public controversy than its intrinsic importance justifies is the resolution of the dilemma that a doctor may be faced with when he has to choose between saving the life of a mother or that of her child. Today this is a very rare situation indeed. But once one accepts the principle that every human life is of equal value, it is morally impossible to justify taking the life of the child in order to save that of the mother, or vice versa. There is no qualitative difference between the two lives to found any such choice. The only difference in fact is that the mother is able to speak for herself, whereas the child is obliged to be silent. The right course for the doctor to pursue is to make every effort to save the lives of both.

104
The Crucial Question About Abortion

Thomas A. Wassmer, S. J.
1916–

The Catholic World, **206**(1):57–61

1967

It would be interesting to participate in a controversial discussion in which there would be no emotive language used. It makes one wonder whether such a discussion is even a possibility. When the social issue is abortion and involves persons with different philosophical and theological presuppositions discussing questions of life, the quality of life, the rights of the person, the interrelation between the legal and the moral orders, it seems that emotive language has a tendency to increase and multiply according to some law of rhetoric. The end result is the generation of more intense heat and less clear light.

Vatican II has called for a dialogue with other Churches, some of whose representatives favor liberalization of present abortion laws. It has also recommended dialogue with secular humanists, many of whom support the relaxation of these laws. The "sincere and prudent dialogue" between these participants cannot be unmindful of the teaching of Vatican II on the sacredness of life. In the *Constitution on the Church in the Modern World* (no. 51) this sentence occurs: "Therefore from the moment of its conception life must be guarded with the greatest care, while abortion and infanticide are unspeakable crimes." Father Robert H. Springer, S.J., commented on this direct statement with the remark: "Though no one would hold that animation at the moment of conception is here defined as a matter of faith, no one can deny that this teaching demands respect. It was discussed, phrased and approved by the bishops with the greatest care and in view of the disregard for life in the world today" (*Theological Studies,* June, 1967).

Is it not true that the crucial question is raised right here? Is it not possible for any participant in the dialogue to agree with everything that is being taught about the person's right to life, and still to disagree on the fundamental issue: When *does* the human person begin his life? All other questions are subordinate to this question that goes to the very heart of the dialogue.

Before advancing to this crucial question, it might be well to summarize our theological and sociological perspectives on this question of abortion. Father James T. McHugh, Director of the Family Life Bureau, did this with remarkable clarity in his statement to the conference of diocesan lawyers and state Catholic welfare conference workers in Washington on April 24th. In the first place, the issue of abortion is specifically different from the issues of contraception and sterilization. Any theological evaluation and any moral analysis should maintain this separation. In the matter of public policy the implications are also different, and no generalization can be made from previous public policy stands. Secondly, there are questions bearing on the matter of abortion, or more precisely on the matter of conception and ensoulment, to which we do not have final answers. More adequate scientific data are required and we should be cautious about overstating the case. Nevertheless, since we are dealing with human life, we must favor the course of action that assures the greatest safety to the fetus. This is the real reason for our opposition to a change in the abortion laws.

Father McHugh reminds the Catholic participants in the dialogue to state Catholic teaching clearly, avoiding emotional arguments or sensationalism, and emphasizing a reasoned presentation that accurately presents the Christian value on human life. However, we should never forget that other persons share with us this fundamental cultural value of life. Differences arise, as Father Springer states, concerning the relative evaluation of unborn life and the health and happiness of the already born, and in the implementation of the respect for life in our modern cultural and legal norms.

But the crucial question is: When *does* the human person begin his life? It is true that in the public forum social arguments should be emphasized: the benefit that redounds to society from the principle of respect for life and the threat that follows from a growing disrespect for its presence in permissive abortion bills. Granted that the dialogue should proceed on the formulation of social arguments, it is still true that the gnawing question that always comes to the surface of responsible discussion is our crucial question: When *does* the human person begin his life?

Some of the more recent writing by Catholics on the subject of abortion have suggested that there may be ground for an improvement in the quality of the dialogue with others, and that questions have been raised in ecumenical exchange which might serve to offer tentative answers that will upon further analysis become more and more acceptable.

Father Robert F. Drinan in *America*, February 4th, suggests that the principle of the lesser of two evils might be applied in abortion reform that permits this medical procedure only in the rare cases of rape, incest or a predictably defective infant. It has always been true that a person's moral role is situationally different with regard to the lesser moral evil than to the greater. Surely, the moral choice between permitting abortion only in rare cases and in permitting it in all situations is obvious. The principle is even more obvious when the discussion takes place with someone who maintains the most extreme position of all, namely, that a mother should have the right in law to terminate a pregnancy at any time during the pregnancy for any reason whatsoever. This extreme position, advanced by some who refer to the "wanted child," has been alluded to in Lawrence Lader's book on *Abortion* as an enlightened and progressive one.

Some moralists might object or place reservations on the adoption of a public policy of approval, or at least of toleration, regarding a law that works evil, if lesser evil is the overall result. It seems that Father Springer considers that it is quite a step from the lesser-evil principle to its application to abortion laws. Nevertheless, the article by Father Drinan was praised by Professor George Williams of the Harvard Divinity School who considered that it advanced the dialogue in the ecumenical and political orders.

An interesting letter of Father Joseph Donceel in *America* (March 25, 1967), commenting on the clear choice of the lesser of two evils, added that there is "a slowly increasing number of Catholic thinkers who are returning to the position of St. Thomas Aquinas, who claimed that there is no human being at all during the first few weeks of pregnancy, when most of the abortions mentioned by Father Drinan might be performed." The implication of these words is that there is a growing respectability for the doctrine of *mediate animation* in place of *immediate animation* which is regarded in questions of practice as the safer of the two alternatives.

Let me explain the meaning of *mediate* and *immediate animation*. The rational principle in man, his vital principle or entelechy, is his soul, and if this is considered to be present at the very moment of conception, it is regarded as animating or vivifying the somatic counterpart *immediately*. If the rational principle is not present at the very moment of conception, and this is the position of St. Thomas Aquinas to which Father Donceel refers to above in his quotation, the animation is called *mediate*. Father Donceel's position is the position of St. Thomas and he briefly touches upon the philosophical basis for this position in his letter in *America*. In a short article in the spring issue of *Continuum* he expands more amply upon the reasons, and adds others, but draws no conclusions from the philosophical respectability of *mediate animation* in theory to its adoption in practice. However, if the choice between the two kinds of abortion laws mentioned above does become clearer by an examination of the evidence for *mediate* animation, why has this inference not been more frequently made? Is it reasonable to suggest that in certain cases a return to this position of St. Thomas might apply in practice?

In this article my intention is to review and evaluate the evidence, supplement it with other evidence and then suggest provisional applications for consideration and discussion. What are the reasons for a return to the traditional doctrine of *mediate animation?* Donceel examines this position as well as the position of *immediate animation* historically and then identifies his own position (*mediate animation*) in this way: "With St. Thomas I teach that at the moment of conception there originates a vegetative organism that will slowly evolve into a sentient organism to become, at a moment I cannot determine, a rational organism, a real human being."

The evidence for *mediate animation* is first of all that it is more compatible with the hylomorphic conception of man and that *immediate animation* is less compatible, or even incompatible, with this theory. St. Thomas, following Aristotle, considered the soul as the first or substantial act of a physically *organized* body which has the capacity of life. He insisted that the human embryo must have a certain degree of organization before it can become the seat of a rational principle. It should have at least the beginning of a human shape and the essential organs should be present. St. Thomas never questioned the presence of life in the embryo from the very moment of conception. But this first life is vegetative and

288

when the proper organization is attained, a sensitive principle replaces the vegetative. When there is adequate organization commensurate for the presence of the rational principle, God creates and infuses this rational soul. This theory of *mediate animation* was replaced by the *immediate animation* theory in the seventeenth century.

Why has this latter position been acceptable for so long apart from the fact that it is safer in practice to adopt? The Cartesian influence upon philosophy is the root reason for the appeal that *immediate animation* has for so many. In such a theory of Cartesian dualism the soul is present and operating more precisely as an *efficient* cause. The soul is no longer the *formal* cause of the body but only the efficient cause in the aggregate of cells, and this hypothesis raises the question why a rational principle is even required. However, such a Cartesian view of man hardly agrees with either hylomorphic conception of man or the notion of the soul as a formal cause that was stated at the Council of Vienne.

If the theory of *mediate animation* seems to be more compatible with this hylomorphic conception of man that considers the soul as the formal cause of a real human body with some degree of commensurate organization, the theory has not been favored by Church legislation. Canon 747 enjoins that all living embryos, of whatever age, must be baptized unconditionally. This legislation in itself raises the question whether each menstrual discharge should be baptized because it might contain a fertilized ovum. Research scientists hold that approximately one third of all conceptions result in natural abortions.

The scientific reasons that appealed to many philosophers of the seventeenth and eighteenth centuries and led them to reject the *mediate animation* theory of St. Thomas have lost their value. St. Thomas would be a welcome guest with his notion of man in process of evolving into a human status. On the other hand, for those holding the *immediate animation* theory, there seems to be no problem in stating that the rational soul may be the substantial form of an unorganized embryo, even when it is composed of a few cells.

Another piece of evidence for *mediate animation* is the case of identical twins. This occurrence may take place several days after fertilization, and some research men in reproduction maintain that it might happen even after the implantation on the wall of the uterus. On a theory of *immediate animation* this phenomenon provides the problem of explaining how this one fertilized ovum can split into two or more parts which then develop of themselves. The spirituality of the rational principle seems to rule out this divisibility if the principle is *intrinsically* independent of matter. Besides, is it to be considered an impossibility that embryologists might succeed in splitting the fertilized human ovum, just as they have artificially divided the fertilized ova of lower organisms? Will this not once again raise problems for the *immediate animation* theory where the spirituality, the nondivisibility of the rational form, would apparently be in conflict?

Reference was recently made above to the large number of conceptions that result in natural or unavoidable abortions. There are theological difficulties for the position of *immediate animation* if these abortions take place spontaneously in a menstrual discharge and no baptism takes place. One theologian remarked about this phenomenon with just a trace of irreverence: "If this is true that there are so many unknown unavoidable abortions, if the rational soul is present from the beginning and if intrauterine baptism is impossible, then there are more souls in limbo than in heaven and hell together."

Such are the arguments for *mediate animation* and for its speculative respectability—compatibility with a genuine hylomorphic conception of man and a more satisfactory explanation for the phenomenon of identical twins. The question now is: Why should the theory of *mediate animation* not be used in difficult moral cases where abortion is suggested by ethically responsible persons?

It is here where some hesitation sets in and the bewilderment of many serious Protestant ecumenists begins to mount. Catholic moralists have to satisfy Canon 747 mentioned above, of course. It is not this canon that the ecumenists stumble over. It is the argument as it proceeds philosophically. Traditional moralists insist that this problem of the moment of rational life in the fetus is a *doubt of fact* regarding *mediate* or *immediate animation*. In cases of *doubts of law, probabilism* may be used, but never in situations involving *doubts of fact,* if the doubts involve considerations of life, justice or the validity of contracts. In these situations, *probabilism* may not be used, but the safer course must be followed. Obviously, the safer course here is to act on the theory that rational life is present from the moment of conception. The safer course is not necessarily the true one.

Just one word on the *principle of probabilism* that operates only in case of *doubts of law*. It amounts to this: In situations where there is a *doubt of law,* where there is a genuine conflict between freedom and law, if there is a solidly probable argument for the nonexistence of the law, then freedom is in possession because *a doubtful law does not oblige*. After this explanation the traditional moralist would deny its application in cases of *doubts of fact* involving considerations of life as in the case of *when precisely* animation takes place.

Now, I would like to raise the crucial question: Are we always obliged to follow the safer course when we confront a *doubt of fact* regarding a question of life? Are we *never* permitted to follow the less safe course in such an ethical situation? As I have suggested in an article in *Commonweal* (June 30, 1967), moralists have on occasion allowed the procedure of the less safe alternative. Of course, they have permitted this alternative only where there were other "situational" values at stake, and where apparently the obligation to adopt the safer course ceased to be present.

Let me summarize two cases briefly:

1. Moralists such as McFadden and others will permit a woman to use a douche after rape as late as 10 hours after the assault. Conception has been known to take place within that length of time and the woman is given the benefit of the doubt. The precise existential moment of conception cannot be known for certain. In our case regarding animation the precise existential moment of animation and the quality of animation cannot be known for certain. Nevertheless in the assault situation, in the absence of certitude and in the presence of the *doubt of fact,* moralists will allow the woman to act without adopting the safer course, i.e., to act within the period of 10 hours. To follow the safer course would have meant that impregnation and conception took place at the earliest possible existential moment after the attack or even during the attack.

2. The second case involves a patient with a *terminal* illness and provision has been made for all *ordinary* means for the continuation of his life. If there is no probability of his returning to rational consciousness, most moralists will permit the family and the doctor to omit the *extraordinary* means to keep him alive. The *doubt of fact,* doubt whether rational consciousness will be restored, does not entail the obligation to follow the safer of the two alternatives which would have required the continuation of all possible means.

Let me conclude these observations with certain tentative propositions of my own, especially on this subject of abortion and dialogue in the political order.

1. It seems that there are and have been situations in which, in the presence of a *doubt of fact* regarding life, the safer course is not always of obligation, if other human values are situationally at stake. Is it conceivable then that if there is philosophical, theological, and scientific respectability for the theory of *mediate animation,* then this theory, admittedly not the safer of the two alternatives, might in certain situations be applied. Would dialogue with others who are just as passionately concerned with the question of life and the *quality* of life be improved at least

a millimeter? Is it temerarious to suggest that abortion in the rare cases of rape, incest or a predictably defective infant during the first few weeks of pregnancy should not be regarded as foreclosed by moralists?

2. Where men of goodwill and ethical integrity disagree, is it always prudential for Catholics to try to impose their "traditional" answers on other citizens by way of a general civil law? Is it not the best index of a man's love of freedom that he respects the freedom of others, and is ethically perceptive and morally sensitive to the freedom of Catholics? And this responsibility is of course reciprocal.

3. The problem of abortion has been called the problem of hard-core ecumenism. Does the ecumenist improve the dialogue if he insists upon maintaining philosophical, theological, and scientific respectability for *mediate animation,* while refusing to admit its application in the rare cases of rape, incest and a predictably defective infant?

4. It seems that the absolutization and polarization of a value apart from its situational presence in a whole constellation of human values leads to moral embarrassment. It seems to me that we have not done this by so absolutizing and polarizing life that where there was a doubt of its presence (and now I would like to say, of its *rational* quality), other values have not situationally permitted its forfeiture.

5. It appears that if in case of *doubts of fact* regarding life the less safe course may be adopted where other human values are situationally at stake, then such abortions are not the lesser of two evils, but can be within the situation ethically and morally good.

6. Doctor Joseph Fletcher has referred to hardcore ecumenism as the period of ecumenical exchange when the blandness ceases and the "nitty-gritty," "nuts-and-bolts" operations take place. What I have submitted here is a set of proposals to improve the "nitty-gritty," "nuts-and-bolts" exchange in the ecumenical and political dialogue with persons as ethically and morally sensitive as ourselves.

At least I hope so.

Father Wassmer is Professor of Moral Philosophy at Saint Peter's College in Jersey City, N. J.

105

Abortion—Or Compulsory Pregnancy?

Garrett Hardin
1915–

Journal of Marriage and the Family, **30**:246–251

1968

The year 1967 produced the first fissures in the dam that had prevented all change in the abortion-prohibition laws of the United States for three-quarters of a century. Two states adopted laws that allowed abortion in the "hardship cases" of rape, incest, and probability of a deformed child. A third approved the first two "indications," but not the last. All three took some note of the mental health of the pregnant woman, in varying language; how this language will be translated into practice remains to be seen. In almost two dozen other states, attempts to modify the laws were made but foundered at various stages in the legislative process. It is quite evident that the issue will continue to be a live one for many years to come.

The legislative turmoil was preceded and accompanied by a fast-growing popular literature. The word "abortion" has ceased to be a dirty word—which is a cultural advance. However, the *word* was so long under taboo that the ability to think about the *fact* seems to have suffered a sort of logical atrophy from disuse. Popular articles, regardless of their conclusions, tend to be over-emotional and to take a moralistic rather than an operational view of the matter. Nits are picked, hairs split. It is quite clear that many of the authors are not at all clear what question they are attacking.

It is axiomatic in science that progress hinges on asking the right question. Surprisingly, once the right question is asked the answer seems almost to tumble forth. That is a retrospective view; in prospect, it takes genuine (and mysterious) insight to see correctly into the brambles created by previous, ill-chosen verbalizations.

The abortion problem is, I think, a particularly neat example of a problem in which most of the difficulties are actually created by asking the wrong question. I submit further that once the right question is asked the whole untidy mess miraculously dissolves, leaving in its place a very simple public policy recommendation.

Rape as a Justification

The wrong question, the one almost invariably asked, is this: "How can we justify an abortion?" This assumes that there are weighty public reasons for encouraging pregnancies, or that abortions, per se, somehow threaten public peace. A direct examination of the legitimacy of these assumptions will be made later. For the present, let us pursue the question as asked and see what a morass it leads to.

Almost all the present legislative attempts take as their model a bill proposed by the American Law Institute which emphasizes three justifications for legal abortion: rape, incest, and the probability of a defective child. Whatever else may be said about this bill, it is clear that it affects only the periphery of the social problem. The Arden House Conference Committee[1] estimated the number of illegal abortions in the United States to be between 200,000 and 1,200,000 per year. A California legislator, Anthony C. Beilenson,[2] has estimated that the American Law Institute bill (which he favors) would legalize not more than four percent of the presently illegal abortions. Obviously, the "problem" of illegal abortion will be scarcely affected by the passage of the laws so far proposed in the United States.

I have calculated [3] that the number of rape-induced pregnancies in the United States is about 800 per year. The number is not large, but for the woman raped the total number is irrelevant. What matters to her is that she be relieved of her unwanted burden. But a law which puts the burden of proof on her compels her to risk a second harrowing experience. How can she *prove* to the district attorney that she was raped? He could really know whether or not she gave consent only if he could get inside her mind; this he cannot do. Here is the philosopher's "egocentric predicament" that none of us can escape. In an effort to help the district attorney sustain the illusion that he can escape this predicament, a talented woman may put on a dramatic performance, with copious tears and other signs of anguish. But what if the raped woman is not an actress? What if her temperament is stoic? In its operation, the law will act against the interests of calm, undramatic women. Is that what we want? It is safe to say also that district attorneys will hear less favorably the pleas of poor women, the general assumption of middle-class agents being that the poor are less responsible in sex anyway.[4] Is it to the interest of society that the poor bear more children, whether rape-engendered or not?

A wryly amusing difficulty has been raised with respect to rape. Suppose the woman is married and having regular intercourse with her husband. Suppose that following a rape by an unknown intruder she finds herself pregnant. Is she legally entitled to an abortion? How does she know whose child she is carrying anyway? If it is her husband's child, abortion is illegal. If she carries it to term, and if blood tests then exclude the husband as the father, as they would in a fraction of the cases, is the woman then entitled to a *delayed* abortion? But this is ridiculous: this in infanticide, which no one is proposing. Such is the bramble bush into which we are led by a *reluctant* consent for abortion in cases of rape.

How Probable Must Deformity Be?

The majority of the public support abortion in cases of a suspected deformity of the child [5] just as they do in cases of rape. Again, however, if the burden of proof rests on the one who requests the operation, we encounter difficulties in administration. Between 80,000 and 160,000 defective children are born every year in the United States. The number stated depends on two important issues: (a) how severe a defect must be before it is counted as such and (b) whether or not one counts as birth defects those defects that are not *detected* until later. (Deafness and various other defects produced by fetal rubella may not be detected until a year or so after birth.) However many defective infants there may be, what is the prospect of detecting them before birth?

The sad answer is: the prospects are poor. A small percentage can be picked up by microscopic examination of tissues of the fetus. But "amniocentesis"—the form of biopsy required to procure such tissues—is itself somewhat dangerous to both mother and fetus; most abnormalities will not be detectable by a microscopic examination of the fetal cells; and 96 to 98 percent of all fetuses are normal anyway. All these considerations are a contra-indication of routine amniocentesis.

When experience indicates that the probability of a deformed fetus is above the "background level" of 2 to 4 percent, is abortion justified? At what level? 10 percent? 50? 80? Or only at 100 percent? Suppose a particular medical history indicates a probability of 20 percent that the baby will be defective. If we routinely abort such cases, it is undeniable that four normal fetuses will be destroyed for every one abnormal. Those who assume that a fetus is an object of high value are appalled at this "wastage." Not uncommonly they ask, "Why not wait until the baby is born and then suffocate those that are deformed?" Such a question is unquestionably rhetoric and sardonic; if serious, it implies that infanticide has no more emotional meaning to a woman than abortion, an assumption that is surely contrary to fact.

Should the Father Have Rights?

Men who are willing to see abortion-prohibition laws relaxed somewhat, but not completely, frequently raise a question about the "rights" of the father. Should we allow a woman to make a unilateral decision for an abortion? Should not her husband have a say in the matter? (After all, he contributed just as many chromosomes to the fetus as she.)

I do not know what weight to give this objection. I have encountered it repeatedly in the discussion section following a public meeting. It is clear that some men are disturbed at finding themselves powerless in such a situation and want the law to give them some power of decision.

Yet powerless men are—and it is nature that has made them so. If we give the father a right of veto in abortion decisions, the wife has a very simple reply to her husband: "I'm sorry, dear, I wasn't going to tell you this, but you've forced my hand. This is not your child." With such a statement she could always deny her husband's right to decide.

Why husbands should demand power in such matters is a fit subject for depth analysis. In the absence of such, perhaps the best thing we can say to men who are "hung up" on this issue is this: "Do you really want to live for another eight months with a woman whom you are compelling to be pregnant against her will?"

Or, in terms of public policy, do we want to pass laws which give men the right to compel their wives to be pregnant? Psychologically, such compulsion is akin to rape. Is it in the public interest to encourage rape?

"Socio-Economic"—an Anemic Phrase

The question "How can we justify an abortion?" proves least efficient in solving the real problems of this world when we try to evaluate what are usually called "socio-economic indications." The hardship cases— rape, incest, probability of a deformed child—have been amply publicized, and as a result the majority of the public accepts them as valid indicators; but hardship cases constitute only a few percent of the need. By contrast, if a woman has more children than she feels she can handle, or if her children are coming too close together, there is little public sympathy for her plight. A poll [5] conducted by the National Opinion Research Center in December, 1965, showed that only 15 percent of the respondents replied "Yes" to this

296

question: "Please tell me whether or not you think it should be possible for a pregnant woman to obtain a legal abortion if she is married and does not want any more children." Yet this indication, which received the lowest rate of approval, accounts for the vast majority of instances in which women want—and illegally get—relief from unwanted pregnancy.

There is a marked discrepancy between the magnitude of the need and the degree of public sympathy. Part of the reason for this discrepancy is attributable to the emotional impact of the words used to describe the need. "Rape," "incest," "deformed child"—these words are rich in emotional connotations. "Socio-economic indications" is a pale bit of jargon, suggesting at best that the abortion is wanted because the woman lives by culpably materialistic standards. "Socio-economic indications" tugs at no one's heartstrings; the hyphenated abomination hides the human reality to which it obliquely refers. To show the sort of human problem to which this label may be attached, let me quote a letter I received from one woman. (The story is unique, but it is one of a large class of similar true stories.)

> I had an illegal abortion 2½ years ago. I left my church because of the guilt I felt. I had six children when my husband left me to live with another woman. We weren't divorced and I went to work to help support them. When he would come to visit the children he would sometimes stay after they were asleep. I became pregnant. When I told my husband, and asked him to please come back, he informed me that the woman he was living with was five months pregnant and ill, and that he couldn't leave her—not at that time anyway.
>
> I got the name of a doctor in San Francisco from a Dr. friend who was visiting here from there. This Dr. (Ob. and Gyn.) had a good legitimate practice in the main part of the city and was a kindly, compassionate man who believes as you do, that it is better for everyone not to bring an unwanted child into the world.
>
> It was over before I knew it. I thought I was just having an examination at the time. He even tried to make me not feel guilty by telling me that the long automobile trip had already started a spontaneous abortion. He charged me $25. That was on Fri. and on Mon. I was back at work. I never suffered any ill from it.
>
> The other woman's child died shortly after birth and six months later my husband asked if he could come back. We don't have a perfect marriage but my children have a father. My being able to work has helped us out of a deep financial debt. I shall always remember the sympathy I received from that Dr. and wish there were more like him with the courage to do what they believe is right.

Her operation was illegal, and would be illegal under most of the "reform" legislation now being proposed, if interpreted strictly. Fortunately some physicians are willing to indulge in more liberal interpretations, but they make these interpretations not on medical grounds, in the strict sense, but on social and economic grounds. Understandably, many physicians are unwilling to venture so far from the secure base of pure physical medicine. As one Catholic physician put it:

> Can the patient afford to have another child? Will the older children have sufficient educational opportunities if their parents have another child? Aren't two, three or four children enough? I am afraid such statements are frequently made in the discussion of a proposed therapeutic abortion. [But] we should be doctors of medicine, not socio-economic prophets.[6]

To this a non-Catholic physician added: "I sometimes wish I were an obstetrician in a Catholic hospital so that I would not have to make any of these decisions. The only position to take in which I would have no misgivings is to do no interruptions at all." [7]

Who Wants Compulsory Pregnancy?

The question "How can we justify an abortion?" plainly leads to great difficulties. It is operationally unmanageable: it leads to inconsistencies in practice and inequities by any moral standard. All these can be completely avoided if we ask the right question, namely: *"How can we justify compulsory pregnancy?"*

By casting the problem in this form, we call attention to its relationship to the slavery issue. Somewhat more than a century ago men in the Western world asked the question: "How can we justify compulsory servitude?" and came up with the answer: *"By no means whatever."* Is the answer any different to the related question: "How can we justify compulsory pregnancy?" Certainly pregnancy is a form of servitude; if continued to term it results in parenthood, which is also a kind of servitude, to be endured for the best years of a woman's life. It is difficult to see how it can be argued that this kind of servitude will be more productive of social good if it is compulsory rather than voluntary. A study[8] made of Swedish children born when their mothers were refused the abortions they had requested showed that unwanted children, as compared with their controls, as they grew up were more often picked up for drunkenness, or antisocial or criminal behavior; they received less education; they received more psychiatric care; and they were more often exempted from military service by reason of defect. Moreover, the females in the group married earlier and had children earlier, thus no doubt tending to create a vicious circle of poorly tended children who in their turn would produce more poorly tended children. How then does society gain by increasing the number of unwanted children? No one has volunteered an answer to this question.

Of course if there were a shortage of children, then society might say that it needs all the children it can get—unwanted or not. But I am unaware of any recent rumors of a shortage of children.

Alternatives: True and False

The end result of an abortion—the elimination of an unwanted fetus—is surely good. But is the act itself somehow damaging? For several generations it was widely believed that abortion was intrinsically dangerous, either physically or psychologically. It is now very clear that the widespread belief is quite unjustified. The evidence for this statement is found in a bulky literature which has been summarized in Lawrence Lader's *Abortion*[9] and the collection of essays brought together by Alan Guttmacher.[10]

In tackling questions of this sort, it is imperative that we identify correctly the alternatives facing us. (All moral and practical problems involve a comparison of alternative actions.) Many of the arguments of the prohibitionists implicitly assume that the alternatives facing the woman are these:

abortion———no abortion

This is false. A person can never do nothing. The pregnant woman is going to do something, whether she wishes to or not. (She cannot roll time backward and live her life over.)

People often ask: "Isn't contraception better than abortion?" Implied by this question are these alternatives:

abortion———contraception

But these are not the alternatives that face the woman who asks to be aborted. She *is* pregnant. She cannot roll time backward and use contraception more successfully than she did before. Contraceptives are never foolproof anyway. It is commonly accepted that the failure rate of our best contraceptive, the "pill," is around one percent, i.e., one failure per hundred woman-years of use. I have earlier shown[11] that this failure rate produces about a quarter of a million unwanted pregnancies a year in the United States. Abortion is not so much an alternative to contraception as it is a subsidiary method of birth control, to be used when the primary method fails—as it often does.

The woman *is* pregnant: this is the base level at which the moral decision begins. If she is pregnant against her will, does it matter to society

299

whether or not she was careless or unskillful in her use of contraception? In any case, she is threatening society with an unwanted child, for which society will pay dearly. The real alternatives facing the woman (and society) are clearly these:

abortion——compulsory pregnancy

When we recognize that these are the real, operational alternatives, the false problems created by pseudo-alternatives vanish.

Is Potential Value Valuable?

Only one weighty objection to abortion remains to be discussed, and this is the question of "loss." When a fetus is destroyed, has something valuable been destroyed? The fetus has the potentiality of becoming a human being. A human being is valuable. Therefore is not the fetus of equal value? This question must be answered.

It can be answered, but not briefly. What does the embryo receive from its parents that might be of value? There are only three possibilities: substance, energy, and information. As for the substance in the fertilized egg, it is not remarkable: merely the sort of thing one might find in any piece of meat, human or animal, and there is very little of it—only one and a half micrograms, which is about a half of a billionth of an ounce. The energy content of this tiny amount of material is likewise negligible. As the zygote develops into an embryo, both its substance and its energy content increase (at the expense of the mother); but this is not a very important matter—even an adult, viewed from this standpoint, is only a hundred and fifty pounds of meat!

Clearly, the humanly significant thing that is contributed to the zygote by the parents is the information that "tells" the fertilized egg how to develop into a human being. This information is in the form of a chemical tape called "DNA," a double set of two chemical supermolecules each of which has about three billion "spots" that can be coded with any one of four different possibilities, symbolized by *A, T, G,* and *C.* (For comparison, the Morse code offers three possibilities in coding: dot, dash, and space.) It is the particular sequence of these four chemical possibilities in the DNA that directs the zygote in its development into a human being. The DNA constitutes the information needed to produce a valuable human being. The question is: is this information precious? I have argued elsewhere[12] that it is not:

> Consider the case of a man who is about to begin to build a $50,000 house. As he stands on the site looking at the blueprints a practical

joker comes along and sets fire to the blueprints. The question is: can the owner go to the law and collect $50,000 for his lost blueprints? The answer is obvious: since another set of blueprints can be produced for the cost of only a few dollars, that is all they are worth. (A court might award a bit more for the loss of the owner's time, but that is a minor matter.) The moral: *a nonunique copy of information that specifies a valuable structure is itself almost valueless.*

This principle is precisely applicable to the moral problem of abortion. The zygote, which contains the complete specification of a valuable human being, is not a human being, and is almost valueless. . . . The early stages of an individual fetus have had very little human effort invested in them; they are of very little worth. The loss occasioned by an abortion is independent of whether the abortion is spontaneous or induced. (Just as the loss incurred by the burning of a set of blueprints is independent of whether the causal agent was lightning or an arsonist.)

A set of blueprints is not a house; the DNA of a zygote is not a human being. The analogy is singularly exact, though there are two respects in which it is deficient. These respects are interesting rather than important. First, we have the remarkable fact that the blueprints of the zygote are constantly replicated and incorporated in every cell of the human body. This is interesting, but it has no moral significance. There is no moral obligation to conserve DNA—if there were, no man would be allowed to brush his teeth and gums, for in this brutal operation hundreds of sets of DNA are destroyed daily.

The other anomaly of the human information problem is connected with the fact that the information that is destroyed in an aborted embryo *is* unique (unlike the house blueprints). But it is unique in a way that is without moral significance. A favorite argument of abortion-prohibitionists is this: "What if Beethoven's mother had had an abortion?" The question moves us; but when we think it over we realize we can just as relevantly ask: "What if Hitler's mother had had an abortion?" Each conceptus is unique, but not in any way that has a moral consequence. The *expected* potential value of each aborted child is exactly that of the average child born. It is meaningless to say that humanity loses when a *particular* child is not born, or is not conceived. A human female, at birth, has about 30,000 eggs in her ovaries. If she bears only 3 children in her lifetime, is there any meaningful sense in which we can say that mankind has suffered a loss in those other 29,997 fruitless eggs? (Yet one of them might have been a super-Beethoven!)

People who worry about the moral danger of abortion do so because they think of the fetus as a human being, hence equate feticide with murder. Whether the fetus is or is not a human being is a matter of definition, not fact; and we can define any way we wish. In terms of the human problem involved, it would be unwise to define the fetus as human (hence tactically unwise ever to refer to the fetus as an "unborn child"). Analysis based on the deepest insights of molecular biology indicates the wisdom of sharply distinguishing the information for a valuable structure from the completed structure itself. It is interesting, and gratifying, to note that this modern insight is completely congruent with common law governing the disposal of dead fetuses. Abortion-prohibitionists generally insist that abortion is murder, and that an embryo is a person; but no state or nation, so far as I know, requires the dead fetus to be treated like a dead person. Although all of the states in the United States severely limit what can be done with a dead human body, no cognizance is taken of dead fetuses up to about five months' prenatal life. The early fetus may, with impunity, be flushed down the toilet or thrown out with the garbage—which shows that we never have regarded it as a human being. Scientific analysis confirms what we have always known.

The Management of Compulsory Pregnancy

What is the future of compulsory pregnancy? The immediate future is not hopeful. Far too many medical people misconceive the real problem. One physician has written:

> Might not a practical, workable solution to this most difficult problem be found by setting up, in every hospital, an abortion committee comprising a specialist in obstetrics and gynecology, a psychiatrist, and a clergyman or priest? The patient and her husband—if any—would meet with these men who would do all in their power to persuade the woman not to undergo the abortion. (I have found that the promise of a postpartum sterilization will frequently enable even married women with all the children they can care for to accept this one more, final pregnancy.) If, however, the committee members fail to change the woman's mind, they can make it very clear that they disapprove of the abortion, but prefer that it be safely done in a hospital rather than bungled in a basement somewhere.[13]

What this author has in mind is plainly not a system of legalizing abortion but a system of managing compulsory pregnancy. It is this philosophy which governs pregnancies in the Scandinavian countires,[14] where the experience of a full generation of women has shown that women do not want their pregnancies to be managed by the state. Illegal abortions have remained at a high level in these countries, and recent years have seen the development of a considerable female tourist trade to Poland, where

302

abortions are easy to obtain. Unfortunately, American legislatures are now proposing to follow the provably unworkable system of Scandinavia.

The drift down this erroneous path is not wholly innocent. Abortion-prohibitionists are showing signs of recognizing "legalization" along Scandinavian lines as one more roadblock that can be thrown in the way of the abolition of compulsory pregnancy. To cite an example: on February 9, 1966, the *Courier,* a publication of the Winona, Minnesota Diocese, urged that Catholics support a reform law based on the American Law Institute model, because the passage of such a law would "take a lot of steam out of the abortion advocate's argument" and would "defeat a creeping abortionism of disastrous importance." [15]

Wherever a Scandinavian or American Law Institute type of bill is passed, it is probable that cautious legislators will then urge a moratorium for several years while the results of the new law are being assessed (though they are easily predictable from the Scandinavian experience). As Lord Morley once said: "Small reforms are the worst enemies of great reforms." Because of the backwardness of education in these matters, caused by the long taboo under which the subject of abortion labored, it seems highly likely that our present system of compulsory pregnancy will continue substantially without change until the true nature of the alternatives facing us is more widely recognized.

---

[1] Mary Steichen Calderone (ed.), *Abortion in the United States,* New York: Hoeber-Harper, 1958, p. 178.

[2] Anthony C. Beilenson, "Abortion and Common Sense," *Per/Se,* **1** (1966):24.

[3] Garrett Hardin, "Semantic Aspects of Abortion," *ETC.,* **24** (1967):263.

[4] Lee Rainwater, *And the Poor Get Children,* Chicago: Quadrangle Books, 1960, p. *ix* and chap. 1.

[5] Alice S. Rossi, "Abortion Laws and Their Victims," *Trans-action,* **3** (September–October 1966): 7.

[6] Calderone (ed.), *op. cit.,* p. 103.

[7] *Ibid.,* p. 123.

[8] Hans Forssman and Inga Thuwe, "One Hundred and Twenty Children Born after Application for Therapeutic Abortion Refused," *Acta Psychiatrica Scandinavica,* **42** (1966):71.

[9] Lawrence Lader, *Abortion,* Indianapolis: Bobbs-Merrill, 1966.

[10] Alan F. Guttmacher (ed.), *The Case for Legalized Abortion,* Berkeley, California: Diablo Press, 1967.

[11] Garrett Hardin, "A Scientist's Case for Abortion," *Redbook,* May 1967, p. 62.

[12] Garrett Hardin, "Blueprints, DNA, and Abortion: A Scientific and Ethical Analysis," *Medical Opinion and Review,* **3**(2)(1967):74.

[13] H. Curtis Wood, Jr., "Letter to the Editor," *Medical Opinion and Review,* **3**(11)(1967):19.

[14] David T. Smith (ed.), *Abortion and the Law,* Cleveland: Western Reserve University, 1967, p. 179.

[15] Anonymous, *Association for the Study of Abortion Newsletter,* **2**(3)(1967):6.

106
Sterilization in India

News Reports

From various Indian journals, quoted in *Population Review,* **11**(2)

1967

Fifteen States Support Sterilization

NEW DELHI—The Union Minister of Health and Family Planning, Dr. S. Chandrasekhar, said in New Delhi on Sunday (13 August) that all the State Chief Ministers, except two—Punjab and Madhya Pradesh—were in favour of compulsory sterilization after a couple had three children, reports PTI.

Fifteen States had accepted the proposal, he added.

Addressing the concluding session of the seminar on Science and Science Writing, he said the Government inconclusively considered at the highest level on Saturday the recent decision to deny maternity benefits to women Government employees with more than three children. "It was a draw," he said.

Muslims Oppose Sterilization

TRIVANDRUM—The Kerala Muslim League has opposed the move to make sterilization compulsory.

The State Committee of the League has, at the same time, urged that if compulsory sterilization is to be enforced the Muslim community should be exempted from its purview.

Mr. E. Ahmed, the League MLA, who met the Health Minister, Mr. B. Wellington, here today said that the Minister assured him that the Government had not made up its mind on this question of compulsory sterilization.

The Minister further agreed that before taking a definite decision on the matter the opinions of different sections of the population would be ascertained.

Muslims Accept Sterilization

NEW DELHI—Nearly 300 Muslims, all men, of the walled city have undergone sterilization.

This was stated by Dr. B. D. Mukhija, Zonal Family Planning Officer of the Delhi Administration, at a seminar here today.

Dr. Mukhija said that after the Shahi Imam of Jama Miasjid, Delhi, issued a fatwa (verdict) last month justifying sterilization, the movement had gained a fresh impetus.

A Family Planning Fortnight will be observed throughout the country from September 16.

Incentives For Sterilization

MADRAS—Dr. Chandrasekhar, Union Minister for Health and Family Planning, today denied that he had advocated "compulsory sterilization."

He told a Press conference that he all along had been in favour of providing incentives to the people for voluntary sterilization. It was the Maharashtra Government which had proposed compulsory sterilization and had sought the Centre's approval for it. The request was being examined.

Dr. Chandrasekhar said he had received numerous letters "mostly from Hindus in West Bengal demanding compulsory sterilization so as to maintain the existing communal ratio of the population but this was a far-fetched argument."

About the proposal to present transistor radios to those agreeing to sterilization, the Minister said a Hongkong manufacturer had agreed to supply 1 million transistors at Rs. 17 each—as against Rs. 55 for the cheapest Indian make. This offer was being examined, he added.

107

Sterilization Degrading

Lord Justice Denning
1900–

Bravery v. Bravery, 3 All E.R. 59

Though not exactly under a taboo, sterilization as a means of birth control is usually discussed somewhat reluctantly. Although a Gallup poll in 1966 showed that 65 per cent of the people in the United States and Canada were in favor of contraceptive sterilization, only ten percent of the states (Maine, Minnesota, North Carolina, South Dakota, and Vermont) have laws specifically permitting voluntary sterilization. (Twenty-eight states have laws permitting court-ordered eugenic sterilization, but most of these statutes are not used.) In spite of this, it is estimated that more than 100,000 American men and women are voluntarily sterilized every year. There is an organization that promotes this practice: the Association for Voluntary Sterilization, 14 West 40th Street, New York 10018. No state **specifically** forbids it. Most lawyers and doctors think the operating doctor has a negligible liability, provided he secures the written consent of both marriage partners. Nevertheless, a substantial minority of physicians refuse to perform the operation, either for religious reasons or because of legal fears stemming from a statement made by the English jurist Justice Denning. The Justice's opinion has been much quoted, but it should be pointed out that it was the minority opinion of the court, and did not prevail.

1954

Take a case where a sterilization operation is done so as to enable a man to have the pleasure of sexual intercourse without shouldering the responsibilities attaching to it. The operation is plainly injurious to the public interest. It is degrading to the man himself. It is injurious to his wife and to any woman whom he may marry, to say nothing of the way it opens to licentiousness; and, unlike contraceptives, it allows no room for a change of mind on either side. It is illegal, even though the man consents to it.

108
Sterilization in Puerto Rico

Clarence Senior
1903–

From *Studies in Population*
edited by George F. Mair
Princeton: Princeton University Press

1949

Let me illustrate what is possible by a hasty account of certain factors in the spread of the practice of sterilization in Puerto Rico, an island famous for its high fertility, on which the Catholic Church claims a membership of at least 85 percent of the population.

Some 25 or 30 years ago, sterilization began to be practiced by upper class women as a birth control measure. The operation, at that time, was both hazardous and costly. It filled a need, however. The women wanted to go to confession but not have to confess the use of mechanical methods of preventing conception. The rationalization which one finds generally made is that sterilization, being one "sin," is forgiven at the next occasion for penance, whereas the use of contraceptives would entail a constant series of confessions and penances! Many of the same women who thus solved their own problem were bitterly opposed to the introduction of public clinics where the wives of workers and peasants could solve theirs. However, in spite of church opposition, the insular legislature legalized contraception for health purposes, including sterilization, in 1937. . . .

It happens that the physical difficulties of birth control on the island (P.R.) are great. They are at least as serious an obstacle to controlled fertility as are the cultural barriers. Sterilization is looked upon by many as a short-cut which will obviate such difficulties as lack of running water, absence of privacy, shortage of nurses and doctors, etc. Recent advances have reduced the cost and the danger, especially as a post-partum operation.

Gradually, the practice began to spread down from the upper class women to the urban working class families, but of course the problem is far more serious in the country than in the cities. The idea was spread in the rural areas in a most illuminating manner. After a clinic up in the mountains had performed a dozen or so sterilizations, it was attacked in a pastoral letter. The reading of the letter in the rural churches was followed by a wave of inquiries at public health clinics and to private doctors as to the availability of the operation which had been denounced by the bishop. Thus public advertising to back up person-to-person rumor was furnished by the very institution which was fighting the practice. A public discussion of sterilization in the spring of 1949 led to another pastoral letter. This one warned that a sterilized woman would not be admitted to communion, but it added, "unless she has sincerely repented." Thus the church seems to have made its adaptation to the requirements of the insular situation. Women in increasing numbers are seeking sterilization as the answer to their needs. Doctors in a position to judge estimate that in the past few years 60 percent of all the women who have their children delivered in hospitals request that sterilization follow the birth.

This hasty summary of a complex question is based largely upon my own experiences on the island, partly as secretary of the Asociacion de Estudios Poblacionale, a non-governmental organization devoted to the study and discussion of population problems.

109
Some Religious Scruples

Norman St. John-Stevas
1929–

From *Life, Death and the Law*
Bloomington: Indiana University Press

1961

Christian opinion is less unanimous when voluntary instead of compulsory sterilization is considered. Both the Roman Catholic and Anglican Churches recognize the validity of therapeutic sterilization as morally justified if it is the only means of securing the welfare of the body as a whole. Thus if vasectomy and salpingectomy are the only means of curing a disease, their use is legitimate. Their employment would fall within the exception mentioned by St Thomas Aquinas in connection with mutilation. Neither communion, on the other hand, countenances the use of sterilization where a woman's health would be gravely endangered by a further pregnancy. Dr Glanville Williams finds such a view "astonishing" but it is not unreasonable.[1] Sexual intercourse is not a necessity and the woman can adequately safeguard her future either by abstention, or in the view of many Anglicans by the use of contraceptives. Such sterilization is not strictly speaking therapeutic but contraceptive. In the case of subnormal couples, incapable of handling contraceptives efficiently, the case for employment of sterilization is stronger, but only of course amongst those who regard the use of contraceptives as legitimate. The latter might extend sterilization as a legitimate procedure from defectives in danger of physical injury through pregnancy, to defectives who would be placed under overwhelming strain through further child-bearing. As the Church of England Moral Welfare Council points out, this conclusion may prove difficult even for those who approve of contraception. Sterilization might well be considered too grave a course to employ save directly for the cure of a disease. Furthermore, while in sterilization of a defective wife whose health would be threatened by pregnancy, and where intercourse can be regarded as inevitable, the causal connection between the operation and the result aimed at is very close; in the second case, where the burden of looking after children is the main concern, the connection is remote. A further complication in this latter case is that there is no indication which of the parents should be sterilized. . . .[2]

Voluntary sterilization for eugenic reasons is not countenanced by the Roman Catholic Church. The Church of England Committee puts forward the argument that a normal couple who know that one partner is a carrier of defect may regard the sexual organ as "diseased", in that the genes it secretes are defective, and given circumstances of "necessity", may resort to sterilization. This argument is answered by pointing out that the organ is not diseased in relation to the parental body but only to the hypothetical child. What constitutes "necessity"? Here the couple have two alternatives; they can abstain or they can use contraceptives. Accordingly sterilization would not be justified in their case. . . .[3]

A State policy of compulsory sterilization conflicts radically with Christian morals and social policy. It violates the fundamental rights of the human person, and confers powers on the State to which it has no claim. The maintenance of State authority is in no way incompatible with the presence within the community of unsterilized mental defectives and others. As has been established, the uncertainty shrouding the whole hereditary process, the ignorance of the pathology of mental diseases and defect, and the high proportion of the population who would have to be sterilized for a eugenic policy to have substantial effect, must result in the rejection of compulsory sterilization on the level of practical ethics. Christians, accordingly, have not only a right but a duty to resist the legislative sponsoring of such projects, and to work for their repeal where they have been enacted. The experience of Nazi Germany has convinced many of the validity of the Christian contention that once sterilization powers have been conferred on the State, the danger of their ruthless exploitation is a real one. A Christian campaign on this issue could accordingly expect general public support. It is a little surprising to observe that the Catholics of Connecticut who have fought so fiercely for the retention on the statute book of a birth control statute which invades the privacy of the home, should have acquiesced for all practical purposes in the presence of sterilization provisions in the State Code which can be invoked without hearing or appeal.

---

[1] Glanville Williams, *The Sanctity of Life and the Criminal Law,* New York, 1957, p. 100.

[2] *Human Sterilization: Some Principles of Christian Ethics,* Church of England Moral Welfare Council, London, 1951, pp. 7–9 and 15.

[3] *Ibid.,* pp. 11–12.

110
Technical Characteristics of Sterilization

Garrett Hardin
1915–

From "Birth Control—The Prospects"
Medicine Today, **1:**38–45

1967

In some respects surgical sterilization is the most satisfactory of all methods. The operation, particularly in the male, is a minor one. It eliminates the need for further contraceptive effort. It is almost 100 percent successful. The "almost" in the preceding sentence calls attention to a medical puzzle. The operation is so simple that we would expect, *a priori,* that it would never fail—yet it does. In a small percentage of cases the vas deferens or the Fallopian tube re-anastomoses.[1] Is this because Nature is very clever? Or are some physicians very clumsy?

There is another possibility. Hans Lehfeldt[2] has called attention to the occasional failure of female contraception when the woman is ambivalent about her desire to avoid having a child, and so is unconsciously clumsy or "forgetful." In the United States many physicians refuse to perform sterilizations, for religious or emotional reasons. Could it be that even those who perform vasectomies are sometimes ambivalent in their intentions and unconsciously bungle the operation?

What is the effect of the operation upon the libido? From the standpoint of strict physical medicine it should be nil. In fact it is not. A study in Japan[3] showed that sexual activity was depressed in 3.5 percent of the couples, but augmented 28.5 percent. The augmentation occurred, no doubt, because of the lifting of the burden of anxiety about another pregnancy. Depression was probably related to complex psychological reactions stemming from sub-scientific notions of the nature of the operation. A study made in two Indian villages[4] showed that only a third of the people understood correctly the relation of sterilization to sexuality. Plainly, any public campaign for mass sterilization must be preceded and accompanied by an adequate educational effort. Those who do the educating must not be strictly objective but rather must deport themselves in the light of what I have elsewhere[5] called "Class II Truths"—truths which become so on being said. Prospective patients should never be told that the operation may decrease their libido; on the contrary, they should be told there is a good chance that it will increase it.

One of the principal impediments to sterilization is the understandable dread of taking an irrevocable step. To this objection, Glanville Williams[6] has replied: "After all, if tubal ligation is irrevocable so is the birth of an unwanted child." Nevertheless this dread leads most couples to postpone the operation until one or two unwanted children beyond the time it should be performed; this fact has in the past limited the usefulness of sterilization as a population control measure. In the future, the situation looks brighter. There will be greater willingness to accept early sterilization if the medical profession can assure the patient that the operation is reversible. Early reports on surgical reversal of sterilization gave a success rate of only a few percent; recent reports[7] have ranged as high as 88 percent. Of course the reverse operation is very expensive because it requires the most delicate technique. Even this requirement may diminish. Already there have been promising results of sterilization by occlusion of the intact vas deferens with a plastic substance that can later be easily removed.

These unpublished experiments have been carried out with dogs; human experiments will follow.

---

[1] Herbert Brewer, "Reversibility Following Sterilization by Vasectomy," *Eugenics Review,* **56** (1964):147–150.

[2] Hans Lehfeldt, "Willful Exposure to Unwanted Pregnancy (WEUP)," *American Journal of Obstetrics & Gynecology,* **78** (1959):661–665.

[3] Yoshio Koya, "Sterilization in Japan," *Eugenics Quarterly,* **8** (1961):135–141.

[4] Thomas Poffenberger and Haribhai G. Patel, "The Effects of Local Beliefs on Attitudes Toward Vasectomy in Two Indian Villages in Gujarat State," *Population Review,* **8** (1964):37–44.

[5] Garrett Hardin, "Three Classes of Truth: Their Implications for the Behavioral Sciences," *ETC.,* **18** (1961):5–20.

[6] Glanville Williams, *The Sanctity of Life,* New York: Knopf, 1957.

[7] Brewer, *op. cit.,* pp. 147–150.

111
Dick and Jane: What Is Pornography?

The problem of birth control is more than merely technical. Trained to have faith in gadgets, we tend to think that the problem of overpopulation will be solved someday by some new gimmick that can be produced and marketed like nuts and bolts. This won't happen. We shouldn't belittle technical devices—the pill is truly much more effective than the diaphragm (because it is psychologically more acceptable). But in the end, no technical device will solve the overpopulation problem unless we change the pictures in people's heads, the pictures to which they unconsciously try to make their lives conform.

We have to begin early to do that. We have to gain control of the earliest stages of education where the heads of children are filled with powerful images. For many years in the United States Dick and Jane dominated the six-year-old scene. In the first grade readers, there was Mother and Daddy—and Dick and Jane. Two children, at least; never less. If there was a married couple next door, they had children too. The people across the street had children. The visiting aunts and uncles had children. Everybody worth mentioning—everybody who **was** mentioned—had children.

Where, we must now ask, was Uncle Harry, that gay old bachelor who had never married and never intended to marry—but was having a helluva fine time? Where was Aunt Debbie, that headstrong and charming spinster who liked children well enough in small doses, but who would **never** tie herself down? Alas, neither of these inspiring characters ever appeared on the scene. The childish mind was filled with only one picture of the Good life: to be married, and to have children. Against the defenses created by such early "brain-washing," the pill and the coil are feeble weapons indeed.

"I would that all men were even as myself," said Paul of Tarsus—but he recognized and accepted that they were not. Less tolerant, we unthinkingly try to press all men and women into a single mold—the breeding mold —whether their temperaments are suited to a life of breeding and parenthood or not. To support those who are not naturally inclined toward parenthood we must introduce Aunt Debbie and Uncle Harry into the elementary schools, and we had better make it clear that their childlessness has the community's blessing. It is not a matter of completely replacing the parents of Dick and Jane with spinsters and bachelors; not replacement, but augmentation, is the order of the day.

Reform will not come easily because our moralists, with few exceptions, are caught in a trap baited by the philosopher Immanuel Kant (1724–1804). Kant's bait was the plausible sounding **Categorical Imperative:** "Act only on that maxim through which you can at the same time will that it should become a universal law." The maxim is plausible because it sounds a bit like the Golden Rule; but it is really something quite different. "Do unto others as you would have them do unto you" surely leads to a practice that permits variation in actions; Kant's Categorical Imperative, by contrast, just as surely acts as a pressure toward conformity. Kant didn't discover any great new principle of ethics; he merely put into high-flown language Everyman's panicky desire to make his neighbor like himself.

If either Dick and Jane or Aunt Debbie and Uncle Harry were generalized into universal models the result would be devastation. If everyone became a childless Debbie or Harry, there would soon be no human world to worry about. If everyone became the parents of many Dicks and Janes the overcrowding of the physical world would soon produce a ruin not worth living in. To universalize either model in today's Pasteurian and Darwinian world is to generate pornography.

We need to introduce multiple models into children's literature. How can we do this? Here is one of the major unsolved problems of our time, a problem made worse by the decline of the family and the rise of literacy. When the family was the major seat of moral instruction and individual counseling it was possible for wise parents to give different advice to different children. In particular instances, their counseling might or might not be wise; but at least oral communications in a family setting made it possible to **focus** tailor-made advice on the individual whom it was believed to fit.

With the replacement of the family by the public school as a source of moral and vocational guidance there has been a significant change. Oral

313

advice is almost entirely replaced by printed advice. It is the nature of print to be **broadcast** rather than focused. The natural technical characteristics of literacy, powered by the intolerant spirit of the Categorical Imperative, threaten the world with ruin.

The ruin can be averted, of course; but we need first to become aware of the roads that lead toward ruin—and then we must deliberately alter them.

112

Advice on the Choice of a Mistress

Benjamin Franklin
1706–1790

1745

Philadelphia, June 25, 1745

My dear Friend:

I know of no medicine fit to diminish the violent natural inclinations you mention; and if I did, I think I should not communicate it to you. Marriage is the proper remedy. It is the most natural state of man, and therefore the state in which you are most likely to find solid happiness. Your reasons against entering into it at present appear to me not well founded. The circumstantial advantages you have in view by postponing it are not only uncertain, but they are small in comparison with that of the thing itself, the being married and settled. It is the man and woman united that make the complete human being. Separate, she wants his force of body and strength of reason; he, her softness, sensibility, and acute discernment. Together they are more likely to succeed in the world. A single man has not nearly the value he would have in the state of union. He is an incomplete animal. He resembles the odd half of a pair of scissors. If you get a prudent, healthy wife, your industry in your profession, with her good economy, will be a fortune sufficient.

But if you will not take the counsel and persist in thinking a commerce with the sex inevitable, then I repeat my former advice, that in all your amours you should prefer old women to young ones.

You call this a paradox and demand my reasons. They are these:

1. Because they have more knowledge of the world, and their minds are better stored with observations, their conversation is more improving and more lastingly agreeable.

2. Because when women cease to be handsome they study to be good. To maintain their influence over men, they supply the diminution of beauty by an augmentation of utility. They learn to do a thousand services small and great, and are the most tender and useful of friends when you are sick. Thus they continue amiable. And hence there is hardly such a thing to be found as an old woman who is not a good woman.

3. Because there is no hazard of children, which irregularly produced may be attended with much inconvenience.

4. Because through more experience they are more prudent and discreet in conducting an intrigue to prevent suspicion. The commerce with them is therefore safer with regard to your reputation. And with regard to theirs, if the affair should happen to be known, considerate people might be rather inclined to excuse an old woman, who would kindly take care of a young man, form his manners by her good counsels, and prevent his ruining his health and fortune among mercenary prostitutes.

5. Because in every animal that walks upright the deficiency of the fluids that fill the muscles appears first in the highest part. The face first grows lank and wrinkled; then the neck; then the breast and arms; the lower parts continuing to the last as plump as ever: so that covering all above with a basket, and regarding only what is below the girdle, it is impossible of two women to tell an old one from a young one. And as in the dark all cats are gray, the pleasure of corporal enjoyment with an old woman is at least equal, and frequently superior; every knack being, by practice, capable of improvement.

6. Because the sin is less. The debauching a virgin may be her ruin, and make her for life unhappy.

7. Because the compunction is less. The having made a young girl miserable may give you frequent bitter reflection; none of which can attend the making an old woman happy.

8th and lastly. They are so grateful!!

Thus much for my paradox. But still I advise you to marry directly; being sincerely
Your affectionate friend,

Benjamin Franklin

113

A Theory of Sexual Sharing

John Humphrey Noyes
1811–1886

From History of American Socialisms
Philadelphia: J. B. Lippincott

One of the most astonishing experiments of the century of Victoria and Comstock was that of the Oneida Community in upper New York state. Many native-born communistic communities were started in the nineteenth century, but most of them failed in a few years, some in a few months. The Oneida Community survived and prospered for thirty years. Why did it finally fail? Perhaps because of the succession of a less able son to the leadership of the founder, John Humphrey Noyes, who was clearly a remarkable man. Perhaps because of the irresistible opposition of the outer world, which looked with horror at the sharing of sex at Oneida. Perhaps because the whole idea was unworkable anyway. (Let every man be his own historian.)

Noyes was trained as a minister, and based his communism solidly on religious idealism. Elements of the theory are given in his words, below; an outsider's view of the practice is presented in the next selection.

1870

The abolishment of exclusiveness is involved in the love-relation required between all believers by the express injunction of Christ and the apostles, and by the whole tenor of the New Testament. "The new commandment is, that we love one another," and that, not by pairs, as in the world. but *en masse*. We are required to love one another fervently. The fashion of the world forbids a man and woman who are otherwise appropriated, to love one another fervently. But if they obey Christ they must do this; and whoever would allow them to do this, and yet would forbid them (on any other ground than that of present expediency), to express their unity, would "strain at a gnat and swallow a camel;" for unity of hearts is as much more important than any external expression of it, as a camel is larger than a gnat.

The abolishment of social restrictions is involved in the anti-legality of the gospel. It is incompatible with the state of perfected freedom toward which Paul's gospel of "grace without law" leads, that man should be allowed and required to love in all directions, and yet be forbidden to express love except in one direction. In fact Paul says, with direct reference to sexual intercourse—"All things are lawful for me, but all things are not expedient; all things are lawful for me, but I will not be brought under the power of any;" (1 Cor. 6: 12;) thus placing the restrictions which were necessary in the transition period on the basis, not of law, but of expediency and the demands of spiritual freedom, and leaving it fairly to be inferred that in the final state, when hostile surroundings and powers of bondage cease, all restrictions also will cease.

The abolishment of the marriage system is involved in Paul's doctrine of the end of ordinances. Marriage is one of the "ordinances of the worldly sanctuary." This is proved by the fact that it has no place in the resurrection. Paul expressly limits it to life in the flesh. Rom. 7: 2, 3. The assumption, therefore, that believers are dead to the world by the death of Christ (which authorized the abolishment of Jewish ordinances), legitimately makes an end of marriage. Col. 2: 20.

The law of marriage is the same in kind with the Jewish law concerning meats and drinks and holy days, of which Paul said that they were "contrary to us, and were taken out of the way, being nailed to the cross." Col. 2: 14. The plea in favor of the worldly social system, that it is not arbitrary, but founded in nature, will not bear investigation. All experience testifies (the theory of the novels to the contrary notwithstanding), that sexual love is not naturally restricted to pairs. Second marriages are contrary to the one-love theory, and yet are often the happiest marriages. Men and women find universally (however the fact may be concealed), that their susceptibility to love is not burnt out by one honey-moon, or satisfied by one lover. On the contrary, the secret history of the human heart will bear out the assertion that it is capable of loving any number of times and any number of persons, and that the more it loves the more it can love. This is the law of nature, thrust out of sight and codemned by common consent, and yet secretly known to all.

The law of marriage "worketh wrath." 1. It provokes to secret adultery, actual or of the heart. 2. It ties together unmatched natures. 3. It sunders matched natures. 4. It gives to sexual appetite only a scanty and monotonous allowance, and so produces the natural vices of poverty, contraction of taste and stinginess or jealousy. 5. It makes no provision for the sexual appetite at the very time when that appetite is the strongest. By the custom of the world, marriage, in the average of cases, takes place at about the age of twenty-four; whereas puberty commences at the age of fourteen. For ten years, therefore, and that in the very flush of life, the sexual appetite is starved. The law of society bears hardest on females, because they have less opportunity of choosing their time of marriage than men. This discrepancy between the marriage system and nature, is one of the principal sources of the peculiar diseases of women, of prostitution, masturbation, and licentiousness in general. . . .

The restoration of true relations between the sexes is a matter second in importance only to the reconciliation of man to God. The distinction of male and female is that which makes man the image of God, i.e., the image of the Father and the Son. Gen. 1: 27. The relation of male and female was the first social relation. Gen. 2: 22. It is therefore the root of all other social relations. The derangement of this relation was the first result of the original breach with God. Gen. 3: 7; comp. 2: 25. Adam and Eve were, at the beginning, in open, fearless, spiritual fellowship, first with God, and secondly, with each other. Their transgression produced two corresponding alienations, viz., first, an alienation from God, indicated by their fear of meeting him and their hiding themselves among the trees of the garden; and secondly, an alienation from each other, indicated by their shame at their nakedness and their hiding themselves from each other by clothing. These were the two great manifestations of original sin—the only manifestations presented to notice in the record of the apostacy. The first thing then to be done, in an attempt to redeem man and reörganize society, is to bring about reconciliation with God; and the second thing is to bring about a true union of the sexes. In other words, religion is the first subject of interest, and sexual morality the second, in the great enterprise of establishing the Kingdom of Heaven on earth.

From what precedes, it is evident that any attempt to revolutionize sexual morality before settlement with God, is out of order. Holiness must go before free love. Bible Communists are not responsible for the proceedings of those who meddle with the sexual question, before they have laid the foundation of true faith and union with God.

Dividing the sexual relation into two branches, the amative and propagative, the amative or love-relation is first in importance, as it is in the order of nature. God made woman because "he saw it was not good for man to be alone;" (Gen. 2: 18); i.e., for social, not primarily for propagative, purposes. Eve was called Adam's "help-meet." In the whole of the specific account of the creation of woman, she is regarded as his companion, and her maternal office is not brought into view. Gen. 2: 18–25. Amativeness was necessarily the first social affection developed in the garden of Eden. The second commandment of the eternal law of love, "Thou shalt love thy neighbor as thyself," had amativeness for its first channel; for Eve was at first Adam's only neighbor. Propagation and the affections connected with it, did not commence their operation during the period of innocence. After the fall God said to the woman, "I will greatly multiply thy sorrow and thy conception;" from which it is to be inferred that in the original state, conception would have been comparatively infrequent.

The amative part of the sexual relation, separate from the propagative, is eminently favorable to life. It is not a source of life (as some would make it), but it is the first and best distributive of life. Adam and Eve, in their original state, derived their life from God. Gen. 2: 7. As God is a dual being, the Father and the Son, and man was made in his image, a dual life passed from God to man. Adam was the channel specially of the life of the Father, and Eve of the life of the Son. Amativeness was the natural agency of the distribution and mutual action of these two forms of life. In this primitive position of the sexes (which is their normal position in Christ), each reflects upon the other the love of God; each excites and develops the divine action in the other.

The propagative part of the sexual relation is in its nature the expensive department. 1. While amativeness keeps the capital stock of life circulating between two, propagation introduces a third partner. 2. The propagative act is a drain on the life of man, and when habitual, produces disease. 3. The infirmities and vital expenses of woman during the long period of pregnancy, waste her constitution. 4. The awful agonies of childbirth heavily tax the life of woman. 5. The cares of the nursing period bear heavily on woman. 6. The cares of both parents, through the period of the childhood of their offspring, are many and burdensome. 7. The labor of man is greatly increased by the necessity of providing for children. A portion of these expenses would undoubtedly have been curtailed, if human nature had remained in its original integrity, and will be, when it is restored. But it is still self-evident that the birth of children, viewed either as a vital or a mechanical operation, is in its nature expensive; and the fact that multiplied conception was imposed as a curse, indicates that it was so regarded by the Creator.

The amative and propagative functions are distinct from each other, and may be separated practically. They are confounded in the world, both in the theories of physiologists and in universal practice. The amative function is regarded merely as a bait to the propagative, and is merged in it. But if amativeness is, as we have seen, the first and noblest of the social affections, and if the propagative part of the sexual relation was originally secondary, and became paramount by the subversion of order in the fall, we are bound to raise the amative office of the sexual organs into a distinct and paramount function. . . .

114

A Gynecological Study
of the Oneida Community

Ely Van de Warker, M.D.
1841–1910

American Journal of Obstetrics, **17**:785–793

1884

The Oneida Community was in some of its relations a great physiological experiment. As such it has a commanding interest to medical men, and especially to the gynecologist. Here were tried elaborate experiments in sexualism, and an act that is done crudely, passionately, or by reason of blind instinct elsewhere, was reduced to an art. With this strange people, the sexual relation was made to realize, in a certain sense, an artistic fulfillment, to conserve their general social relations, and to contribute to their most refined pleasure.

That sexualism formed the warp in the texture of their religion in nothing concerns us as scientific men; nor is it at all singular, for in all ages religions have existed in which this function entered as a rite.

And here, for the first time in the history of the race, was a deliberate attempt made to apply the rules that govern scientific breeding to an entire community of men and women. A new science was discovered, or rather created, that of "stirpiculture." [1] Its laws were formulated upon those which govern the skilled breeder of short-horns, or the still more delicate art of the bird fancier who breeds to a feather; its practice consisted in combining known conditions of temperaments and mental aptitudes in the men and women who were "combined" in accordance with these traits, in order to produce given results in the children. The Community lived long enough to bring its fine art of coition to something like perfection; but, unfortunately for stirpiculture, it was too brief in existence to reach results. Here, under the rule of male continence and scientific propagation, was made the first attempt to apply the laws of Malthus to human increase. If, in the Community, the art of coition was sometimes a failure, it simply proved that all were not artists; and if scientific propagation resulted in unexpected and undesirable "combinations," it simply proved that human love and passion were eternal factors that mock alike at prison bars and scientific laws.

It is necessary to say something now about "male continence." The sexual practices of the Community were those usually understood under this term, plus male continence. Mr. J. H. Noyes, who invented, or discovered— it is difficult to decide which is the better word—this refinement of sexualism, has written of it without reserve. He says frankly that "the Oneida Community in an important sense owed its existence to the discovery of male continence, and has evidently been the Committee of Providence to test its value in actual life." [2] As this gynecological study of the Community is made only with reference to the sexual practices which prevailed there, it is important that we understand just what is meant by the term. It is better to let Mr. Noyes describe it:

"We begin," he says, "by analyzing the act of sexual intercourse. It has a beginning, a middle, and an end. Its beginning and most elementary form is the simple presence of the male organ in the female. Then usually follows a series of reciprocal motions. Finally this exercise brings on a nervous action or ejaculatory crisis which expels the seed. Now we insist that this whole process, up to the very moment of emission, is voluntary, entirely under the control of the moral faculty, and can be stopped at any point. In other words, the presence and the motions can be continued or stopped at will, and it is only the final crisis of emission that is automatic or uncontrollable. Suppose, then, that a man, in lawful intercourse with a woman, choosing, for good reasons, not to beget a child or to disable himself, should stop at the primary stage, and content himself with simple presence continued as long as agreeable? Would there be any harm? It cannot be injurious to refrain from voluntary excitement. Would it do any good? I appeal to the memory of every man who has had good sexual experience to say whether, on the whole, the sweetest and noblest period of intercourse with woman is not that first moment of simple presence and spiritual effusion before the muscular exercise begins? But we may go further. Suppose the man chooses for good reasons, as before, to enjoy not only the simple presence, but also the reciprocal motion, and yet to stop short of the final crisis. Again, I ask, would there be any harm, or would it do no good? I suppose physiologists might say, and I would acknowledge, that excitement by motion might be carried so far that a voluntary suppression of the commencing crisis would be injurious. But what if a man, knowing his own power and limits, should not even approach the crisis, and yet be able to enjoy the presence and the motion *ad libitum?* If you say that this is impossible, I answer that I know it is possible, nay, that it is easy." Further on, Mr. Noyes gives the following illustration of male continence

321

which is picturesque, to say the least, and deserves quotation: "The situation (male continence) may be compared to a stream in three conditions, viz., 1, a fall; 2, a course of rapids above the fall; and 3, still water above the rapids. The skillful boatman may choose whether he will remain in the still water, or venture more or less down the rapids, or run his boat over the fall. But there is a point on the verge of the fall where he has no control over his course; and just above that there is a point where he will have to struggle with the current in a way which will give his nerves a severe trial, even though he may escape the fall. If he is willing to learn, experience will teach him the wisdom of confining his excursions to the region of easy rowing, unless he has an object in view that is worth the cost of going over the fall." [3] The reader has now both the theory of male continence and some practical instruction as well. There are some arguments in favor of the practice which the author calls Bible arguments, and we will remain just as wise if we omit them. One argument is so forcible, and gives the reader such a clear idea of the author's style and method, that I cannot resist the temptation to insert it. "It is seriously believed by many that nature requires a periodical and somewhat frequent discharge of the seed, and that the retention of it is liable to be injurious. Even if this were true, it would be no argument against male continence, but rather an argument in favor of masturbation; for it is obvious that before marriage men have no lawful method of discharge but masturbation, and after marriage it is as foolish and cruel to expend one's seed on a wife merely for the sake of getting rid of it as it would be to fire a gun at one's best friend merely for the sake of unloading it." [4] As a scientific study of the subject, we have nothing to do with Mr. Noyes' arguments, and must concern ourselves only with results. For thirty years the Community existed under the rule of male continence. "Two hundred and fifty sober men and women have lived together in constant observation of its tendencies and effects." [5]

Having said so much about the peculiar sexual habits of these people, it is necessary to say something upon the other side. The illumination must be direct and oblique to give us the lights and shadows—the good and evil that exist in it. There are no persons so well qualified to give the subject this oblique illumination as the women themselves. A lady of whom I asked some questions upon this matter requested me to write out those points upon which I wished information and she would answer them. I did so, and she returned home with the questions. The following is the result, and is just as I received it, except that some parts are omitted which contained repetition.[6]

1. "The Community, or Mr. Noyes, who represented it, thought that girls usually had, as they termed it, 'amative desires,' when quite young, and that they would get bad habits unless these feelings were

satisfied in the way of sexual intercourse, and so of course they were looked after and introduced into the social system *certainly* at the age of puberty and in quite a number of cases before.

2. I am knowing particularly of at least four women of my own age who had sexual intercourse at ten years of age, and one case at nine years of age. One of these cases did not arrive at the age of puberty until five years after, another not until two years after, and the other two were unwell very soon after, before they were in the least developed. This was not confined to the girls; boys of thirteen and fourteen years old were put with old women who had passed the change of life, and instructed all about such things before they had begun to think of it at all.

3. The sexual relations were encouraged very much. The young women were always instructed that the more unselfish they were in giving the men all the satisfaction they could in that respect, the nearer they were to God. They were encouraged so much that those in office would advise and urge it to both men and women if they thought they did not care much for it.

4. In theory this relation was under a rule, and to a certain extent in practice. Still there was a *great* deal of rule-breaking in regard to it.

5. There was a great deal of complaint by the young women and girls, a few years before the breaking up of the system, of too frequent demands upon them by the other sex. Ten years before, they *felt* just the same, but partly in bondage to their religious beliefs about it, and partly from fear of criticism and the knowledge the relation with a loved one would be broken up, they were quiet, and submitted. I have known of girls no older than sixteen or seventeen years of age being called upon to have intercourse as often as seven times in a week and oftener, perhaps with a feeling of repugnance to all of those whom she was with during the time. She would do this without complaint simply to gain the confidence of those in charge of such things so that she would be allowed to associate with some one she loved.

6. Sexual relations did occur clandestinely, but were nearly always confessed and the parties criticised and separated; by this I mean the more common people. Those who held office did as they pleased, only they made some show of always having a 'third party.'

7. A lady might refuse at one time without incurring criticism, and at another time be severely criticised, and, too, it made a difference who the person was that she refused. If it were one of the leading members she was just as likely to be taken out of any responsible position she held at the time, and not be allowed to do anything until it was thought she had a good spirit and was humble.

8. Pregnancy was sometimes accidental. Ever since I remember anything about it there have been at least from six to eight pregnant women

during the year, and perhaps one or two of these by accident, and in some cases no possible way of telling who the father of the child was. This, of course, was in accidental pregnancy.

9. Abortion was never practised while the social theory was in existence to my certain knowledge. What was done after people were married I will not attempt to say.

10. Love affairs were frequent and caused a great amount of trouble, sometimes causing one or both of the parties to leave the Community (of their own accord). It was generally like this: If a young couple loved each other and were intimate, so much that they did not care for others, they were severely criticised and separated, one being sent to Wallingford, and all correspondence forbidden. It was frequently the case with those who had children that they were getting too "special" to each other, and to the child. The consequence was that the child would be put into other hands, the father and mother separated, and one or both to have children by others.

11. I cannot say that there was any *special rule* governing the ages of the parties to the sexual relations. It was very seldom that a young man under twenty years of age associated with a woman who had not passed the change of life, or who was not so near it that she would not be likely to become pregnant. Of course there were some exceptions to this. As to young women and girls—girls, after they were twenty or twenty-five years old, were allowed to associate with men who were not very much older than they were, but with the older ones, too. Girls under those ages did not, as a general thing, associate with men who were much under forty years, and then very seldom. They were considered better off, morally and physically, if they sought after men fifty and seventy years of age, and in fact were put under moral pressure about it."

If this investigation into the health of these people has any scientific value at all, it comes from the light thrown upon the physiology of the sexual relation. What they are physically must be understood in the light of what they do sexually.

It seems proper that I should say something about my connection with this investigation of the sexual health of the Oneida Community. In the autumn of 1877, Dr. Theo. R. Noyes, with whom I had been acquainted at that time nearly a year, spoke to me about the feeling of dissatisfaction, then growing in the institution, concerning the effect of their peculiar sexual practices upon the health. As the subject was one of great physiological interest, I expressed a willingness to undertake the necessary investigation. He returned to the Community, and in about a week after I received a letter inviting me to Oneida, to make a study of the subject upon the lady inmates. At that time, I have been since informed, there already existed the two factions, one in favor of, and one opposed to the sexual habits that were then practised, and which division finally resulted in breaking up the Community. Whether the examinations were allowed after consultations with one or both parties I do not know, but that visit was the only one I ever made for this purpose. About one-fourth of the lady inmates were examined when the investigation was stopped by, as I have learned, the interference of the venerable head of the Community himself, Mr. John Humphrey Noyes, whom, by the way, I have never seen.

I commenced my work directly after breakfast, and continued until day-light began to fail. Each lady was brought into a small steam heated room, the dormitory of Dr. Noyes, who was present and assisted at the examinations. From the order and manner in which they presented themselves, I am quite confident that there was no attempt to select cases by Dr. Noyes; but those, young or old, were brought in who were willing to submit to the examination. They were bright and intelligent women, and were modest and lady-like in their manner.

The lady, whose report I have included in this paper, says: "In theory this relation (the sexual) was under a rule, and to a certain extent in practice." It is but justice to the Community that I state what I know upon this subject, in contradiction to the extraordinary stories about drawing lots, and the ungoverned license which have been related by newspaper correspondents. I sought information upon this matter as a preliminary to my investigation. My informants were Dr. Noyes and Dr. Cragin, the then resident medical member. I have every confidence in the truth of these gentlemen. As the lady reporter says, these rules may have been violated, as all laws and rules are in sexual affairs, but such violations did not pass without criticism on the part of those in authority. In the Community, as in the world everywhere, the sexual approach came from the man. This was not made directly to the subject, but through a third party, and by whom the wishes of the gentleman were made known personally to the lady. She was at liberty to decline or accept, as she thought best. All reasonable grounds of objection were respected, but what those in authority did attempt to overcome were those objections which originated in too warm feeling toward any party other than the one making the advances. All those sexual solicitations made, as one may say, through the official channels were properly recorded so that the history of each individual was known to every one. Certain advances, such as known to the authorities, were discouraged if for any reason they were believed to be inexpedient. For instance, two individuals of very warm and impulsive temperament were not allowed relations for fear of the consequences; or when both were too young and inexperienced. There were probably other regulations governing the sexual affairs of the Community, but which were not confided to me. Many of them are incidentally referred to by the lady reporter. The sexes roomed separately.

In the table of antecedent conditions every item of interest in the history of each individual that seemed to bear upon the subject under investigation has been tabulated. It will be observed that about one half the women examined were originally from the rural population. This accords with what has been observed concerning heterodox religious movements.[7] The morbid indwelling and religious inquiry necessary to those who depart in erratic religions seem to be fostered by the quiet and isolation of country life. Another point of interest to be noted is the early age at which a large proportion menstruated for the first time, namely, one at ten years, eleven at twelve years, and twelve at thirteen years. It follows that about fifty-seven percent menstruated nearly two years in advance of the average age for girls in this latitude. Other causes may have operated to produce this, but the one most evident is the mental and physical stimulation due to the peculiar sexualism that surrounded them. Sixteen of these instances of early menstruation were exposed to communistic marriages from ten to thirteen years of age. By comparing the column of weights, opposite these cases of early sexual intercourse, we find that they correspond to the average. By following out the numbers which identify these cases . . . , we find an average of thirty-four inches in chest expansion, a bust measure that, if anything, is in excess of the average for the adult woman. In some examinations I have made upon this subject, I have concluded that the girl at thirteen years of age has about four inches to add to her height, and twenty pounds to her weight, before she reaches the average development of the adult woman. However repugnant it may be to our sense of manhood, we cannot resist the conclusion that sexual intercourse at this tender age does not arrest the steady tendency to a fine and robust womanhood. From what we all have observed of the stunted appearance of women who have borne children prematurely, it would seem that the extraordinary care with which impregnation was prevented in the Community was a redeeming feature of Mr. Noyes' system of sexual intercourse, in its humanitarian and physical relations. As a gynecologist, I think I may say further that in no other way than by male continence could impregnation be insured against.

---

[1] John Humphrey Noyes, "Essay on Scientific Propagation," Oneida, N. Y.

[2] Noyes, *Male Continence,* Oneida.

[3] *Ibid.,* p. 10.

[4] *Ibid.,* p. 21.

[5] *Ibid.,* p. 20.

[6] In order that no eye of suspicion should rest upon any lady at present resident of the Oneida Community Co., Limited, I will state that this paper has been in my possession several years, and was written by a lady who had left the O. C. never to return.

[7] See Hepworth Dixon's "Spiritual Wives."

115
Judge Lindsey and the Companionate Marriage

In the history of western morals World War I stands as a watershed. Woman suffrage, the birth-control movement, the smoking of cigarettes, divorce—all these, comparatively rare or uninfluential before the war, markedly increased in frequency or importance after it. The acceleration in the rate of change upset the older generation and made them doubt whether civilization could survive.

The decay of Christian marriage caused much "viewing with alarm." Most moralists called for a return to traditional standards; only a few thought of adapting the old institution of marriage to the new fact of life. One of these few was Judge Ben B. Lindsey (1869–1943), a Colorado jurist who enjoyed a well-deserved reputation for having humanized the juvenile courts. Concerned with the breakdown of marriage, he proposed a new kind of association in his book **The Companionate Marriage**, written in collaboration with Wainwright Evans (1927).

One of the most powerful, practical defenses for the indissolvability of marriage is the necessity of providing a stable home for children. Without birth control, children are so probable that it is quite natural to design the institution of marriage on the assumption that there will be children (perhaps allowing annulment, but only if the marriage is sterile). With birth control, another assumption is possible. It becomes reasonable to assume that some marriages, at least for a time, will be reliably fruitless. If so, what interest does society have in opposing divorce? The question is not easily answered.

Judge Lindsey (following in the path of some sociologists) proposed that there be two kinds of marriage, or two stages of one marriage (his writing is somewhat ambivalent). The first stage would be a "companionate marriage," in which the expressed intention of the couple would be companionship without children. So long as their contraceptive efforts were effective divorce would be easy. If they desired children they should go through a second, more solemn ceremony. Perhaps society should set stringent conditions for admission to the second state of marriage. In any case, a couple joined in a procreative marriage should find divorce difficult to obtain, because of society's interest in the psychological health of children.

Such was Judge Lindsey's dream, which evoked a great public outcry. A deeply grounded social institution strongly resists change; Judge Lindsay's attempts were apparently without effect. . . Or were they?

116

Companionship Tailored
to Occupation

Richard L. Meier
1920–

From *Modern Science and the Human Fertility Problem*
New York: Wiley

1959

. . . The most promising proposal so far uncovered leading in the direction of population stabilization seems to be the following:

Satisfying lifetime roles should be established which do not require parenthood, and which in effect, discourage it. The bases for discouraging child raising should be consistent with the mores of the period and other responsibilities inherent in the role of parenthood. A fraction of the adult population could be depended upon to be sterile and thus fraction must be modifiable by incentives normally available to democratic governments.

This is a surprising proposal whose implications should be further explored. Most members of the society are sufficiently blind, culturally speaking, so that they fail to see how the social roles of the business man, the banker, scientist, engineer, or unionized factory worker are circumscribed, changed, and even created by legislation and other government action. Politics, as the subject is argued in public, is mainly a patching up of difficulties and a correction of evils; it is not ordinarily thought of as a manipulation of social structure. The very concept frightens conservative-thinking persons who are, more often than not, the most numerous and most influential persons in the society. Therefore, the political feasibility of this approach to population equilibrium depends upon finding an ensemble of reforms which can be argued on their own merits and incidentally carry with them the added advantage of containing significant population growth-reduction characteristics. In addition, only a minority of persons must be directly affected by the actions of the government, and they in a way that offers greater opportunity for personal gratification than was otherwise expected. . . .

The idea of prescribing that certain social roles should be infertile is far from novel. It is understood by virtually every human society and practiced by a large share of them. At certain periods in history large numbers of persons voluntarily entered monasteries and convents. The quantities may have been great enough to have relieved regional population pressures. At other times it was expected that domestic servants and retainers would remain without issue; careers in armies and navies, in nursing, and in teaching carried with them equivalent expectations. However, the availability of efficient contraceptives means that institutions reinforcing continence would no longer be necessary to assure infertility. The moral pressures which establish behavioral norms can allow much greater latitude, thus making the infertile roles more attractive for a wider range of personalities. Recruitment should be much easier than it has been for monastic pursuits.

In the search for a logical basis for specifying what social roles might best contain a large sterile contingent, the arguments that seem most persuasive for the general population rest upon geographic mobility and inconvenient occupational time commitments. Marriage without a stable home and community life will certainly have greater, often insuperable, difficulties in providing satisfactory environments for growing children. If conditions are to be maintained at a decent level for this mobile element with children, many special social services need to be created. This is a cost that many of the sedentary elements in the population are unwilling to pay. At this junction a government interested in achieving long-run population equilibrium gains some leverage. It can set into motion a series of measures which reinforce existing attitudes so that it is considered less respectable for persons choosing the mobile occupations to have families. Under these circumstances the decision to bring up a family would normally be coincident with a decision to abandon an occupation deemed to be of a mobile character. In [the following table] are listed some typical occupations which appear to impose unbalanced home life.

The compilation of known occupations ordinarily requiring continual movement . . . reveals one major defect. According to Western tradition, at least, these occupational roles have been filled almost exclusively by males. If these are to be truly sterile roles, the monogamous society must find means for providing a roughly equal number of female sterile roles, such as nuns, maiden aunts, and prostitutes. Some societies officially condone such a system but they are condemned as cruel and inhuman by the neighboring cultures and so such standards are likely to be dropped as time passes. Most societies would probably prefer to transform many of the occupations in Table 3 into typical roles for women so that equal numbers of men and women in the same age brackets are mobile. Such positions should be of a type which require low absentee rates and graduated increases of responsi-

1. Agriculture	Skilled fruit pickers
	Harvest combine crews
	Dusters and sprayers
	Ranch hands
	Trappers and hunters
	Deep sea fisherman
2. Transportation	Marine workers and bargemen
	Air pilots and crew
	Railroad operating personnel (line)
	Truck drivers (over the road)
	Bus drivers (cross-country)
3. Construction	Specialists in heavy work
	Riggers
	Well drilling crews
	Surveyors and prospectors
	Supervisory engineers
4. Service	Traveling salesmen and buyers
	Technical maintenance and repair
	Newspapermen
	Firemen
	Medical staff (on call)
	Nurses (on call)
	Consultants
	Inspectors and auditors
	Diplomatic Service
	Members of armed forces
5. Arts	Dramatic work
	Musicians and entertainers
	Film photography crews
	Professional athletes

bility according to experience—in other words, they should become jobs with futures! At present in Western societies most jobs allocated to women tend to have limited responsibility and limited opportunities for advancement. Employers nowadays do this mainly in self-defense because almost all domestic crises require the attention of the mother, with either an interruption of her work or her absence from it. There is tacit agreement in most cultures that problems of children hold precedence over the mother's attention to her job. These arrangements may still be necessary for many of the working women in this future population, but it need not occur for the contingent which does not bear children and so maintains continuity for employment.

Societies can use various kinds of emoluments, mainly salary and prestige, to attract women into these career lines. However, in order to reinforce and stabilize the choice, a number of other measures will be necessary. These positions must be made rewarding ways of life. Otherwise there may be a large-scale disenchantment when these women are in their thirties, followed by a flight back to the hearth and cradle pattern of life where every effort is devoted to "catching up" to the normal family size for their social class. . . .

One basic principle for making ways of life associated with the mobile occupations more attractive would be to incorporate within them "the best of both worlds." If, for many of these there could be provided not only the warmth and intimacy of marriage but even a close association with the upbringing of children, if that were desired, then there seems to be a reasonable chance that the equilibrium relationship between homemaking and other careers might be achieved. A sufficient fraction of the women are then likely to choose a way of life which presumes infertility—if other pressures are not too strong. There are a great many traditions which need modification before such roles are likely to be completely satisfactory.

One of the possibilities is the development of a variety of alternatives for the sterile, or companionate, marriage. One or another such arrangement has often been discussed, and even practiced, particularly in Europe, but almost always in response to arguments other than those concerned with achieving population equilibrium. Such marriages, when they last, have the desired effect; but, as it now stands, the women tend to make other unions in which they usually bear children in numbers almost as large as otherwise. The government, when it becomes concerned, might do a few things to help. For instance, the institution of companionate marriage could be recognized in laws as a kind of limited liability partnership to which certain tax and inheritance advantages accrue. Such marriages should cost relatively little to form and only a moderate amount to dissolve. Thus, if divergent vocational duties require physical separation, the union may be broken up by mutual consent with little trouble beyond that of cutting emotional ties. Dissolution of one such union may be followed by the formation of another by each party. In states with easy divorce laws much of this pattern is already in operation, and it exists in some parts of the world irrespective of legal regulations. Currently, this shifting about of partners is complicated by inadequacies in contraceptive technique and, as a consequence, unwanted pregnancies. In the system proposed here there would be two or more forms of marriage, at least one of which anticipates no children.

117
The Road Not Taken

Robert Frost
1874–1963

From *Complete Poems of Robert Frost*
New York: Holt

1944

Two roads diverged in a yellow wood,
And sorry I could not travel both
And be one traveler, long I stood
And looked down one as far as I could
To where it bent in the undergrowth;

Then took the other, as just as fair,
And having perhaps the better claim,
Because it was grassy and wanted wear;
Though as for that the passing there
Had worn them really about the same,

And both that morning equally lay
In leaves no step had trodden black.
Oh, I kept the first for another day!
Yet knowing how way leads on to way,
I doubted if I should ever come back.

I shall be telling this with a sigh
Somewhere ages and ages hence:
Two roads diverged in a wood, and I—
I took the one less traveled by,
And that has made all the difference.

118
Raising Per Capita Income Through Fewer Births

Stephen Enke
1916–

General Electric—TEMPO
Publication 68TMP-9

1968

During the late 1960's it has become a common observation that many less developed countries (LDC's) are not doing well in the race between increasing output and increasing consumers. In fact, output of food in many countries has increased less rapidly than has the number of mouths to feed. A typical LDC may have an annual increase in overall gross national product (GNP) of 4.0 percent and an increase in population of 2.5 percent for an increase in income per head of only 1.5 percent a year.

In most LDC's the birth rate is not falling. Specific-age fertilities may be rising because of reduced pregnancy wastage and better living conditions. Crude annual birth rates at 45 per 1,000 of population approach a biological maximum. Death rates are often around 20 per 1,000 and are falling slowly. The result is a doubling of population every 30-odd years.

A doubling of population would ordinarily not be burdensome if the stock of capital and the natural resource endowment could double at the same rate. Unfortunately, LDC's cannot usually save enough each year to double their cumulative investments every 30 years. The national endowment of arable land, proven mineral reserves, and usable water cannot increase at all.

Thus an LDC must somehow try to promote a favorable balance among the rates of (1) capital accumulations through annual investment, (2) the population increase, and (3) new innovations that increase productivity. If capital can be increased only slowly, and there are no usable resources still unused, economic development requires that the rate of innovation outpace population increases.[1]

The effect of innovations is to increase the output obtainable with a unit of labor, capital, or "land" (i.e., natural resource). Increases in productivity attributable to innovations are considered to be about 2.5 percent a year in advanced countries. They are lower in most poor and backward countries—perhaps 1.5 percent typically.

High birth rates also result in high child dependency ratios. A country with a birth rate of over 40 per 1,000 may have 40 percent of its population under 15 years of age. These children can produce very little, but they do eat and need some clothing: From birth to 15 years children are consumers but not significant producers.

The conclusion for most LDC's, and especially those with limited natural resources, is that the rate of natural increase must be considerably slowed (emigration being seldom possible on sufficient scale). As death rates decline, birth rates must be reduced even more. A necessary and hopefully practical goal would be a reduction of at least 10 points in the crude birth rate in 10 years and of 15 points in 15 years.

Any campaign by government for voluntary family planning will require expenditures for clinics and staff, distribution or fitting of contraceptive and for campaign publicity. The direct cost per couple "accepting" birth control (depending upon the preferred mix of methods for both sexes) could vary from $1 to $3 per "acceptor" per year.

Crucial questions that arise concerning government financed birth control programs are: What is the return to governments on outlays for birth control: How can the return be estimated? How does this return compare with the return on resources invested in steel plants, irrigation canals, factories, and other traditional forms of capital?

Some of the earliest LDC economic planning work compared exactly this choice between resources used to slow population growth (through government-financed programs of voluntary birth control) or used to acclerate production (through capital investment). The results showed that the return on resources used to reduce births could be a hundred times greater than the return on resources used to increase output. These conclusions were sensitive to assumptions regarding (1) the cost of a birth control program, (2) the productivity of capital in industry and agriculture, and (3) the "otherwise" fertility of women subject to birth control.[2]

These incredible rates of return on birth control resources resulted from a simple equation representing a rather static case. It did not adequately take into account the full demographic consequences over many years of varying the numbers of women of different ages and fertility practicing birth control. Nor did it take into account either the loss in GNP from having a smaller labor force *or* the gain in GNP from having more invested saving as a result of more income per head with a birth control program in operation.

Many LDC governments are now urging or adopting voluntary birth control as an important element in their plans for economic development. Overdue is a more complete analysis of returns to birth control,—one that includes all the demographic dynamics and a more complete national production function. The model described below does this for an abstract LDC. The tabulated computer results indicate the value of directing a birth control program at different age groups. They also indicate that, with what could be a practicable rate of increasing birth control acceptance, the return on birth control expenditures is about 25 times after 10 years and 50 times after 20 years. . . .

Rate of Return for Program

Economic development planners need to know what rate of return can be expected from resources used to promote birth control—rather than to construct irrigation canals, factories, etc.

The cost of a birth control program depends on the number of participants, the methods of contraception they use (because these vary in cost and effectiveness), and the presumed fertility of participants were they not practicing birth control. The natural fertility of participants increases as the government program is assumed increasingly to include younger adult women. Here it is assumed that a typical cost is $2 a year for each participant, averaging across methods such as the pill and the coil. Thus if the annual fertility rate per 1,000 women between 35 and 39 years of age is 199, the cost of preventing births by them is almost $10. After 25 years, with increasing birth control, the current cost of preventing a birth is roughly $11.

A simple *undiscounted* rate of return can be derived by dividing the extra income for the existing population by the cost of increasing birth control. Here again the cumulative return is more meaningful than the ratio obtained for any given 5 years. At 25 years the cumulative return with these assumptions is about 65 times (see table).

These are extraordinarily high rates of return. Many alternative investments in productive facilities and equipment would do well if, after 25 years by a similar calculation, they earned not 65 times but 4 times. Hence economic development programs may do 15 or more times better when they invest in slowing population growth rather than in accelerating output growth. . . .

How Few Births Are Optimum?

Suspicion can attach to an argument that fewer births are desirable when the effects of zero births would obviously be most undesirable.[3] Needed is an anlysis that can indicate when higher birth rates are good for

335

Rate of return on cost of programs (increasing controls versus no controls).

At end of:	Each 5 Years			Cumulative		
	ΔY ($ million)	ΔC ($ million)	$R = \Delta Y/C$	ΔY ($ million)	ΔC ($ million)	$R = \Delta Y/C$
5 years	8.10	0.622	13	8.10	0.622	13
10 years	19.89	0.940	21	39.8	1.56	26
15 years	49.9	1.24	40	105.7	2.80	38
20 years	91.2	1.49	61	215.6	4.29	50
25 years	143.7	1.66	87	380.8	5.95	64
30 years	209.0	1.74	120	613.9	7.69	80

an economy. This additional understanding can be derived from the model and computations described previously.

For a representative 1,000 infants born in any year, their aggregate contribution to production can be estimated for each future year, given numbers of survivors, then current capital to labor ratios, state of art, etc. The aggregate consumption of survivors of this initial 1,000 can also be estimated year by year into the future. The present discounted value of these future production and consumption streams can be computed from the other results of the model used.

Discounting at 15 percent, for one typical infant born the first year, the expected present discounted value of its future consumption exceeds that of its production by $299. Such an infant then has a negative value to the economy of almost $300—twice the current income per head. (And such an estimate gives some indication of how much at most a government might be prepared to spend permanently to prevent such a birth.[4])

However, if crude birth rates were reduced, say, by half for several decades from present levels, there would be significantly more income per family member. More saving and investment would occur. Labor would become more scarce relative to capital for this reason and also because the labor force would be smaller than otherwise after 15 years or so of birth control. A higher marginal product of labor means, of course, that a representative infant, born 15 years or more after the start of a successful birth reduction program, will have earnings worth more in present discounted terms than an infant born the first year. After 25 to 50 years for a typical LDC with falling birth rates, the net discounted present value of an infant could well cease to be negative and become positive.

Infants must be considered as sources of enjoyment for their parents and others and not solely as a particular kind of investment asset. The worth of a first child to an LDC family of any means is surely worth twice the annual per capita income of the nation ordinarily. But for most parents there is some Nth infant that presumably is certainly not.

Because a model indicates that lower birth rates are now economically desirable, it does not follow that under all future circumstances these same birth rates will remain desirable. Obviously the fact that many children are a source of utility cannot be overlooked. The model described here can take all these considerations into account.

Implications for Policy

The policy implication of these computations is *not* that LDC governments should concentrate exclusively on birth control programs and cease to invest in productive capital, or in health and education.

One reason is that the fullest birth control participation that one

337

can imagine—one that included half of all fertile women (or their spouses) —would involve, at most, 15 percent of the total population. At $2 per year per participant, the resultant annual budget would be 30 cents per head of population. In most LDC's, expenditures for economic development vary around $10 per head each year. Thus a "full" birth control program, including one half of all fertile women in every age group, would take no more than about 3 percent of all expenditures for economic development in a typical backward country. Even a program that halved the crude birth rate, reducing it by 20 to 25 points per 1,000, would leave about 97 percent of most development budgets for health and education and for real capital investment.

In so far as birth control participation can be increased—perhaps by including financial inducements—every ethical means should be employed by governments to increase the knowledge and practice of family planning in less developed countries.

---

[1] See S. Enke, "Population and Development: A General Model," *Quarterly Journal of Economics,* February 1963.

[2] See for example, S. Enke, "The Gains to India from Population Control: Some Money Measures and Incentive Schemes," *Review of Economics and Statistics,* May 1960; "The Economics of Government Payments to Limit Population," *Economic Development and Cultural Change,* July 1960; and "Some Economic Aspects of Slowing Population Growth," *Economic Journal,* March 1966.

[3] This point is somewhat irrelevantly made by Professor Kingsley Davis against the family planning programs of some LDC's. One need not defer feeding a starving man because of uncertainty as to what future weight will indicate a need to diet! Until crude birth rates have fallen well below 45 per 100 a year, need one consider whether they should be 15, 20, or even 25? (See Kingsley Davis, "Population Policy: Will Current Programs Succeed?," *Science,* **158,** 10 November 1967.)

[4] It does not follow that, because lower birth rates might eventually advantage all families together (i.e., the national economy), the full force of this fact will bear on individual adults having children. There are externalities that promote anti-social behavior by parents and invite the application of conventional welfare economies. Specifically, governments could and should offer bonuses to fertile and exposed women who remain non-pregnant, to cohabiting men who volunteer for a vasectomy, etc. Many of these ideas have already been developed elsewhere. (See S. Enke, *Economics for Development,* Prentice-Hall, 1963, pp. 368–385.)

119
The Non-Baby Bonus

Raymond B. Cowles
1896–

From *The Meaning of Wilderness to Science,*
David Brower, editor
San Francisco: Sierra Club

1960

I would like to take a minute or two if I might, Mr. Chairman, for a curious thing that has been boiling around in my mind for some time—three years. This is the economics that might be applied in limiting populations. I have thought of all the possible things that might be done, and have come to the conclusion that none of them are feasible unless we can appeal to the crass financial motive—the motive which does tend to limit births when the economic conditions get hard. We give bonuses for having children. I don't see why we shouldn't give bonuses for not having them. One seems as logical as the other in terms of our dilemma. Could this be economically feasible? I inquired as to cost of education through high school: roughly $5,000 in the State of California. Then every child that isn't born would save us $5,000. Some sort of award for not having children could be given just as logically as exemptions; allow a person to take his choice. I assure you that although it seems funny to us, if you give it thought you will find, in view of the economics of the situation (the new schools, new streets, new resources) that a bonus for not having children is fully as logical as exemptions for having them. It would be financially a self-liquidating proposition. I suggest that you look into the economics of it, and I think you will be surprised at the conclusions you will reach. I have worked at this from several different angles, and it seems to me economically feasible and desirable. Just to make one suggestion, if a bonus of say $600 (equal to the exemption) were given for not having children (this would have to be given only to the women) we would save the cost of education for the child not born, and we could thus repay the bonus. Best of all, it would act on a eugenic basis. The reward would be most effective in the poorest and least educated and least forward-thinking part of our population: those that are usually dependent, those that require social security and unemployment compensation (the least employable usually have the biggest families) would benefit the most. We could dispense with some of these awards, and let the burden of financing the family fall on the bonus for not having a child.

120

Marketable Licenses for Babies

Kenneth E. Boulding
1910–

From *The Meaning of the 20th Century*
New York: Harper & Row

1964

I have only one positive suggestion to make, a proposal which now seems so farfetched that I find it creates only amusement when I propose it. I think in all seriousness, however, that a system of marketable licenses to have children is the only one which will combine the minimum of social control necessary to the solution to this problem with a maximum of individual liberty and ethical choice. Each girl on approaching maturity would be presented with a certificate which will entitle its owner to have, say, 2.2 children, or whatever number would ensure a reproductive rate of one. The unit of these certificates might be the "deci-child," and accumulation of ten of these units by purchase, inheritance, or gift would permit a woman in maturity to have one legal child. We would then set up a market in these units in which the rich and the philoprogenitive would purchase them from the poor, the nuns, the maiden aunts, and so on. The men perhaps could be left out of these arrangements, as it is only the fertility of women which is strictly relevant to population control. However, it may be found socially desirable to have them in the plan, in which case all children both male and female would receive, say, eleven or twelve deci-child certificates at birth or at maturity, and a woman could then accumulate these through marriage.

This plan would have the additional advantage of developing a long-run tendency toward equality in income, for the rich would have many children and become poor and the poor would have few children and become rich. The price of the certificate would of course reflect the general desire in a society to have children. Where the desire is very high the price would be bid up; where it was low the price would also be low. Perhaps the ideal situation would be found when the price was naturally zero, in which case those who wanted children would have them without extra cost. If the price were very high the system would probably have to be supplemented by some sort of grants to enable the deserving but impecunious to have children, while cutting off the desires of the less deserving through taxation. The sheer unfamiliarity of a scheme of this kind makes it seem absurd at the moment. The fact that it seems absurd, however, is merely a reflection of the total unwillingness of mankind to face up to what is perhaps its most serious long-run problem.

121

Population Policy: Will Current Programs Succeed?

Kingsley Davis
1908–

Science, **158**:730–739

1967

Throughout history the growth of population has been identified with prosperity and strength. If today an increasing number of nations are seeking to curb rapid population growth by reducing their birth rates, they must be driven to do so by an urgent crisis. My purpose here is not to discuss the crisis itself but rather to assess the present and prospective measures used to meet it. Most observers are surprised by the swiftness with which concern over the population problem has turned from intellectual analysis and debate to policy and action. Such action is a welcome relief from the long opposition, or timidity, which seemed to block forever any governmental attempt to restrain population growth, but relief that "at last something is being done" is no guarantee that what is being done is adequate. On the face of it, one could hardly expect such a fundamental reorientation to be quickly and successfully implemented. I therefore propose to review the nature and (as I see them) limitations of the present policies and to suggest lines of possible improvement.

The Nature of Current Policies

With more than 30 nations now trying or planning to reduce population growth and with numerous private and international organizations helping, the degree of unanimity as to the kind of measures needed is impressive. The consensus can be summed up in the phrase "family planning." President Johnson declared in 1965 that the United States will "assist family planning programs in nations which request such help." The Prime Minister of India said a year later, "We must press forward with family planning. This is a programme of the highest importance." The Republic of Singapore created in 1966 the Singapore Family Planning and Population Board "to initiate and undertake population control programmes." [1]

As is well known, "family planning" is a euphemism for contraception. The family-planning approach to population limitation, therefore, concentrates on providing new and efficient contraceptives on a national basis through mass programs under public health auspices. The nature of these programs is shown by the following enthusiastic report from the Population Council: [2]

> No single year has seen so many forward steps in population control as 1965. Effective national programs have at last emerged, international organizations have decided to become engaged, a new contraceptive has proved its value in mass application, . . . and surveys have confirmed a popular desire for family limitation . . .
>
> An accounting of notable events must begin with Korea and Taiwan . . . Taiwan's program is not yet two years old, and already it has inserted one IUD [intrauterine device] for every 4–6 target women (those who are not pregnant, lactating, already sterile, already using contraceptives effectively, or desirous of more children). Korea has done almost as well . . . has put 2,200 full-time workers into the field, . . . has reached operational levels for a network of IUD quotas,

342

supply lines, local manufacture of contraceptives, training of hundreds of M.D.'s and nurses, and mass propaganda . . .

Here one can see the implication that "population control" is being achieved through the dissemination of new contraceptives, and the fact that the "target women" exclude those who want more children. One can also note the technological emphasis and the medical orientation.

What is wrong with such programs? The answer is, "Nothing at all, if they work." Whether or not they work depends on what they are expected to do as well as on how they try to do it. Let us discuss the goal first, then the means.

Goals

Curiously, it is hard to find in the population-policy movement any explicit discussion of long-range goals. By implication the policies seem to promise a great deal. This is shown by the use of expressions like *population control* and *population planning* (as in the passages quoted above). It is also shown by the characteristic style of reasoning. Expositions of current policy usually start off by lamenting the speed and the consequences of runaway population growth. This growth, it is then stated, must be curbed—by pursuing a vigorous family-planning program. That family planning can solve the problem of population growth seems to be taken as self-evident.

For instance, the much-heralded statement by 12 heads of state, issued by Secretary-General U Thant on 10 December 1966 (a statement initiated by John D. Rockefeller III, Chairman of the Board of the Population Council), devotes half its space to discussing the harmfulness of population growth and the other half to recommending family planning.[3] A more succinct example of the typical reasoning is given in the Provisional Scheme for a Nationwide Family Planning Programme in Ceylon:[4]

> The population of Ceylon is fast increasing. . . . [The] figures reveal that a serious situation will be created within a few years. In order to cope with it a Family Planning programme on a nationwide scale should be launched by the Government.

The promised goal—to limit population growth so as to solve population problems—is a large order. One would expect it to be carefully analyzed, but it is left imprecise and taken for granted, as is the way in which family planning will achieve it.

When the terms *population control* and *population planning* are used, as they frequently are, as synonyms for current family-planning pro-

343

grams, they are misleading. Technically, they would mean deliberate influence over all attributes of a population, including its age-sex structure, geographical distribution, racial composition, genetic quality, and total size. No government attempts such full control. By tacit understanding, current population policies are concerned with only the *growth* and *size* of populations. These attributes, however, result from the death rate and migration as well as from the birth rate; their control would require deliberate influence over the factors giving rise to all three determinants. Actually, current policies labeled population control do not deal with mortality and migration, but deal only with the birth input. This is why another term, *fertility control,* is frequently used to describe current policies. But, as I show below, family planning (and hence current policy) does not undertake to influence most of the determinants of human reproduction. Thus the programs should not be referred to as population control or planning, because they do not attempt to influence the factors responsible for the attributes of human populations, taken generally; nor should they be called fertility control, because they do not try to affect most of the determinants of reproductive performance.

The ambiguity does not stop here, however. When one speaks of controlling population size, any inquiring person naturally asks, What is "control"? Who is to control whom? Precisely what population size, or what rate of population growth, is to be achieved? Do the policies aim to produce a growth rate that is nil, one that is very slight, or one that is like that of the industrial nations? Unless such questions are dealt with and clarified, it is impossible to evaluate current population policies.

The actual programs seem to be aiming simply to achieve a reduction in the birth rate. Success is therefore interpreted as the accomplishment of such a reduction, on the assumption that the reduction will lessen population growth. In those rare cases where a specific demographic aim is stated, the goal is said to be a short-run decline within a given period. The Pakistan plan adopted in 1966 [5] aims to reduce the birth rate from 50 to 40 per thousand by 1970; the Indian plan[6] aims to reduce the rate from 40 to 25 "as soon as possible"; and the Korean aim[7] is to cut population growth from 2.9 to 1.2 percent by 1980. A significant feature of such stated aims is the rapid population growth they would permit. Under conditions of modern mortality, a crude birth rate of 25 to 30 per thousand will represent such a multiplication of people as to make use of the term *population control* ironic. A rate of increase of 1.2 percent per year would allow South Korea's already dense population to double in less than 60 years.

One can of course defend the programs by saying that the present goals and measures are merely interim ones. A start must be made somewhere. But we do not find this answer in the population-policy literature. Such a defense, if convincing, would require a presentation of the *next* steps, and these are not considered. One suspects that the entire question of goals is instinctively left vague because thorough limitation of population growth would run counter to national and group aspirations. A consideration of hypothetical goals throws further light on the matter.

INDUSTRIALIZED NATIONS AS THE MODEL

Since current policies are confined to family planning, their maximum demographic effect would be to give the underdeveloped countries the same level of reproductive performance that the industrial nations now have. The latter, long oriented toward family planning, provide a good yardstick for determining what the availability of contraceptives can do to population growth. Indeed, they provide more than a yardstick; they are actually the model which inspired the present population policies.

What does this goal mean in practice? Among the advanced nations there is considerable diversity in the level of fertility.[8] At one extreme are countries such as New Zealand, with an average gross reproduction rate (GRR) of 1.91 during the period 1960–64; at the other extreme are countries such as Hungary, with a rate of 0.91 during the same period. To a considerable extent, however, such divergencies are matters of timing. The birth rates of most industrial nations have shown, since about 1940, a wave-like movement, with no secular trend. The average level of reproduction during this long period has been high enough to give these countries, with their low mortality, an extremely rapid population growth. If this level is maintained, their population will double in just over 50 years —a rate higher than that of world population growth at any time prior to 1950, at which time the growth in numbers of human beings was already considered fantastic. The advanced nations are suffering acutely from the effects of rapid population growth in combination with the production of ever more goods per person.[9] A rising share of their supposedly high per capita income, which itself draws increasingly upon the resources of the underdeveloped countries (who fall farther behind in relative economic position), is spent simply to meet the costs, and alleviate the nuisances, of the unrelenting production of more and more goods by more people. Such facts indicate that the industrial nations provide neither a suitable demographic model for the nonindustrial peoples to follow nor the leadership to plan and organize effective population-control policies for them.

ZERO POPULATION GROWTH AS A GOAL

Most discussions of the population crisis lead logically to zero population growth as the ultimate goal, because *any* growth rate, if continued, will eventually use up the earth. Yet hardly ever do arguments for population policy consider such a goal, and current policies do not dream of it. Why not? The answer is evidently that zero population growth is unacceptable to most nations and to most religious and ethnic communities. To argue for this goal would be to alienate possible support for action programs.

GOAL PECULIARITIES INHERENT IN FAMILY PLANNING

Turning to the actual measures taken, we see that the very use of family planning as the means for implementing population policy poses serious but unacknowledged limits on the intended reduction in fertility. The family-planning movement, clearly devoted to the improvement and dissemination of contraceptive devices, states again and again that its purpose is that of enabling couples to have the number of children they want. "The opportunity to decide the number and spacing of children is a basic human right," say the 12 heads of state in the United Nations declaration. The 1965 Turkish Law Concerning Population Planning declares:[10]

> *Article 1.* Population Planning means that individuals can have as many children as they wish, whenever they want to. This can be ensured through preventive measures taken against pregnancy. . . .

Logically, it does not make sense to use *family* planning to provide *national* population control or planning. The "planning" in family planning is that of each separate couple. The only control they exercise is control over the size of *their* family. Obviously, couples do not plan the size of the nation's population, any more than they plan the growth of the national income or the form of the highway network. There is no reason to expect that the millions of decisions about family size made by couples in their own interest will automatically control population for the benefit of society. On the contrary, there are good reasons to think they will not do so. At most, family planning can reduce reproduction to the extent that unwanted births exceed wanted births. In industrial countries the balance is often negative—that is, people have fewer children as a rule than they would like to have. In underdeveloped countries the reverse is normally true, but the elimination of unwanted births would still leave an extremely high rate of multiplication.

Actually, the family-planning movement does not pursue even the limited goals it professes. It does not fully empower couples to have only the number of offspring they want because it either condemns or disregards certain tabooed but nevertheless effective means to this goal. One of its tenets is that "there shall be freedom of choice of method so that individuals can choose in accordance with the dictates of their consciences," [11] but in practice this amounts to limiting the individual's choice, because the "conscience" dictating the method is usually not his but that of religious and governmental officials. Moreover, not every individual may choose: even the so-called recommended methods are ordinarily not offered to single women, or not all offered to women professing a given religious faith.

Thus, despite its emphasis on technology, current policy does not utilize all available means of contraception, much less all birth-control measures. The Indian government wasted valuable years in the early stages of its population-control program by experimenting exclusively with the "rhythm" method, long after this technique had been demonstrated to be one of the least effective. A greater limitation on means is the exclusive emphasis on contraception itself. Induced abortion, for example, is one of the surest means of controlling reproduction, and one that has been proved capable of reducing birth rates rapidly. It seems peculiarly suited to the threshold stage of a population-control program—the stage when new conditions of life first make large families disadvantageous. It was the principal factor in the halving of the Japanese birth rate, a major factor in the declines in birth rate of East-European satellite countries after legalization of abortions in the early 1950's, and an important factor in the reduction of fertility in industrializing nations from 1870 to the 1930's.[12] Today, according to *Studies in Family Planning*,[13] "abortion is probably the foremost method of birth control throughout Latin America." Yet this method is rejected in nearly all national and international population-control programs. American foreign aid is used to help *stop* abortion.[14] The United Nations excludes abortion from family planning, and in fact justifies the latter by presenting it as a means of combating abortion.[15] Studies of abortion are being made in Latin America under the presumed auspices of population-control groups, not with the intention of legalizing it and thus making it safe, cheap, available, and hence more effective for population control, but with the avowed purpose of reducing it.[16]

Although few would prefer abortion to efficient contraception (other things being equal), the fact is that both permit a woman to control the size of her family. The main drawbacks to abortion arise from its illegality. When performed, as a legal procedure, by a skilled physician, it is safer than childbirth. It does not compete with contraception but serves as a backstop when the latter fails or when contraceptive devices or information are not available. As contraception becomes customary, the incidence of abortion recedes even without its being banned. If, therefore, abortions enable women to have only the number of children they want, and if family planners do not advocate—in fact decry—legalization of abortion, they are to that extent denying the central tenet of their own movement. The irony of antiabortionism in family-planning circles is seen particularly in hair-splitting arguments over whether or not some contraceptive agent (for example, the IUD) is in reality an abortifacient. A Mexican leader in family planning writes:[17]

> One of the chief objectives of our program in Mexico is to prevent abortions. If we could be sure that the mode of action [of the IUD] was not interference with nidation, we could easily use the method in Mexico.

The questions of sterilization and unnatural forms of sexual intercourse usually meet with similar silent treatment or disapproval, although nobody doubts the effectiveness of these measures in avoiding conception. Sterilization has proved popular in Puerto Rico and has had some vogue in India (where the new health minister hopes to make it compulsory for those with a certain number of children), but in both these areas it has been for the most part ignored or condemned by the family-planning movement.

On the side of goals, then we see that a family-planning orientation limits the aims of current population policy. Despite reference to "population control" and "fertility control," which presumably mean determination of demographic results by and for the nation as a whole, the movement gives control only to couples, and does this only if they use "respectable" contraceptives.

The Neglect of Motivation

By sanctifying the doctrine that each woman should have the number of children she wants, and by assuming that if she has only that number this will automatically curb population growth to the necessary degree, the leaders of current policies escape the necessity of asking why women desire so many children and how this desire can be influenced.[18, 19] Instead, they claim that satisfactory motivation is shown by the popular desire (shown by opinion surveys in all countries) to have the means of family limitation, and that therefore the problem is one of inventing and distributing the best possible contraceptive devices. Overlooked is the fact that a desire for availability of contraceptives is compatible with *high* fertility.

Given the best of means, there remain the questions of how many children couples want and of whether this is the requisite number from the standpoint of population size. That it is not is indicated by continued rapid population growth in industrial countries, and by the very surveys showing that people want contraception—for these show, too, that people also want numerous children.

The family planners do not ignore motivation. They are forever talking about "attitudes" and "needs." But they pose the issue in terms of the "acceptance" of birth control devices. At the most naive level, they assume that lack of acceptance is a function of the contraceptive device itself. This reduces the motive problem to a technological question. The task of population control then becomes simply the invention of a device that *will* be acceptable.[20] The plastic IUD is acclaimed because, once in place, it does not depend on repeated *acceptance* by the woman, and thus it "solves" the problem of motivation.[21]

But suppose a woman does not want to use *any* contraceptive until after she has had four children. This is the type of question that is seldom raised in the family-planning literature. In that literature, wanting a specific number of children is taken as complete motivation, for it implies a wish to control the size of one's family. The problem woman, from the standpoint of family planners, is the one who wants "as many as come," or "as many as God sends." Her attitude is construed as due to ignorance and "cultural values," and the policy deemed necessary to change it is "education." No compulsion can be used, because the movement is committed to free choice, but movie strips, posters, comic books, public lectures, interviews, and discussions are in order. These supply information and supposedly change values by discounting superstitions and showing that unrestrained procreation is harmful to both mother and children. The effort is considered successful when the woman decides she wants only a certain number of children and uses an effective contraceptive.

In viewing negative attitudes toward birth control as due to ignorance, apathy, and outworn tradition, and "mass-communication" as the solution to the motivation problem,[22] family planners tend to ignore the power and complexity of social life. If it were admitted that the creation and care of new human beings is socially motivated, like other forms of behavior, by being a part of the system of rewards and punishments that is built into human relationships, and thus is bound up with the individual's economic and personal interests, it would be apparent that the social structure and economy must be changed before a deliberate reduction in the birth rate can be achieved. As it is, reliance on family planning allows people to feel that "something is being done about the population problem" without the need for painful social changes.

Designation of population control as a medical or public health task leads to a similar evasion. This categorization assures popular support because it puts population policy in the hands of respected medical personnel, but, by the same token, it gives responsibility for leadership to people who think in terms of clinics and patients, of pills and IUD's, and who bring to the handling of economic and social phenomena a self-confident naiveté. The study of social organization is a technical field; an action program based on intuition is no more apt to succeed in the control of human beings than it is in the area of bacterial or viral control. Moreover, to alter a social system, by deliberate policy, so as to regulate births in accord with the demands of the collective welfare would require political power, and this is not likely to inhere in public health officials, nurses, midwives, and social workers. To entrust population policy to them is "to take action," but not dangerous "effective action."

Similarly, the Janus-faced position on birth-control technology represents an escape from the necessity, and onus, of grappling with the social and economic determinants of reproductive behavior. On the one side, the rejection or avoidance of religiously tabooed but otherwise effective means of birth prevention enables the family-planning movement to avoid official condemnation. On the other side, an intense preoccupation with contraceptive technology (apart from the tabooed means) also helps the family planners to avoid censure. By implying that the only need is the invention and distribution of effective contraceptive devices, they allay fears, on the part of religious and governmental officials, that fundamental changes in social organization are contemplated. Changes basic enough to affect motivation for having children would be changes in the structure of the family, in the position of women, and in the sexual mores. Far from proposing such radicalism, spokesmen for family planning frequently state their purpose as "protection" of the family—that is, closer observance of family norms. In addition, by concentrating on *new* and *scientific* contraceptives, the movement escapes taboos attached to old ones (the Pope will hardly authorize the condom, but may sanction the pill) and allows family planning to be regarded as a branch of medicine: overpopulation becomes a disease, to be treated by a pill or a coil.

We thus see that the inadequacy of current population policies with respect to motivation is inherent in their overwhelmingly family-planning character. Since family planning is by definition private planning, it eschews any societal control over motivation. It merely furnishes the means, and, among possible means, only the most respectable. Its leaders, in avoiding social complexities and seeking official favor, are obviously activated not solely by expediency but also by their own sentiments as members of society and by their background as persons attracted to the family-planning movement. Unacquainted for the most part with technical economics, sociology, and demography, they tend honestly and instinctively to believe that something they vaguely call population control can be achieved by making better contraceptives available.

The Evidence of Ineffectiveness

If this characterization is accurate, we can conclude that current programs will not enable a government to control population size. In countries where couples have numerous offspring that they do not want, such programs may possibly accelerate a birth-rate decline that would occur anyway, but the conditions that cause births to be wanted or unwanted are beyond the control of family planning, hence beyond the control of any nation which relies on family planning alone as its population policy.

This conclusion is confirmed by demographic facts. As I have noted above, the widespread use of family planning in industrial countries has not given their governments control over the birth rate. In backward countries today, taken as a whole, birth rates are rising, not falling; in those with population policies, there is no indication that the government is controlling the rate of reproduction. The main "successes" cited in the well-publicized policy literature are cases where a large number of contraceptives have been distributed or where the program has been accompanied by some decline in the birth rate. Popular enthusiasm for family planning is found mainly in the cities, or in advanced countries such as Japan and Taiwan, where the people would adopt contraception in any case, program or no program. It is difficult to prove that present population policies have even speeded up a lowering of the birth rate (the least that could have been expected), much less that they have provided national "fertility control."

Let us next briefly review the facts concerning the level and trend of population in underdeveloped nations generally, in order to understand the magnitude of the task of genuine control.

Rising Birth Rates in Underdeveloped Countries

In ten Latin-American countries, between 1940 and 1959,[23] the average birth rates (age-standardized), as estimated by our research office at the University of California, rose as follows: 1940–44, 43.4 annual births per 1000 population; 1945–49, 44.6; 1950–54, 46.4; 1955–59, 47.7.

In another study made in our office, in which estimating methods derived from the theory of quasi-stable populations were used, the recent trend was found to be upward in 27 underdeveloped countries, downward in six, and unchanged in one.[24] Some of the rises have been substantial, and most have occurred where the birth rate was already extremely high. For instance, the gross reproduction rate rose in Jamaica from 1.8 per thousand in 1947 to 2.7 in 1960; among the natives of Fiji, from 2.0 in 1951 to 2.4 in 1964; and in Albania, from 3.0 in the period 1950–54 to 3.4 in 1960.

The general rise in fertility in backward regions is evidently not due to failure of population-control efforts, because most of the countries either have no such effort or have programs too new to show much effect. Instead, the rise is due, ironically, to the very circumstance that brought on the population crisis in the first place—to improved health and lowered mortality. Better health increases the probability that a woman will conceive and retain the fetus to term; lowered mortality raises the proportion of babies who survive to the age of reproduction and reduces the probability of widowhood during that age.[25] The significance of the general rise in fertility, in the context of this discussion, is that it is giving would-be population planners a harder task than many of them realize. Some of the upward pressure on birth rates is independent of what couples do about family planning, for it arises from the fact that, with lowered mortality, there are simply more couples.

Underdeveloped Countries with Population Policies

In discussions of population policy there is often confusion as to which cases are relevant. Japan, for instance, has been widely praised for the effectiveness of its measures, but it is a very advanced industrial nation and, besides, its government policy had little or nothing to do with the decline in the birth rate, except unintentionally. It therefore offers no test of population policy under peasant-agrarian conditions. Another case of questionable relevance is that of Taiwan, because Taiwan is sufficiently developed to be placed in the urban-industrial class of nations. However, since Taiwan is offered as the main showpiece by the sponsors of current policies in underdeveloped areas, and since the data are excellent, it merits examination.

Taiwan is acclaimed as a showpiece because it has responded favorably to a highly organized program for distributing up-to-date contraceptives and has also had a rapidly dropping birth rate. Some observers have carelessly attributed the decline in the birth rate—from 50.0 in 1951 to 32.7 in 1965—to the family-planning campaign,[26] but the campaign began only in 1963 and could have affected only the end of the trend. Rather, the decline represents a response to modernization similar to that made by all countries that have become industrialized.[27] By 1950 over half of Taiwan's population was urban, and by 1964 nearly two-thirds were urban, with 29 percent of the population living in cities of 100,000 or more. The pace of economic development has been extremely rapid. Between 1951 and 1963, per capita income increased by 4.05 percent per year. Yet

Table 1. Decline in Taiwan's Fertility Rate, 1951 Through 1966.

Year	Registered births per 1000 women aged 15–49	Change in rate (percent) *
1951	211	
1952	198	−5.6
1953	194	−2.2
1954	193	−0.5
1955	197	+2.1
1956	196	−0.4
1957	182	−7.1
1958	185	+1.3
1959	184	−0.1
1960	180	−2.5
1961	177	−1.5
1962	174	−1.5
1963	170	−2.6
1964	162	−4.9
1965	152	−6.0
1966	149	−2.1

* The percentages were calculated on unrounded figures. Source of data through 1965, *Taiwan* Demographic Fact Book (1964, 1965); for 1966, *Monthly Bulletin of Population Registration Statistics of Taiwan* (1966, 1967).

the island is closely packed, having 870 persons per square mile (a population density higher than that of Belgium). The combination of fast economic growth and rapid population increase in limited space has put parents of large families at a relative disadvantage and has created a brisk demand for abortions and contraceptives. Thus the favorable response to the current campaign to encourage use of the IUD is not a good example of what birth-control technology can do for a genuinely backward country. In fact, when the program was started, one reason for expecting receptivity was that the island was already on its way to modernization and family planning.[28]

At most, the recent family-planning campaign—which reached significant proportions only in 1964, when some 46,000 IUD's were inserted (in 1965 the number was 99,253, and in 1966, 111,242)[29, 30]—could have caused the increase observable after 1963 in the rate of decline. Between

1951 and 1963 the average drop in the birth rate per 1000 women (see Table 1) was 1.73 percent per year; in the period 1964–66 it was 4.35 percent. But one hesitates to assign all of the acceleration in decline since 1963 to the family-planning campaign. The rapid economic development has been precisely of a type likely to accelerate a drop in reproduction. The rise in manufacturing has been much greater than the rise in either agriculture or construction. The agricultural labor force has thus been squeezed, and migration to the cities has skyrocketed.[31] Since housing has not kept pace, urban families have had to restrict reproduction in order to take advantage of career opportunities and avoid domestic inconvenience. Such conditions have historically tended to accelerate a decline in birth rate. The most rapid decline came late in the United States (1921–33) and in Japan (1947–55). A plot of the Japanese and Taiwanese birth rates shows marked similarity of the two curves, despite a difference in level. All told, one should not attribute all of the post-1963 acceleration in the decline of Taiwan's birth rate to the family-planning campaign.

The main evidence that *some* of this acceleration is due to the campaign comes from the fact that Taichung, the city in which the family-planning effort was first concentrated, showed subsequently a much faster drop in fertility than other cities.[32] But the campaign has not reached throughout the island. By the end of 1966, only 260,745 women had been fitted with an IUD under auspices of the campaign, whereas the women of reproductive age on the island numbered 2.86 million. Most of the reduction in fertility has therefore been a matter of individual initiative. To some extent the campaign may be simply substituting sponsored (and cheaper) services for those that would otherwise come through private and commerical channels. An island-wide survey in 1964 showed that over 150,000 women were already using the traditional Ota ring (a metallic intrauterine device popular in Japan); almost as many had been sterilized; about 40,000 were using foam tablets; some 50,000 admitted to having had at least one abortion; and many were using other methods of birth control.[33]

The important question, however, is not whether the present campaign is somewhat hastening the downward trend in the birth rate but whether, even if it is, it will provide population control for the nation. Actually, the campaign is not designed to provide such control and shows no sign of doing so. It takes for granted existing reproductive goals. Its aim is "to integrate, through education and information, the idea of family limitation *within the existing attitudes, values, and goals* of the people"[34] (italics mine). Its target is *married* women who do not want any more children; it ignores girls not yet married, and women married and wanting more children.

With such an approach, what is the maximum impact possible? It is the difference between the number of children women have been having and the number they want to have. A study in 1957 found a median figure of 3.75 for the number of children wanted by women aged 15 to 29 in Taipei, Taiwan's largest city; the corresponding figure for women from a satellite town was 3.93; for women from a fishing village, 4.90; and for women from a farming village, 5.03. Over 60 percent of the women in Taipei and over 90 percent of those in the farming village wanted 4 or more children.[35] In a sample of wives aged 25 to 29 in Taichung, a city of over 300,000, Freedman and his co-workers found the average number of children wanted was 4; only 9 percent wanted less than 3, 20 percent wanted 5 or more.[36] If, therefore, Taiwanese women used contraceptives that were 100-percent effective and had the number of children they desire, they would have about 4.5 each. The goal of the family-planning effort would be achieved. In the past the Taiwanese woman who married and lived through the reproductive period had, on the average, approximately 6.5 children; thus a figure of 4.5 would represent a substantial decline in fertility. Since mortality would continue to decline, the population growth rate would decline somewhat less than individual reproduction would. With 4.5 births per woman and a life expectancy of 70 years, the rate of natural increase would be close to 3 percent per year.[37]

In the future, Taiwanese views concerning reproduction will doubtless change, in response to social change and economic modernization. But how far will they change? A good indication is the number of children desired by couples in an already modernized country long oriented toward family planning. In the United States in 1966, an average of 3.4 children was considered ideal by white women aged 21 or over.[38] This average number of births would give Taiwan, with only a slight decrease in mortality, a long-run rate of natural increase of 1.7 percent per year and a doubling of population in 41 years.

Detailed data confirm the interpretation that Taiwanese women are in the process of shifting from a "peasant-agrarian" to an "industrial" level of reproduction. They are, in typical fashion, cutting off higher-order births at age 30 and beyond.[39] Among young wives, fertility has risen, not fallen. In sum, the widely acclaimed family-planning program in Taiwan may, at most, have somewhat speeded the later phase of fertility decline which would have occurred anyway because of modernization.

Moving down the scale of modernization, to countries most in need of population control, one finds the family-planning approach even more inadequate. In South Korea, second only to Taiwan in the frequency with which it is cited as a model of current policy, a recent birth-rate decline of unknown extent is assumed by leaders to be due overwhelmingly to the government's family-planning program. However, it is just as plausible to say that the net effect of government involvement in population control has been, so far, to delay rather than hasten a decline in reproduction made inevitable by social and economic changes. Although the government is advocating vasectomies and providing IUD's and pills, it refuses to legalize abortions, despite the rapid rise in the rate of illegal abortions and despite the fact that, in a recent survey, 72 percent of the people who stated an opinion favored legalization. Also, the program is presented in the context of maternal and child health; it thus emphasizes motherhood and the family rather than alternative roles for women. Much is made of the fact that opinion surveys show an overwhelming majority of Koreans (89 percent in 1965) favoring contraception,[40] but this means only that Koreans are like other people in wishing to have the means to get what they want. Unfortunately, they want sizable families: "The records indicate that the program appeals mainly to women in the 30–39 year age bracket who have four or more children, including at least two sons. . . ."[41]

In areas less developed than Korea the degree of acceptance of contraception tends to be disappointing, especially among the rural majority. Faced with this discouragement, the leaders of current policy, instead of reexamining their assumptions, tend to redouble their effort to find a contraceptive that will appeal to the most illiterate peasant, forgetting that he wants a good-sized family. In the rural Punjab, for example, "a disturbing feature . . . is that the females start to seek advice and adopt family planning techniques at the fag end of their reproductive period." [42] Among 5196 women coming to rural Punjabi family-planning centers, 38 percent were over 35 years old, 67 percent over 30. These women had married early, nearly a third of them before the age of 15;[43] some 14 percent had eight or more *living* children when they reached the clinic, 51 percent six or more.

A survey in Tunisia showed that 68 percent of the married couples were willing to use birth-control measures, but the average number of children they considered ideal was 4.3.[44] The corresponding averages for a village in eastern Java, a village near New Delhi, and a village in Mysore were 4.3, 4.0, and 4.2, respectively.[45, 46] In the cities of these regions women are more ready to accept birth control and they want fewer children than village women do, but the number they consider desirable is still wholly unsatisfactory from the standpoint of population control. In an urban family-planning center in Tunisia, more than 600 of 900 women accepting contraceptives had four living children already.[47] In Bangalore, a city of nearly a million at the time (1952), the number of offspring desired by married women was 3.7 on the average; by married men, 4.1.[48] In the metropolitan area of San Salvador (350,000 inhabitants) a 1964 survey[49] showed the number desired by women of reproductive age to be 3.9, and in seven other capital cities of Latin America the number ranged from 2.7 to 4.2. If women in the cities of underdeveloped countries used birth-control measures with 100-percent efficiency, they still would have enough babies to expand city populations senselessly, quite apart from the added contribution of rural-urban migration. In many of the cities the difference between actual and ideal number of children is not great; for instance, in the seven Latin-American capitals mentioned above, the ideal was 3.4 whereas the actual births per women in the age range 35 to 39 was 3.7.[50] Bombay City has had birth-control clinics for many years, yet its birth rate (standardized for age, sex, and marital distribution) is still 34 per 1000 inhabitants and is tending to rise rather than fall. Although this rate is about 13 percent lower than that for India generally, it has been about that much lower since at least 1951.[51]

Is Family Planning the "First Step" in Population Control?

To acknowledge that family planning does not achieve population control is not to impugn its value for other purposes. Freeing women from the need to have more children than they want is of great benefit to them and their children and to society at large. My argument is therefore directed not against family-planning programs as such but against the assumption that they are an effective means of controlling population growth.

But what difference does it make? Why not go along for awhile with family planning as an initial approach to the problem of population control? The answer is that any policy on which millions of dollars are being spent should be designed to achieve the goal it purports to achieve. If it is only a first step, it should be so labeled, and its connection with the next step (and the nature of that next step) should be carefully examined. In the present case, since no "next step" seems ever to be mentioned, the question arises, Is reliance on family planning in fact a basis for dangerous postponement of effective steps? To continue to offer a remedy as a cure long after it has been shown merely to ameliorate the disease is either quackery or wishful thinking, and it thrives most where the need is greatest. Today the desire to solve the population problem is so intense that we are all ready to embrace any "action program" that promises relief. But postponement of effective measures allows the situation to worsen.

Unfortunately, the issue is confused by a matter of semantics. "Family *planning*" and "fertility *control*" suggest that reproduction is being regulated according to some rational plan. And so it is, but only from the standpoint of the individual couple, not from that of the community. What is rational in the light of a couple's situation may be totally irrational from the standpoint of society's welfare.

The need for societal regulation of individual behavior is readily recognized in other spheres—those of explosives, dangerous drugs, public property, natural resources. But in the sphere of reproduction, complete individual initiative is generally favored even by those liberal intellectuals who, in other spheres, most favor economic and social planning. Social reformers who would not hesitate to force all owners of rental property to rent to anyone who can pay, or to force all workers in an industry to join a union, balk at any suggestion that couples be permitted to have only a certain number of offspring. Invariably they interpret societal control of reproduction as meaning direct police supervision of individual behavior. Put the word *compulsory* in front of any term describing a means of limiting births —*compulsory sterilization, compulsory abortion, compulsory contraception* —and you guarantee violent opposition. Fortunately, such direct controls need not be invoked, but conservatives and radicals alike overlook this in their blind opposition to the idea of collective determination of a society's birth rate.

That the exclusive emphasis on family planning in current population policies is not a "first step" but an escape from the real issues is suggested by two facts. (i) No country has taken the "next step." The industrialized countries have had family planning for half a century without acquiring control over either the birth rate or population increase. (ii) Support and encouragement of research on population policy other than family planning is negligible. It is precisely this blocking of alternative thinking and experimentation that makes the emphasis on family planning a major obstacle to population control. The need is not to abandon family-planning programs but to put equal or greater resources into other approaches.

New Directions in Population Policy

In thinking about other approaches, one can start with known facts. In the past, all surviving societies had institutional incentives for marriage, procreation, and child care which were powerful enough to keep the birth rate equal to or in excess of a high death rate. Despite the drop in death rates during the last century and a half, the incentives tended to remain intact because the social structure (especially in regard to the family) changed little. At most, particularly in industrial societies, children became less productive and more expensive.[52] In present-day agrarian societies, where the drop in death rate has been more recent, precipitate, and independent of social change,[53] motivation for having children has changed little. Here, even more than in industrialized nations, the family has kept on producing abundant offspring, even though only a fraction of these children are now needed.

If excessive population growth is to be prevented, the obvious requirement is somehow to impose restraints on the family. However, because family roles are reinforced by society's system of rewards, punishments, sentiments, and norms, any proposal to demote the family is viewed as a threat by conservatives and liberals alike, and certainly by people with enough social responsibility to work for population control. One is charged with trying to "abolish" the family, but what is required is selective restructuring of the family in relation to the rest of society.

The lines of such restructuring are suggested by two existing limitations on fertility. (i) Nearly all societies succeed in drastically discouraging reproduction among unmarried women. (ii) Advanced societies unintentionally reduce reproduction among married women when conditions worsen in such a way as to penalize childbearing more severely than it was penalized before. In both cases the causes are motivational and economic rather than technological.

It follows that population-control policy can de-emphasize the family in two ways: (i) by keeping present controls over illegitimate childbirth yet making the most of factors that lead people to postpone or avoid marriage, and (ii) by instituting conditions that motivate those who do marry to keep their families small.

Postponement of Marriage

Since the female reproductive span is short and generally more fecund in its first than in its second half, postponement of marriage to ages beyond 20 tends biologically to reduce births. Sociologically, it gives women time to get a better education, acquire interests unrelated to the family, and develop a cautious attitude toward pregnancy.[54] Individuals who have not married by the time they are in their late twenties often do not marry at all. For these reasons, for the world as a whole, the average age at marriage for women is negatively associated with the birth rate: a rising age at marriage is a frequent cause of declining fertility during the middle phase of the demographic transition; and, in the late phase, the "baby boom" is usually associated with a return to younger marriages.

Any suggestion that age at marriage be raised as a part of population policy is usually met with the argument that "even if a law were passed, it would not be obeyed." Interestingly, this objection implies that the only way to control the age at marriage is by direct legislation, but other factors govern the actual age. Roman Catholic countries generally follow canon law in stipulating 12 years as the minimum *legal* age at which girls may marry, but the actual average age at marriage in these countries (at least in Europe) is characteristically more like 25 to 28 years. The actual age is determined, not by law, but by social and economic conditions. In agrarian societies, postponement of marriage (when postponement occurs) is apparently caused by difficulties in meeting the economic prerequisites for matrimony, as stipulated by custom and opinion. In industrial societies it is caused by housing shortages, unemployment, the requirement for overseas military service, high costs of education, and inadequacy of consumer services. Since almost no research has been devoted to the subject, it is difficult to assess the relative weight of the factors that govern the age at marriage.

Encouraging Limitation of Births within Marriage

As a means of encouraging the limitation of reproduction within marriage, as well as postponement of marriage, a greater rewarding of nonfamilial than of familial roles would probably help. A simple way of accomplishing this would be to allow economic advantages to accrue to the single as opposed to the married individual, and to the small as opposed to the large family. For instance, the government could pay people to permit themselves to be sterilized;[55] all costs of abortion could be paid by the government; a substantial fee could be charged for a marriage license; a "child-tax" [56] could be levied; and there could be a requirement that illegitimate pregnancies be aborted. Less sensationally, governments could simply reverse some existing policies that encourage childbearing. They could, for example, cease taxing single persons more than married ones; stop giving parents special tax exemptions; abandon income-tax policy that discriminates against couples when the wife works; reduce paid maternity leaves; reduce family allowances;[57] stop awarding public housing on the basis of family size; stop granting fellowships and other educational aids (including special allowances for wives and children) to married students; cease outlawing abortions and sterilizations; and relax rules that allow use of harmless contraceptives only with medical permission. Some of these policy reversals would be beneficial in other than demographic respects and some would be harmful unless special precautions were taken. The aim would be to reduce the number, not the quality, of the next generation.

A closely related method of deemphasizing the family would be modification of the complementarity of the roles of men and women. Men are now able to participate in the wider world yet enjoy the satisfaction of having several children because the housework and childcare fall mainly on their wives. Women are impelled to seek this role by their idealized view of marriage and motherhood and by either the scarcity of alternative roles or the difficulty of combining them with family roles. To change this situation women could be required to work outside the home, or compelled by circumstances to do so. If, at the same time, women were paid as well as men and given equal educational and occupational opportunities, and if social life were organized around the place of work rather than around the home or neighborhood, many women would develop interests that would compete with family interests. Approximately this policy is now followed in several Communist countries, and even the less developed of these currently have extremely low birth rates.[58]

That inclusion of women in the labor force has a negative effect on reproduction is indicated by regional comparisons.[59] But in most countries the wife's employment is subordinate, economically and emotionally, to her family role, and is readily sacrificed for the latter. No society has restructured both the occupational system and the domestic establishment to the point of permanently modifying the old division of labor by sex.

In any deliberate effort to control the birth rate along these lines, a government has two powerful instruments—its command over economic planning and its authority (real or potential) over education. The first determines (as far as policy can) the economic conditions and circumstances affecting the lives of all citizens; the second provides the knowledge and attitudes necessary to implement the plans. The economic system largely determines who shall work, what can be bought, what rearing children will cost, how much individuals can spend. The schools define family roles and develop vocational and recreational interests; they could, if it were desired, redefine the sex roles, develop interests that transcend the home, and transmit realistic (as opposed to moralistic) knowledge concerning marriage, sexual behavior, and population problems. When the problem is viewed in this light, it is clear that the ministeries of economics and education, not the ministry of health, should be the source of population policy.

The Dilemma of Population Policy

It should now be apparent why, despite strong anxiety over runaway population growth, the actual programs purporting to control it are limited to family planning and are therefore ineffective. (i) The goal of zero, or even slight, population growth is one that nations and groups find difficult to accept. (ii) The measures that would be required to implement such a goal, though not so revolutionary as a Brave New World or a Communist Utopia, nevertheless tend to offend most people reared in existing societies. As a consequence, the goal of so-called population control is implicit and vague; the method is only family planning. This method, far from de-emphasizing the family, is familistic. One of its stated goals is that of helping sterile couples to *have* children. It stresses parental aspirations and responsibilities. It goes along with most aspects of conventional morality, such as condemnation of abortion, disapproval of premarital intercourse, respect for religious teachings and cultural taboos, and obeisance to medical and clerical authority. It deflects hostility by refusing to recommend any change other than the one it stands for: availability of contraceptives.

The things that make family planning acceptable are the very things that make it ineffective for population control. By stressing the right of parents to have the number of children they want, it evades the basic question of population policy, which is how to give societies the number of children they need. By offering only the means for *couples* to control fertility, it neglects the means for societies to do so.

Because of the predominantly profamily character of existing soccieties, individual interest ordinarily leads to the production of enough offspring to constitute rapid population growth under conditions of low mortality. Childless or single-child homes are considered indicative of personal failure, whereas having three to five living children gives a family a sense of continuity and substantiality.[60]

Given the existing desire to have moderate-sized rather than small families, the only countries in which fertility has been reduced to match reduction in mortality are advanced ones temporarily experiencing worsened economic conditions. In Sweden, for instance, the net reproduction rate (NRR) has been below replacement for 34 years (1930–63), if the period is taken as a whole, but this is because of the economic depression. The average replacement rate was below unity (NRR = 0.81) for the period 1930–42, but from 1942 through 1963 it was above unity (NRR = 1.08). Hardships that seem particularly conducive to deliberate lowering of the birth rate are (in managed economies) scarcity of housing and other consumer goods despite full employment, and required high participation of women in the labor force, or (in freer economies) a great deal of unemployment and economic insecurity. When conditions are good, any nation tends to have a growing population.

It follows that, in countries where contraception is used, a realistic proposal for a government policy of lowering the birth rate reads like a catalogue of horrors: squeeze consumers through taxation and inflation; make housing very scarce by limiting construction; force wives and mothers to work outside the home to offset the inadequacy of male wages, yet provide few childcare facilities; encourage migration to the city by paying low wages in the country and providing few rural jobs; increase congestion in cities by starving the transit system; increase personal insecurity by encouraging conditions that produce unemployment and by haphazard political arrests. No government will institute such hardships simply for the purpose of controlling population growth. Clearly, therefore, the task of contemporary population policy is to develop attractive substitutes for family interests, so as to avoid having to turn to hardship as a corrective. The specific measures required for developing such substitutes are not easy to determine in the absence of research on the question.

In short, the world's population problem cannot be solved by pretense and wishful thinking. The unthinking identification of family planning with population control is an ostrich-like approach in that it permits people to hide from themselves the enormity and unconventionality of the task. There is no reason to abandon family-planning programs; contraception is a valuable technological instrument. But such programs must be supplemented with equal or greater investments in research and experimentation to determine the required socioeconomic measures.[61]

---

[1] *Studies in Family Planning, No. 16,* 1967.

[2] *Studies in Family Planning, No. 9,* 1966, p. 1.

[3] The statement is given in *Studies in Family Planning,* **1**:1, and in *Population Bulletin,* **23** (1967):6.

[4] The statement is quoted in *Studies in Family Planning,* **1**:2.

[5] *Hearings on S. 1676, U. S. Senate, Subcommittee on Foreign Aid Expenditures, 89th Congress, Second Session, April 7, 8, 11,* pt. 4, 1966, p. 889.

[6] B. L. Raina, in B. Berelson, R. K. Anderson, O. Harkavy, G. Maier, W. P. Mauldin, S. G. Segal (eds.), *Family Planning and Population Programs,* Chicago: Univ. of Chicago Press, 1966.

[7] D. Kirk, *Ann. Amer. Acad. Polit. Soc. Sci.,* **369** (1967):53.

[8] As used by English-speaking demographers, the word *fertility* designates actual reproductive performance, not a theoretical capacity.

[9] K. Davis, *Rotarian,* **94** (1959):10; *Health Education Monographs,* **9** (1960):2; L. Day and A. Day, *Too Many Americans,* Boston: Houghton Mifflin, 1964; R. A. Piddington, *Limits of Mankind,* Bristol, England: Wright, 1956.

[10] *Official Gazette,* April 15, 1965; quoted in *Studies in Family Planning,* **1**:7.

[11] J. W. Gardner (Secretary of Health, Education, and Welfare), "Memorandum to Heads of Operating Agencies," January 1966; reproduced in *Hearings on S. 1676,* **5**:783.

[12] C. Tietze, *Demography,* **1** (1964):119; *J. Chronic Diseases* **18** (1964):1161; M. Muramatsu, *Milbank Memorial Fund Quarterly,* **38** (1960):153; K. Davis, *Population Index,* **29** (1963):345; R. Armijo and T. Monreal, *J. Sex Research,* **1964** (1964):143; Proceedings World Population Conference, Belgrade, 1965; Proceedings International Planned Parenthood Federation.

[13] *Studies in Family Planning, No. 4,* 1964, p. 3.

[14] D. Bell (then administrator for Agency for International Development), in *Hearings on S. 1676,* **5**:862.

[15] *Asian Population Conference,* New York: United Nations, 1964, p. 30.

[16] R. Armijo and T. Monreal, in *Components of Population Change in Latin America,* New York: Milbank Fund, 1964, p. 272; E. Rice-Wray, *Amer. J. Public Health,* **54** (1964):313.

[17] E. Rice-Wray, in "Intra-Uterine Contraceptive Devices," *Excerpta Med. Intern. Congr. Ser. No. 54,* 1962, p. 135.

[18] J. Blake, in M. C. Sheps and J. C. Ridley (eds.), *Public Health and Population Change,* Pittsburgh: Univ. of Pittsburgh Press, 1965, p. 41.

[19] J. Blake and K. Davis, *Amer. Behavioral Scientist,* **5** (1963):24.

[20] See "Panel discussion on comparative acceptability of different methods of contraception," in *Research in Family Planning* (C. V. Kiser, ed.), Princeton: Princeton Univ. Press, 1962, pp. 373–86.

[21] "From the point of view of the woman concerned, the whole problem of continuing motivation disappears, . . ." (D. Kirk, in M. Muramatsu and P. A. Harper (eds.), *Population Dynamics,* Baltimore: Johns Hopkins Press, 1965).

[22] "For influencing family size norms, certainly the examples and statements of public figures are of great significance . . . also . . . use of mass-communication methods which help to legitimize the small-family style, to provoke conversation, and to establish a vocabulary for discussion of family planning" (M. W. Freymann, in M. Muramatsu and P. A. Harper (eds.) *Population Dynamics,* Baltimore: Johns Hopkins Press, 1965).

[23] O. A. Collver, *Birth Rates in Latin America,* Berkeley: International Population and Urban Research, 1965, pp. 27–28; the ten countries were Colombia, Costa Rica, El Salvador, Ecuador, Guatemala, Honduras, Mexico, Panama, Peru, and Venezuela.

[24] J. R. Rele, *Fertility Analysis through Extension of Stable Population Concepts,* Berkeley: International Population and Urban Research, 1967.

[25] J. C. Ridley, M. C. Sheps, J. W. Lingner, J. A. Menken, *Milbank Memorial Fund Quarterly,* **45** (1967):77; E. Arriaga, unpublished paper.

[26] "South Korea and Taiwan appear successfully to have checked population growth by the use of intrauterine contraceptive devices" (U. Borell, *Hearings on S. 1676,* vol. 5, p. 556).

[27] K. Davis, *Population Index,* **29** (1963):345.

[28] R. Freedman, *Population Index,* **31** (1965):421.

[29] Before 1964 the Family Planning Association had given advice to fewer than 60,000 wives in 10 years and a Pre-Pregnancy Health Program had reached some 10,000, and, in the current campaign, 3650 IUD's were inserted in 1965, in a total population of 2.5 million women of reproductive age. See *Studies in Family Planning, No. 19,* 1967, p. 4, and R. Freedman et al., *Population Studies,* **16** (1963):231.

[30] R. W. Gillespie, *Family Planning on Taiwan,* Taichung: Population Council, 1965.

[31] During the period 1950–1960 the ratio of growth of the city to growth of the non-city population was 5:3; during the period 1960–64 the ratio was 5:2; these ratios are based on data of Shaohsing Chen, *J. Sociol. Taiwan,* **1** (1963):74, and data in the United Nations *Demographic Yearbooks.*

[32] Gillespie, *op. cit.,* p. 69; R. Freedman, *Population Index,* **31** (1965):434. Taichung's rate of decline in 1963–64 was roughly double the average in four other cities, whereas just prior to the campaign its rate of decline had been much less than theirs.

[33] Gillespie, *op. cit.,* pp. 18, 31.

[34] *Ibid.,* p. 8.

[35] S. H. Chen, *J. Soc. Sci. Taipei,* **13** (1963):72.

[36] R. Freedman et al., *Population Studies,* **16** (1963):227, 232.

[37] In 1964 the life expectancy at birth was already 66 years in Taiwan, as compared to 70 for the United States.

[38] J. Blake, *Eugenics Quarterly,* **14** (1967):68.

[39] Women accepting IUD's in the family-planning program are typically 30 to 34 years old and have already had four children (*Studies in Family Planning, No. 19,* 1967, p. 5).

[40] Y. K. Cha, in Berelson et al., *op. cit.,* p. 27.

[41] *Ibid.,* p. 25.

[42] H. S. Ayalvi and S. S. Johl, *J. Family Welfare,* **12** (1965):60.

[43] Sixty percent of the women had borne their first child before age 19. Early marriage is strongly supported by public opinion. Of couples polled in the Punjab, 48 percent said that girls *should* marry before age 16, and 94 percent said they should marry before age 20 (H. S. Ayalvi and S. S. Johl, *ibid.,* p. 57). A study of 2,380 couples in 60 villages of Uttar Pradesh found that the women had consummated their marriage at an average age of 14.6 years (J. R. Rele, *Population Studies,* **15** (1962): 268).

[44] J. Morsa, in B. Berelson et al. (eds.), *op cit.,* 1966.

[45] H. Gille and R. J. Pardoko, *ibid.,* p. 515; S. N. Agarwala, *Med. Dig. Bombay,* **4** (1961):653.

[46] *Mysore Population Study,* New York: United Nations, 1961, p. 140.

[47] A. Daly, in B. Berelson et al. (eds.), *op. cit.,* 1966.

[48] *Mysore Population Study,* New York: United Nations, 1961.

[49] C. J. Goméz, paper presented at the World Population Conference, Belgrade, 1965.

[50] C. Miro, in B. Berelson et al. (eds.), *op. cit.,* 1966.

[51] *Demographic Training and Research Centre (India) Newsletter,* **20** (August 1966):4.

[52] K. Davis, *Population Index,* **29** (1963):345. For economic and sociological theory of motivation for having children, see J. Blake (in preparation).

[53] K. Davis, *Amer. Economic Review,* **46** (1956):305; *Scientific American,* **209** (1963):68.

[54] J. Blake, *World Population Conference, Belgrade, 1965* (vol. 2), New York: United Nations, 1967, pp. 132–36.

[55] S. Enke, *Rev. Economics Statistics,* **42** (1960):175; *Econ. Develop. Cult. Change,* **8** (1960):339; *ibid.,* **10** (1962):427; A. O. Krueger and L. A. Sjaastad, *ibid.,* p. 423.

[56] T. S. Samuel, *J. Family Welfare India,* **13** (1966):12.

[57] Sixty-two countries, including 27 in Europe, give cash payments to people for having children (U. S. Social Security Administration, *Social Security Programs Throughout the World, 1967,* Government Printing Office, Washington, D. C., 1967, pp. xxvii–xxviii).

[58] Average gross reproduction rates in the early 1960's were as follows: Hungary, 0.91; Bulgaria, 1.09; Romania, 1.15; Yugoslavia, 1.32.

[59] J. Blake, in M. C. Sheps and J. C. Ridley, *op. cit.,* p. 1195; O. A. Collver and E. Langlois, *Econ. Develop. Cult. Change,* **10** (1962):367; J. Weeks, in preparation.

[60] Roman Catholic textbooks condemn the "small" family (one with fewer than four children) as being abnormal (J. Blake, *Population Studies,* **20** (1966):27).

[61] Judith Blake's critical readings and discussions have greatly helped in the preparation of this article.

122
How to Save the Ship

Paul R. Ehrlich
1932–

From *The Population Bomb*
New York: Ballantine Books

1968

A ship has hit the rocks and is sinking. The passengers scream for help. Some jump overboard and are devoured by the circling sharks. A group of distinguished scientists is on board. One of their number suggests that they can help man the pumps. "Oh, no!" shout the others. "That might hurt the captain's feelings. Besides, pumping is not our business. It's outside our field of competence." You can guess what they do. They appoint a committee to study the problem, with subcommittees on marine engineering and navigation. They announce to the passengers that in two or three years the committee will produce a wonderful report which will be acceptable to the passengers, the captain, and the steamship line. Not so passive are the politicians. Some jump up to say that the passengers don't understand the political realities of the situation. Other more progressive politicians grab thimbles and start bailing, stopping every few seconds to accept praise for their valiant efforts.

That about sums up the situation on the population control front in the United States and in much of the rest of the world.

123

The Tragedy of the Commons

Garrett Hardin
1915–

Science, **162**:1243–1248

1968

At the end of a thoughtful article on the future of nuclear war, Jerome Wiesner and Herbert York[1] concluded that: "Both sides in the arms race are . . . confronted by the dilemma of steadily increasing military power and steadily decreasing national security. *It is our considered professional judgment that this dilemma has no technical solution.* If the great powers continue to look for solutions in the area of science and technology only, the result will be to worsen the situation."

I would like to focus your attention not on the subject of the article (national security in a nuclear world) but on the *kind* of conclusion they reached, namely that there is no "technical solution" to the problem. An implicit and almost universal assumption of discussions published in professional and semipopular scientific journals is that the problem under discussion has a "technical solution." A technical solution may be defined as one that requires a change only in the techniques of the natural sciences, demanding little or nothing in the way of change in human values or ideas of morality.

In our day (though not in earlier times) technical solutions are always welcome. Because of previous failures in prophecy it takes courage to assert that a desired technical solution is not possible. Wiesner and York exhibited this courage; publishing in a science journal they insisted that the solution to the problem was not to be found in the natural sciences. They cautiously qualified their statement with the phrase, "It is our considered professional judgment. . . ." Whether they were right or not is not the concern of the present article. Rather, the concern here is with the important concept of a class of human problems which can be called "no technical solution problems"; and more specifically, with the identification and discussion of one of these.

It is easy to show that the class is not a null class. Recall the game of tick-tack-toe. Consider the problem, "How can I win the game of tick-tack-toe?" It is well known that I cannot, if I assume (in keeping with the conventions of game theory) that my opponent understands the game perfectly. Put another way, there is no "technical solution" to the problem. I can win only by giving a radical meaning to the word "win." I can hit my opponent over the head; or I can drug him; or I can falsify the records. Every way in which I "win" involves, in some sense, an abandonment of the *game,* as we intuitively understand it. (I can also, of course, openly abandon the game—refuse to play it. This is what most adults do.)

The class of "No technical solution problems" has members. It is the thesis of the present article that the "population problem," as conventionally conceived, is a member of this class. How it is conventionally conceived needs some comment. I think it is fair to say that most people who anguish over the population problem are trying to find a way to avoid the evils of overpopulation without relinquishing any of the privileges they now enjoy. They think that farming the seas or developing new strains of wheat will solve the problem—technologically. I shall try to show here that the solution they seek cannot be found. The population problem cannot be solved in a technical way, any more than can the problem of winning the game of tick-tack-toe.

What Shall We Maximize?

Population, as Malthus said, naturally tends to grow "geometrically"; or as we would say, exponentially. In a finite world this means that the per capita share of the world's goods must steadily decrease. Is ours a finite world?

A fair defense can be put forward for the view that the world is infinite; or that we don't know that it isn't. But, in terms of the practical problems we must face in the next few generations with the foreseeable technology, it is clear that we will greatly increase human misery if we do not, during the immediate future, assume that the world *available to the terrestrial human population* is finite. "Space" is no escape.[2]

A finite world can support only a finite population; therefore, population growth must eventually equal zero. (The case of perpetual wide fluctuations above and below zero is a trivial variant that need not be discussed.) When this condition is met, what will be the situation of mankind? Specifically, can Bentham's goal of "the greatest good for the greatest number" be realized?

No—for two reasons, each sufficient by itself. The first is a theoretical one. It is not mathematically possible to maximize for two (or more) variables at the same time. This was clearly stated by von Neumann and Morgenstern,[3] but the principle is implicit in the theory of partial differential equations, dating back at least to D'Alembert (1717–1783).

The second reason springs directly from biological facts. To live, any organism must have a source of energy (e.g., food). This energy is utilized for two purposes: mere maintenance, and work. For man, maintenance of life requires about 1,600 kilocalories a day ("maintenance calories"). Anything that he does over and above merely staying alive will be defined as work, and is supported by "work calories," which he takes in. Work calories are used not only for what we call work in common speech; they are also required for all forms of enjoyment, from gormandizing and automobile racing to playing music and writing poetry. If our goal is to maximize population it is obvious what we must do: we must make the work calories per person approach as close to zero as possible. No gourmet meals, no vacations, no sports, no music, no literature, no art. . . . I think everyone will grant, without argument or proof, that maximizing population does not maximize goods. Bentham's goal is impossible.

In reaching this conclusion I have made the usual assumption that it is the acquisition of energy that is the problem. The appearance of atomic energy has led some to question this assumption. Given an infinite source of energy, however, population growth still produces an inescapable problem. The problem of the acquisition of energy is replaced by the problem of its dissipation, as J. H. Fremlin has so wittily shown.[4] The arithmetic signs in the analysis are, as it were, reversed; but Bentham's goal is still unattainable.

The optimum population is, then, less than the maximum. The difficulty of defining the optimum is enormous; so far as I know no one has seriously tackled this problem. Reaching an acceptable and stable solution will surely require more than one generation of hard analytical work; and much persuasion.

We want the maximum good per person; but what is "good"? To one person it is wilderness, to another it is ski lodges for thousands. To one it is estuaries to nourish ducks for hunters to shoot at; to another it is factory land. Comparing one good with another is, we usually say, impossible because goods are incommensurable. Incommensurables cannot be compared.

Theoretically this may be true; but in real life *incommensurables are commensurable*. All that is needed is a criterion of judgment and a system of weighting. In nature the criterion is survival. Is it better for a species to be small and hideable, or large and powerful? Natural selection commensurates the incommensurables. The compromise achieved depends on a natural weighting of the values of the variables.

Man must imitate this process. There is no doubt that in fact he already does, but unconsciously. It is when the hidden decisions are made explicit that the arguments begin. The problem for the years ahead is to work out an acceptable theory of weighting. Synergistic effects, nonlinear variation, and difficulties in discounting the future make the intellectual problem difficult, but not (in principle) insoluble.

Has any cultural group solved this practical problem at the present time, even on an intuitive level? One simple fact proves that none has: there is no prosperous population in the world today that has, and has had for some time, a growth rate of zero. Any people that has intuitively identified its optimum point will soon reach it, after which its growth rate becomes and remains zero.

Of course, a positive growth rate might be taken as evidence that a population is below its optimum. It is widely recognized, however that, by any reasonable standards, the most rapidly growing populations on earth today are (in general) the most miserable. This association (which need not be invariable) casts doubt on the optimistic assumption that the positive growth rate of a population is evidence that it has yet to reach its optimum.

We can make little progress in working toward optimum population size until we explicitly exorcize the spirit of Adam Smith in the field of practical demography. In economic affairs, *The Wealth of Nations* (1776) popularized the "invisible hand," the idea that an individual who "intends only his own gain," is, as it were, "led by an invisible hand to promote . . . the public interest." [5] Adam Smith did not assert that this was invariably true, and perhaps neither did any of his followers. But he contributed to a dominant tendency of thought that has ever since interfered with positive action based on rational analysis, namely the tendency to assume that decisions reached individually will, in fact, be the best decisions for an entire society. If this assumption is correct it justifies the continuance of our present policy of *laissez-faire* in reproduction. If it is correct we can assume that men will control their individual fecundity so as to produce the optimal population. If the assumption is not correct, we need to re-examine our individual freedoms to see which ones are defensible.

Tragedy of Freedom in a Commons

The rebuttal to the "invisible hand" in population control is to be found in a "scenario" first sketched in a little known pamphlet[6] in 1833 by a mathematical amateur named William Forster Lloyd (1794–1852). We may well call it "The Tragedy of the Commons," using the word "tragedy" as the philosopher Whitehead used it:[7] "The essence of dramatic tragedy is not unhappiness. It resides in the solemnity of the remorseless

370

working of things." He then goes on to say: "This inevitableness of destiny can only be illustrated in terms of human life by incidents which in fact involve unhappiness. For it is only by them that the futility of escape can be made evident in the drama."

The tragedy of the commons develops in this way. Picture a pasture open to all. It is to be expected that each herdsman will try to keep as many cattle as possible on the commons. Such an arrangement may work reasonably satisfactorily for centuries because tribal wars, poaching, and disease keep the numbers of both man and beast well below the "carrying capacity" of the land. Finally, however, comes the day of reckoning, i.e., the day when the long-desired social stability becomes a reality. At this point, the inherent logic of the commons remorselessly generates tragedy.

As a rational being each herdsman seeks to maximize his gain. Explicitly or implicitly, more or less consciously, he asks: "What is the utility *to me* of adding one more animal to my herd?" This utility has two components:

> 1. A positive component, which is a function of the increment of one animal. Since the herdsman receives all the proceeds from the sale of the additional animal, the positive utility is nearly $+1$.
>
> 2. A negative component, which is a function of the additional overgrazing created by one more animal. But since the effects of overgrazing are shared by all the herdsmen, the negative utility for any particular decision-making herdsman is only a fraction of -1.

Adding together the component partial utilities, the rational herdsman concludes that the only sensible course for him to pursue is to add another animal to his herd. And another; and another . . . But this is the conclusion reached by each and every rational herdsman sharing a commons. Therein is the tragedy. Each man is *locked in* to a system that compels him to increase his herd without limit—in a world that is limited. Ruin is the destination toward which all men rush, each pursuing his own best interest in a society that believes in the freedom of the commons. *Freedom in a commons brings ruin to all.*

Some would say that this is platitudinous, that is, a truth known to all. Would that it were! In a sense it was learned thousands of years ago, but natural selection favors the forces of psychological denial.[8] The individual benefits *as an individual* from his ability to deny the truth even though society as a whole, of which he is a part, suffers. Education can counteract the natural tendency to do the wrong thing, but the inexorable succession of generations requires that the basis for this knowledge be constantly refreshed.

A simple incident that occurred a few years ago in Leominster,

Massachusetts, shows how perishable the knowledge is. During the Christmas shopping season the parking meters downtown were covered with plastic bags that bore tags reading: "Do not open until after Christmas. Free parking courtesy of the mayor and city council." In other words, facing the prospect of an increased demand for already scarce space, the city fathers reinstituted the system of the commons. (Cynically, we suspect that they gained more votes than they lost by this retrogressive act.)

In an approximate way, the logic of the commons has been understood for a long time, perhaps since the discovery of agriculture or the invention of private property in real estate. But it is understood mostly only in special cases, which are not sufficiently generalized. Even at this late date, cattlemen leasing national land on the western ranges demonstrate no more than an ambivalent understanding, constantly pressuring federal authorities to increase the head-count to the point where overgrazing produces erosion and weed-dominance. Similarly, the oceans of the world continue to suffer from the survival of the philosophy of the commons. Maritime nations still respond automatically to the shibboleth of the "freedom of the seas." Professing to believe in the "inexhaustible resources of the oceans," they bring species after species of fish and whales closer to extinction.[9]

The National Parks present another instance of the working out of the tragedy of the commons. At present, they are open to all, without limit. The Parks themselves are limited in extent—there is only one Yosemite Valley—while population seems to grow without limit. The values that visitors seek in the Parks are steadily eroded. Plainly, we must soon cease to treat the Parks as commons or they will be of no value to anyone.

What shall we do? We have several options. We might sell them off as private property. We might keep them as public property, but allocate the right to enter them. The allocation might be on the basis of wealth, using an auction system. It might be on the basis of merit, as defined by some agreed-upon standards. It might be by lottery. Or it might be on a first-come, first-served basis, administered to long queues. These, I think, are all the reasonable possibilities. They are all objectionable. *But we must choose*—or acquiesce in the destruction of the commons that we call our National Parks.

Pollution

In a reverse way, the tragedy of the commons reappears in problems of pollution. Here it is not a question of taking something out of the commons, but of putting something in—sewage, or chemical, radioactive and heat wastes into water; noxious and dangerous fumes into the air; and distracting and unpleasant advertizing signs into the line of sight. The utility calculations are much the same as before. The rational man finds that his share of the cost of the wastes he discharges into the commons is less than the cost of purifying his wastes before releasing them. Since this is true for everyone, we are locked into a system of "fouling our own nest," so long as we behave only as independent, rational, free-enterprizers.

The tragedy of the commons as a foodbasket is averted by private property, or something formally like it. But the air and waters surrounding us cannot readily be fenced, and so the tragedy of the commons as a cesspool must be prevented by different means, by coercive laws or taxing devices that make it cheaper for the polluter to treat his pollutants than to discharge them untreated. We have not progressed as far with the solution of this problem as we have with the first. Indeed, our particular concept of private property, which deters us from exhausting the positive resources of the earth, favors pollution. The owner of a factory on the bank of a stream —whose "property" extends to the middle of the stream—often has difficulty seeing why it is not his natural "right" to muddy the waters flowing past his door. The law, always behind the times, requires elaborate stitching and fitting to mold it to this newly perceived aspect of the commons.

The pollution problem is a consequence of population. It did not much matter how a lonely American frontiersman disposed of his waste. "Flowing water purifies itself every ten miles," my grandfather used to say, and the myth was near enough to the truth when he was a boy, for there weren't too many people. But as population become denser the natural chemical and biological recycling processes became overloaded, calling for a redefinition of property rights.

How Legislate Temperance?

Analysis of the pollution problem as a function of population density uncovers a not generally recognized principle of morality, namely: *the morality of an act is a function of the state of the system at the time it is performed.*[10] Using the commons as a cesspool does not harm the general public under frontier conditions, because there is no public; the same behavior in a metropolis is unbearable. A hundred and fifty years ago a plainsman could kill an American bison, cut out only the tongue for his dinner, and discard the rest of the animal. He was not in any important sense being wasteful. Today, with only a few thousand bison left, we would be appalled at such behavior.

In passing, it is worth noting that the morality of an act cannot be determined from a photograph. One does not know whether a man killing an elephant or setting fire to the grassland is harming others until one knows the total system in which his act appears. "One picture is worth a thousand words," said an ancient Chinese; but it may take 10,000 words to validate it. It is as tempting to ecologists as it is to reformers in general to try to persuade others via the photographic shortcut. But the guts of an argument can't be photographed: they must be presented rationally—in words.

That morality is system-sensitive escaped the attention of most codifiers of ethics in the past. "Thou shalt not . . ." is the form of traditional ethical directives, which make no allowance for particular circumstances. (Christ did; and his continued existence was unbearable to the Establishment.) The laws of our society follow the pattern of ancient ethics, and therefore are poorly suited to governing a complex, crowded, changeable world. Our epicyclic solution is to augment statutory law with administrative law. Since it is practically impossible to spell out all the conditions under which it is safe to burn trash in the back yard or run an automobile without smog-control, by law we delegate the details to bureaus. The result is administrative law, which is rightly feared for an ancient reason: *Quis custodiet ipsos custodes?*—"Who shall watch the watchers themselves?" John Adams said we must have "a government of laws and not men." Bureau administrators, trying to evaluate the morality of acts in the total system, are singularly liable to corruption, producing a government by men, not laws.

Prohibition is easy to legislate (though not necessarily to enforce!); but how do we legislate temperance? Experience indicates that it can be accomplished best through the mediation of administrative law. We limit possibilities unnecessarily if we suppose that the sentiment of *Quis custodiet* denies us the use of administrative law. We should rather retain the phrase as a perpetual reminder of fearful dangers we cannot avoid. The great challenge facing us now is to invent the corrective feedbacks that are needed to keep custodians honest. We must find ways to legitimate the needed authority of both the custodians and the corrective feedbacks.

Freedom to Breed Is Intolerable

The tragedy of the commons is involved in population problems in another way. In a world governed solely by the principle of "dog eat dog" —if indeed there ever was such a world—it would not be a matter of public concern how many children a family had. Parents who bred too exuberantly would leave fewer descendants, not more, because they would be unable to care adequately for their children. David Lack and others have found that such a negative feedback demonstrably controls the fecundity of birds.[11] But men are not birds, and have not acted like them for millennia, at least.

If each human family were dependent only on its own resources; *if* the children of improvident parents starved to death; *if,* thus, overbreeding brought its own "punishment" to the germ line—*then* there would be no public interest in controlling the breeding of families. But our society is deeply committed to the welfare state,[12] and hence confronted with another aspect of the tragedy of the commons.

In a welfare state, how shall we deal with the family, the religion, the race, or the class (or indeed any distinguishable and cohesive group) that adopts overbreeding as a policy to secure its own aggrandizement? [13] To couple the concept of freedom to breed with the belief that everyone born has an equal right to the commons is to lock the world into a tragic course of action.

Unfortunately this is just the course of action that is being pursued by the United Nations. In late 1967 some thirty nations agreed to the following:

> The Universal Declaration of Human Rights describes the family as the natural and fundamental unit of society. It follows that any choice and decision with regard to the size of the family must irrevocably rest with the family itself, and cannot be made by anyone else.[14]

It is painful to have to deny categorically the validity of this "right"; denying it, one feels as uncomfortable as a resident of Salem who denied the reality of witches in the seventeenth century. At the present time, in liberal quarters, something like a taboo acts to inhibit criticism of the United Nations. There is a feeling that the U.N. is "our last and best hope," that we shouldn't find fault with it; we shoudn't play into the hands of the arch-conservatives. Let us not forget, however, what Robert Louis Stevenson said: "The truth that is suppressed by friends is the readiest weapon of the enemy." If we love the truth we must openly deny the validity of the Universal Declaration of Human Rights, even though it is promoted by the United Nations. We should also join with Kingsley Davis[15] in attempting to get Planned Parenthood to see the error of its ways in embracing the same tragic ideal.

Conscience Is Self-eliminating

It is a mistake to think that we can control the breeding of mankind *in the long run* by an appeal to conscience. Charles Galton Darwin made this point when he spoke on the centennial of the publication of his grandfather's great book. The argument is straightforward and Darwinian.

People vary. Confronted with appeals to limit breeding, some people will undoubtedly respond to the plea more than others. Those who have more children will produce a larger fraction of the next generation

375

than those with more susceptible consciences. The difference will be accentuated, generation by generation. In C. G. Darwin's words:

> It may well be that it would take hundreds of generations for the progenitive instinct to develop in this way, but if it should do so, nature would have taken her revenge, and the variety *Homo contracipiens* would become extinct and would be replaced by the variety *Homo progenitivus*.[16]

The argument assumes that conscience or the desire for children (no matter which) is hereditary—but hereditary *only in the most general formal sense*. The result will be the same whether the attitude is transmitted via germ cells, or exosomatically, to use A. J. Lotka's term. (If one denies the latter possibility as well as the former, then what's the point of education?) The argument has here been stated in the context of the population problem, but it applies equally well to any instance in which society appeals to an individual exploiting a commons to restrain himself for the general good—by means of his conscience. To make such an appeal is to set up a selective system that works toward the elimination of conscience from the race.

Pathogenic Effects of Conscience

The long-term disadvantage of an appeal to conscience should be enough to condemn it; but it has serious short-term disadvantages as well.

If we ask a man who is exploiting a commons to desist "in the name of conscience," what are we saying to him? What does he hear—not only at the moment but also in the wee small hours of the night when, half asleep, he remembers not merely the words we used but also the nonverbal communication cues we gave him unawares? Sooner or later, consciously or subconsciously he senses that he has received two communications, and that they are contradictory:

> 1. (Intended communication) "If you don't do as we ask, we will openly condemn you for not acting like a responsible citizen."
> 2. (The unintended communication) "If you *do* behave as we ask, we will secretly condemn you for a schlemiel, a sucker, a sap, who can be shamed into standing aside while the rest of us exploit the commons."

In a word, he is damned if he does and damned if he doesn't. He is caught in what Gregory Bateson has called a "double bind." Bateson and his co-workers have made a plausible case for viewing the double bind as an important causative factor in the genesis of schizophrenia.[17] The double bind may not always be so damaging, but it always endangers the mental health of anyone to whom it is applied. "A bad conscience," said Nietzsche, "is a kind of illness."

To conjure up a conscience in others is tempting to anyone who wishes to extend his control beyond the legal limits. Leaders at the highest level succumb to this temptation. Has any President during the past generation failed to call upon labor unions to moderate "voluntarily" their demands for higher wages, or to steel companies to honor "voluntary" guide-lines on prices? I can recall none. The rhetoric used on such occasions is designed to produce feelings of guilt in noncooperators.

For centuries it was assumed without proof that guilt was a valuable, perhaps even an indispensable, ingredient of the civilized life. Now, in this post-Freudian world, we doubt it. Paul Goodman speaks from the modern point of view when he says:

> No good has ever come from feeling guilty, neither intelligence, policy, nor compassion. The guilty do not pay attention to the object but only to themselves, and not even to their own interests, which might make sense, but to their anxieties.[18]

One does not have to be a professional psychiatrist to see the consequences of anxiety. We in the western world are just emerging from a dreadful two-centuries-long Dark Ages of Eros, which was sustained partly by prohibition laws, but perhaps more effectively by the anxiety-generating mechanisms of education. Alex Comfort has told the story well in *The Anxiety Makers*;[19] it is not a pretty one.

Since proof is difficult, we may even concede that the results of anxiety may sometimes, from certain points of view, be desirable. The larger question we should ask is whether, as a matter of policy, we should ever encourage the use of a technique the tendency of which (if not the intention) is psychologically pathogenic. We hear much talk these days of "responsible parenthood"; the coupled words are incorporated into the titles of some organizations devoted to birth control. Some people have proposed massive propaganda campaigns to instill responsibility into the nation's (or the world's) breeders. But what is the meaning of the word "responsibility" in this context? Is it not merely a synonym for the word "conscience"? When we use the word "responsibility" in the absence of substantial sanctions are we not trying to browbeat a free man in a commons into acting against his own interest? "Responsibility" is a verbal counterfeit for a substantial *quid pro quo*. It is an attempt to get something for nothing.

If the word "responsibility" is to be used at all, I suggest that it be in the sense Charles Frankel uses it.[20] *"Responsibility,"* says this philosopher, *"is the product of definite social arrangements."* Notice that Frankel calls for social arrangements—not propaganda.

Mutual Coercion, Mutually Agreed Upon

The social arrangements that produce responsibility are arrangements that create coercion, of some sort. Consider bank-robbing. The man who takes money from a bank acts as if the bank were a commons. How do we prevent such action? Certainly not by trying to control his behavior solely by a verbal appeal to his sense of responsibility. Rather than rely on propaganda we follow Frankel's lead and insist that a bank is not a commons; we seek the definite social arrangements that will keep it from becoming a commons. That we thereby infringe on the freedom of would-be robbers we neither deny nor regret.

The morality of bank-robbing is particularly easy to understand because we accept complete prohibition of this activity. We are willing to say "Thou shalt not rob banks," without providing for exceptions. But temperance also can be created by coercion. Taxing is a good coercive device. To keep downtown shoppers temperate in their use of parking space we introduce parking meters for short periods, and traffic fines for longer ones. We need not actually forbid a citizen to park as long as he wants to; we need merely make it increasingly expensive for him to do so. Not prohibition, but carefully biased options are what we offer him. A Madison Avenue man might call this "persuasion"; I prefer the greater candor of the word "coercion."

Coercion is a dirty word to most liberals now, but it need not forever be so. As with the four-letter words, its dirtiness can be cleansed away by exposure to the light, by saying it over and over without apology or embarrassment. To many, the word coercion implies arbitrary decisions of distant and irresponsible bureaucrats; but this is not a necessary part of its meaning. The only kind of coercion I recommend is mutual coercion, mutually agreed upon by the majority of the people affected.

To say that we mutually agree to coercion is not to say that we are required to enjoy it, or even to pretend we enjoy it. Who enjoys taxes? We all grumble about them. But we accept compulsory taxes because we recognize that voluntary taxes would favor the conscienceless. We institute and (grumblingly) support taxes and other coercive devices to escape the horror of the commons.

An alternative to the commons need not be perfectly just to be preferable. With real estate and other material goods, the alternative we have chosen is the institution of private property coupled with legal inheritance. Is this system perfectly *just?* As a genetically trained biologist I deny that it is. It seems to me that, if there are to be differences in individual inheritance, legal possession should be perfectly correlated with biological inheritance—that those who are biologically more fit to be the custodians of property and power should legally inherit more. But genetic recombination continually makes a mockery of the doctrine of "like father, like son" implicit in our laws of legal inheritance. An idiot can inherit millions, and a trust fund can keep his estate intact. We must admit that our legal system of private property plus inheritance *is* unjust—but we put up with it because we are not convinced, at the moment, that anyone has invented a better system. The alternative of the commons is too horrifying to contemplate. Injustice is preferable to total ruin.

One of the peculiarities of the warfare between reform and the status quo is that it is thoughtlessly governed by a double standard. Whenever a reform measure is proposed it is often defeated when its opponents triumphantly discover a flaw in it. As Kingsley Davis has pointed out,[21] worshippers of the status quo sometimes imply that no reform is possible without unanimous agreement, an implication contrary to historical fact. As nearly as I can make out, automatic rejection of proposed reforms is based on one of two unconscious assumptions:

1. That the status quo is perfect; or
2. That the choice we face is between reform and no action; if the proposed reform is imperfect, we presumably should take no action at all, while we wait for a perfect proposal.

But we can never do nothing. That which we have done for thousands of years is also action. It also produces evils. Once we are aware that the status quo *is* action, we can then compare its discoverable advantages and disadvantages with the predicted advantages and disadvantages of the proposed reform, discounting as best we can for our lack of experience. On the basis of such a comparison, we can make a rational decision, which will not involve the unworkable assumption that only perfect systems are tolerable.

The Recognition of Necessity

Perhaps the simplest summary of this analysis of man's population problems is this: the commons, if justifiable at all, is justifiable only under conditions of low population density. As the human population has increased, the commons has had to be abandoned in one aspect after another.

First we abandoned the commons in food gathering, enclosing farm land and restricting pastures and hunting and fishing areas. These restrictions are still not complete throughout the world.

Somewhat later we saw that the commons as a place for waste disposal would also have to be abandoned. Restrictions on the disposal of domestic sewage are widely accepted in the western world; we are still struggling to close the commons to pollution by automobiles, factories, insecticide sprayers, fertilizing operations, and atomic energy installations.

In a still more embryonic state is our recognition of the evils of the commons in matters of pleasure. There is almost no restriction on the propagation of sound waves in the public medium. The shopping public is assaulted with "mindless music," without its consent. Our government is paying out billions of dollars to create the SST plane, which will disturb fifty thousand people for every one person who is whisked from coast to coast three hours faster. Advertizers muddy the airwaves of radio and TV and pollute the view of travellers. We are a long way from outlawing the commons in matters of pleasure. Is this because our puritan inheritance makes us view pleasure as something of a sin, and pain (i.e., the pollution of advertizing) as the sign of virtue?

Every new enclosure of the commons involves the infringement of somebody's personal liberty. Infringements made in the distant past are accepted because no contemporary complains of a loss. It is the newly proposed infringements that we vigorously oppose: cries of "rights" and "freedom" fill the air. But what does "freedom" mean? When men mutually agreed to pass laws against robbing, mankind became more free, not less so. Individuals locked into the logic of the commons are free only to bring on universal ruin; once they see the necessity of mutual coercion, they become free to pursue other goals. I believe it was Hegel who said, *"Freedom is the recognition of necessity."*

The most important aspect of necessity that we must now recognize, is the necessity of abandoning the commons in breeding. No technical solution can rescue us from the misery of overpopulation. Freedom to breed will bring ruin to all. At the moment, to avoid hard decisions many of us are tempted to propagandize for conscience and "responsible parenthood." The temptation must be resisted, because an appeal to independently acting consciences selects for the disappearance of all conscience in the long run, and an increase in anxiety in the short.

The only way we can preserve and nurture other and more precious freedoms is by relinquishing the freedom to breed, and that very soon. "Freedom is the recognition of necessity"—and it is the role of education to reveal to all the necessity of abandoning the freedom to breed. Only so, can we put an end to this aspect of the tragedy of the commons.

[1] J. B. Wiesner and H. F. York, *Scientific American,* **211** (April 1964):27.

[2] G. Hardin, *J. Heredity,* **50** (1959):68; this volume, Reading 52; S. von Hoernor, *Science,* **137** (1962):18.

[3] J. von Neumann and O. Morgenstern, *Theory of Games and Economic Behavior,* Princeton: Princeton Univ. Press, 1947, p. 11.

[4] J. H. Fremlin, *New Scientist,* no. 415 (1964):285; this volume, Reading 27.

[5] Adam Smith, *The Wealth of Nations,* New York: Modern Library, 1937, p. 423.

[6] W. F. Lloyd, *Two Lectures on the Checks to Population,* Oxford, 1833; this volume, Reading 13.

[7] A. N. Whitehead, *Science and the Modern World,* New York: Mentor, 1948, p. 17.

[8] See Reading 21.

[9] S. McVay, *Scientific American,* **216** (August 1966):13.

[10] J. Fletcher, *Situation Ethics,* Philadelphia: Westminster Press, 1966.

[11] D. Lack, *The Natural Regulation of Animal Numbers,* Oxford: Clarendon Press, 1954.

[12] H. Girvetz, *From Wealth to Welfare,* Stanford: Stanford Press, 1950.

[13] G. Hardin, *Persp. Biol. Med.,* **6** (1963):366.

[14] U Thant, *Intern. Planned Parenthood News,* no. 168, February 1968, p. 3.

[15] K. Davis, *Science,* **158** (1967):730; this volume, Reading 121.

[16] S. Tax (ed.), *Evolution After Darwin,* Chicago: Univ. of Chicago Press, 1960, vol. 2, p. 469.

[17] G. Bateson, D. D. Jackson, J. Haley, and J. Weakland, *Behav. Sci.,* **1** (1956):251.

[18] P. Goodman, *New York Review of Books,* **10** (23 May 1968):22.

[19] A. Comfort, *The Anxiety Makers,* London: Nelson, 1967.

[20] C. Frankel, *The Case for Modern Man,* New York: Harper, 1955, p. 203.

[21] J. D. Roslansky, *Genetics and the Future of Man,* New York: Appleton-Century-Crofts, 1966, p. 177.

Index of Names

Lader, Lawrence, 303
La Fontaine, 48
Lamarck, J. B., 133, 165
Lange, Frederick Albert, 163–165
Langer, William L., 194–197
Latz, Leo J., 221, 226
Lazarus, Emma, 106
Lecky, William, 232
Lehfeldt, Hans, 312
Lindsey, Judge Ben B., 327
Little, William John Knox, 197–198
Lloyd, William Forster, 28–32, 370
Lofthouse, W. F., 215
Lotka, A. J., 376
Lovejoy, Arthur O., 181–185
Loyola, St. Ignatius, 82
Lucretius, 136
Luther, Martin, 19
Lyell, Charles, 146, 147, 149, 151

McHugh, James T., 286
McManus, Msgr. William F., 276
Malthus, Thomas Robert, 3, 4–16, 30, 32, 67–70, 87–88, 137–138, 147, 160, 167, 168, 186–188, 194, 196, 368
Manheim, Karl, 68, 69
"Marcus" (pseudo.), 197
Marx, Karl, 67–70
Matthew, Patrick, 157
Meier, Richard L., 328–331
Mill, James, 189, 190
Miller, John Eli, 41
Mivart, St. George, 258
More, Thomas, 19
Morgenstern, O., 381
Müller, Fritz, 149
Muller, H. J., 173
Myrdal, Gunnar, 124

Nethercot, Arthur H., 198–204
Neumann, J., von, 381
Newman, James R., 279
Niciporovic, A. A., 60
Nietzsche, Friedrich Wilhelm, 377
Noah, vii
Noonan, John T., Jr., 179
Noyes, John Humphrey, 316–319, 321, 324

O'Brien, John A., 226

Ogino, K., 220
O'Loane, J. Kenneth, 242–247
Orr, Sir John Boyd, 56
Orwell, George, 256

Paddock, William and Paul, 84–87, 123–126, 127
Paley, William, 139–140, 162–163, 167, 187
Paul, St., 313, 317
Peckham, Morse, 133
Peel, John, 235
Peirce, Isaac, 232
Peterson, William, 67–70
Place, Francis, 188–191, 192–193, 255
Plato, 48
Poliakoff, S. R., 248
Pope Innocent III, 284
Pope John XXIII, 248, 263
Pope Paul VI, 263
Pope Pius IX, 284
Pope Pius XI, 240, 256
Price, Richard, 16

Rainwater, Lee, 303
Rangel, Charles, 277
Reiner, Joseph, 224
Rhodes, Alan, 241
Riesman, David, 175
Robinson, William Josephus, 208
Rock, John, 248, 251, 253, 257
Rockefeller, John D., III, 343
Roosevelt, Theodore, 98
Rossi, Alice S., 303
Ruether, Rosemary, 249
Russell, Flora S., 207
Ryan, John A., 236

St. John-Stevas, Norman, 285, 308–310
Sanger, Margaret, 179, 209–211, 223, 233
Sauvy, Alfred, 107
Sax, Karl, 40
Sears, Paul B., 49
Senior, Clarence, 307–308
Shakespeare, W., 182
Shaw, George Bernard, 258
Shelley, Percy, 168
Shepherd, L. R., 112

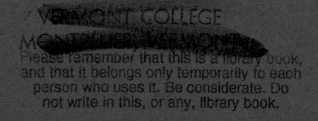